Fodor's 97

Hong Kong

"When it comes to information on regional history, what to see and do, and shopping, these guides are exhaustive."

—*USAir Magazine*

"Usable, sophisticated restaurant coverage, with an emphasis on good value."
—Andy Birsh, *Gourmet Magazine* columnist

"Valuable because of their comprehensiveness."
—*Minneapolis Star-Tribune*

"Fodor's always delivers high quality...thoughtfully presented...thorough."

—*Houston Post*

"An excellent choice for those who want everything under one cover."

—*Washington Post*

Fodor's Travel Publications, Inc.
New York • Toronto • London • Sydney • Auckland
http://www.fodors.com/

Fodor's Hong Kong '97

Editors: Deborah Field Washburn and Caroline Haberfeld

Editorial Contributors: Jan Alexander, Steven K. Amsterdam, Shann Davies, Patricia Davis, Barry Girling, Tim Healy, Laura M. Kidder, Sue Marshall

Gold Guide Contributors: Robert Andrews, David Brown, Audra Epstein, Heidi Sarna, Helayne Schiff, Mary Ellen Schultz, M. T. Schwartzman (editor), Dinah Spritzer

Creative Director: Fabrizio La Rocca

Associate Art Director: Guido Caroti

Photo Researcher: Jolie Novak

Cartographer: David Lindroth

Cover Photograph: Jeffrey Aaronson/Network Aspen

Text Design: Between the Covers

Copyright

ISBN 0–679–03230–4

"Impacts and Images" is an extract from *Hong Kong* by Jan Morris. Copyright © 1988 by Jan Morris. Reprinted by kind permission of Random House, Inc., and A. P. Watt Limited on behalf of Jan Morris.

Special Sales

Fodor's Travel Publications are available at special discounts for bulk purchases for sales promotions or premiums. Special editions, including personalized covers, excerpts of existing guides, and corporate imprints, can be created in large quantities for special needs. For more information contact your local bookseller or write to Special Markets, Fodor's Travel Publications, 201 East 50th Street, New York, NY 10022. Inquiries from Canada should be directed to your local Canadian bookseller or sent to Random House of Canada, Ltd., Marketing Department, 1265 Aerowood Drive, Mississauga, Ontario L4W 1B9. Inquiries from the United Kingdom should be sent to Fodor's Travel Publications, 20 Vauxhall Bridge Road, London, England SW1V 2SA.

PRINTED IN THE UNITED STATES OF AMERICA

10 9 8 7 6 5 4 3 2 1

CONTENTS

On the Road with Fodor's   vi

About Our Writers *vi*
New This Year *vi*
How to Use This Book *vi*
Please Write to Us *vii*

The Gold Guide   xii

Important Contacts A to Z *xii*
Smart Travel Tips A to Z *xxvi*

1 Destination: Hong Kong   1

"A Brief History" *2*
"1997: The Year of Reckoning" *5*
What's Where *8*
Pleasures and Pastimes *9*
New and Noteworthy *9*
Fodor's Choice *10*
Festivals and Seasonal Events *13*

2 Exploring Hong Kong   14

Hong Kong Island *17*
Kowloon *36*
The New Territories *40*
The Outer Islands *46*

3 Dining   51

4 Lodging   74

5 Nightlife and the Arts   92

6 Outdoor Activities and Sports   103

7 Shopping   114

8 Side Trip to Macau   141

Exploring *145*
Dining *155*
Lodging *159*
Nightlife *163*
Outdoor Activities and Sports *165*
Shopping *168*
Macau A to Z *170*

Contents

9   Side Trips to South China   175

Exploring *178*
South China A to Z *185*

10   Portraits of Hong Kong   188

"Impacts and Images," by Jan Morris *189*
"Food and Drink in Hong Kong and Macau," by Barry Girling *192*
"Doing Business in Hong Kong, 1997 Style," by Tim Healy *196*
"A Shopper's Paradise," by Patricia Davis *199*
Further Reading *201*

Index   202

Maps

Hong Kong *viii–ix*
World Time Zones *x–xi*
Hong Kong Island *16*
Hong Kong Mass Transit
  Railway *19*
Central and Western
  Districts *24–25*
Wanchai, Causeway Bay, Happy
  Valley, and North Point *30–31*
The South Side of Hong Kong
  Island *35*

Kowloon Peninsula *39*
The New Territories and
  the Outer Islands *44–45*
Dining *56–57*
Lodging *80–81*
Shopping *118–119*
Macau *146*
Taipa and Coloane Islands *154*
The Pearl River Delta *179*

ON THE ROAD WITH FODOR'S

WE'RE ALWAYS THRILLED to get letters from readers, especially one like this:

It took us an hour to decide what book to buy and we now know we picked the best one. Your book was wonderful, easy to follow, very accurate, and good on pointing out eating places, informal as well as formal. When we saw other people using your book, we would look at each other and smile.

Our editors and writers are deeply committed to making every Fodor's guide "the best one"—not only accurate but always charming, brimming with sound recommendations and solid ideas, right on the mark in describing restaurants and hotels, and full of fascinating facts that make you view what you've traveled to see in a rich new light.

About Our Writers

Our success in achieving our goals—and in helping to make your trip the best of all possible vacations—is a credit to the hard work of our extraordinary writers.

Jan Alexander is a journalist who has lived on and off in Hong Kong since 1992. She has written about the region for *Newsweek, The Wall Street Journal, Far Eastern Economic Review,* and the *Hong Kong Daily Eastern Express.* A novel based on her travels in China and Hong Kong is in press.

Shann Davies is a British-born travel writer who has lived and worked in 15 countries around the world, but always comes back to Asia. She first visited Macau in 1960 and has since made it her spiritual home, although for the past few years she's been based in Hong Kong.

Sue Marshall lives and works in the highrise, high-flying world of Hong Kong. Underneath the neon-illuminated skyline of this unique city, she has been reviewing films, events, and restaurants for *HK Magazine,* a weekly guide to arts and entertainment.

New This Year

This year we've reformatted our guides to make them easier to use. You may also notice our fresh graphics, new in 1996. More readable and more helpful than ever? We think so—and we hope you do, too.

Nineteen ninety-seven is a year of great significance for Hong Kong, as sovereignty over the territory passes from Great Britain to China at midnight on June 30th. Journalist Jan Alexander has written a thought-provoking essay, "1997: The Year of Reckoning," analyzing the significance of the changeover for residents of Hong Kong. Her piece is in Chapter 1. Tim Healy, a writer for the Hong Kong–based journal *AsiaWeek,* has contributed a portrait titled "Doing Business in Hong Kong, 1997 Style" to Chapter 10. His essay looks at the effect of the transition on the territory's business culture.

On the Web

Also check out Fodor's Web site (http://www.fodors.com/), where you'll find travel information on major destinations around the world and an ever-changing array of travel-savvy interactive features.

How to Use This Book

Organization

Up front is the **Gold Guide.** Its first section, **Important Contacts A to Z,** gives addresses and telephone numbers of organizations and companies that offer destination-related services and detailed information and publications. **Smart Travel Tips A to Z,** the Gold Guide's second section, gives specific information on how to accomplish what you need to in Hong Kong as well as tips on savvy traveling. Both sections are in alphabetical order by topic.

The Exploring chapter is subdivided by neighborhood and lists neighborhood sights alphabetically, many of which are bulleted and correspond to a map. Off the Beaten Path sights appear after the places from which they are most easily accessible. The remaining chapters are arranged in alphabetical order by subject (dining, lodging, nightlife and the arts, outdoor activities and sports, shopping, and side trips).

At the end of the book you'll find Portraits, wonderful essays about food, business, shopping, and the history of Hong Kong, followed by suggestions for pretrip reading, both fiction and nonfiction.

Icons and Symbols

★   Our special recommendations
✕   Restaurant
▨   Lodging establishment
☺   Good for kids (rubber duckie)
☞   Sends you to another section of the guide for more information
✉   Address
☎   Telephone number
FAX   Fax number
☉   Opening and closing times
💰   Admission prices (those we give apply only to adults; substantially reduced fees are almost always available for children, students, and senior citizens)

Credit Cards

The following abbreviations are used: **AE,** American Express; **DC,** Diners Club; **MC,** MasterCard; and **V,** Visa.

Please Write to Us

You can use this book in the confidence that all prices and opening times are based on information supplied to us at press time; Fodor's cannot accept responsibility for any errors. Time inevitably brings changes, so always confirm information when it matters—especially if you're making a detour to visit a specific place. In addition, when making reservations be sure to speak up if you have a disability or are traveling with children, if you prefer a private bath or a certain type of bed, or if you have specific dietary needs or any other concerns.

Were the restaurants we recommended as described? Did our hotel picks exceed your expectations? Did you find a museum we recommended a waste of time? If you have complaints, we'll look into them and revise our entries when the facts warrant it. If you've discovered a special place that we haven't included, we'll pass the information along to our correspondents and have them check it out. So send your feedback, positive *and* negative, to Fodor's Hong Kong Editor, 201 East 50th Street, New York, New York 10022—and have a wonderful trip!

Karen Cure

Karen Cure
Editorial Director

Hong Kong

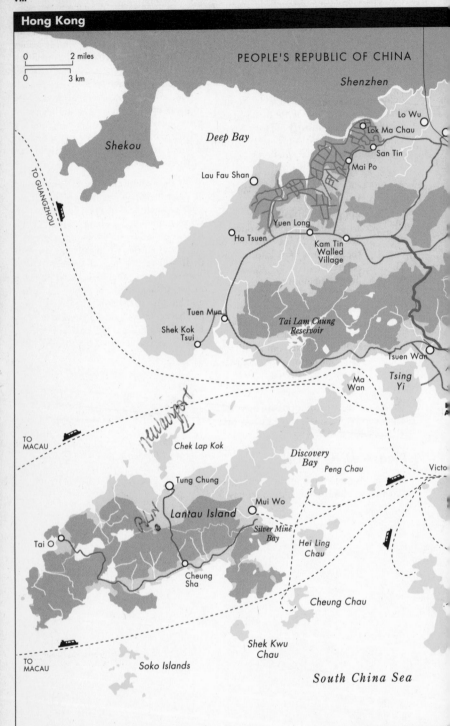

0   2 miles
0   3 km

PEOPLE'S REPUBLIC OF CHINA

Shenzhen

Shekou

Deep Bay

Lo Wu

Lok Ma Chau

San Tin

Mai Po

TO GUANGZHOU

Lau Fau Shan

Yuen Long

Ha Tsuen

Kam Tin
Walled
Village

Tuen Mun

*Tai Lam Chung
Reservoir*

Shek Kok
Tsui

Tsuen Wan

*Ma
Wan*

*Tsing
Yi*

TO
MACAU

Chek Lap Kok

*Discovery
Bay*

Peng Chau

Victo

Tung Chung

Mui Wo

Lantau Island

*Silver Mine
Bay*

Tai O

*Hei Ling
Chau*

Cheung
Sha

Cheung Chau

TO
MACAU

*Shek Kwu
Chau*

Soko Islands

South China Sea

Crooked Island

Sheung Shui

Fanling

Wu Kau Tang

Plover Cove Reservoir

Tolo Channel

Grass Island

Taipo

Kam Shan

Pan Chung

Tolo Harbour

NEW TERRITORIES

Chek Keng

Shatin

Sai Kung

Ho Chung

High Island

Sung Dynasty Village

Lai Chi Kok Amusement Park

KOWLOON

Hong Kong Int'l Municipal Airport

Port Shelter

Basalt Island

Victoria

Victoria Harbour

Kowloon Bay

Yau Tong

Junk Bay

Tai Wan Tau

HONG KONG

Tei Tong Tsui

Tung Lung Chau

Shek O

Stanley

Lamma Island

Stanley Peninsula

Po Toi Islands

N

KEY

Ferry Lines

World Time Zones

Numbers below vertical bands relate each zone to Greenwich Mean Time (0 hrs.).
Local times frequently differ from these general indications,
as indicated by light-face numbers on map.

Algiers, **29**
Anchorage, **3**
Athens, **41**
Auckland, **1**
Baghdad, **46**
Bangkok, **50**
Beijing, **54**

Berlin, **34**
Bogotá, **19**
Budapest, **37**
Buenos Aires, **24**
Caracas, **22**
Chicago, **9**
Copenhagen, **33**
Dallas, **10**

Delhi, **48**
Denver, **8**
Djakarta, **53**
Dublin, **26**
Edmonton, **7**
Hong Kong, **56**
Honolulu, **2**

Istanbul, **40**
Jerusalem, **42**
Johannesburg, **44**
Lima, **20**
Lisbon, **28**
London
(Greenwich), **27**
Los Angeles, **6**
Madrid, **38**
Manila, **57**

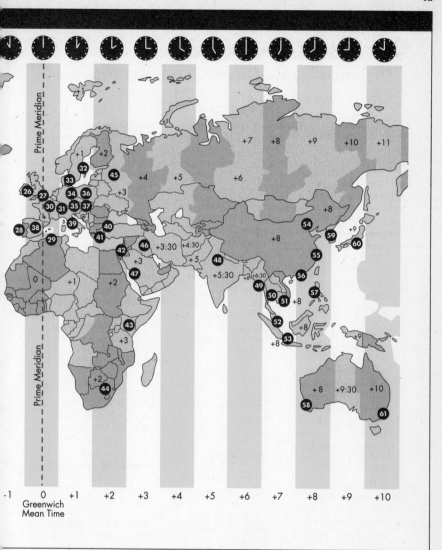

Prime Meridian

+7 +8 +9 +10 +11

+1 +2

+4 +5 +6

+3

+8

+8

+9

+3:30 +4:30

+8

+5

+5:30 +6 +6:30

+8

+8

+9

+3

+8

+8

Prime Meridian

+2

+8 +9:30 +10

+9

-1   0   +1   +2   +3   +4   +5   +6   +7   +8   +9   +10
Greenwich
Mean Time

Mecca, **47**
Mexico City, **12**
Miami, **18**
Montréal, **15**
Moscow, **45**
Nairobi, **43**
New Orleans, **11**
New York City, **16**

Ottawa, **14**
Paris, **30**
Perth, **58**
Reykjavík, **25**
Rio de Janeiro, **23**
Rome, **39**
Saigon (Ho Chi Minh City), **51**

San Francisco, **5**
Santiago, **21**
Seoul, **59**
Shanghai, **55**
Singapore, **52**
Stockholm, **32**
Sydney, **61**
Tokyo, **60**

Toronto, **13**
Vancouver, **4**
Vienna, **35**
Warsaw, **36**
Washington, D.C., **17**
Yangon, **49**
Zürich, **31**

IMPORTANT CONTACTS A TO Z

An Alphabetical Listing of Publications, Organizations, and Companies that Will Help You Before, During, and After Your Trip

A

AIR TRAVEL

The major gateway to Hong Kong is **Hong Kong International Airport** (☎ 011–852/ 2769–7531). Nearby **Macau International Airport** (☎ 011– 853/785–448) allows travelers to fly directly into the neighboring island.

FLYING TIME

Flying time to Hong Kong is between 17 and 20 hours from New York or Chicago, via Vancouver or Honolulu, and 13 hours direct from Los Angeles or San Francisco. Macau is a 20-minute flight from Hong Kong.

CARRIERS

To Hong Kong➤ **Canadian Airlines International** (☎ 800/ 426–7000 in Canada), **Cathay Pacific Airways** (☎ 800/233–2742 in the U.S.; 800/663–1338 in Canada), **China Airlines** (☎ 800/227– 5118), **Delta Airlines** (☎ 800/221–1212), **Northwest** (☎ 800/225– 2525), **Qantas** (☎ 800/227–4500), **Singapore Airlines** (☎ 800/742–3333), **United Airlines** (☎ 800/241– 6522), and **Virgin Atlantic** (☎ 800/862– 8621).

To Macau➤ **Asiana** (☎ 800/227–2462), **Korean Air** (☎ 800/ 438–5000), and **Singa-**pore Airlines (☎ 800/ 742–3333) fly via Hong Kong. Another option is to fly **TAP Air Portugal** (☎ 800/221– 7370) to Lisbon and on to Brussels, where you'll board a Sabena flight for the last leg to Macau.

FROM THE U.K.

British Airways (☎ 0181/897–4000 or 0345/222111 outside London), **Cathay Pacific Airways** (☎ 0345/ 581581), and **Virgin Atlantic** (☎ 01293/ 747747), have daily flights from London Heathrow to Hong Kong. Various Asian national airlines fly to Hong Kong via their capital cities, usually at reasonable rates.

COMPLAINTS

To register complaints about charter and scheduled airlines, contact the U.S. Department of Transportation's **Aviation Consumer Protection Division** (☒ C-75, Washington, DC 20590, ☎ 202/366– 2220). Complaints about lost baggage or ticketing problems and safety concerns may also be logged with the **Federal Aviation Administration (FAA) Consumer Hotline** (☎ 800/322–7873).

CONSOLIDATORS

For the names of reputable air-ticket consolidators, contact the **United States Air Consolidators Association** (☒ 925 L St., Suite 220, Sacramento, CA 95814, ☎ 916/441–4166, FAX 916/441–3520). For discount air-ticketing agencies, *see* Discounts & Deals, *below.*

PUBLICATIONS

For general information about charter carriers, ask for the Department of Transportation's free brochure **"Plane Talk: Public Charter Flights"** (☒ Aviation Consumer Protection Division, C-75, Washington, DC 20590, ☎ 202/366– 2220). The Department of Transportation also publishes a 58-page booklet, **"Fly Rights,"** available from the Consumer Information Center (☒ Supt. of Documents, Dept. 136C, Pueblo, CO 81009; $1.75).

For other tips and hints, consult the Consumers Union's monthly **"Consumer Reports Travel Letter"** (☒ Box 53629, Boulder, CO 80322, ☎ 800/234–1970; $39 1st year).

AIRPORT TRANSFERS

AIRBUSES

A fast and efficient way to get to and from the airport is to use the **Airbus** (☎ 2745–4466), which runs every 10 to 20 minutes from 7 AM to midnight. Route A1 (HK$12) runs through the Kowloon tourist area and serves the Ambassador, Empress, Grand, Holiday Inn Golden Mile, Hyatt Regency, Imperial, International, Kowloon, Miramar, New World, Park, Peninsula, Regent, Shangri-La, and Sheraton hotels, plus the YMCA and the Star Ferry. Routes A2 and A3 (HK$19) go to Hong Kong Island. A2 serves the Harbour View International House, Furama, Hilton, Mandarin, and Victoria hotels. A3 serves the Causeway Bay hotels: Caravelle, Excelsior, and Park Lane Radisson.

TAXIS

If you're staying at a hotel, follow signs to the area where hotel limousines wait. For normal taxi service, expect to pay HK$50 to HK$60 for Kowloon destinations and up to HK$120 for Hong Kong Island destinations, which includes the HK$20 fee for the Cross-Harbour Tunnel. Drivers will add a luggage-handling charge of HK$5 per piece.

B

For local contacts in the hometown of a tour operator you may be considering, consult the **Council of Better Business Bureaus** (⌧ 4200 Wilson Blvd., Suite 800, Arlington, VA 22203, ☎ 703/276-0100, FAX 703/525-8277).

For information call the **Hong Kong Tourist Association** (☎ 2807-6177).

BUSINESS CENTERS

There are many business centers outside the hotels; some are considerably cheaper than hotel facilities. Others cost about the same but offer private desks (from HK$250 per hour for desk space to HK$8,000 a month and up for a private office).

Amenities include a private address and phone answering and forwarding services. Many centers are affiliated with accountants and lawyers who can speed company registration. Some will even process visas and wrap gifts for you.

Harbour International Business Centre (⌧ 2802-2803 Admiralty Centre Tower I, 18 Harcourt Rd., Wanchai, ☎ 2529-0356, FAX 2861-3420) provides typing, secretarial support, and office rentals. Reservations are not required.

The **American Chamber of Commerce** (⌧ 1030 Swire House, Chater Rd., Central, Hong Kong Island ☎ 2526-0165, FAX 2810-1289) can arrange a Breakfast Briefing Program at your hotel for a fee that is negotiable according to the size of the group. The chamber hosts many luncheons and seminars, and the Young Professionals Committee holds cocktail parties at least once a month. There is also a library and a China trade services section.

Other business organizations of note are **AMS Management Service Ltd.** (⌧ 18th Floor, Wilson House, 19-27 Wyndham St., Central, ☎ 2846-3100, FAX 2810-7002), **Brauner's Business Centre** (⌧ Room 903-5, 9th Floor, Kowloon Centre, 29-43 Ashley Rd., Tsim Sha Tsui, ☎ 2376-2855, FAX 2376-3360), **Business Executive Centre** (⌧ Room 3715, Sun Hung Kai Centre, 30 Harbour Rd., Wanchai, ☎ 2827-7322, FAX 2827-4227), **Business Station** (⌧ 5th Floor, East Wing Duke Wellington House, 14-24 Wellington St., Central, ☎ 2521-0630, FAX 2521-7601), and 6th Floor, Cosmos Bldg., 8-11 Lan Kwai Fong; Central, ☎ 2523-6810, FAX 2530-5071), **Central Executive Business Centre** (⌧ 11th Floor, Central Bldg., 1 Pedder St., Central, ☎ 2841-7888, FAX 2810-1868), and **United Network Business Centre** (⌧ 4th Floor, Albion Plaza, 2-6 Granville Rd., Central, ☎ 2734-4888, FAX 2367-2151).

CELLULAR PHONES, BEEPERS, & FAXES

Phone Rent HK Ltd. (⌧ 10th Floor, Unit A, Time Centre, 53-55 Hollywood Rd., Central, ☎ 2545-5988) is the only remaining telecommunications rental outfit that has an English-speaking staff. Phone Rent has cellular phones, beepers, laptop computers and faxes, and it will deliver to your hotel for a small charge.

THE GOLD GUIDE / IMPORTANT CONTACTS

CHAMBERS OF COMMERCE

American Chamber of Commerce in Hong Kong (⊠ 1030 Swire House, Chater Rd., Central, Hong Kong Island, ☎ 2526–0165, FAX 2810–1289).

British Chamber of Commerce (⊠ Shui On Centre, 19th Floor, 8 Harbour Rd., Wanchai, Hong Kong Island, ☎ 2824–2211, FAX 2824–1333).

Chinese Manufacturers' Association (⊠ 5th Floor, CMA Bldg., 64–66 Connaught Rd., Central, Hong Kong Island, ☎ 2542–8600, FAX 2541–4541.

Federation of H.K. Industries (⊠ 407 Hankow Centre, 5–15 Hankow Rd., Kowloon, ☎ 2732–3188, FAX 2721–3494.

Hong Kong General Chamber of Commerce (⊠ United Centre, 22nd Floor, Queensway, Hong Kong Island, ☎ 2529–9229, FAX 2527–9843).

Hong Kong Japanese Chamber of Commerce and Industry (⊠ Hennessy Centre, 38th Floor, 500 Hennessy Rd., Hong Kong Island, ☎ 2577–6129, FAX 2577–0525).

Hong Kong Productivity Council (⊠ HKPC Bldg., 78 Tat Chee Ave., Kowloon Tong, ☎ 2788–5678, FAX 2788–5900).

Indian Chamber of Commerce Hong Kong (⊠ Hoseinee House, 2nd Floor, 69 Wyndham St., Central, Hong Kong Island, ☎ 2523–3877, FAX 2845–0300).

Swedish Chamber of Commerce (⊠ Shun Ho Tower, 24–30 Ice House St., Central, Hong Kong Island, ☎ 2525–0349, FAX 2537–1843).

CONVENTION CENTER

The **Hong Kong Convention and Exhibition Centre** (⊠ Harbour Rd., Wanchai, Hong Kong Island, ☎ 2582–8888, FAX 2582–8828) is a state-of-the-art 4.4-million-square-foot complex on the Wanchai waterfront. There are two 97,000-square-foot exhibition halls, with a main convention hall capable of seating 2,600. A large addition to the center is scheduled to be completed in June of '96. The complex, Asia's largest, houses two hotels, the 600-room Grand Hyatt and the 900-room New World, an apartment block, and a 54-story trade center/office building.

COPY SERVICES

All hotels and business centers have photocopy machines, as do many stores scattered throughout the territory. For heavy-duty, oversize, and color copying, try **Rank Xerox** (⊠ Central: New Henry House, 10 Ice House St., ☎ 2524–9799, FAX 2845–9271; Chung Hing Commercial Bldg., 62–63 Connaught Rd., ☎ 2541–6550, FAX 2850–5537; Wanchai: Shanghai Ind. Investment Bldg., 58 Hennessy Rd., ☎ 2528–0761, FAX 2865–0799; Tsim Sha Tsui: China Hong Kong City, 4 Canton Rd., ☎

2736–6011, FAX 2736–6278).

FACSIMILE

The Post Office and Hong Kong Telecom International (HKTI) offer a joint service called "Postfax." Check the **General Post Office** (⊠ Next to Star Ferry Terminal, Central, Hong Kong, ☎ 2921–2222) to find out which post offices have the service. Postfax is available at Hong Kong Telecom's 24-hour office (⊠ TST Hermes House, Kowloon, ☎ 2843–9466).

MESSENGERS

Deliveries can sometimes be arranged through your hotel concierge. Most business centers offer delivery service, too. However, there is a good chance that both of them will contact **DHL's** local courier service, run simultaneously with their international one. There are numerous **DHL Express Centres** (☎ 2710–8111) in major buildings and at various Mass Transit Railway stations. DHL will also pick up from your hotel. The minimum charge is HK$100 up to 1 kilogram; weight and distance determine exact price. If your timing is right at the Express Centre, you should be able to get same-day delivery.

OVERNIGHT MAIL

The post office has an overnight express service called **Speedpost.** Large international couriers, including **DHL** (☎ 2765–8111, FAX 2764–0641), **Federal Express**

(☎ 2730–3333, FAX 2730–6588), and **UPS** (☎ 2735–3535, FAX 2738–5070) have offices here. Minimum charge for a 1-kilogram parcel to New York City is between HK$293 and HK$394, depending on the zip code.

TELEX

If you want to avoid the hotel surcharge or your business center is closed, the public telex for sending is at **Hong Kong Telecom International** offices. There are many offices throughout the territory; the 24-hour office is at Hermes House, 10 Middle Road (across the street from the Sheraton), in Tsim Sha Tsui, Kowloon (☎ 2888–7184 or 2888–7185).

TRADE INFORMATION

Hong Kong Trade Development Council (⊠ 38th Floor, Office Tower Convention Plaza, 1 Harbour Rd., Hong Kong Island, ☎ 2584–4333, FAX 2824–0249). The TDC has 51 overseas offices, including 12 in the United States and one in the United Kingdom.

Trade Department (⊠ Trade Department Tower, 700 Nathan Rd., Kowloon, ☎ 2789–7444, FAX 2789–2491).

Industry Department (⊠ Ocean Centre, 14th Floor, 5 Canton Rd., Kowloon, ☎ 2737–2573, FAX 2730–4633).

C

CAR RENTAL

The only major car-rental company represented in Hong Kong is **Avis** (☎ 800/331–1084; in Canada, 800/879–2847). Rates begin at $79 a day and $329 a week for an economy car with unlimited mileage.

Local agencies include **Ace Hire Car** (⊠ 16 Min Fat St., Happy Valley, ☎ 2893–0541; turn left at the Hong Kong Bank), and **Fung Hing Hire Co.** (☎ 2572–0333), which rents chauffeured cars only.

CHILDREN & TRAVEL

FLYING

Look into **"Flying with Baby"** (⊠ Third Street Press, Box 261250, Littleton, CO 80163, ☎ 303/595–5959; $4.95 includes shipping), cowritten by a flight attendant. **"Kids and Teens in Flight,"** free from the U.S. Department of Transportation's Aviation Consumer Protection Division (⊠ C-75, Washington, DC 20590, ☎ 202/366–2220), offers tips on children flying alone. Every two years the February issue of **Family Travel Times** (☞ Know-How, *below*) details children's services on three dozen airlines. **"Flying Alone, Handy Advice for Kids Traveling Solo"** is available free from the American Automobile Association (AAA) (⊠ send stamped, self-addressed, legal-size envelope: Flying Alone, Mail Stop 800, 1000 AAA Dr., Heathrow, FL 32746).

KNOW-HOW

Family Travel Times, published quarterly by Travel with Your Children (⊠ TWYCH, 40 5th Ave., New York, NY 10011, ☎ 212/477–5524; $40 per year), covers destinations, types of vacations, and modes of travel.

LOCAL INFORMATION

The Great Hong Kong Dragon Adventure, published by the Hong Kong Tourist Association (HKTA, ☞ Visitor Information, below), is a story about a dragon that flies children from place to place. The HKTA also offers maps, brochures, and leaflets of activities sure to enthrall young visitors.

CONSULATES & COMMISSIONS

U.S. Consulate (⊠ 26 Garden Rd., Hong Kong Island, ☎ 2523–9011, FAX 2845–0735).

Canadian Commission (⊠ Tower 1, Exchange Sq., 11th–14th Floors, 8 Connaught Pl., Hong Kong Island, ☎ 2810–4321, FAX 2810–8736).

U.K. Commission (⊠ Overseas Visa Section, Hong Kong Immigration Dept., Wanchai Tower, 7 Gloucester Rd., Hong Kong Island, ☎ 2824–6111, FAX 2724–2333).

CUSTOMS

U.S. CITIZENS

The **U.S. Customs Service** (⊠ Box 7407, Washington, DC 20044, ☎ 202/927–6724) can answer questions on duty-free limits and publishes a helpful brochure, "Know Before You Go." For information on registering foreign-made articles, call

202/927–0540 or write U.S. Customs Service, Resource Management, 1301 Constitution Ave. NW, Washington DC, 20229.

COMPLAINTS➤ Note the inspector's badge number and write to the commissioner's office (✉ 1301 Constitution Ave. NW, Washington, DC 20229).

CANADIANS

Contact **Revenue Canada** (✉ 2265 St. Laurent Blvd. S, Ottawa, Ontario K1G 4K3, ☎ 613/993–0534) for a copy of the free brochure **"I Declare/Je Déclare"** and for details on duty-free limits. For recorded information (within Canada only), call 800/461–9999.

U.K. CITIZENS

HM Customs and Excise (✉ Dorset House, Stamford St., London SE1 9NG, ☎ 0171/202–4227) can answer questions about U.K. customs regulations and publishes a free pamphlet, **"A Guide for Travellers,"** detailing standard procedures and import rules.

D

DISABILITIES & ACCESSIBILITY

COMPLAINTS

To register complaints under the provisions of the Americans with Disabilities Act, contact the U.S. Department of Justice's **Disability Rights Section** (✉ Box 66738, Washington, DC 20035, ☎ 202/514–0301 or 800/514–0301, FAX 202/307–1198, TTY 202/514–0383 or 800/514–

0383). For airline-related problems, contact the U.S. Department of Transportation's **Aviation Consumer Protection Division** (☞ Air Travel, *above*). For complaints about surface transportation, contact the Department of Transportation's **Civil Rights Office** (✉ 400 7th St., SW, Room 10215, Washington, DC 20590 ☎ 202/366–4648).

LOCAL INFORMATION

A Guide for Physically Handicapped Visitors in Hong Kong is available through the HKTA (☞ Visitor Information, *below*.)

ORGANIZATIONS

TRAVELERS WITH HEARING IMPAIRMENTS➤ The **American Academy of Otolaryngology** (✉ 1 Prince St., Alexandria, VA 22314, ☎ 703/836–4444, FAX 703/683–5100, TTY 703/519–1585) publishes a brochure, "Travel Tips for Hearing Impaired People."

TRAVELERS WITH MOBILITY PROBLEMS➤ Contact **Mobility International USA** (✉ Box 10767, Eugene, OR 97440, ☎ and TTY 541/343–1284, FAX 541/343–6812), the U.S. branch of a Belgium-based organization (☞ *below*) with affiliates in 30 countries; **MossRehab Hospital Travel Information Service** (☎ 215/456–9600, TTY 215/456–9602), a telephone information resource for travelers with physical disabilities; the **Society for the Advancement of Travel for the Handicapped** (✉ 347

5th Ave., Suite 610, New York, NY 10016, ☎ 212/447–7284, FAX 212/725–8253; membership $45); and **Travelin' Talk** (✉ Box 3534, Clarksville, TN 37043, ☎ 615/552–6670, FAX 615/552–1182), which provides local contacts worldwide for travelers with disabilities.

TRAVELERS WITH VISION IMPAIRMENTS➤ Contact the **American Council of the Blind** (✉ 1155 15th St. NW, Suite 720, Washington, DC 20005, ☎ 202/467–5081, FAX 202/467–5085) for a list of travelers' resources, or the **American Foundation for the Blind** (✉ 11 Penn Plaza, Suite 300, New York, NY 10001, ☎ 212/502–7600 or 800/232–5463, TTY 212/502–7662), which provides general advice and publishes "Access to Art" ($19.95), a directory of museums that accommodate travelers with vision impairments.

IN THE U.K.

Contact the **Royal Association for Disability and Rehabilitation** (✉ RADAR, 12 City Forum, 250 City Rd., London EC1V 8AF, ☎ 0171/250–3222) or **Mobility International** (✉ rue de Manchester 25, B-1080 Brussels, Belgium, ☎ 00–322–410–6297, FAX 00–322–410–6874), an international travel-information clearinghouse for people with disabilities.

PUBLICATIONS

Several publications for travelers with disabilities are available from the **Consumer Information Center** (⊠ Box 100, Pueblo, CO 81009, ☎ 719/948–3334). Call or write for its free catalog of current titles. The Society for the Advancement of Travel for the Handicapped (☞ Organizations, *above*) publishes the quarterly magazine **"Access to Travel"** ($13 for 1-year subscription).

The 500-page ***Travelin' Talk Directory*** (⊠ Box 3534, Clarksville, TN 37043, ☎ 615/552–6670, FAX 615/552–1182; $35) lists people and organizations who help travelers with disabilities. For travel agents worldwide, consult the ***Directory of Travel Agencies for the Disabled*** (⊠ Twin Peaks Press, Box 129, Vancouver, WA 98666, ☎ 360/694–2462 or 800/637–2256, FAX 360/696–3210; $19.95 plus $3 shipping).

TRAVEL AGENCIES & TOUR OPERATORS

The Americans with Disabilities Act requires that all travel firms serve the needs of all travelers. That said, you should note that some agencies and operators specialize in making travel arrangements for individuals and groups with disabilities, among them **Access Adventures** (⊠ 206 Chestnut Ridge Rd., Rochester, NY 14624, ☎ 716/889–9096), run by a former physical-rehab counselor.

TRAVELERS WITH MOBILITY PROBLEMS➤ Contact **Accessible Journeys** (⊠ 35 W. Sellers Ave., Ridley Park, PA 19078, ☎ 610/521–0339 or

800/846–4537, FAX 610/521–6959), an escorted-tour operator exclusively for travelers with mobility impairments; **Hinsdale Travel Service** (⊠ 201 E. Ogden Ave., Suite 100, Hinsdale, IL 60521, ☎ 708/325–1335), a travel agency that benefits from the advice of wheelchair traveler Janice Perkins; and **Wheelchair Journeys** (⊠ 16979 Redmond Way, Redmond, WA 98052, ☎ 206/885–2210 or 800/313–4751), which can handle arrangements worldwide.

TRAVELERS WITH DEVELOPMENTAL DISABILITIES➤ Contact the nonprofit **New Directions** (⊠ 5276 Hollister Ave., Suite 207, Santa Barbara, CA 93111, ☎ 805/967–2841).

TRAVEL GEAR

The **Magellan's** catalog (☎ 800/962–4943, FAX 805/568–5406), includes a section devoted to products designed for travelers with disabilities.

DISCOUNTS & DEALS

AIRFARES

For the lowest airfares to Hong Kong, call 800/FLY–4–LESS.

CLUBS

Contact **Entertainment Travel Editions** (⊠ Box 1068, Trumbull, CT 06611, ☎ 800/445–4137; $28–$53, depending on destination), **Great American Traveler** (⊠ Box 27965, Salt Lake City, UT 84127, ☎ 800/548–2812; $49.95 per year), **Moment's Notice Discount Travel Club** (⊠ 7301 New

Utrecht Ave., Brooklyn, NY 11204, ☎ 718/234–6295; $25 per year, single or family), **Privilege Card International** (⊠ 3391 Peachtree Rd. NE, Suite 110, Atlanta, GA 30326, ☎ 404/262–0222 or 800/236–9732; $74.95 per year), **Travelers Advantage** (⊠ CUC Travel Service, 49 Music Sq. W, Nashville, TN 37203, ☎ 800/548–1116 or 800/648–4037; $49 per year, single or family), or **Worldwide Discount Travel Club** (⊠ 1674 Meridian Ave., Miami Beach, FL 33139, ☎ 305/534–2082; $50 per year for family, $40 single).

PASSES

See Subway Travel in Smart Travel Tips A to Z, *below.*

STUDENTS

Members of Hostelling International–American Youth Hostels (☞ Students, *below*) are eligible for discounts on car rentals, admissions to attractions, and other selected travel expenses.

PUBLICATIONS

Consult ***The Frugal Globetrotter,*** by Bruce Northam (⊠ Fulcrum Publishing, 350 Indiana St., Suite 350, Golden, CO 80401, ☎ 800/992–2908; $16.95 plus $4 shipping). For publications that tell how to find the lowest prices on plane tickets, ☞ Air Travel, *above.*

E EMERGENCIES

Police, fire, or **ambulance** (☎ 999).

Royal Hong Kong Police Visitor Hot Line (☎

2527–7177). English-speaking police wear a red shoulder tab.

DOCTORS

The main government hospitals are the **Queen Mary Hospital** (⌂ 102 Pok Fu Lam Rd., Hong Kong, ☎ 2855–3338), the **Queen Elizabeth Hospital** (⌂ 30 Gascoigne Rd., Kowloon, ☎ 2958–8888), the **Tang Shiu Kin Hospital** (⌂ 284 Queen's Rd. East, Hong Kong, ☎ 2831–6800), the **Princess Margaret Hospital** (⌂ 2-10 Princess Margaret Hospital Rd.; Laichikok, Kowloon, ☎ 2990–3200), and the **Prince of Wales Hospital** (⌂ 30–32 Ngan Shing St., Shatin, New Territories, ☎ 2636–2211).

G
GAY & LESBIAN TRAVEL

LOCAL INFORMATION

Contacts, a magazine covering the local gay scene, is available for HK$35 at the boutique **Fetish Fashion** (⌂ 1st Floor, 52–60 Lyndhurst Terr., Central, ☎ 2544-1155). Among popular nightspots are **Petticoat Lane** (⌂ 2 Tun Wo La., Mid-Levels, ☎ 2973-0642), and **Propaganda** (⌂ 30–32 Wyndham St., Central, ☎ 2868-1316), the largest gay and lesbian bar in Hong Kong. Meeting spots include **Middle Bay Beach** (a 10-minute walk from Repulse Bay along South Bay Rd. toward South Bay), **South Bay Beach**, the **Morrison Hill Swimming Bath** (⌂ Oi Kwan Rd.,

Wanchai), and **Tom Turk's Fitness Club** (⌂ Citibank Tower, Citibank Plaza, 3 Garden Rd., 3rd Floor, Central, ☎ 2521-4541).

Hong Kong's **AIDS Hotline** can be reached at 2780–2211.

ORGANIZATIONS

The **International Gay Travel Association** (⌂ Box 4974, Key West, FL 33041, ☎ 800/448-8550, FAX 305/296-6633), a consortium of more than 1,000 travel companies, can supply names of gay-friendly travel agents, tour operators, and accommodations.

PUBLICATIONS

The 16-page monthly newsletter **"Out & About"** (⌂ 8 W. 19th St., Suite 401, New York, NY 10011, ☎ 212/645-6922 or 800/929-2268, FAX 800/929-2215; $49 for 10 issues and quarterly calendar) covers gay-friendly resorts, hotels, cruise lines, and airlines.

TOUR OPERATORS

Toto Tours (⌂ 1326 W. Albion Ave., Suite 3W, Chicago, IL 60626, ☎ 312/274-8686 or 800 /565-1241, FAX 312/ 274-8695) offers group tours to worldwide destinations.

TRAVEL AGENCIES

The largest agencies serving gay travelers are **Advance Travel** (⌂ 10700 Northwest Fwy., Suite 160, Houston, TX 77092, ☎ 713/682-2002 or 800/292-0500), **Club Travel** (⌂ 8739 Santa Monica Blvd., W. Hollywood, CA 90069, ☎ 310/

358–2200 or 800/429-8747), **Islanders/ Kennedy Travel** (⌂ 183 W. 10th St., New York, NY 10014, ☎ 212/ 242–3222 or 800/988-1181), **Now Voyager** (⌂ 4406 18th St., San Francisco, CA 94114, ☎ 415/626–1169 or 800/255–6951), and **Yellowbrick Road** (⌂ 1500 W. Balmoral Ave., Chicago, IL 60640, ☎ 312/561–1800 or 800/ 642–2488). **Skylink Women's Travel** (⌂ 2460 W. 3rd St., Suite 215, Santa Rosa, CA 95401, ☎ 707/ 570–0105 or 800/225-5759) serves lesbian travelers.

H
HEALTH

FINDING A DOCTOR

For its members, the **International Association for Medical Assistance to Travellers** (⌂ IAMAT, membership free; 417 Center St., Lewiston, NY 14092, ☎ 716/754–4883; 40 Regal Rd., Guelph, Ontario N1K 1B5, ☎ 519/836–0102; 1287 St. Clair Ave. W., Toronto, Ontario M6E 1B8, ☎ 416/652–0137; 57 Voirets, 1212 Grand-Lancy, Geneva, Switzerland, no phone) publishes a worldwide directory of English-speaking physicians meeting IAMAT standards.

MEDICAL-ASSISTANCE COMPANIES

The following companies are concerned primarily with emergency medical assistance, although they may provide some insurance as part of their coverage. For a list of full-service travel insurance companies, ☞ Insurance, *below.*

You can also contact **International SOS Assistance** (⊠ Box 11568, Philadelphia, PA 19116, ☎ 215/244–1500 or 800/523–8930; Box 466, Pl. Bonaventure, Montréal, Québec H5A 1C1, ☎ 514/874–7674 or 800/363–0263; 7 Old Lodge Pl., St. Margarets, Twickenham TW1 1RQ, England, ☎ 0181/744–0033), **Medex Assistance Corporation** (⊠ Box 5375, Timonium, MD 21094, ☎ 410/453–6300 or 800/537–2029), **Near Travel Services** (⊠ Box 1339, Calumet City, IL 60409, ☎ 708/868–6700 or 800/654–6700), **Traveler's Emergency Network** (⊠ 1133 15th St. NW, Suite 400, Washington DC, 20005, ☎ 202/828–5894 or 800/275–4836, FAX 202/828–5896), **TravMed** (⊠ Box 5375, Timonium, MD 21094, ☎ 410/453–6380 or 800/732–5309), or **Worldwide Assistance Services** (⊠ 1133 15th St. NW, Suite 400, Washington, DC 20005, ☎ 202/331–1609 or 800/821–2828, FAX 202/828–5896).

I
INSURANCE

IN THE U.S.

Travel insurance covering baggage, health, and trip cancellation or interruptions is available from **Access America** (⊠ 6600 W. Broad St., Richmond, VA 23230, ☎ 804/285–3300 or 800/334–

7525), **Carefree Travel Insurance** (⊠ Box 9366, 100 Garden City Plaza, Garden City, NY 11530, ☎ 516/294–0220 or 800/323–3149), **Tele-Trip** (⊠ Mutual of Omaha Plaza, Box 31716, Omaha, NE 68131, ☎ 800/228–9792), **Travel Guard International** (⊠ 1145 Clark St., Stevens Point, WI 54481, ☎ 715/345–0505 or 800/826–1300), **Travel Insured International** (⊠ Box 280568, East Hartford, CT 06128, ☎ 203/528–7663 or 800/243–3174), and **Wallach & Company** (⊠ 107 W. Federal St., Box 480, Middleburg, VA 22117, ☎ 540/687–3166 or 800/237–6615).

IN CANADA

Contact **Mutual of Omaha** (⊠ Travel Division, 500 University Ave., Toronto, Ontario M5G 1V8, ☎ 800/465–0267 (in Canada) or 416/598–4083).

IN THE U.K.

The **Association of British Insurers** (⊠ 51 Gresham St., London EC2V 7HQ, ☎ 0171/600–3333) gives advice by phone and publishes the free pamphlet "**Holiday Insurance and Motoring Abroad,**" which sets out typical policy provisions and costs.

M
MAIL

RECEIVING MAIL

The **General Post Office** (⊠ next to the Star Ferry Concourse in Central, ☎ 2921–2222, or at Hermes House, 100 Middle Rd.

in Kowloon, ☎ 2366–4111 or 2843–9466 for addressee information) is speedy and efficient, with deliveries twice daily, six days a week, and overnight delivery in main business areas.

Travelers can receive mail at the **American Express** office (⊠ 16–18 Queen's Rd., Central; Ground Floor, New World Tower, Central, ☎ 2844–0688). This service is available only for AMEX cardholders or traveler's check holders. Mail should be addressed c/o Client Mail Service at the office listed above.

MONEY

ATMS

For specific foreign **Cirrus** locations, call 800/424–7787; for foreign **Plus** locations, consult the Plus directory at your local bank.

CURRENCY EXCHANGE

If your bank doesn't exchange currency, contact **Thomas Cook Currency Services** (☎ 800/287–7362 for locations). **Ruesch International** (☎ 800/424–2923 for locations) can also provide you with foreign banknotes before you leave home and publishes a number of useful brochures, including a "Foreign Currency Guide" and "Foreign Exchange Tips."

WIRING FUNDS

Funds can be wired via **MoneyGram℠** (for locations and information in the U.S. and Canada, ☎ 800/926–9400) or **Western Union** (for agent locations or to send money using MasterCard or Visa, ☎ 800/325–6000; in Canada, 800/321–2923; in the U.K., 0800/833833; or visit the Western Union office at the nearest major post office).

P

PASSPORTS & VISAS

U.S. CITIZENS

For fees, documentation requirements, and other information, call the State Department's **Office of Passport Services** information line (☎ 202/647–0518).

CANADIANS

For fees, documentation requirements, and other information, call the Ministry of Foreign Affairs and International Trade's **Passport Office** (☎ 819/994–3500 or 800/567–6868).

U.K. CITIZENS

For fees, documentation requirements, and to request an emergency passport, call the **London Passport Office** (☎ 0990/210410).

PHOTO HELP

The **Kodak Information Center** (☎ 800/242–2424) answers consumer questions about film and photography. The **Kodak Guide to Shooting Great Travel Pictures** (available in bookstores; or contact Fodor's Travel Publications, ☎ 800/533–6478; $16.50 plus $4 shipping) explains how to take expert travel photographs.

S

SAFETY

"Trouble-Free Travel," from the AAA, is a booklet of tips for protecting yourself and your belongings when away from home. Send a stamped, self-addressed, legal-size envelope to Trouble-Free Travel (✉ Mail Stop 75, 1000 AAA Dr., Heathrow, FL 32746).

SENIOR CITIZENS

CLUBS

Sears's **Mature Outlook** (✉ Box 10448, Des Moines, IA 50306, ☎ 800/336–6330; annual membership $14.95) includes a lifestyle/travel magazine and membership in ITC-50 travel club, which offers discounts of up to 50% at participating hotels and restaurants. (☞ Discounts & Deals *in* Smart Travel Tips A to Z).

ORGANIZATIONS

Contact the **American Association of Retired Persons** (✉ AARP, 601 E St. NW, Washington, DC 20049, ☎ 202/434–2277; annual dues $8 per person or couple). Its Purchase Privilege Program secures discounts for members on lodging, car rentals, and sightseeing.

SHOPPING

If you are considering the purchase of ivory products, check with the **Hong Kong Department of Agriculture and Fisheries** (☎ 2733–2283), as well as your home consulate or trade commission.

SIGHTSEEING

ORIENTATION TOURS

The **Hong Kong Island Tour** is a three- to four-hour bus tour that departs from all major hotels daily in the mornings and afternoons. Routes vary, but the following areas are generally covered: Victoria Peak, Wanchai, Aw Boon Haw Gardens, Repulse Bay and Deep Water Bay, Aberdeen, the University of Hong Kong, and Western and Central districts.

The **Kowloon and New Territories Tour** takes in sights as varied as Kwai Chung Container Terminal, the Castle Peak fishing village, a Taoist temple, the town of Yuen Long, the Chinese border at Lokmachau, and the Royal Hong Kong Golf Club at Fanling. The six-hour "Land Between Tour" offers a glimpse of rural Hong Kong. Tours can be booked through the Hong Kong Tourist Association (☞ Visitor Information, *below*).

Harbour and Islands, Watertours of Hong Kong Ltd., (☎ 2739–3302 or 2724–2856) and the **Seaview Harbour Tour Co. Ltd.** (☎ 2561–5033) operate a variety of tours that cover the Inner Harbour and outer islands via junks and cruisers. Tours can be booked through the Hong Kong Tourist Association (☞ Visitor Information, *below*).

Star Ferry Harbour Cruises (☎ 2366–9885 or 2345–2324) offers sundown cruises and a late-night "Harbour Lights" cruise that enjoys the romantic view from the water.

SPECIAL-INTEREST TOURS

DOLPHIN WATCH➤ The Chinese white dolphin is on its way to extinction in the South China sea. **Hong Kong Dolphin Watch** (✉ GPO Box 4102, Central, ☎ 2984–1414, ⅢＸ 2984–1414) sponsors tours, by junk, to dolphin habitats around Lantau Island and beyond.

GOVERNMENT➤ The civic-minded may be interested in a last glimpse of parliamentary government in action in Hong Kong, at the Legislative Council, before China reassumes control of the territory on July 1, 1997. Contact the **Secretary General** Information Officer (✉ Legco Bldg., 8 Jackson Rd., ☎ 2869–9284) to arrange to sit in on a council session and take a guided tour of the building. Visitors after July 1 will need to telephone for an update.

HELICOPTER➤ **Heliservices Hong Kong Limited** (✉ Helipad, Fenwick Pier, Wanchai, ☎ 2802–0200 for reservations, 2523–6407 main office) offers helicopter tours around the colony; the chopper seats up to five passengers.

HERITAGE➤ The **HKTA** (☎ 2807–6390 for tour department, 2807–6177) offers a four-hour "Heritage Tour" that takes in the Lei Cheng Uk tomb, Sam

Tunk Uk Folk Museum, Tai Fu Tai mansion, and Man Shek Tong ancestral hall.

HORSE RACING➤ The HKTA runs a tour to both Shatin and Happy Valley tracks during the September–May season. This tour is for nonresidents only, so bring your passport.

HOUSING➤ The **Family Insight Home Visit** focuses on the daily life of local people by visiting a public housing estate, the home of an estate family, and the Wong Tai Sin Temple. About half of Hong Kong's population lives in public housing, and this tour offers visitors a rare view of this economic miracle. Contact the HKTA (☎ 2807–6390).

MACAU➤ The **Macau Tourist Bureau** (☎ 2540–8180) offers day and night sightseeing tours of this nearby ex-Portuguese colony. Included in the package are embarkation taxes, lunch, and transfers.

NIGHTLIFE➤ The "Hong Kong Night Tour" offers a Chinese dinner at the Jumbo floating restaurant in Aberdeen, followed by a visit to a Chinese night market. Contact the **Watertours** (☎ 2739–3302).

Open Top Tram Tours (☎ 2801–7430) offers open-air cocktail rides atop a tram and a four-hour night tour that includes dinner in a luxe restaurant and a night-owl tour of the city.

SAILING➤ **B. Tours** (☎ 2851–9601) operates

pleasure cruises for private parties on its sailing junk, the Duk Ling. The vessel accommodates up to 35 people.

Contact the **HKTA** (☎ 2807–6390) for a list of other boat tours, including their *Harbour Junk and Sung Dynasty Tour,* an all-day event consisting of a sail on one of those fabled junks, followed by a coach trip to a living-history, 1,000-year-old-village for lunch and a traditional cultural performance.

SHOPPING➤ There are a number of private shopping tour operators. Non-Stop Shoppers (☎ 2523–3850, ⅢＸ 2868–1164) charters a bus once a week to visit factory outlets, mostly in Kowloon and the New Territories. The itinerary, which varies from week to week, takes in outlets for cookware, towels, brass ware, porcelain, furniture, and carpets. Cost is HK$280 per person. Call or fax for current schedule.

At the high end of the shopping spectrum, **Asian Cajun Ltd.** (✉ 12 Scenic Village Drive, 4th Floor, Pokfulam, ☎ 2817–3687, ⅢＸ 2855–9571) offers customized shopping tours for visitors looking for good buys in antiques, art, jewelry, designer clothes and specialty items. Escorted tours are US$80 per hour, with a three-hour minimum. There is an extra hourly charge for a car and driver.

THE GOLD GUIDE / IMPORTANT CONTACTS

GROUPS

A major tour operator specializing in student travel is **AESU Travel** (✉ 2 Hamill Rd., Suite 248, Baltimore, MD 21210-1807, ☎ 410/323–4416 or 800/638–7640).

HOSTELING

In the United States, contact **Hostelling International–American Youth Hostels** (✉ 733 15th St. NW, Suite 840, Washington, DC 20005, ☎ 202/783–6161, FAX 202/783–6171); in Canada, **Hostelling International–Canada** (✉ 205 Catherine St., Suite 400, Ottawa, Ontario K2P 1C3, ☎ 613/237–7884); and in the United Kingdom, the **Youth Hostel Association of England and Wales** (✉ Trevelyan House, 8 St. Stephen's Hill, St. Albans, Hertfordshire AL1 2DY, ☎ 01727/855215 or 01727/845047). Membership (in the U.S., $25; in Canada, C$26.75; in the U.K., £9.30) gives you access to 5,000 hostels in 77 countries that charge $5–$40 per person per night.

LODGING

Booth Lodge (✉ The Salvation Army; 11 Wing Sing La., Yau Ma Tei, Kowloon, ☎ 2771–9266, FAX 2385–1140) has rooms for HKS$ 680–$950. The **Garden View International House** (✉ YWCA, 1 MacDonnell Rd., Central, ☎ 2877–3737, FAX 2845–6263) charges between HK$800 to $1650. **STB Hostel** (✉ HK Ltd., 1st Floor, Great Eastern Mansion, 255–261 Reclamation St., Mongkok, Kowloon, ☎ 2710–9199, FAX 2385–0153) has dormitory-style sleeping quarters at HK$200 and rooms for HK$500. Bargain lodging has become increasingly rare in Hong Kong. The **YMCA** (✉ 41 Salisbury Rd., Tsim Sha Tsui, Kowloon, ☎ 2369–2211, FAX 2739–9315), across from the Peninsula Hotel, is the most popular place among accommodations that are moderately priced by Hong Kong standards (HK$800–$945), but it is hard to get a booking. Other YMCA rooms can be found at **YMCA International House** (✉ 23 Waterloo Rd., Yau Ma Tei, Kowloon, ☎ 2771–9111, FAX 2771–5238) for HK$1000.

ORGANIZATIONS

A major contact is the **Council on International Educational Exchange** (✉ mail orders only: CIEE, 205 E. 42nd St., 16th Floor, New York, NY 10017, ☎ 212/822–2600, FAX 212/822–2699). The **Educational Travel Centre** (✉ 438 N. Frances St., Madison, WI 53703, ☎ 608/256–5551 or 800/747–5551, FAX 608/256–2042) offers rail passes and low-cost airline tickets, mostly for flights that depart from Chicago.

In Canada, also contact **Travel Cuts** (✉ 187 College St., Toronto, Ontario M5T 1P7, ☎ 416/979–2406 or 800/667–2887).

For information and schedules, contact the **Mass Transit Railway** (MTR, ☎ 2750–0170) or the **Hong Kong Tourist Association** information service (HKTA, ☎ 2807–6177). *See* Smart Travel Tips, *below,* for general information.

T

COMPLAINTS

You can file complaints through the **police hot line** (☎ 2527–7177).

The country code for Hong Kong is 852. For local access numbers abroad, contact **AT&T USADirect** (☎ 800/874–4000), **MCI** Call USA (☎ 800/444–4444), or **Sprint** Express (☎ 800/793–1153).

LONG-DISTANCE

For long-distance calling, go to the **Hong Kong Telecom International** (✉ Century Square, 1 D'Aguilar St., Central, ☎ 2810–0660, and TST Hermes House, Kowloon, ☎ 2888–7184 or 2888–7185).

Among the companies that sell tours and packages to Hong Kong, the following are nationally known, have a proven reputation, and offer plenty of options.

GROUP TOURS

SUPER-DELUXE➤ **Abercrombie & Kent** (✉ 1520 Kensington Rd., Oak Brook, IL 60521-2141, ☎ 708/954–2944 or 800/323–

7308, FAX 708/954–3324) and **Travcoa** (✉ Box 2630, 2350 S.E. Bristol St., Newport Beach, CA 92660, ☎ 714/476–2800 or 800/992–2003, FAX 714/476–2538)

DELUXE➤ **Globus** (✉ 5301 S. Federal Circle, Littleton, CO 80123, ☎ 303/797–2800 or 800/221–0090, FAX 303/795–0962), **Maupintour** (✉ Box 807, 1515 St. Andrews Drive, Lawrence, KS 66047, ☎ 913/843–1211 or 800/255–4266, FAX 913/843–8351), and **Tauck Tours** (✉ Box 5027, 276 Post Rd. W, Westport, CT 06881, ☎ 203/226–6911 or 800/468–2825, FAX 203/221–6828).

FIRST-CLASS➤ **Brendan Tours** (✉ 15137 Califa St., Van Nuys, CA 91411, ☎ 818/785–9696 or 800/421–8446, FAX 818/902–9876), **DER Tours** (✉ 11933 Wilshire Blvd., Los Angeles, CA 90025, ☎ 310/479–4411 or 800/937–1235), **Orient Flexi-Pax Tours** (✉ 630 Third Ave., New York, NY 10017, ☎ 212/692–9550 or 800/545–5540), **Pacific Bestour** (✉ 228 Rivervale Rd., River Vale, NJ 07675, ☎ 201/664–8778 or 800/688–3288), and **Pacific Delight Tours** (✉ 132 Madison Ave., New York, NY 10016, ☎ 212/684–7707 or 800/221–7179).

BUDGET➤ **Cosmos** (☞ Globus, *above*).

PACKAGES

Independent vacation packages are available from major airlines and tour operators. Contact **Delta Dream Vacations** (☎ 800/872–7786) and **United Vacations** (☎ 800/328–6877). Many of the operators listed under group tours, *above*, also sell independent tours. Contact **DER Tours,** Orient Flexi-Pax Tours, Pacific Bestour, and **Pacific Delight Tours.**

FROM THE U.K.

Contact **British Airways Holidays** (✉ Astral Towers, Betts Way, London Rd., Crawley, West Sussex RH10 2XA, ☎ 01293/723–171), **Kuoni Travel** (✉ Kuoni House, Dorking, Surrey RH5 4AZ,2 ☎ 01306/742–222), and **Tradewinds** (✉ Helmshore, Rossendale, Lancashire BB4 4NB, ☎ 01706/219–111).

THEME TRIPS

Customized, deluxe tours of Hong Kong, tailored to individual interests, are available from **Pacific Experience** (✉ 366 Madison Ave., #1203, New York, NY 10017, ☎ 212/661–2604 or 800/279–3639, FAX 212/661–2587).

BICYCLING➤ Bike tours of Asia that include Hong Kong are available from **Backroads** (✉ 1516 Fifth St., Berkeley, CA 94710-1740, ☎ 510/527–1555 or 800/462–2848, FAX 510/527–1444).

JUDAISM➤ Jewish Life in the Far East, including Hong Kong, is the subject of a tour from the **American Jewish Congress** (✉ 15 E. 84th St., New York, NY 10028, ☎ 212/879–4588 or 800/221–4694).

LEARNING VACATIONS➤ For an in-depth look at Hong Kong, contact **Smithsonian Study Tours and Seminars** (✉ 1100 Jefferson Dr. SW, Room 3045, MRC 702, Washington, DC 20560, ☎ 202/357–4700, FAX 202/633–9250).

ORGANIZATIONS

The **National Tour Association** (✉ NTA, 546 E. Main St., Lexington, KY 40508, ☎ 606/226–4444 or 800/755–8687) and the **United States Tour Operators Association** (✉ USTOA, 211 E. 51st St., Suite 12B, New York, NY 10022, ☎ 212/750–7371) can provide lists of members and information on booking tours.

PUBLICATIONS

Contact the USTOA (☞ Organizations, *above*) for its **"Smart Traveler's Planning Kit."** Pamphlets in the kit include the "Worldwide Tour and Vacation Package Finder," "How to Select a Tour or Vacation Package," and information on the organization's consumer protection plan. Also get a copy of the Better Business Bureau's **"Tips on Travel Packages"** (✉ Publication 24-195, 4200 Wilson Blvd., Arlington, VA 22203; $2).

TRANSLATION SERVICES

Contact **CIAP Hong Kong** (✉ Flat 15, 7F, Mt. Nicholson Gap, 103 Mt. Nicholson Rd., Happy Valley, ☎ 2838–5852), **Translanguage-IRH Ltd.** (✉ Room 1003, Working Field

Commercial Bldg., 408–412 Jaffe Rd., Wanchai, ☎ 2893–5000), or **Polyglot Translations** (✉ Time Centre, 53 Hollywood Rd., Central, ☎ 2851–7232).

FERRIES

For information and schedules, contact the **HKTA** (☎ 2807–6543 or hot line 2807–6177), **Star Ferry Harbour Cruises** (☎ 2366–2576 or 2845–2324), and the **Hong Kong and Yaumatei Ferry Company** (☎ 2542–3081). For information about ferry service to Macau and locations in China, ☞ China A to Z *in* Chapter 9 *and* Macau A to Z *in* Chapter 8.

For travel apparel, appliances, personal-care items, and other travel necessities, get a free catalog from **Magellan's** (☎ 800/962–4943, FAX 805/568–5406), **Orvis Travel** (☎ 800/541–3541, FAX 540/343–7053), or **TravelSmith** (☎ 800/950–1600, FAX 415/455–0554).

ELECTRICAL CONVERTERS

Send a self-addressed, stamped envelope to the **Franzus Company** (✉ Customer Service, Dept. B50, Murtha Industrial Park, Box 142, Beacon Falls, CT 06403, ☎ 203/723–6664) for a copy of the free brochure "Foreign Electricity Is No Deep, Dark Secret."

For names of reputable agencies in your area,

contact the **American Society of Travel Agents** (✉ ASTA, 1101 King St., Suite 200, Alexandria, VA 22314, ☎ 703/739–2782), the **Association of Canadian Travel Agents** (✉ Suite 201, 1729 Bank St., Ottawa, Ontario K1V 7Z5, ☎ 613/521–0474, FAX 613/521–0805), or the **Association of British Travel Agents** (✉ 55-57 Newman St., London W1P 4AH, ☎ 0171/637–2444, FAX 0171/637–0713).

U

The U.S. Department of State's American Citizens Services office (✉ Room 4811, Washington, DC 20520; enclose SASE) issues **Consular Information Sheets** on all foreign countries. These cover issues such as crime, security, political climate, and health risks as well as listing embassy locations, entry requirements, and currency regulations and providing other useful information. For the latest information, stop in at any U.S. passport office, consulate, or embassy, or call the interactive hot line (☎ 202/647–5225, FAX 202/647–3000).

V

IN THE U.S.

Contact the **HKTA** (✉ 590 5th Ave., Suite 590, New York, NY 10036, ☎ 212/869–5008, FAX

212/730–2605; ✉ 610 Enterprise Dr., Suite 200, Oak Brook, IL 60521, ☎ 708/575–2828, FAX 708/575–2829; ✉ 10940 Wilshire Blvd., Suite 1220, Los Angeles, CA 90024, ☎ 310/208–4582, FAX 310/208–1869).

For information on Macau, contact the **Macau Tourist Information Bureau,** (MTIB, ✉ 70A Greenwich Ave., Box 316, New York, NY 10011, ☎ 212/206–6828 or 800/295–7891, FAX 212/727–3222; ✉ 3133 Lake Hollywood Dr., Box 1860, Los Angeles, CA 90068, ☎ 213/851–3402 or 800/331–7150, FAX 213/851–3684; ✉ 999 Wilder Ave., Suite 1103, Honolulu, HI 96822, ☎ 808/536–0719, FAX 808/538–7613; and ✉ Box 350, Kenilworth, IL 60043, ☎ 708/251–6421, FAX 708/256–5601).

IN CANADA

Contact the **HKTA** (✉ 347 Bay St., Suite 909, Toronto, Ontario M5H 2R7, ☎ 416/366–2389, FAX 416/366–1098).

For information on Macau, contact the **MTIB** (✉ 13 Mountalan Ave , Toronto, Ontario, M4J 1H3, ☎ FAX 416/466–6552, and ✉ 157-10551 Shellbridge Way, Richmond, British Columbia V6X 2W9, ☎ 604/231–9040, FAX 604/231–9031).

IN HONG KONG

Information centers are just beyond customs at Hong Kong International Airport, on the Star Ferry Concourse in

Kowloon, and in the basement of Jardine House on Hong Kong Island. For help by phone, try the **multilingual telephone information service** (☎ 2801–7177). If you prefer to get help by fax, try the **24-hour facsimile information service** (☎ 2177–1128). Dial by voice first for the menu.

IN THE U.K.

Contact the **HKTA** (✉ 4th Floor, 125 Pall Mall, London SW1Y 5EA, ☎ 0891/661–188, (calls are charged at 39p per minute cheap

rate and 49p per minute at other times) or 0171/930–4775, FAX 0171/930–4777.

For information on Macau, contact the **MTIB** (✉ 6 Sherlock Mews, Paddington St., London W1M 3RH, ☎ 0171/224–3390, FAX 0171/224–0601.

W
WEATHER

For current conditions and forecasts, plus the local time and helpful travel tips, call the **Weather Channel Con-**

nection (☎ 900/932–8437; 95¢ per minute) from a Touch-Tone phone.

The *International Traveler's Weather Guide* (✉ Weather Press, Box 660606, Sacramento, CA 95866, ☎ 916/974–0201 or 800/972–0201; $10.95 includes shipping), written by two meteorologists, provides month-by-month information on temperature, humidity, and precipitation in more than 175 cities worldwide.

SMART TRAVEL TIPS A TO Z

Basic Information on Traveling in Hong Kong and Savvy Tips to Make Your Trip a Breeze

A
AIR TRAVEL

If time is an issue, **always look for nonstop flights,** which require no change of plane. If possible, **avoid connecting flights,** which stop at least once and can involve a change of plane, even though the flight number remains the same; if the first leg is late, the second waits.

For better service, **fly smaller or regional carriers,** which often have higher passenger satisfaction ratings. Sometimes they have such in-flight amenities as leather seats or greater legroom and they often have better food.

CUTTING COSTS

The Sunday travel section of most newspapers is a good place to look for deals.

MAJOR AIRLINES➤ The least-expensive airfares from the major airlines are priced for round-trip travel and are subject to restrictions. Usually, you must **book in advance and buy the ticket within 24 hours** to get cheaper fares, and you may have to **stay over a Saturday night.** The lowest fare is subject to availability, and only a small percentage of the plane's total seats is sold at that price. It's smart to **call a number of airlines,** and when you are quoted a good price, **book it on the spot**—the same fare may not be available on the same flight the next day. Airlines generally allow you to change your return date for a $25 to $50 fee. If you don't use your ticket, you can apply the cost toward the purchase of a new ticket, again for a small charge. However, most low-fare tickets are nonrefundable. To get the lowest airfare, **check different routings.** If your destination has more than one gateway, **compare prices to different airports.**

FROM THE U.K.➤ To save money on flights, **look into an APEX or Super-PEX ticket.** APEX tickets must be booked in advance and have certain restrictions. Super-PEX tickets can be purchased right at the airport.

CONSOLIDATORS➤ Consolidators buy tickets for scheduled flights at reduced rates from the airlines, then sell them at prices below the lowest available from the airlines directly—usually without advance restrictions. Sometimes you can even get your money back if you need to return the ticket. Carefully read the fine print detailing penalties for changes and cancellations. If you doubt the reliability of a consolidator, **confirm your reservation with the airline.**

ALOFT

AIRLINE FOOD➤ If you hate airline food, **ask for special meals when booking.** These can be vegetarian, low-cholesterol, or kosher, for example; commonly prepared to order in smaller quantities than standard fare, they can be tastier.

JET LAG➤ To avoid this syndrome, which occurs when travel disrupts your body's natural cycles, try to maintain a normal routine. At night, **get some sleep.** By day, move about the cabin to **stretch your legs, eat light meals, and drink water—not alcohol.**

SMOKING➤ **Contact your carrier regarding their smoking policy.** Some carriers have prohibited smoking throughout their system; others allow smoking only on certain routes or even certain departures of that route.

B
BUSES

For schedules, call the Hong Kong Tourist Association's information service (☞ Buses *in* Important Contacts A to Z, *above*); it is difficult to get bus operators on the phone and they don't usually speak English, but HKTA will be helpful. Minibuses,

14- to 16-seat yellow vehicles with single red stripes, travel all over Hong Kong and stop almost anywhere on request; **look for a minibus for quick transportation.** They are, however, slightly more expensive than ordinary buses. Their destination is written on the front, but the English-language characters are small. **Wave the minibus down when you see the one you want.** Since fares are adjusted throughout the journey, you could pay as little as HK$2 or as much as HK$6.

Maxicabs look the same as minibuses but have single green stripes and run fixed routes. Rates run from HK$1.60 to HK$6.

BUSINESS HOURS

Most banks are open 9 AM to 4:30 PM, but some open in the evening, and major ones are open 9 AM to 12:30 PM on Saturday, and even on Sundays for special purposes. There is 24-hour automated banking in most branches. Office hours are more or less the same as in the West, 9 AM–5 or 6 PM, but shops usually open about 10 AM and stay open until 9 or 9:30 PM, especially in the tourist and residential areas.

Although there are no hard and fast rules about hours, shops in Hong Kong tend to open and close late. On Hong Kong Island, the Central area is open from 10 AM to 6 PM; Causeway Bay and Wanchai from 10 AM to 9:30 PM. Kowloon's Tsim Sha Tsui East is open from 10 AM to 7:30 PM; Tsim Sha Tsui, Yau Ma Tei, and Mongkok from 10 AM to 9 PM.

C
CAMERAS, CAMCORDERS, & COMPUTERS

IN TRANSIT

Always **keep your film, tape, or disks out of the sun;** never put these on the dashboard of a car. Carry an extra supply of batteries, and **be prepared to turn on your camera, camcorder, or laptop computer for security personnel.**

X-RAYS

Always **ask for hand inspection at security.** Such requests are virtually always honored at U.S. airports, and are usually accommodated abroad. Photographic film becomes clouded after successive exposure to airport X-ray machines. Videotape and computer disks are not harmed by X-rays, but **keep your tapes and disks away from metal detectors.**

CUSTOMS

Before departing, **register your foreign-made camera or laptop with U.S. Customs.** If your equipment is U.S.-made, call the consulate of the country you'll be visiting to find out whether it should be registered with local customs upon arrival.

CAR RENTAL

Because of difficult driving conditions, traffic jams, and parking problems, you should **avoid renting a car in Hong Kong.** Public transportation is excellent and taxis are inexpensive. If you do decide to rent a car, it is advisable to take one *with* a driver. Several operators offer such services, which can be arranged through your hotel. Charges are HK$800–HK$1200 for the first four hours (depending on car model) and HK$200–HK$300 for each subsequent hour (☞ Important Contacts A to Z, *above,* for car rental companies).

CHILDREN & TRAVEL

When traveling with children, **plan ahead** and **involve your youngsters** as you outline your trip. When packing, **include a supply of things to keep them busy** en route (☞ Children & Travel *in* Important Contacts A to Z). On sightseeing days, try to **schedule activities of special interest to your children,** such as a trip to a zoo or a playground. If you **plan your itinerary around seasonal festivals,** you'll never lack for things to do. In addition, **check local newspapers for special events** mounted by public libraries, museums, and parks.

BABY-SITTING

For recommended local sitters, **check with your hotel desk.**

DRIVING

If you are renting a car, don't forget to **arrange for a car seat when you reserve.** Sometimes they're free.

FLYING

As a general rule, infants under two not occupying a seat fly at greatly reduced fares and occasionally for free. If your children are two or older **ask about special children's fares.** Age limits for these fares vary among carriers. Rules also vary regarding unaccompanied minors, so again, check with your airline.

BAGGAGE➤ In general, the adult baggage allowance applies to children paying half or more of the adult fare. If you are traveling with an infant, **ask about carry-on allowances** before departure. In general, for infants charged 10% of the adult fare you are allowed one carry-on bag and a collapsible stroller, which may have to be checked; you may be limited to less if the flight is full.

SAFETY SEATS➤ According to the FAA, it's a good idea to **use safety seats aloft** for children weighing less than 40 pounds. Airline policies vary. U.S. carriers allow FAA-approved models but usually require that you buy a ticket, even if your child would otherwise ride free, since the seats must be strapped into regular seats. However, some U.S. and foreign-flag airlines may require you to hold your baby during takeoff and landing—defeating the seat's purpose. Other foreign carriers may not allow infant seats at all, or may charge a child rather than an infant fare for their use.

FACILITIES➤ When making your reservation, **request children's meals or freestanding bassinets** if you need them; the latter are available only to those seated at the bulkhead, where there's enough legroom. If you don't need a bassinet, **think twice before requesting bulkhead seats**—the only storage space for in-flight necessities is in inconveniently distant overhead bins.

GAMES

Milton Bradley and Parker Brothers have travel versions of some of their most popular games, including Yahtzee, Trouble, Sorry, and Monopoly. Prices run $5 to $8.

LODGING

Most hotels allow children under a certain age to stay in their parents' room at no extra charge; others charge them as extra adults. Be sure to **ask about the cutoff age.**

CUSTOMS & DUTIES

To speed your clearance through customs, **keep receipts for all your purchases abroad** and **be ready to show the inspector what you've bought.** If you feel that you've been incorrectly or unfairly charged a duty, you can **appeal assessments in dispute.** First ask to see a supervisor. If you are still unsatisfied, **write to the port director** at your point of entry, sending your customs receipt and any other appropriate documentation. The address will be listed on your receipt. If you still don't get satisfaction, you can take your case to customs headquarters in Washington.

IN HONG KONG

Except for the usual prohibitions against narcotics, explosives, firearms, and ammunition (all of which must be declared upon arrival and handed over for safekeeping until departure), and modest limits on alcohol, tobacco products, and perfume, you can bring anything you want into Hong Kong, including an unlimited amount of money.

Nonresident visitors may bring in, duty-free, 200 cigarettes or 50 cigars or 250 grams of tobacco, and 1 liter of alcohol.

IN THE U.S.

You may bring home $400 worth of foreign goods duty-free if you've been out of the country for at least 48 hours and haven't already used the $400 allowance, or any part of it, in the past 30 days.

Travelers 21 or older may bring back 1 liter of alcohol duty-free, provided the beverage laws of the state through which they reenter the United States allow it. In addition, regardless of their age, they are allowed 100 non-Cuban cigars and 200 cigarettes. Antiques, which the U.S. Customs Service defines as objects more than 100 years old, are duty-free. Original works of art done entirely by hand are also duty-free. These include, but are not limited to, paintings, drawings, and sculptures.

Travelers may mail packages valued at up to $200 to themselves, and up to $100 to others, duty-free, with a limit of one parcel per addressee per day (and no alcohol or tobacco products or perfume valued at more than $5); on the outside, the package must be labeled as being either for personal use or an unsolicited gift, and a list of its contents and their retail value must be attached. Mailed items do not affect your duty-free allowance on your return.

IN CANADA

If you've been out of Canada for at least seven days, you may bring in C$500 worth of goods duty-free. If you've been away for fewer than seven days but for more than 48 hours, the duty-free allowance drops to C$200; if your trip lasts between 24 and 48 hours, the allowance is C$50. You cannot pool allowances with family members. Goods claimed under the C$500 exemption may follow you by mail; those claimed under the lesser exemptions must accompany you.

Alcohol and tobacco products may be included in the seven-day and 48-hour exemptions but not in the 24-hour exemption. If you meet the age requirements of the province or territory through which you reenter Canada, you may bring in, duty-free, 1.14 liters (40 imperial ounces) of wine or liquor *or* 24

12-ounce cans or bottles of beer or ale. If you are 16 or older, you may bring in, duty-free, 200 cigarettes, 50 cigars or cigarillos, and 400 tobacco sticks or 400 grams of manufactured tobacco. Alcohol and tobacco must accompany you on your return.

An unlimited number of gifts with a value of up to C$60 each may be mailed to Canada duty-free. These do not affect your duty-free allowance on your return. Label the package "Unsolicited Gift—Value Under $60." Alcohol and tobacco are excluded.

IN THE U.K.

From countries outside the EU, including Hong Kong, you may import, duty-free, 200 cigarettes, 100 cigarillos, 50 cigars, or 250 grams of tobacco; 1 liter of spirits or 2 liters of fortified or sparkling wine or liqueurs; 2 liters of still table wine; 60 milliliters of perfume; 250 milliliters of toilet water; plus £136 worth of other goods, including gifts and souvenirs.

D

DISABILITIES & ACCESSIBILITY

Hong Kong is not the easiest of cities for people in wheelchairs; there are few ramps or other provisions for access. Progress is being made, however; the airport, City Hall, Hong Kong Arts Centre, and the Academy for Performing Arts have made efforts to assist people in

wheelchairs. For more information, get a copy of the local guide to accessibility, *A Guide for Physically Handicapped Visitors in Hong Kong,* available from the Hong Kong Tourist Association (HKTA). The guide lists the rare places that have special facilities for people with disabilities, in addition to the best access to hotels, shopping centers, government offices, consulates, restaurants, and churches.

When discussing accessibility with an operator or reservationist, **ask hard questions.** Are there any stairs, inside *or* out? Are there grab bars next to the toilet *and* in the shower/tub? How wide is the doorway to the room? To the bathroom? For the most extensive facilities, meeting the latest legal specifications, **opt for newer accommodations,** which more often have been designed with access in mind. Older properties or ships must usually be retrofitted and may offer more limited facilities as a result. Be sure to **discuss your needs before booking.**

DISCOUNTS & DEALS

You shouldn't have to pay for a discount. In fact, you may already be eligible for all kinds of savings. Here are some time-honored strategies for getting the best deal.

LOOK IN YOUR WALLET

When you **use your credit card to make travel purchases,** you may get free travel-accident insurance, collision damage insurance, and medical or legal assistance, depending on the card and bank that issued it. American Express, Visa, and MasterCard provide one or more of these services, so **get a copy of your card's travel benefits.** If you are a member of the AAA or an oil-company-sponsored road-assistance plan, always **ask hotel or car-rental reservationists for auto-club discounts.** Some clubs offer additional discounts on tours, cruises, or admission to attractions. And don't forget that auto-club membership entitles you to free maps and trip-planning services.

SENIORS CITIZENS & STUDENTS

As a senior-citizen traveler, you may be eligible for special rates, but you should mention your senior-citizen status up front. If you're a students or under 26 can also get discounts, especially if you have an official ID card (☞ Senior-Citizen Discounts *and* Students on the Road, *below*).

DIAL FOR DOLLARS

To save money, **look into "1-800" discount reservations services,** which often have lower rates. These services use their buying power to get a better price on hotels, airline tickets, and sometimes even car rentals. When booking a room, always **call the hotel's local toll-free number** (if one is available) rather than the central reservations number—you'll often get a better price. Ask the reservationist about special packages or corporate rates, which are usually available even if you're not traveling on business.

JOIN A CLUB?

Discount clubs can be a legitimate source of savings, but you must use the participating hotels and visit the participating attractions in order to realize any benefits. Remember, too, that you have to pay a fee to join, so **determine if you'll save enough to warrant your membership fee.** Before booking with a club, **make sure the hotel or other supplier isn't offering a better deal.**

GET A GUARANTEE

When shopping for the best deal on hotels and car rentals, **look for guaranteed exchange rates,** which protect you against a falling dollar. With your rate locked in, you won't pay more even if the price goes up in the local currency.

G
GAY & LESBIAN TRAVEL

Criminal sanctions on homosexual relations between consenting adults were lifted in Hong Kong in 1991.

H
HEALTH

Although the Hong Kong government declares that the water is safe to drink, even locals prefer to **boil tap water or to drink mineral water in bottles.**

I
INSURANCE

Travel insurance can protect your monetary investment, replace your luggage and its contents, or provide for medical coverage should you fall ill during your trip. Most tour operators, travel agents, and insurance agents sell specialized health-and-accident, flight, trip-cancellation, and luggage insurance as well as comprehensive policies with some or all of these coverages. Comprehensive policies may also reimburse you for delays due to weather—an important consideration if you're traveling during the winter months. Some health-insurance policies do not cover preexisting conditions, but waivers may be available in specific cases. Coverage is sold by the companies listed in Important Contacts A to Z *above*; these companies act as the policy's administrators. The actual insurance is usually underwritten by a well-known name, such as The Travelers or Continental Insurance.

Before you make any purchase, **review your existing health and homeowner's policies** to find out whether they cover expenses incurred while traveling.

BAGGAGE

Airline liability for baggage is limited to $1,250 per person on domestic flights. On international flights, it amounts to $9.07 per pound or $20 per kilogram for checked baggage (roughly $640 per 70-pound bag) and $400 per passenger for unchecked baggage. Insurance for losses exceeding the terms of your airline ticket can be bought directly from the airline at check-in for about $10 per $1,000 of coverage; note that it excludes a rather extensive list of items, shown on your airline ticket.

COMPREHENSIVE

Comprehensive insurance policies include all the coverages described above plus some that may not be available in more specific policies. If you have purchased an expensive vacation, especially one that involves travel abroad, comprehensive insurance is a must; **look for policies that include trip delay insurance,** which will protect you in the event that weather problems cause you to miss your flight, tour, or cruise. A few insurers will also sell you a waiver for preexisting medical conditions. Some of the companies that offer both these features are Access America, Carefree Travel, Travel Insured International, and Travel Guard (☞ Important Contacts A to Z).

FLIGHT

You should **think twice before buying flight insurance.** Often purchased as a last-minute impulse at the airport, it pays a lump sum when a plane crashes, either to a beneficiary if the insured dies or sometimes to a surviving passenger who loses his or her eyesight or a

limb. Supplementing the airlines' coverage described in the limits-of-liability paragraphs on your ticket, it's expensive and basically unnecessary. Charging an airline ticket to a major credit card often automatically provides you with coverage that may also extend to travel by bus, train, and ship.

HEALTH

Medicare generally does not cover health care costs outside the United States; nor do many privately issued policies. If your own health insurance policy does not cover you outside the United States, **consider buying supplemental medical coverage.** It can reimburse you for $1,000– $150,000 worth of medical and/or dental expenses incurred as a result of an accident or illness during a trip. These policies also may include a personal-accident, or death-and-dismemberment, provision, which pays a lump sum ranging from $15,000 to $500,000 to your beneficiaries if you die or to you if you lose one or more limbs or your eyesight, and a medical-assistance provision, which may either reimburse you for the cost of referrals, evacuation, or repatriation and other services, or automatically enroll you as a member of a particular medical-assistance company. (☞ Health Issues *in* Important Contacts A to Z.)

U.K. TRAVELERS

You can buy an annual travel insurance policy valid for most vacations

during the year in which it's purchased. If you are pregnant or have a preexisting medical condition make sure you're covered before buying such a policy.

TRIP

Without insurance, you will lose all or most of your money if you cancel your trip regardless of the reason. Especially if your airline ticket, cruise, or package tour is nonrefundable and cannot be changed, it's essential that you **buy trip-cancellation-and-interruption insurance.** When considering how much coverage you need, look for a policy that will cover the cost of your trip plus the nondiscounted price of a one-way airline ticket should you need to return home early. Read the fine print carefully, especially sections that define "family member" and "preexisting medical conditions." Also **consider default or bankruptcy insurance,** which protects you against a supplier's failure to deliver. Be aware, however, that if you buy such a policy from a travel agency, tour operator, airline, or cruise line, it may not cover default by the firm in question.

L

LANGUAGE

The official languages of Hong Kong are English and Chinese. The most commonly spoken Chinese dialect is Cantonese, but Mandarin is gaining popularity because it is the official language of

China. In Macau, the languages are, officially, Portuguese and Chinese, but many people speak some English.

In hotels, major restaurants, shops, and tourist centers, almost everyone speaks fluent English. However, this is not the case with taxi drivers and workers in small shops, cafés and market stalls.

The HKTA has introduced a color-coded badge system for their information officers. **Look for badges or window stickers that show which languages are spoken by staff members** (in *addition* to English): a red stripe indicates Japanese; a green stripe, Mandarin; purple, German; and blue, French.

M

MEDICAL ASSISTANCE

No one plans to get sick while traveling, but it happens, so **consider signing up with a medical assistance company.** These outfits provide referrals, emergency evacuation or repatriation, 24-hour telephone hot lines for medical consultation, cash for emergencies, and other personal and legal assistance. They also dispatch medical personnel and arrange for the relay of medical records. Coverage varies by plan, so **read the fine print carefully.**

FINDING A DOCTOR

Hotels have a list of accredited doctors and can arrange for a doctor to visit your hotel room. Otherwise, **consult the nearest government hospital.** Check the Government section of the business telephone directory under Medical and Health Department for a list.

MONEY

The units of currency in Hong Kong are the Hong Kong dollar ($) and the cent. There are bills of 1,000, 500, 100, 50, 20, and 10 dollars. Coins are 10, 5, 2, and 1 dollar and 50, 20, and 10 cents. At press time the Hong Kong dollar was fixed at approximately 8 dollars to the U.S. dollar, 6.52 to the Canadian dollar, and 12.5 to the pound sterling.

There are no currency restrictions in Hong Kong. Money-changing facilities are available at the airport, in hotels, in banks, and at private money changers scattered through the tourist areas. You will get better rates from a bank or money changer than from a hotel. However, **be aware of money changers who advertise "no selling commission"** and do not mention the "buying commission" you must pay when you exchange foreign currency or traveler's checks for Hong Kong dollars.

The official currency unit in Macau is the pataca, which is divided into 100 avos. Bank notes come in five denominations: 500, 100, 50, 10, and 5 patacas; coins are 5 and 1 patacas and 50, 20, and 10 avos. The pataca is pegged to the Hong Kong dollar (within a few cents). At press time there were 8 patacas to the Hong Kong dollar. Hong Kong currency circulates freely in Macau but not vice versa, so remember to change your patacas before you return to Hong Kong.

ATMS

CASH ADVANCES➤ Before leaving home, **make sure that your credit cards have been programmed for ATM use in Hong Kong.** Note that Discover is accepted mostly in the United States. Local bank cards often do not work overseas either; **ask your bank about a MasterCard/Cirrus or Visa debit card,** which works like a bank card but can be used at any ATM displaying a MasterCard/Cirrus or Visa logo.

TRANSACTION FEES➤ Although fees charged for ATM transactions may be higher abroad than at home, Cirrus and Plus exchange rates are excellent, because they are based on wholesale rates offered only by major banks.

EXCHANGING CURRENCY

For the most favorable rates, **change money at banks.** You won't do as well at exchange booths in airports or rail and bus stations, in hotels, in restaurants, or in stores, although you may find their hours more convenient. To avoid lines at airport exchange booths, **get a small amount of the local currency before you leave home.**

TAXES

HOTEL➤ Hong Kong levies a 10% tax on hotel rooms.

TRAVELER'S CHECKS

Whether or not to buy traveler's checks depends on where you are headed; **take cash to rural areas and small towns, traveler's checks to cities.** The most widely recognized checks are issued by American Express, Citicorp, Thomas Cook, and Visa. These are sold by major commercial banks for 1%–3% of the checks' face value—it pays to **shop around.** Both American Express and Thomas Cook issue checks that can be countersigned and used by either you or your traveling companion. So you won't be left with excess foreign currency, **buy a few checks in small denominations** to cash toward the end of your trip. Before leaving home, **contact your issuer for information on where to cash your checks** without a incurring a transaction fee. Record the numbers of all your checks, and keep this listing in a separate place, crossing off the numbers of checks you have cashed.

WIRING MONEY

For a fee of 3%–10%, depending on the amount of the transaction, you can have money sent to you from home through Money-Gram℠ or Western Union (☞ Money *in* Important Contacts A to Z). The transferred funds and the service fee can be charged to a MasterCard or Visa account.

P
PACKING FOR HONG KONG

From May to September, high humidity warrants light clothing. However, air-conditioning in hotels and restaurants can be glacial, so bring a sweater or shawl for evening use indoors. Don't forget your swimsuit and high-protection suntan lotion; several hotels have pools, and you may want to spend some time on one of the many beaches. Dress in Hong Kong is fairly informal, but a few hotels and restaurants do insist on a jacket and tie for men in the evenings.

In October, November, March, and April, a jacket or sweater should suffice, but from December through February bring a raincoat or a light overcoat. Whatever the time of year, it is wise to **pack a folding umbrella.**

Bring an extra pair of eyeglasses or contact lenses in your carry-on luggage, and if you have a health problem, **pack enough medication** to last the trip or have your doctor write you a prescription using the drug's generic name, because brand names vary from country to country (you'll then need a duplicate prescription from a local doctor). It's important that you **don't put prescription drugs or valuables in luggage to be checked,** for it could go astray. To avoid problems with customs officials, carry medications in the original packaging. Also, don't forget the addresses of offices that handle refunds of lost traveler's checks.

ELECTRICITY

To use your U.S.-purchased electric-powered equipment, **bring a converter and an adapter.** The electrical current in Hong Kong is 200 volts, 50 cycles alternating current (AC); in Macau it is 220 volts, 50 cycles. Some outlets in Hong Kong take plugs with three round prongs, while others use plugs with two square prongs. There is no standard plug size in Macau; check with your hotel regarding their setup.

If your appliances are dual-voltage, you'll need only an adapter. Hotels sometimes have 110-volt outlets for low-wattage appliances near the sink, marked FOR SHAVERS ONLY; don't use them for high-wattage appliances such as blow dryers. If your laptop computer is older, carry a converter; new laptops operate equally well on 110 and 220 volts, so you need only an adapter.

LUGGAGE

Airline baggage allowances depend on the airline, the route, and the class of your ticket; ask in advance. In general, on domestic flights and on international flights between the United States and foreign destinations, you are entitled to check two bags. A third piece may be brought on board, but it must fit easily under the seat in front of you or in the overhead compartment. In the United States, the FAA gives airlines broad latitude regarding carry-on allowances, and they tend to tailor them to different aircraft and operational conditions. Charges for excess, oversize, or overweight pieces vary.

If you are flying between two foreign destinations, note that baggage allowances may be determined not by piece but by weight—generally 88 pounds (40 kilograms) in first class, 66 pounds (30 kilograms) in business class, and 44 pounds (20 kilograms) in economy. If your flight between two cities abroad *connects* with your transatlantic or transpacific flight, the piece method still applies.

SAFEGUARDING YOUR LUGGAGE➤ Before leaving home, **itemize your bags' contents** and their worth, and label them with your name, address, and phone number. (If you use your home address, cover it so that potential thieves can't see it readily.) Inside each bag, **pack a copy of your itinerary.** At check-in, **make sure that each bag is correctly tagged** with the destination airport's three-letter code. If your bags arrive damaged—or fail to arrive at all—file a written report with the airline before leaving the airport.

PASSPORTS & VISAS

If you don't already have one, **get a passport.** It is advisable that you **leave one photocopy of your passport's data page** with someone at home and keep another with you, separated from your passport, while traveling. If you lose your passport, promptly call the nearest embassy or consulate and the local police; having the data page information can speed replacement.

U.S. CITIZENS

All U.S. citizens, even infants, need only a valid passport to enter Hong Kong or Macau for stays of up to 30 days. Application forms for both first-time and renewal passports are available at any of the 13 U.S. Passport Agency offices and at some post offices and courthouses. Passports are usually mailed within four weeks; allow five weeks or more in spring and summer.

CANADIANS

You need only a valid passport to enter Hong Kong for stays of up to 90 days. Passport application forms are available at 28 regional passport offices, as well as post offices and travel agencies. Whether for a first or a renewal passport, you must apply in person. Children under 16 may be included on a parent's passport but must have their own to travel alone. Passports are valid for five years and are usually mailed

within two to three weeks of application.

U.K. CITIZENS

Citizens of the United Kingdom need only a valid passport to enter Hong Kong for stays of up to six months. Applications for new and renewal passports are available from main post offices and at the passport offices in Belfast, Glasgow, Liverpool, London, Newport, and Peterborough. You may apply in person at all passport offices, or by mail to all except the London office. Children under 16 may travel on an accompanying parent's passport. All passports are valid for 10 years. Allow a month for processing.

S

SENIOR-CITIZEN DISCOUNTS

To qualify for age-related discounts, **mention your senior-citizen status up front** when booking hotel reservations, not when checking out, and before you're seated in restaurants, not when paying the bill. Note that discounts may be limited to certain menus, days, or hours. When renting a car, **ask about promotional car-rental discounts**—they can net even lower costs than your senior-citizen discount.

SHOPPING

If you buy Chinese lacquer or other breakable keepsakes, **buy an all-risks insurance policy for any delicate purchases that you ship home.** Ivory has long been a prized souvenir of trips to the Orient. However, in 1990 the Hong Kong government imposed a stringent policy on the import and export of this bone derivative. As a result, you must **get an import license from your country of residence, as well as an export license to take ivory out of Hong Kong.** Failure to comply may result in a fine and forfeiture of the purchase. Remember that all goods, with the exception of alcohol, tobacco, petroleum, perfume, cosmetics, and soft drinks, are duty-free everywhere in Hong Kong, not just in "duty-free" stores. Bargaining, even at street markets, has become increasingly rare in Hong Kong. **Beware of merchants who claim to be giving you a "special" price;** you may not be getting what you're paying for.

STUDENTS ON THE ROAD

To save money, **look into deals available through student-oriented travel agencies.** To qualify, you'll need to have a bona fide student ID card. Members of international student groups are also eligible (☞ Students *in* Important Contacts A to Z).

SUBWAY TRAVEL

The Mass Transit Railway (MTR) links Hong Kong Island to the shopping area of Tsim Sha Tsui and to parts of the New Territories. Trains run frequently, and are safe and easy to use (there are only four lines).

Station entrances are marked with a simple line symbol resembling a man with arms and legs outstretched. There are clearly marked ticket machines inside the station; change is available at the Hang Seng Bank counters inside the stations. Fares range from HK$4 to HK$11.

DISCOUNT PASSES

The special Tourist Ticket (HK$25) can save you money. Another possibility is the Stored Value Ticket, which also provides access to the overground Kowloon Canton Railway (KCR). Tickets may be purchased for HK$70, HK$100, and HK$200.

T
TAXIS

Taxis in Hong Kong are usually red and have a roof sign that lights up when the taxi is available. Fares in the urban areas are HK$14 for the first 2 kilometers and HK$1.20 for each additional 0.20 kilometer (.12 mile). There is a surcharge of HK$5 per large piece of baggage and a HK$20 surcharge for driving through the Cross-Harbour Tunnel. Aberdeen Tunnel carries a surcharge of HK$5, and the Lion Rock Tunnel toll is HK$6. Taxis cannot pick up passengers where there is a solid yellow line painted on the road.

It is difficult to find taxis from 3:30 to 6 PM. Most taxi drivers speak some English, but to avoid problems, **get someone at your hotel**

to write out your destination in Chinese.

Outside the urban areas taxis are mainly green and white (blue on Lantau Island). New Territories taxis cost less than urban red taxis, with fares of HK$11.80 for the first 2 kilometers (1.2 miles), and HK$1.10 every 0.20 kilometer (.12 mile). Urban taxis may travel into rural zones, but rural taxis must not cross into the urban zones. There are no interchange facilities for these taxis, so **do not try to reach the urban area using a green taxi.**

COMPLAINTS

Taxis are usually reliable in Hong Kong, but just in case, **get the taxi's license number,** which is usually on the dashboard. The police hot line for complaints is 2527–7177. Your complaint will not be investigated without the license number.

TELEPHONES

To make a local call from a pay phone, use a HK$1 coin. Although pay phones are not hard to find, the tradition is to pop into any store and ask to use the telephone. Many small stores keep their telephone on the counter facing the street, hoping your eyes will browse while your ear and mouth are occupied.

LONG-DISTANCE

The long-distance services of AT&T, MCI, and Sprint make calling home relatively convenient, but in many hotels you may find it impossible to dial the access number. The hotel operator may also

THE GOLD GUIDE / SMART TRAVEL TIPS

THE GOLD GUIDE / SMART TRAVEL TIPS

refuse to make the connection. Instead, the hotel will charge you a premium rate—as much as 400% more than a calling card—for calls placed from your hotel room. To avoid such price gouging, travel with more than one company's long-distance calling card—a hotel may block Sprint but not MCI. If the hotel operator claims that you cannot use any phone card, ask to be connected to an international operator, who will help you to access your phone card. You can also dial the international operator yourself. If none of this works, try calling your phone company collect in the United States. If collect calls are also blocked, call from a pay phone in the hotel lobby. Before you go, **find out the local access codes** for your destinations.

Many hotels offer direct dial, as do many business centers, but always with a hefty surcharge. Call 013 for international inquiries and for assistance with direct dialing. Call 010 for operator-assisted calls to most countries, including the United States, Canada, and the United Kingdom. Dial 011 for international conference calls or outgoing collect calls. Long-distance calls can also be made from Hong Kong Telecom International (☞ Long Distance *under* Telephones *in* Important Contacts A to Z). You can dial direct from specially marked silver-color phone booths that take phone cards, available from the Hong

Kong Telephone Companies retail shops and Seven Eleven convenience stores located throughout the island. The cards come in values of HK$25, 50, and 100 and have no expiration date. Multilingual instructions are posted in the phone booths.

OPERATORS & INFORMATION

Dial 1081 for directory assistance from English-speaking operators. If a number is constantly busy and you think it might be out of order, call 109 and the operator will check the line.

TIPPING

Hotels and major restaurants add a 10% service charge. In the more traditional Chinese restaurants, a waiter will bring small snacks at the beginning of the meal and charge them to you, even if you did not order them. This money is in lieu of a service charge. It is customary to leave an additional 10% tip in all restaurants, and in taxis and beauty salons.

TOUR OPERATORS

A package or tour to Hong Kong can make your vacation less expensive and more hassle-free. Firms that sell tours and packages reserve airline seats, hotel rooms, and rental cars in bulk and pass some of the savings on to you. In addition, the best operators have local representatives available to help you at your destination.

A GOOD DEAL?

The more your package or tour includes, the

better you can predict the ultimate cost of your vacation. Make sure you know exactly what is covered, and **beware of hidden costs.** Are taxes, tips, and service charges included? Transfers and baggage handling? Entertainment and excursions? These can add up.

Most packages and tours are rated deluxe, first-class superior, first class, tourist, or budget. The key difference is usually accommodations. If the package or tour you are considering is priced lower than in your wildest dreams, **be skeptical.** Also, **make sure your travel agent knows the accommodations** and other services. Ask about the hotel's location, room size, beds, and whether it has a pool, room service, or programs for children, if you care about these. Has your agent been there in person or sent others you can contact?

BUYER BEWARE

Each year a number of consumers are stranded or lose their money when operators—even very large ones with excellent reputations—go out of business. To avoid becoming one of them, take the time to **check out the operator**—find out how long the company has been in business and ask several agents about its reputation. Next, **don't book unless the firm has a consumer-protection program.** Members of the USTOA and the NTA are required to set aside funds for the sole purpose of covering your payments and travel arrangements in case of default. Nonmember operators may instead carry insurance; look for the details in the operator's brochure—and for the name of an underwriter with a solid reputation. Note: When it comes to tour operators, **don't trust escrow accounts.** Although there are laws governing those of charter-flight operators, no governmental body prevents tour operators from raiding the till.

Next, **contact your local Better Business Bureau and the attorney general's offices** in both your own state and the operator's; have any complaints been filed? Finally, **pay with a major credit card.** Then you can cancel payment, provided that you can document your complaint. Always **consider trip-cancellation insurance** (☞ Insurance, *above*).

BIG VS. SMALL➤ Operators that handle several hundred thousand travelers per year can use their purchasing power to give you a good price. Their high volume may also indicate financial stability. But some small companies provide more personalized service; because they tend to specialize, they may also be more knowledgeable about a given area.

USING AN AGENT

Travel agents are excellent resources. In fact, large operators accept bookings made only through travel agents.

But it's good to **collect brochures from several agencies** because some agents' suggestions may be skewed by promotional relationships with tour and package firms that reward them for volume sales. If you have a special interest, **find an agent with expertise in that area;** ASTA can provide leads in the United States. (Don't rely solely on your agent, though; agents may be unaware of small-niche operators, and some special-interest travel companies only sell direct.)

SINGLE TRAVELERS

Prices are usually quoted per person, based on two sharing a room. If traveling solo, you may be required to pay the full double-occupancy rate. Some operators eliminate this surcharge if you agree to be matched up with a roommate of the same sex, even if one is not found by departure time.

TRAINS

The Kowloon-Canton Railway (KCR) has 13 commuter stops on its 22-mile (34-kilometer) journey through urban Kowloon (from Kowloon to Lo Wu) and the new cities of Shatin and Taipo on its way to the Chinese border. The main station is at Hunghom, Kowloon, where you can catch express trains to China. Fares range from HK$7.50 to HK$40. The crossover point with the MTR is at Kowloon Tong Station (☎ 2602–7799).

TRANSPORTATION

Being a collection of islands scattered in the South China Sea, along with a chunk of the Chinese mainland, Hong Kong has more types of transportation than probably any other city in the world. Ferries (☞ Ferries, *below*) and a subway system (☞ Subways, *above*) connect Hong Kong Island with the Kowloon peninsula and the Outer Islands. Buses (☞ Buses *in* Important Contacts A to Z, *above*) run throughout Hong Kong Island, Kowloon, and the New Territories, and along a number of routes linking the two sides of the harbor. On Hong Kong Island are two kinds of trams (☞ Trams, *below*): a street-level tram that runs across the north shore of the island, and the Peak Tram, a funicular railway that climbs Victoria Peak. Trains (☞ Trains, *above*) travel north from Kowloon serving cities all the way to the Chinese border. Choose, as well, from limousines (the Mandarin and the Peninsula hotels have chauffeur-driven Rolls-Royces for rent), and the now touristy rickshaws (☞ Rickshaws, *below*). You can also rent cars with drivers (☞ Car Rental, *above*).

FERRIES

The Star Ferry Harbour Cruises (☞ Transportation *in* Important Contacts A to Z, *above*) is one of Hong Kong's landmarks. Double-bowed, green-and-white vessels connect Hong Kong Island with the Kowloon peninsula.

THE GOLD GUIDE / SMART TRAVEL TIPS

The cost for the seven-minute ride is HK$2 upper deck and HK$1.70 lower deck. The Star Ferry also runs a service to Hunghom for HK$1.70–HK$2 and between Wanchai and Tsim Sha Tsui (HK$1.70).

The ferries of the Hong Kong & Yaumati Ferry Company (HKF) (☞ Transportation *in* Important Contacts A to Z, *above*) go to Hong Kong's beautiful outer islands. Call for ferry schedules and departure points; you can also contact the HKTA (☞ Visitor Information *in* Important Contacts A to Z, *above*). Return fares vary from HK$15 to HK$50. Hover-ferries, operated by the same organization, travel from Central to Tsuen Wan for HK$6–HK$7.50 and to Tsim Sha Tsui East for HK$4.

Ferries are extremely crowded and noisy on weekends. If you have to go to the more distant parts of Hong Kong, **choose a linking ferry service to beat surface traffic and save time.**

RICKSHAWS

Because rickshaws are largely a tourist attraction rather than a common mode of transportation, prices run high. Rates are supposed to be around HK$50 for a five-minute ride, but rickshaw operators are merciless. A posed snapshot can cost from HK$10 to HK$20. When you hire a rickshaw or take an opera-

tor's picture, **agree on the price in advance.**

TRAMS

For schedules, call the Hong Kong Tourist Association information service (☞ Buses or Subway Travel *in* Important Contacts A to Z).

STREET TRAMS➤ Trams run along Hong Kong Island's north shore from Kennedy Town in the west all the way through Central, Wanchai, Causeway Bay, North Point, and Quarry Bay, ending in the former fishing village of Shaukiwan. There is also a branch line that turns off in Wanchai toward Happy Valley, where horse races are held during the season. Destinations are marked on the front; the fare is HK$1.20. Avoid them at rush hours which are generally 7:30 AM to 9:00 AM and 5:00 PM to 7:00 PM, Monday through Friday.

PEAK TRAMS➤ This funicular railway dates back to 1888 and rises from ground level to Victoria Peak (1,305 feet), offering a panoramic view of Hong Kong. Both residents and tourists use the tram, which has five stations. The fare is HK$14 one way or HK$21 round-trip. The tram runs every 10–15 minutes daily from 7 AM to midnight. There is a free shuttle bus to and from the Star Ferry.

TRAVEL GEAR

Travel catalogs specialize in useful items that can **save space when packing** and make life on the road more con-

venient. Compact alarm clocks, travel irons, travel wallets, and personal-care kits are among the most common items you'll find. They also carry dual-voltage appliances, currency converters and foreign-language phrase books. Some catalogs even carry miniature coffeemakers and water purifiers.

U

U.S. GOVERNMENT

The U.S. government can be an excellent source of travel information. Some of this is free and some is available for a nominal charge. When planning your trip, **find out what government materials are available.** For just a couple of dollars, you can get a variety of publications from the Consumer Information Center in Pueblo, Colorado. Free consumer information also is available from individual government agencies, such as the Department of Transportation or the U.S. Customs Service. For specific titles, see the appropriate publications entry in Important Contacts A to Z, *above*.

W

WALKING

If you're not defeated by the heat, it is pleasant to stroll around Hong Kong. On Hong Kong Island you can enjoy a walk through the very traditional Western district, where life has not changed much over the years. If you are a very keen walker and relish the idea of a self-guided tour, you can **go for a long stroll in the New Territories or on Lantau Island.** Contact the HKTA for walking-tour guides to these distinct areas of Hong Kong. Each includes a map and detailed instructions for getting from place to place.

WHEN TO GO

The high tourist season, October through late December, is popular for a reason: The weather is pleasant, with sunny days and comfortable, cool nights. January, February, and sometimes early March are cold and dank, with long periods of overcast skies and rain. March and April can be either cold and miserable or beautiful and sunny. By May the cold has broken and the temperature is warm and comfortable. The months of June through September are the typhoon season, when the weather is hot and sticky, with lots of rain. All visitors to Hong Kong should know in advance that typhoons (called hurricanes in the Atlantic) must be treated with respect. Fortunately, Hong Kong is prepared for these blustery assaults. If a storm is approaching, the airwaves will be crackling with information, and your hotel will make certain through postings in the lobby that you know the applicable signals. In addition, public places will have postings.

When a No. 8 signal is posted, Hong Kong and Macau close down completely. Head immediately for your hotel, and stay put. This is serious business— bamboo scaffolding can come hurtling through the streets like spears, ships can be sunk in the harbor, and large areas of the colony are often flooded.

Macau's summers are slightly cooler and wetter than Hong Kong's.

The following are average daily maximum and minimum temperatures for Hong Kong.

Climate in Hong Kong

Jan.	64F	18C	May	82F	28C	Sept.	85F	29C
	56	13		74	23		77	25
Feb.	63F	17C	June	85F	29C	Oct.	81F	27C
	55	13		78	26		73	23
Mar.	67F	19C	July	87F	31C	Nov.	74F	23C
	60	16		78	26		65	18
Apr.	75F	24C	Aug.	87F	31C	Dec.	68F	20C
	67	19		78	26		59	15

THE GOLD GUIDE / SMART TRAVEL TIPS

1 Destination: Hong Kong

A BRIEF HISTORY

WHEN YOU FLY to Hong Kong, try to get a window seat on the aircraft; the landing will take your breath away.

When you hear the prelanding announcement, you will probably still be out over the gray South China Sea. As you approach the coast of China, you will spot a few small, rocky islands, tiny fishing boats, and sailboats in the channels leading into Hong Kong Harbour—the most spectacular harbor you will ever see.

The final approach into Hong Kong's Kai Tak Airport is sudden and rather startling. If you come in over the sea, you follow the channel between Hong Kong Island and the mainland on wings that seem close enough to touch the boats or the windows of the skyscrapers rising above the hills. If you fly in over Kowloon, the plane will seem dangerously close to the scrub-covered hills, and you will see children playing in school grounds and perhaps even be able to read the advertisements on the sides of buses. Of course, like much else in Hong Kong, the view is temporary. A new airport, farther out on Chek Lap Kok Island, is under construction and scheduled to open in April 1998.

Under the modern veneer of skyscrapers and high fashion, Hong Kong is deeply rooted in ancient Chinese traditions–more so, in many ways, than China, which destroyed much of its heritage during the three decades following the Communist revolution.

In Cantonese, Hong Kong means "Fragrant Harbor," a name inspired either by the incense factories that once dotted Hong Kong Island or by the profusion of scented pink *bauhinias*, the national flower.

Hong Kong is on the southeast coast of China, at the mouth of the Pearl River, on the same latitude as Hawaii and Cuba. By air, it's 2¾ hours from Beijing, 17 hours from New York, 12¼ hours from San Francisco, and 13 hours from London. It consists of three parts: Hong Kong Island, roughly 32 square miles; Kowloon, 3½ square miles; and the New Territories, about 365 square miles.

The name Hong Kong refers to the overall territory as well as to the main island, which is across the harbor from Kowloon. The island's principal business district is officially named Victoria, but everyone calls it Central. Also on the island are the districts of Wanchai, Causeway Bay, Repulse Bay, Stanley, and Aberdeen.

Kowloon includes Tsim Sha Tsui, Tsim Sha Tsui East, Hung Hom, Mongkok/Yau Ma Tei, and the area north to Boundary Street. The New Territories begin at Boundary Street and extend north to the border with China, encompassing the container port, the airport, most of the major factories, and the outlying islands.

Hong Kong is 98% Chinese. Other nationalities include British, American, Indian, and Japanese. Although the official languages are English and Cantonese, many other languages and dialects are spoken here, including Mandarin, Hakka (the language of a group of early settlers from China), Tanka (the language of the original boat people who came here some 5,000 years ago), Shanghainese, and Chinglish (a mixture of Cantonese and English). Some 30,000 Filipinos live and work in Hong Kong, so you're also likely to hear Philippine languages, especially near the Star Ferry and Statue Square park.

Buddhism, Taoism, ancestor worship, Christianity, and animism are the major religions, and you'll see signs of them everywhere. The distinctions between religions are often blurred because Chinese people tend to be eclectic in their beliefs. It is not uncommon for the same Hong Kong citizen to put out food and incense for his departed ancestors at Spring Festival time, invite a Taoist priest to his home to exorcise unhappy ghosts, pray in a Buddhist temple for fertility, and take communion in a Christian church.

Hong Kong's earliest visitors are believed to have been boat people of Malaysian-Oceanic origin who came here about 5,000 years ago. They left geometric-style drawings that are still visible on rocks in Big Wave Bay (on Hong Kong Island) and Po Toi Island. The earliest structure found so far is the 2,000-year-old Han Dynasty tomb at Lei Cheng Uk. More than 600 years later, the Tang Dynasty left lime kilns full of seashells—an archaeological mystery because there are no clues indicating how or why the lime was used.

There are also records from the 13th century, when Sung Dynasty loyalists fled China with their child-emperor to escape the invading Mongols. The last of the Sung Dynasty emperors, a 10-year-old boy, is said to have spent a night in the late 1270s near what is now the airport. One of his men is credited with naming Kowloon, which means "nine dragons" (he counted eight mountains that resembled dragons and added one for the emperor, who was also considered a dragon). The boy was the only Chinese emperor believed to have set foot in what is now Hong Kong. Many of his courtiers settled here. Today anyone visiting Po Lin monastery, high in the mountains of Lantau Island, will pass Shek Pik reservoir, where innumerable Sung Dynasty coins were found during the reservoir's excavation. You can also get a feel for life during the period by visiting Sung Dynasty Village, a reproduction of a Sung village, in an amusement park in Laichikok near Kowloon. The village is small, but it demonstrates the highly developed Sung civilization with spirit and charm and is well worth a visit.

Western traders first appeared in the Hong Kong area in 1513. The first were Portuguese, soon followed by the Spanish, Dutch, English, and French. All were bent either on making fortunes trading porcelain, tea, and silk, or on saving souls for their respective religions. Until 1757 the Chinese restricted all foreigners to neighboring Macau, the Portuguese territory 40 miles (64 kilometers) across the Pearl River estuary. After 1757, traders—but not their families—were allowed to live just outside Canton for about eight months each year. (Canton, known by its Chinese pronunciation, Guangzhou, is only 20 minutes from Hong Kong by plane, or three hours by train or hovercraft.)

Trading in Canton was frustrating for the foreigners. It took at least 20 days for messages to be relayed to the emperor, local officials had to be bribed, and Chinese justice seemed unfair. The Chinese confined foreign traders to a small, restricted zone and forbade them to learn Chinese. The Chinese wanted nothing from the West except silver, until the foreigners, especially the British, started offering opium.

THE SPREAD OF the opium habit and the growing outflow of silver alarmed high Chinese officials as early as 1729. They issued edicts forbidding importation of the drug, but these were not strictly enforced until 1839. Then a heroic and somewhat fanatical imperial commissioner, Lin Ze-xu (Lin Tse-hsu), laid siege to the foreign factories in Canton and detained the traders until they surrendered more than 20,000 chests of the drug, almost a year's worth of trade. The foreigners also signed bonds promising to desist from dealing opium forever, upon threat of death. The opium was destroyed. The resulting tension between the government and foreign traders led to the Opium Wars and a succession of unequal treaties forced by superior British firepower. The most important of these treaties required China to cede the island of Hong Kong to Britain; later, another treaty added Kowloon. Finally, in 1898, China leased the New Territories to Britain for 99 years.

British-ruled Hong Kong flourished from the start of trade, especially the trade in opium, which was not outlawed in Hong Kong until after World War II. The population grew quickly, from 4,000 in 1841 to more than 23,000 in 1847, as Hong Kong attracted anyone anxious to make money or escape the fetters of feudalism and family.

Each convulsion on the Chinese mainland—the Taiping rebellion in the mid-1800s, the 1911 republican revolution, the rule of warlords of the 1920s, the 1937 Japanese invasion—pushed another group of refugees into Hong Kong. Then Japan invaded Hong Kong itself. The population, which was 1.4 million just before the Japanese arrived, dropped to a low of 600,000 by 1945. Many Hong Kong residents were forced to flee to Macau and the rural areas of China. The Japanese period is still remembered with bitterness by older local residents.

The largest group of Chinese refugees came as a result of the civil war in China between the Nationalists and Communists, which ended with a Communist victory in 1949. Many refugees, especially the Shanghainese, brought capital and business skills. The population of Hong Kong was 1.8 million in 1947. By 1961 it stood at 3.7 million. For 25 days in 1962, when food was short in China, Chinese border guards allowed 70,000 Chinese to walk into Hong Kong. Ordinarily, it is very difficult for Chinese citizens to get permission to leave China.

DURING THE ANTILAND-lord, anticapitalist, and antirightist campaigns in China, and especially during the Cultural Revolution (1967–76), more and more refugees risked imprisonment and the sharks in Mirs Bay to reach Hong Kong. In 1967, inspired by the leftist fanaticism of the Red Guards in China, local sympathizers and activists in Hong Kong set off bombs, organized labor strikes, and demonstrated against the British rulers and Hong Kong's Chinese policemen. They taunted the latter by saying, "Will the British take you when they go?" But the revolutionaries did not have popular support, and the disruptions in Hong Kong lasted less than a year.

In the late 1970s, a half-million Chinese refugees came to Hong Kong, disillusioned with communism and eager for a better standard of living for themselves and their families.

Until October 1980 the Hong Kong government had a curious "touch-base" policy—a critical game of "hide-and-seek." Any Chinese who managed to get past the barbed wire, attack dogs, and tough border patrols to the urban areas was allowed to stay and work. Labor was needed for local industries then. At first, a similarly lenient policy was applied to Vietnamese boat people who arrived between 1975 and 1982. More than 100,000 of these refugees were allowed to work in Hong Kong pending transfer to permanent homes abroad, and 14,000 were given permanent resident status. As the number of countries willing to take the Vietnamese has dwindled, Hong Kong has detained recently arrived refugees indefinitely in closed camps, much like prisons, in the hope that no more boat people will come.

In the early 1980s jobs became less plentiful as a result of worldwide recession. As the population continued to increase, the standard of services in Hong Kong began to deteriorate. After consulting China, the government decreed that everyone had to carry a Hong Kong identification card.

The future of Hong Kong after the expiration of the New Territories lease on June 30, 1997, was understandably the big question hanging over the colony from the moment Britain's then prime minister, Margaret Thatcher, set foot in Beijing in September 1982 to start talks with China's Deng Xiaoping. China stated from the beginning that it wanted to repossess all of Hong Kong. Officially, Britain was willing to return only the New Territories, but no one believed a Hong Kong without them would be economically viable. The New Territories consist of more than 97% of the land in Hong Kong and include most of the manufacturing facilities, the airport, and the container port. China proposed that Hong Kong become a special administrative region under the Chinese flag, with a Chinese governor. The Chinese added a 50-year guarantee of autonomy, effective July 1, 1997, labeling the deal "One country, two systems." Negotiations between China and Britain lasted for nearly two years, with China applying pressure by announcing that if a solution were not found by September 1984, it would declare one unilaterally. An agreement was inevitable.

Hong Kong's economy didn't react well to this political uncertainty. Land prices fell. The stock market plunged by as much as 50% from late 1981 to late 1983. The Hong Kong dollar careened to almost HK$10 to the U.S. dollar in September 1983, from HK$5.7 at the end of 1981. This forced the government to intervene reluctantly by stabilizing the local unit at HK$7.80 to U.S.$1. Emigration reached record levels.

The final agreement gives Hong Kong many safeguards and special freedoms that are not permitted in other regions of the People's Republic of China. Whether China lives up to the guarantees in the agreement remains to be seen, however. All predictions are guesswork, of course, since the Chinese leadership is likely to be in some turmoil itself after Deng Xiaoping dies. However, Hong Kong's importance to China as a center for business and finance is unlikely to diminish, which gives hope to those who are destined to remain there beyond 1997.

1997: THE YEAR OF RECKONING

WILL HONG KONG change when China takes over from Great Britain at the stroke of midnight on June 30, 1997? The Union Jack, symbol of the colonial era, will be replaced in government offices by Hong Kong's bauhinia flower flag. Aside from that, on the morning of July 1 Hong Kong will look the same as it did the night before, except for any residue of revelry, mourning, and other expressions of emotion.

Unquestionably, though, the territory will be different. This transfer of power is a phenomenon unprecedented in world history. Before, palace coups and revolutions have sown their seeds behind the backs of governments; but in Hong Kong, sovereignty is being handed over after 15 years of planning and negotiation between two powerful countries. Moreover, a core group of Hong Kong Chinese business and government leaders has participated in the discussions.

The fact that the negotiations have hardly been amicable has made the changeover especially significant to the outside world. The political and social questions it raises are part of history in the making. Approximately 12 million visitors from around the world—academicians, business leaders, journalists, former residents, and the generally curious—will descend upon Hong Kong during the first half of 1997. Hotels have had waiting lists for several years for the week that starts June 22, and incoming flights are also expected to be booked well in advance.

The influx of visitors is likely to continue over the next several years of the transition. Hong Kong will still be a mecca for those who love shopping, Chinese culture, nightlife, sailing, hiking, horse racing, rugby, Asian cuisine, and cosmopolitan ambience. It will continue to be a duty-free port, with many goods available at bargain prices, and the excellent hotels, convention space, tourism assistance centers, and communications facilities will remain in place. The Hong Kong Chinese people have themselves become great fans of the good life available here, and such colonial institutions as the Royal Hong Kong Yacht Club and the Royal Hong Kong Jockey Club will continue to thrive (though the latter has dropped the "Royal" from its name).

Day-to-day life in Hong Kong is apt to be much as before, especially on the back streets, where small businesses thrive, laundry hangs from windows, outdoor market stalls serve noodles and congee, and incense from tiny makeshift altars curls into the air. Ordinary Hong Kong citizens will continue to work hard and invest their earnings, sweep their ancestors' graves on special holidays, and hope their children grow up to be prosperous. With China's growing market economy unlikely to reverse course, there may be a bright future ahead for Hong Kong's next generation, with plenty of entrepreneurial opportunities for those willing to work hard.

Many Hong Kong residents fear, however, that the free-wheeling capitalism of colonial Hong Kong will become more like the multilayered capitalism that exists in the urban areas of China today. There are opportunities to build factories, stores, and real estate developments in China, but for the most part only for those with either multinational clout or the ability to offer local officials special favors or equity in the business.

The official agreements between China and Britain over Hong Kong, known as the Joint Declaration and the Basic Law, state that Hong Kong will be a Special Administrative Region (SAR) for 50 years, belonging to China but functioning autonomously. China's policy is supposed to be "one country, two systems." However, what actually happens will depend on many different factors: whether a liberal or a hardline faction is in charge in Beijing, as well as in Hong Kong, whether a power struggle takes place in Beijing, and whether the politicians involved in such a struggle find Hong Kong a convenient target for a display of muscle.

In 1996 it became apparent that the present Beijing leadership was determined to fill the Hong Kong government seats with legislators who would be sympathetic to China's views. The Chinese government says it plans to disband the old Legislative Council (LegCo) and replace it with a provisional legislature, appointed by the 400 Hong Kong political and business leaders who make up what is known as the Selection Committee, which will also appoint Hong Kong's new chief executive to replace the British governor. Among the 60 LegCo members, 20 were directly elected to their positions and have stood for democratic reform in Hong Kong. The Beijing government has made it clear that only those legislators who agree with the plan for a provisional legislature will be chosen to sit on the Selection Committee. What this means is that those legislators whose political views are different from Beijing's have been effectively denied a voice in the handover process.

THERE WERE demonstrations in the streets of Hong Kong in the spring of 1996, when the Chinese government announced its decision on the Legislative Council. Whether the new Hong Kong chief executive—who will be appointed in late 1996—tolerates other political demonstrations, including the annual candlelight memorial service for the victims of the June 4, 1989, Beijing Massacre near Tiananmen Square, is another unknown in Hong Kong's future.

Most of Hong Kong's leaders who have served on the Preliminary Working Committee that has been planning the handover with Beijing take the stance that it is best to cooperate with the Chinese government. Most of the committee members are business executives who view the public displays of dissent that inevitably come with Western-style democracy as being detrimental to a stable business environment. They hold that if business is allowed to flourish, jobs will be abundant and the general public will prosper and have little reason for discontent. Of course, the business leaders themselves will be the first to prosper and be content.

But there are also many "ifs" at work on the business front. True, tiny Hong Kong has shown miraculous economic growth in the second half of the 20th century, evolving from a center of manufacturing for export into a world financial capital. Today the multinational investment banks that line the streets of Central Hong Kong are there mostly to handle the flows of capital investment into China and other parts of Asia. Nearly half the direct investment into East Asia in recent years has been channeled through Hong Kong because of its prominence as a regional financial center. Thus, economic growth in the region, especially in China, is important to Hong Kong's future.

The Basic Law, article 109, states that the government of the SAR will provide an economic environment that maintains Hong Kong's status as an international financial center. The document also calls for the provision of an environment that encourages investment and promotes trade. All of this was very important when the Basic Law was signed in 1990, when reform in China was in a precarious infant stage. Now that the giant next door is on the verge of becoming an economic superpower, Shanghai in particular is beginning to rival Hong Kong as a financial capital. As the legal system and infrastructure of China develop, financial institutions that have based their China operations in Hong Kong simply because it was an easier place for the staff to live and conduct business might start to find Shanghai equally attractive.

Business in Hong Kong has always been resilient, adapting to changes as they start to occur. Many of Hong Kong's most prominent business leaders are descended from Shanghai merchant families that fled China after the Communist revolution in 1949. Ironically, in the future pragmatism might dictate a return to their roots.

On the other hand, China could experience turmoil in the next few years: a power struggle after the death of patriarch Deng Xiaoping, dissent among the Chinese people, and trouble in political relations with Taiwan are all possibilities. Though the business world currently seems eager to cultivate the huge potential market in China, most foreign investors were quick to take to their heels immediately after the 1989 Beijing Massacre. Hong Kong suffered aftershocks too, in the form of economic slowdown and a "brain drain" of educated Hong Kong Chinese who thought the future looked brighter in North America, Australia, and the

United Kingdom. Today the economies of both China and Hong Kong have recovered with a vengeance, and many of those who left have returned—albeit with foreign passports in hand in case problems arise in China again.

Between January and July of 1996 nearly 400,000 Hong Kong citizens lined up to get British National Overseas passports, which, while not allowing them to emigrate to Britain, would enable them to travel more freely than on a Chinese passport. Some 364,000 such passports were granted. At the same time many Western expatriate residents were applying for naturalization, so that they could remain in the territory as permanent residents. The expat community, some 60,000 strong before the takeover, includes many who have made their careers and homes in Hong Kong, and want the choice of staying. In a year of uncertainties, most in Hong Kong are taking a wait and see approach, but they want to be free to go or to stay. It's a right of choice that people living in democratic countries take for granted.

Culturally, Hong Kong has evolved into a very different place from China. The language, Cantonese, is unintelligible to China's Mandarin speakers, who consider it a rather unrefined, harsh-sounding dialect. The Hong Kong Chinese have a religious tradition that was not interrupted by Maoism and revolutionary rhetoric, and is observed today in a mind-boggling number of holidays and rituals that involve ancestor worship, multiple deities, numerology, Buddhism, Taoism, Confucianism, and various forms of mysticism. Unlike Mainland Chinese, Hong Kong Chinese are accustomed to viewing movies from all over the world, to dining on European cuisine, and to seeing designer goods for sale on almost every corner.

Although Hong Kong will officially remain a British colony right up until July 1, the Hong Kong Chinese have become the true voice of business, politics, and society here. They fought for their rights under colonial rule. At one time Chinese people were not allowed to live on Victoria Peak, the 1,805-foot high billionaire's paradise; the legislative and judicial positions in government used to be occupied strictly by British men. All of this has changed. Universities, corporations, and civil service branches have in recent years begun to favor hiring local Chinese men and women instead of expats, partly to save on relocation costs but also because of a growing nationalistic sentiment and an abundant pool of well-educated bilingual and multilingual professionals. Even Hong Kong's busy socialite scene of charity balls and exclusive parties is at least half Chinese these days.

ULTIMATELY, it seems unlikely that the Hong Kong Chinese will take any more kindly to an authoritative hand from Beijing than to one from England. Though on the surface this appears to be a conciliatory society, concerned mostly with working, making money, and living well, there is a history of sympathetic activism on behalf of the Chinese people when they've suffered from repression on the mainland. Hong Kong citizens organized fund-raising events for the demonstrators in Tiananmen Square, and sent them hundreds of thousands of dollars as well as bright-colored tents to make the vigil more comfortable.

Many Hong Kong residents were concerned about Beijing's attempts to crack down on the media even before the handover. In 1994 a Hong Kong journalist, Xi Yan, was arrested in China when he obtained information the government did not want him to have, and sentenced to 12 years in prison on a charge of "stealing state secrets." Xi's newspaper did not take the risk of trying to help him, and he remains behind bars. Three mainland movies due to be shown at the Hong Kong International Film Festival in 1996 were withdrawn under strong pressure from China. Beijing was apparently angry because the municipal council that organizes the festival had refused to ban independent mainland films not sanctioned by the government or submit a list to China for consultation.

At the same time, there are reports of factionalism within the Beijing government over many issues, including how to handle Hong Kong. In the spring of 1996, for example, Li Ruihauyan, the chairman of the Chinese People's Political Consultative Conference, a part of the domestic bureaucracy that doesn't actually have a direct role in policy toward Hong Kong, nevertheless made a point of saying publicly that the central government departments must act in accordance with the Basic Law, implying that they were not. Differences of opinion could degenerate into a power struggle, or a liberal faction could ultimately prevail.

The plethora of possibilities is both unnerving and exciting to outsiders who have branded themselves "Hong Kong watchers." The intricate maneuverings, the clash of cultures and personalities, the way China behaves, and the way other foreign powers react will combine to make 1997 in Hong Kong a sort of global political-economic Super Bowl. One hopes that the eyes of the world will be a monitoring force upon the Beijing government and the new Hong Kong leaders, sending a strong message that stifling the territory's individual freedoms or its laissez-faire business environment would backfire in the end.

—Jan Alexander

WHAT'S WHERE

Hong Kong Island

Hong Kong is a dazzling melée of human life and enterprise. From the harbor, the city's latest architectural wonders stand against a green mountainside backdrop, while on the other side of the island beaches and quieter villages slow the pace considerably. There is nearly everything in between. Moving clockwise, beginning with the harbor districts, Western and Central are two of the liveliest areas, full of markets, other shopping, restaurants, businesses—you name it. South of these, Mid-Levels, with its agglomeration of apartment towers, and Victoria Peak rise above the din of downtown. Wanchai is the next district east, formerly of ill repute but now the preferred locale for a night on the town. After that is Causeway Bay, another shopping haven. North Point is on the northeast corner; its principal tourist offerings are a market and a ferry pier. Shek O lies at a distant remove on the southeastern peninsula—a pleasant village with a beach for an afternoon's escape.

On the bottom of the Hong Kong Island, Stanley was a fishing village in the 19th century. Now mostly residential, it too has a pleasant beach, an interesting market, and restaurants that make a trip here worthwhile. Working your way back to the western part of the island, the amusements at Ocean Park and the large town of Aberdeen follow Repulse Bay, named for the HMS *Repulse,* which the British used to break the ring of pirates that occupied the area.

Kowloon

Occupying the tip of the peninsula across from Hong Kong Island, bustling Kowloon is where your airplane will actually land when you arrive in the area. Tsim Sha Tsui lies at the bottom of the peninsula, crammed full of shops, restaurants, and businesses. On the western side of Kowloon, Yau Ma Tei is noted for two temples, more practical shops, and great markets, such as the Jade Market and the Temple Street night market.

The New Territories

Because of its distance, which in fact is not great, from the commercial hubs of Hong Kong Island and Kowloon, tourists often overlook the attractions of the New Territories. Parts of the area retain their isolated, rural character, even if to find them you must first make your way past massive housing developments (new towns built to house the burgeoning population). Shatin is one of these towns, with the ultra-modern Shatin Racecourse and the very old Temple of Ten Thousand Buddhas. Nonetheless the older character is what Hong Kong grew out of, and it is as interesting to see for its remaining traditional lifestyles as for its ancient temples and country parks. To the east, Sai Kung's country park is one of the most spectacular in the area.

The Outlying Islands

As popular getaways for locals and tourists alike, the islands around Hong Kong in the South China Sea have unique charms of their own, from beaches and old fishing villages to hiking trails and remote, ancient Buddhist monasteries.

Macau

A tiny remnant of the 16th-century Portuguese spice trade, Macau provides a pleasant respite from the nonstop bustle of Hong Kong forty miles to the east. Construction on the island has taken away some of its quieter charms, but Portuguese influence—especially in the food—is yet another fascinating Eurasian variation played out in the South China Sea. Macau is the principal island of the territory, but the neighboring Taipa and Coloane islands are also worth visiting if you plan to spend a few days in Macau.

PLEASURES AND PASTIMES

Beaches

Surprising as it may seem, there are splendid beaches all over the area, some of which are well maintained by the government and served by lifeguards. **Repulse Bay** is a sort of Chinese Coney Island; **Turtle Cove** is isolated and beautiful; **Shek O** has a Mediterranean feeling; and among New Territory and Outlying Island beaches, **Pak Sha Chau** has lovely golden sands, while **Lo Sho Ching** is a favorite of local families.

Chinese Culture

There are so many ways of taking in the phenomena of Asian life—at restaurants, in street markets where the very sense of an individual's space is so dramatically different than in the West, in ancient Chinese temples, in a karaoke bar, at the hands of a fortune teller, or in parks watching the morning t'ai chi ritual. Embrace as much of Hong Kong as you can. You'll never forget it.

Restaurants

No other city in the world, except New York, can match the distinct variety and integrity of cuisine found in Hong Kong. One of the most exciting aspects of dining on Chinese soil is the opportunity to eat truly authentic Chinese food. At the same time, at a cultural crossroads like Hong Kong, with all of its exotic connotations, the steamy, aromatic tastes of Pan-Asian cuisine are another unique culinary opportunity. All in all, there is enough to satisfy everyone, if not while sitting at the same table. If you approach this diversity with an open mind, try some things that you usually might shy away from, you may just leave Hong Kong wishing that you could take it all with you.

Shopping

Hong Kong has the best shopping in the world, if you work at it. Although the thought of crowded streets, mind-boggling choices, and endless haggling can be daunting, there is no place more conducive to big-time spending than this center of international commerce. Even nonshoppers get tempted to part with their money—and some have admitted to actually enjoying the experience.

The variety of goods is astonishing: everything from international designer products to intriguing treasures and handcrafted items from all over Asia. Just as remarkable is the fantastic choice of places to shop, which range from sophisticated boutique-lined malls to open-air markets and shadowy alleyways.

Walking

There is a wide range of pedestrian movement possible in Hong Kong—from the sort of sideways shuffling that one does in a street market to outstanding hiking on Hong Kong Island itself, in the New Territories, and on the Outlying Islands. The point is not how fast or far you go, but simply that you experience the area on foot. It is without question the most rewarding way to take in the sights, sounds, and smells of this astonishing territory.

NEW AND NOTEWORTHY

A walking trail of epic proportions. Even the territory's diehard hikers are still clocking in miles along the Wilson Trail, which opened last year. Named after a former governor who was a hiking enthusiast, the trail runs nearly 50 miles from the steep hills of southern Hong Kong Island to Kowloon and the New Territories. It takes at least 31 hours to hike the entire trail, but the well-marked pathways are divided into 10 sections. Choose a route for a day hike. The least rigorous section will take you along a beautiful reservoir to the cliffs overlooking the tranquil Tolo Harbour. On other sections of the trail you'll see the fishing villages that dot the Sai Kung islands, tropical groves, incense-filled temples, sweeping panoramas of the sea islands, and of course, Hong Kong's majestic mountains.

The Airport Core Programme (ACP) Exhibition Centre. Hong Kong is getting more than just a new airport next year. The engineering feat on Chek Lap Kok island, which required mowing down a mountain to level the land for an airstrip and terminal, was just the beginning of a massive development project that will pave over the green hills of adjacent Lantau Island with highways, a subway line, and a long stretch of skyscrapers. There will also be a new tunnel to connect the airport to urban Hong Kong, and the world's longest road/rail suspension bridge. This is all in keeping with explosive growth: Hong Kong's urban planning department expects the territory's population, currently 6.2 million, to triple within 30 years. You can see architectural models, videos, and photographs of what Hong Kong will look like when the 21st century dawns at the ACP Exhibition Centre. Call the Hong Kong Tourist Association (☎ 2807–6177) for information.

The Racing Museum. Whether you're game for trying your luck at the track or not, you can see memorabilia and photographs that reveal great moments in the history of horse racing in Hong Kong. The museum, which opened last year, is adjacent to the Hong Kong Jockey Club's Happy Valley racecourse, and includes a small cinema and a gift shop. ☎ 2966–8111 or 2966–8364.

Ocean Park Hong Kong. The Film Fantasia Simulator Ride, in the Lowland area of the park, is a cinema with 100 hydraulically activated seats to take the audience through a series of virtual fantasy adventures. The Mine Train Roller Coaster, in the Tai Shue Wan area of the park, takes you rolling at dizzying heights along a backdrop of desert scrub—resembling America's Wild West. Hold onto your seat for the straight drop from 81 meters (266 feet) above sea level. The Discovery of the Ancient World theme area is scheduled to open in April 1997. It will recreate the atmosphere of a lost city within a tropical rain forest, complete with animated, interactive jungle animals. ☎ 2873–8888.

Museum. In Chai Wan, a museum showing the history of coastal defense in Hong Kong since the Ming Dynasty is scheduled to open in 1997 at the old Lyemun Barracks. Original gun batteries and heavy weapons will be restored to their 19th-century appearance. Call the HKTA at 2801–7111 for an update on the opening and directions on how to get there.

FODOR'S CHOICE

Dining

★**Pierrot.** There is no reason why you shouldn't crave haute cuisine *française*—even in Hong Kong—and there is no reason why you shouldn't go to Pierrot to taste it, while you gaze out at the harbor. *$$$$*

★**Sagano Restaurant.** For its sushi imported exclusively from Japan, *teppanyaki* deftly prepared at your table, or intriguing *kansai* cuisine from around Kyoto, Sagano has set itself apart as *the* Japanese restaurant in Hong Kong. *$$$$*

★**Cafe Deco Bar and Grill.** Combining Hong Kong chic and Pan-Asian cuisine with panoramic views from atop Victoria Peak, this has become an Island favorite. *$$$*

★**Yung Kee.** What you expect from Cantonese dining—lightning-fast preparations, high-energy service, and reasonable prices—is what you'll get at Yung Kee, which is why so many different kinds of people keep coming back. *$$*

★**Il Mercato.** If you find yourself in Stanley Village, think Italian and stop into Il Mercato for whatever the changing menu has to offer—or for their not-so-Italian New York–style cheesecake. *$*

★**Spice Island Gourmet Club.** When the Indian buffet is one of the best in the city and the food is this good, there is no need to spend time deciding where to go for lunch—or dinner for that matter—just go. *$*

★**Bela Vista, Macau.** In the landmark Bela Vista Hotel overlooking Praia Grande Bay, this romantic restaurant with veranda offers Portuguese seafood dishes, such as grilled garoupa (grouper) with mango. This is the place to come for a truly memorable Macanese dinner. *$$$*

★**Afonso III, Macau.** For a wholly different experience of Portuguese cuisine, where the chef prepares food the way his grandmother did, try this simple café. *$$*

Excursions

★The view of the coastline from the **Ocean Park cable car.** From here you'll think you're riding over the Mediterranean as you gaze down at a panorama of mountains, pastel villas, and the vast, blue sea.

★Crossing the harbor on the **Star Ferry,** first class. Breathing the air of the South China Sea is vital to any experience of Hong Kong, whose very existence owes itself to the crossing of seas—not to mention today's stunning views.

★A **tram ride** from Kennedy Town to North Point. Spare half of an afternoon to see Hong Kong at its bustling, crowded best. Find a spot on the upper deck for the ideal view of stores, office buildings, produce markets, traffic, and swarms of humanity, all with a uniquely Chinese flair.

★The **double-decker bus ride** over the bridge from Macau to Taipa Island. With the wind in your hair and water all around, this roller coaster–like ride is the best way to escape to the quieter island south of Macau.

Lodging

★**Island Shangri-La, Hong Kong Island.** This hotel, which towers above the Pacific Place complex, has spacious rooms and spectacular views of the Peak and Victoria Harbour. $$$$

★**Mandarin Oriental, Hong Kong Island.** The Mandarin matches convenience with luxury, making it one of the world's great hotels. Celebrities and VIPs agree. $$$$

★**Peninsula, Kowloon.** The "Pen" is the ultimate in colonial elegance with its mix of European elegance and Chinese details. $$$$

★**Garden View International House, Hong Kong Island.** This small, attractive hotel overlooks the botanical gardens and the harbor. $$

★**Bela Vista, Macau.** Originally built in the 1880s and now a luxury all-suite inn, the Bela Vista retains its colonial ambience under the management of Mandarin Oriental Hotels. $$$

★**Pousada de São Tiago, Macau.** This traditional Portuguese inn is built into the ruins of a 17th-century fortress and incorporates ancient trees and natural springs into its design. The furnishings were custom made in Portugal and Hong Kong. $$$

Museums

★**The life-size dioramas in the Hong Kong Museum of History.** See what Hong Kong looked like more than 6,000 years ago, when tigers and other animals ranged over the islands. Scenes of Neolithic life are part of a permanent exhibition that traces the territory's development all the way up to the present.

★**The Hong Kong Museum of Art.** This, of course, is the place in town to see ancient Chinese scrolls and sculpture along with the work of the territory's own contemporary masters.

★**The Maritime Museum, Macau.** From its dragon boats to pirate-chasing *lorchas*, Portuguese voyage charts, and navigation equipment, the ship-shaped Maritime Museum provides a fascinating view of seagoing Macau.

Nightlife

★**Wanchai District.** Less Western, less uptight, and—some would say—more fun than the gentrified Lan Kwai Fong in Central District, Wanchai is shedding the sleazy image it once had and becoming the new hot spot after hours.

★**Crazy Paris Show at Hotel Lisboa, Macau.** Girls, girls, girls (wait, was that a boy in there?)—if that's what you're after, this Paris Vegas–style show is the best around.

Parks and Countryside Walks

★**Dragon's Back in Shek O Country Park.** Bring your hiking boots and canteen and escape the urban madness on a moderately hilly trail where banana leaves grow to be three feet long and the view of the sea is nothing short of spectacular.

★**Lantau Island, Shek Pik to Tai O.** If you're a seasoned hiker, try this wondrous all-day trek past the Shek Pik reservoir and a half-dozen tucked-away monasteries down to the picturesque seaside village of Tai O, still unmarred by serious development.

★**Lou Lim Ieoc Garden, Macau.** For a lovely respite in Macau, stroll through this Soochow-style enclosed garden, a miniature landscape of bamboo, a lake, and a traditional nine-turn bridge.

★**Coloane Park, Macau.** On the southernmost of Macau's three islands, Coloane Park has a remarkable walk-in aviary with more than 200 bird species (some quite rare), a nature trail, and a fascinating collection of exotic trees and shrubs.

Special Events

★**Candlelight parades.** Two parades, one in honor of the mid-autumn moon and another at the Dragon Boat Festival in June, are both resplendent with traditional costumes, music, and general merrymaking.

★**Bun Festival (May) on Cheung Chau.** The villagers still offer fresh-baked buns to placate vengeful spirits of the dead each year, with three 50-foot-high bun towers outside of the Pak Tai Temple. Bring a camera to catch the parade of elaborate floats and an altar of papier-mâché gods on film.

★**Horse racing at Happy Valley track.** All of Hong Kong loves a gamble, and there's no better way to see a cross-section of the population, from the boxes to the bleachers, taking a chance on winning. Whether you win or not, you'll find the mood contagious.

★**Fringe Festival.** Experience the best of Hong Kong's avant-garde theater, music, and art at the unique Fringe Club, housed in a historic building that used to be a dairy depot. The festival is held on various dates in January and February.

★**The Good Friday Passion Parade, Macau.** In the first weekend of Lent, a statue of Christ is carried through the streets in procession, with stations of the cross erected along the way.

Street Markets

★**Jade Market, Kansu Street, Kowloon.** Besides 10,000 jade bangles, baubles, and beads, this colorful open-air bazaar has Chinese-style jewelry galore, in every price range.

★**Bird Market on Hong Lok Street, near Mongkok MTR station Kowloon.** On a tiny street filled with the trill of song-birds, you might also hear a mynah cursing in Cantonese as you watch old men feed grasshoppers to their prize songsters. If you'd like, pick up a beautiful handmade bamboo cage for a souvenir.

★**Rua de Cinco de Outubro, Macau.** This is old Macau at its finest—old teahouses and the superb *Farmacia Tai Neng Tong,* a traditional Chinese medicine shop with a wonderfully carved wooden facade and an interior full of apothecary jars and other fantastic items.

Taste Treats

★**Dim sum lunch** anywhere. Since you've come to the source, this is one tradition that you simply must not pass up.

★A market-stall Chinese breakfast of *congee* (rice porridge) at Kowloon Park Road/Haiphong Road, Kowloon. There are plenty of tastes so exotic that we wouldn't recommend them, but this is a worthwhile, quintessential experience of bustling Hong Kong culture.

★**Afternoon tea** in the grand lobby of the Peninsula Hotel. Dignified and utterly civilized, this legacy of the British presence in Hong Kong can transport you beyond the elegance of the Peninsula to a wholly other era.

Temples and Shrines

★**The Temple of 10,000 Buddhas, Shatin.** You will have to climb nearly 500 steps to reach this wonder, but with its 13,000 statues and gilded, mummified holy man, in addition to views of Amah Rock, the temple is worth the effort.

★**Po Lin Buddhist Monastery, Lantau Island.** On a grander scale than most temple complexes in Hong Kong, Po Lin Monastery is home to Southeast Asia's tallest bronze Buddha, more than 100 feet high.

★**A-Ma Temple, Macau.** Named for a sea goddess who, according to custom, saved a humble junk from a storm, A-Ma is the oldest and perhaps the most beautiful Buddhist temple in Macau.

FESTIVALS AND SEASONAL EVENTS

Top seasonal events in Hong Kong include Chinese New Year, the Hong Kong Arts Festival, the Hong Kong Food Festival, and the Dragon Boat Festival. The most colorful festivals of all are the many lunar festivals celebrated throughout the year. For exact dates and further details about the following events, contact the HKTA (☞ Visitor Information *in* the Gold Guide's Important Contacts A to Z).

WINTER

MID-JAN.–FEB.➤ Hong Kong Arts Festival takes place in venues throughout Hong Kong.

LATE JAN.➤ Hong Kong Marathon is sponsored by the Hong Kong Distance Runner's Club.

LATE JAN.–FEB.➤ Chinese New Year, a time to visit friends and relatives and wear new clothes, causes the city to come to a virtual standstill.

FEB.➤ Spring Lantern Festival is on the last day of Chinese New Year celebrations; streets and homes are decorated with brightly colored lanterns.

EARLY MAR.➤ Hong Kong Open Golf Championship, at the Royal Hong Kong Golf Club.

SPRING

MID-MAR.➤ The annual Hong Kong Food Festival is more than two weeks of nonstop feasting and entertainment.

LATE MAR. OR EARLY APR.➤ The Invitation Sevens is a premier rugby tournament.

LATE MAR.➤ Hong Kong International Film Festival, featuring films from several countries, is a rewarding fortnight for film buffs.

EARLY APR.➤ Ching Ming Festival is a time when families visit the burial plots of ancestors and departed relatives.

LATE APR.➤ Birthday of Tin Hau, goddess of the sea. Fishermen decorate their boats and converge on seaside temples to honor her, especially around the Tin Hau Temple in Junk Bay.

MAY➤ Birthday of Lord Buddha, when temples throughout the territory bathe the Buddha's statue.

MAY➤ Bun Festival on Cheung Chau Island is a three-day spirit-placating rite, culminating in a grand procession that attracts thousands of people.

JUNE➤ The Dragon Boat Festival pits long, many-oared dragon-head boats against one another in races to commemorate the hero Ch'u Yuen. International races follow a week later.

SUMMER

JULY 1➤ This is the official day that Hong Kong reverts to Chinese sovereignty. Various events will take place from June 30 to July 2.

MID-AUG.➤ Seven Sisters (Maiden) Festival is a celebration for lovers and a time when young girls pray for a good husband.

AUG.➤ Hungry Ghosts Festival is a time when food is set out to placate roaming spirits.

AUTUMN

SEPT.➤ Lantern Festival sees crowds with candle lanterns gather in parks and other open spaces.

LATE SEPT. OR EARLY OCT.➤ Birthday of Confucius celebrates the revered philosopher.

MID-OCT.➤ Chung Yeung Festival commemorates a Han Dynasty tale about a man taking his family to high ground to avoid disaster.

LATE NOV.➤ The Macau Grand Prix takes over the city streets for a weekend.

MID-DEC.➤ Hong Kong Judo Championship takes place at Queen Elizabeth Stadium.

2 Exploring Hong Kong

HONG KONG IS ONE OF THE WORLD'S most compact, intense travel experiences. The crowds can be overwhelming, but the city vibrates with life, energy, and the frantic quest for personal achievement and gain. Hong Kong is the very essence of Western capitalism, yet the soul of the place is truly Eastern. This blend and contrast are what make Hong Kong so fascinating.

There is so much to see and do here that it's easy to be lured away from a hectic business schedule or a rigid sightseeing plan and instead head down alleyways lined with shops selling everything from jewelry to sportswear and filled with the aroma from food stalls and some of the world's best Chinese restaurants. You won't find much ancient history here. Hong Kong has existed as a city for little more than 150 years, and urban development has brought change even to old neighborhoods. The Chinese have been flocking to Hong Kong for decades, bringing with them their traditions as well as their energy and entrepreneurial spirit. Hong Kong has given full scope to that spirit, leaving it unhindered by political or social limitations.

The feeling of Hong Kong, what it is and why it exists, can be discovered only from the harbor. That body of water, chosen centuries ago by fishermen from China as a perfect shelter from the raging *tai'foos* ("big winds," the origin of the word "typhoon"), is still the territory's centerpiece. Hong Kong began as a trading center and has grown into a bustling commercial capital largely because its harbor, emptying into the South China Sea, is a convenient gateway for traders from both East and West. Today, however, the harbor is almost as densely packed as the streets of Hong Kong's commercial districts. The Port of Hong Kong—the busiest on earth—barely has enough space left to accommodate the traffic of huge cargo ships from around the globe.

On either side of the harbor, the packed streets of Hong Kong Island and lower Kowloon Peninsula have the look of a futuristic metropolis, with skyscrapers built virtually on top of one another and hardly a green space in sight. Construction hasn't stopped just because there seems to be no visible patch of land left. Developers faced with a shortage of space upon which to build are creating more land by dredging it from beneath the harbor. A major land reclamation project is underway on Hong Kong Island just to the west of the pier where the Star Ferry to Kowloon docks. A miniature island is being created at the northern edge of Wanchai to provide for an extension to the Convention and Exhibition Centre. At Western District, land is being dredged up to lengthen the MTR subway line, which will eventually provide service to West Kowloon and Chek Lap Kok. Still other projects are planned for the Kowloon tip.

The intensely developed areas seen by most tourists belie the fact that 80% of the territory is actually rural land. A bird's-eye view reveals the 236 islands that make up the lesser-known part of Hong Kong. Most of these islands are nothing but jagged peaks and tropical scrub, too rocky for cultivation or building. Others are throwbacks to the world of fishing villages and small vegetable farms. Even Hong Kong Island has vast stretches of green, with walking trails that take two days or more to cover. This other side of Hong Kong is easily accessible by boats and buses.

Hong Kong residents have a great fondness for open spaces. Indeed, the popularity of weekend hiking, junk sailing, and skydiving has reached almost manic levels in recent years. Perhaps this is because every-

Hong Kong Island

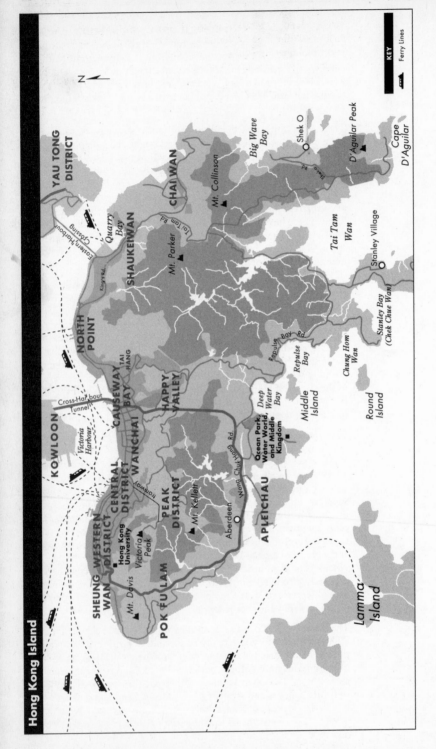

N

KEY

Ferry Lines

YAU TONG DISTRICT

Quarry Bay

Eastern Harbour Crossing

Big Wave Bay

Shek O

Shek O Rd

D'Aguilar Peak

Cape D'Aguilar

CHAI WAN

Mt. Collinson

SHAUKEIWAN

Mt. Parker

Tai Tam Rd

NORTH POINT

King's Rd

Tai Tam Wan

Stanley Village

Stanley Bay (Chek Chue Wan)

Cross-Harbour Tunnel

KOWLOON

Victoria Harbour

CAUSEWAY BAY

TAI HANG

HAPPY VALLEY

WANCHAI

Repulse Bay Rd

Repulse Bay

Chung Hom Wan

CENTRAL DISTRICT

Wong Chuk Hang Rd

Deep Water Bay

Ocean Park, Water World and Middle Kingdom

Middle Island

Round Island

WESTERN DISTRICT

SHEUNG WAN

Hong Kong University

Victoria Peak

PEAK DISTRICT

Mt. Kellett

Aberdeen

APLEICHAU

Mt. Davis

POK FU LAM

Lamma Island

one who lives here knows that nothing lasts forever, especially undeveloped land. The New Territories are full of industry instead of rice fields now; the farms of Lamma Island are disappearing as new apartment buildings go up; and many of the vast uninhabited stretches of Lantau Island, a favorite among hikers, will be filled with offices and residential towers in a few years as part of the development that will come with the new airport. For now, Hong Kong's sudden economic boom has brought it into a sort of golden age, with a perfect balance of the old and the new, the dazzle of the city and the intrepid spirit of the outdoors. You can hike and camp in the woods, stroll through traditional Chinese villages, or spend the afternoon sailing, then, via the city's mega-efficient highways and public transportation, arrive back in civilization in plenty of time for an evening of fine dining and glittering nightlife.

Until 1841, the island that is now modern Hong Kong was home to a few fishermen and their families. It was a sparse little island, 30 square miles (155 square kilometers) in size, with only one natural water source—a waterfall above what is now Aberdeen—and a mountainous center. Except for the natural harbor, all its geographical, historical, and demographic factors should have guaranteed Hong Kong permanent obscurity.

The island was officially ceded to Great Britain in 1841, at the end of the First Opium War with China. At that time it was hardly considered a valuable prize. The British military acknowledged its usefulness as an operational base or transshipping port, but was angry that it wasn't offered a port on the mainland of China. The British foreign minister called Hong Kong "that barren rock," and Queen Victoria's consort, Prince Albert, publicly laughed at this "jewel" in the British Crown.

Hardly an auspicious beginning for the island that author Han Suyin was to describe a century later as the "deep roaring bustling eternal market . . . in which life and love and souls and blood and all things made and grown under the sun are bought and sold and smuggled and squandered."

Han's description is the impression one gets now when arriving on the island for the first time by Star Ferry. One of the unfortunate results of progress is that many visitors now get their initial view of Hong Kong Island as they emerge from the cavernous Cross-Harbour Tunnel or from the steps of the MTR, rather than from the legendary ferry.

It was only blocks away from the Star Ferry terminal that Captain Charles Elliott of Britain's Royal Navy first set foot on the island. Today, the "barren rock" contains some of the world's most expensive real estate and a skyline to rival that of any of the world's major cities.

NOTE: This chapter is divided into four exploring sections covering Hong Kong Island, Kowloon across the harbor, the New Territories north of Kowloon, and the Outer Islands around Hong Kong in the South China Sea.

HONG KONG ISLAND

Many of the British who set up their trading warehouses on Hong Kong Island were of Scottish ancestry. They were among the most nationalistic (or homesick) in the Victorian era, and almost everything of importance was named after Queen Victoria. The central section was named Victoria City, the mountain peak was Victoria Peak, the military barracks, Victoria Barracks, and the prison, Victoria Prison. Victoria College and Victoria Park came later.

Central Hong Kong is still officially named Victoria City, but everyone calls it **Central.** (It will be no surprise if the Chinese-appointed government that takes over on July 1, 1997, changes the territory's colonial names to Chinese ones.) Buildings in the district are both modern and ornate, gleaming in gold, silver, ivory, and ebony, iridescent reflections of the harbor shimmering on their surfaces—this is just one of the faces with which the city enchants new visitors.

Central District is, of course, in the center of the north side of the island. To the west, **Western District** begins with small Chinese shops that give way to large residential high-rises stretching out to Pok Fu Lam, a neighborhood popular among expat families. To the east of Central lies **Wanchai,** famed at one time for its nightlife, as immortalized in Richard Mason's novel *The World of Suzie Wong* and the movie it inspired. Just past Wanchai, **Causeway Bay** was once a middle-class Chinese community but is now primarily a business and tourist area filled with offices, hotels, restaurants, and Hong Kong's highest concentration of department stores.

Farther east, **Quarry Bay** once consisted solely of factories and tenements and is now full of gleaming new office complexes. **Shaukiwan** and **Chai Wan,** at the eastern end of Quarry Bay, were once very poor but have become rapidly gentrifying refuges for middle-class residents and businesses fleeing the high rents of Central.

South of Central's business district, the Mid-Levels area climbs out of the hills, with luxury skyscrapers growing right out of the tropical bush. The series of escalators carrying you up through the center of the development is a striking example of the use of technology to relieve the city's congestion. It saves valuable space and eliminates the traffic of a large road. Escalators run downhill in the morning, taking Mid-Levels residents to their jobs, and then run uphill for the rest of the day. Also worth a visit are **Hong Kong University,** the **Botanical Gardens,** and some of Hong Kong's few remaining examples of Victorian apartment architecture—although the latter are disappearing rapidly.

High above Mid-Levels, **Victoria Peak,** known simply as the Peak, juts 1,805 feet above sea level. Residents here take special pride in the positions to which they have, quite literally, risen: It is the most exclusive residential area on the island.

Aberdeen, on the southwest side of the island, has a busy fisherman's harbor. It is where you will find the "floating garden" restaurants, (including the garishly lit, much-photographed Jumbo)—and **Ocean Park,** containing Asia's largest oceanarium, and the **Middle Kingdom** and **Water World** theme parks. Aberdeen also contains a factory area, Wong Chuk Hang, and the highway interchange for the Aberdeen Tunnel, which slices through the mountains and comes out at the **Happy Valley Race Track.**

Leaving Aberdeen and heading east on a winding oceanfront highway, you reach scenic **Deep Water Bay.** Farther east is **Repulse Bay,** another of Hong Kong's prestigious residential areas with a very popular beach. Still following the winding road, you will come upon the growing suburb of **Stanley,** with bargain shopping; then Big Wave Bay, one of the territory's few surfing beaches; and then the pleasant village of **Shek O,** another old settlement that is a mix of village houses and baronial mansions.

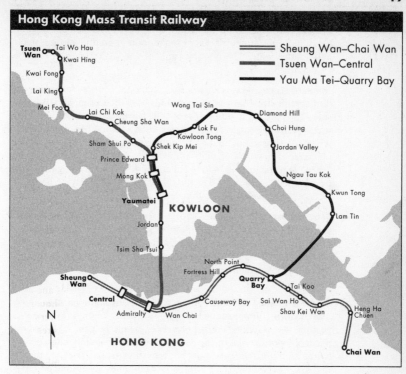

Hong Kong Mass Transit Railway

=== Sheung Wan–Chai Wan
=== Tsuen Wan–Central
=== Yau Ma Tei–Quarry Bay

Tsuen Wan · Tai Wo Hau · Kwai Hing · Kwai Fong · Lai King · Mei Foo · Lai Chi Kok · Cheung Sha Wan · Sham Shui Po · Prince Edward · Mong Kok · **Yaumatei** · Jordan · Tsim Sha Tsui · Shek Kip Mei · Kowloon Tong · Lok Fu · Wong Tai Sin · Diamond Hill · Choi Hung · Jordan Valley · Ngau Tau Kok · Kwun Tong · Lam Tin

KOWLOON

Sheung Wan · **Central** · Admiralty · Wan Chai · Causeway Bay · Fortress Hill · North Point · **Quarry Bay** · Tai Koo · Sai Wan Ho · Shau Kei Wan · Heng Ha Chuen · **Chai Wan**

N

HONG KONG

Central and Western Districts

Sights to See

Numbers in the margin correspond to points of interest on the Central and Western Districts map.

Bank of China. This structure, the old Bank of China building, is easy to recognize with its two Chinese stone lions guarding the front doorway. Built by Chinese Nationalists after World War II, this building was 20 feet higher than the Hongkong and Shanghai Bank edifice until the latter built its imposing new structure in the 1980s. Not to be outdone, the Bank of China commissioned I. M. Pei to design an even more impressive tower, which was completed in 1989. Across the street and a few doors east of the venerable institution, on Queen's Road Central, the Bank of China Tower challenges its rival's influence on the landscape. A visiting architect recently said that the towers of finance in Hong Kong, which dominate the view as no church spires ever have, are an indication of the city's worship of an economy built around banking.

On the 11th floor of the old Bank of China building, the **Tsui Museum of Art** has holdings of more than 3,000 pieces of Chinese art including collections of ceramics, bronze, and carved wood and ivory. ☎ 2868–2688. ✆ *HK$20.* ☉ *Weekdays 10–6, Sat. 10–2. Closed public holidays.*

⑫ Bonham Strand East and West. An area left relatively untouched by the modern world, the streets here are lined with traditional shops, many open-fronted. Among the most interesting are those selling live snakes, both for food and for medicinal uses. The snakes, from pythons to cobras, are imported from China and kept in cages outside of the shops. Go ahead and sample a bowl of snake soup or an invigorating snake-gallbladder wine. The main season for the snake trade is October through February.

Bonham Strand West is known for traditional Chinese medicines and herbal remedies. Many of the old shops have their original facades. Inside, walls are lined with drawers and shelves of jars filled with hundreds of strange-smelling ingredients, such as wood barks and insects, which are consumed dried and ground up, infused in hot water or tea, or taken as powders or pills. Some of the more innocuous remedies are made from ginseng, said to enhance virility and prolong life. Skeptics should keep in mind that the Chinese have been relying on the effects of these medicines for thousands of years.

9 **Central Market.** The Queen Victoria Street crossing with Queen's Road Central used to be the city's largest public food market. On the ground floor there are still produce stalls, but the top floor, a walkway connecting to the Mid-Levels escalator, has become gentrified, with small stalls selling souvenirs, lingerie, jewelry, Chinese magazines, and fast food.

7 **Chater Garden.** This small park, across from the Bank of China Tower, was the former home of the Hong Kong Cricket Club. A favorite local pastime was watching cricket players enjoying the game at a leisurely pace, oblivious to the traffic noise and bustle. The club, chased away by the high price of real estate, has moved to grounds outside the city center. Conservationists won the battle against developers and preserved the park, to the delight of all who come to sit and relax in this small, green oasis. ⊠ *Chater and Jackson Rds.*

NEED A
BREAK?
On the west side of Statue Square is the **Mandarin Oriental Hotel** (⊠ 5 Connaught Rd.), one of the finest hotels in the world. The mezzanine coffee lounge is a pleasant place to have a drink, or you can people-watch at the **Captain's Bar,** where billion-dollar deals are consummated over cognac.

4 **City Hall complex.** Stroll through the garden on almost any afternoon and you'll see at least one or two wedding parties, usually with a young Chinese bride and bridegroom in elaborate Western regalia posing for a photographer. The registry at City Hall is the territory's most popular spot for weddings, with more than 6,500 couples exchanging vows here each year. In addition to municipal offices, it contains a theater, a concert hall, and several libraries. (You can take out books if you bring your passport, proof of address, and a refundable deposit of HK$130 per book.) Many of the events in the annual International Arts and Film Festival are held here. ⊠ *Between Edinburgh Pl. and Connaught Rd.,* ☎ *2921–2840 or 2921–2555.* ⊙ *Library: Mon.–Thurs. 10–7, Fri. 10–9, Sat. 10–5, Sun. 10–1. Closed holidays.*

13 **Des Voeux Road West.** You'll recognize the tram tracks when you get to the western end of Bonham Strand West. On the left side of the street as you walk west, you will find all kinds of shops selling preserved foods such as dried and salted fish, black mushrooms, and vegetables. This is a good area for lunchtime dim sum.

3 **Exchange Square.** Exchange Square consists of three gold- and silver-striped glass towers. This complex is home to the Hong Kong Stock Exchange and contains some of the most expensive rental space on the island (call 2522–1122 to arrange a tour of the Exchange during trading hours, weekdays 10–12:30 and 2:30–3:30). In good weather, local office workers like to buy take-out food from the various epicurean establishments in the square, including Häagen-Dazs, and picnic around the life-size bronze water buffalo between the towers. Go up the escalator to the lobby of Exchange Square 1 to see the rotunda, which has exhibitions of a fairly trendy collection of contemporary art.

Take a good look at the harbor from the plaza at Exchange Square, because soon the view will be gone. You can see the construction taking place on a development project on land that has been "reclaimed" (i.e., dredged up from the harbor) to create a new site for development. Much of the prime real estate in Hong Kong sits on land created this way—at one time Des Voeux Road, where the trams run through Central, was waterfront property.

⑤ HMS *Tamar*. Named after a ship that used to be docked here is the 28-story headquarters of the British Army and Royal Navy. The building and a small harbor are all that remain of the old naval dockyard that occupied the entire shore area, as far as Wanchai. Today, visiting warships often anchor offshore here, their crews coming ashore for nightlife and shopping, as sailors have always done in Hong Kong.

⑮ Hollywood Road. Here funerary shops sell traditional Chinese coffins and other elaborate ceremonial funerary items. Farther along, other shops sell different grades of rice, displayed in brass-banded, wooden tubs. Rice is sold by the catty (about 1¼ lb.). Look to the left for a sign saying POSSESSION STREET. This was where Captain Charles Elliott of the British Royal Navy stepped ashore in 1841 and claimed Hong Kong for the British Empire. It is interesting to note how far today's harbor is from this earlier shoreline—the result of a century of aggressive land reclamation.

Farther east along Hollywood Road are many antiques, curio, and junk shops, as well as shops selling every type of Asian art and handicraft. Some items are genuinely old, but most are not. Porcelain, embroidered robes, paintings, screens, snuff bottles, and wood and ivory carvings are among the many items that can be found here in profusion. Bargain hard if you want a good price.

Hongkong and Shanghai Bank. This modern glass-and-steel headquarters at the end of Statue Square, known simply as the Bank, is the largest and most powerful financial institution in Hong Kong.

Hong Kong Club. A modern building bordering Statue Square houses one of the last social bastions of the fading British colonial system. The club, as attractive as an ice-rink cafeteria, will accept anyone today, but even now there is only 10% Chinese membership.

❷ Jardine House. To the left of the Star Ferry and easy to spot with its many round windows, the building, formerly Connaught Centre, was completed in 1973 and was one of Central's first skyscrapers.

Jubilee Street. Next to Central Market, this street is packed with food stalls offering bowls of noodles, rice dishes, and a wide variety of snacks.

❽ The Landmark. At Pedder Street stands this rather overwhelming shopping complex with an atrium and European-style cafés. Here the same Gucci, Tiffany, and top designer boutiques that line Fifth Avenue and the Champs-Elysées have even higher prices because of stratospheric Hong Kong retail rents. Concerts and other events are presented free of charge. You'll find the latest addition to the complex—a moving carillon, with meter-high figurines representing the 12 animals of the Chi-

nese zodiac, rotating to a Chinese melody played by the bells that ring
on the hour—on the corner of Queen's Road Central and Ice House
Street.

Legislative Council Building. Next door to the Hong Kong Club on Statue
Square, with its domes and colonnades, is the former home of the
Supreme Court. It is one of the few remaining grand Victorian-style
buildings left in this area. Until recently the council had no real power,
but since 1991 it has had a majority of elected members who now challenge the administration at sessions held every Wednesday. Its position
after 1997, when the Crown Colony reverts to Chinese rule, is uncertain. In front of the Council building is the **Cenotaph** monument to all
who lost their lives in the two world wars.

16 **Man Mo Temple.** Built in 1847 and dedicated to the gods of literature
and of war, Man and Mo, this is Hong Kong Island's oldest temple.
The statue of Man is dressed in green and holds a writing brush, while
Mo is dressed in red and holds a sword. To their left is a shrine to Pao
Kung, god of justice, whose face is painted black. To the right, Shing
Wong is god of the city. Coils of incense hang from roof beams, filling the air with a heavy fragrance. The temple bell, cast in Canton in
1847, and the drum next to it are sounded to attract the attention of
the gods when a prayer is being offered. To check your fortune, stand
in front of the altar, take one of the small bamboo cylinders available
there, and shake it until one of the sticks falls out. The number on the
stick corresponds to a written fortune. Here's the catch—the English
translation of your fortune is in a book on sale in the temple. ⊠ *Hollywood Rd.* ⊙ *Daily 9* AM–6 PM.

Mid-Levels. From Central Market you can ride the half-mile of escalators and walkways that go through the steep incline between Central and Mid-Levels. This painless uphill climb provides an interesting
view of small Chinese shops and gleaming residential high-rises, as well
as the all-green Jamia Mosque at Shelley Street (built in 1915). Go between 10:20 AM and 10 PM. After 11 PM, the escalators shut down, and
in the mornings, from 6 to 10, they reverse course and move downhill, so that commuters living in Mid-Levels can get to work in Central.

Queen's Road Central. One of the main shopping arteries, this road
has narrow lanes on either side lined with tiny shops and stalls filled
with inexpensive clothes and leather goods. Queen's Road Central was
also once the seafront and site of the old military parade grounds.

14 **Queen's Road West.** Both sides of this street are filled with embroidery shops selling richly brocaded wedding clothes and all types of embroidered linens, clothing, and household goods. There are Chinese
medicine shops, bird shops selling mynah birds and parrots, and shops
where colorful items are made and sold for burning at Chinese funerals. Houses, cars, furniture, and TV sets—all made of paper and bamboo—are among the items believed necessary to ensure the departed
a good life in the hereafter.

1 **Star Ferry.** This the logical place to start exploring Central District. Since
1898, the ferry terminal has been the gateway to the island for visitors and commuters crossing the harbor from Kowloon. Crossing the
harbor on the Star Ferry and riding around Hong Kong Island on a
two-decker tram are almost essential for first-time visitors. The charge
is minimal: HK$2 for first class and HK$1.70 for second class on the
ferry, and HK$1.20 for the tram from Central to Causeway Bay and
beyond. In front of the terminal you will usually see a few red rickshaws. Once numbering in the thousands, these two-wheel, man-pow-

ered "taxis" are all but gone. One of the Tote (off-track betting) offices is in front of the terminal, and to the right as you face inland are the main post office and the towering ☞ **Jardine House.**

OFF THE
BEATEN PATH

HONG KONG DOLPHIN WATCH – The Chinese white dolphin (it's actually pink to dark gray, and found in waters from South Africa to Australia) is on its way to extinction in the South China Sea, largely because of dredging for the new airport. The group sponsors a Dolphin Discovery Cruise, departing three to four times a week. There is no guarantee that you'll see a dolphin, but on most trips, passengers see at least two or three jumping out of the water, rolling around, and showing their fins. The trip makes for an enjoyable day at sea, and tickets help raise money to build a sanctuary that would ensure the dolphins' survival. The cost includes buffet lunch. Reservations should be made at least two weeks in advance. ⊠ *Hong Kong Dolphin Watch, Box 4102, Central, Hong Kong,* ☎ *2984–1414,* FAX *2984–7799.* ☎ *HK$350.*

⑥ Statue Square. A small oasis of green between Connaught Road Central and Chater Road, filled with shaded walks and fountains, attracts office workers during lunchtime and hundreds of housemaids from the Philippines on the weekends. The square is surrounded by some of the most important buildings in Hong Kong (☞ **Hong Kong Club, Legislative Council, Bank of China**), and it is near the Central MTR station.

⑰ Upper Lascar Row. To get to Upper Lascar Row, also known as Cat Street, walk down the steps of Ladder Street, just across from Man Mo Temple. In the days before wheeled traffic, most of the steep, narrow lanes on the hillside were filled with steps. Cat Street is a vast flea market. You won't find Ming vases here—or anything else of significant monetary value—but you may come across an old Mao badge or an antique pot or teakettle.

More worthwhile for the art or antiques collector is the section of shops and stalls known as **Cat Street Galleries,** adjacent to the flea market. This is a growing new complex, with galleries selling every kind of crafted work, old and, most often, new. You can rest your feet and have coffee in the convenient little European café, Somethin' Brewin'. ⊠ *38 Lok Ku Rd.* ☺ *Mon.–Sat. 10–6. Closed holidays.*

⑪ Western Market. You can get to this market on Connaught Road West by turning right on Man Wa Lane and walking three blocks to the busy highway that faces the harbor; then walk left another two blocks to Number 323. Built in 1906, the market is a fine example of mid-Victorian architecture. Once a produce market, it now consists of arcades, wide galleries, and a variety of souvenir shops: a small version of London's Covent Garden.

⑩ Wing Lok Street. Although Wing Sing Street, which used to be known for its dazzling array of preserved eggs, has been torn down to make way for developers, you can still find fascinating traditional items for sale on this street (off Queen's Road Central) lined with Chinese shops selling rattan goods, medicines, and the engraved seals that they call chops. You can have your initials engraved in Roman letters or Chinese characters on a chop made of plastic, bone, or jade. (Ivory is also available all over Hong Kong, but it is illegal to bring it into the United States.) It takes about an hour to engrave a chop, which you can pick up later or on the following day.

Central and Western Districts

Macau Ferry Pier

11

Connaught Rd. West

Outlying Islands
Ferry Pier

Central Harbour
Ferry Pier

Vehicular
Ferry Pier

Wing Lok St.

13

**Sheung
Wan**

Connaught Rd. Central

12

10

Man Wa Ln.

Des Voeux Rd.

Bonham Strand East

Queen's
Rd. West

Jervois St.

Hillier St.

Queen's Rd. Central

Gough St.

Jubilee St.

Queen Victoria St.

3

Tung St. · Cat St.

14

17

9

Square St.

16 **15** Hollywood Rd.

Aberdeen St.

Gage St.

Peel St.

Graham St.

Stanley St.

Queen's Rd. Central

Des Voeux Rd. Central

Ladder St.

Bridges St.

Hollywood Rd.

Wellington St.

Central

Seymour Rd.

Caine Rd.

Staunton St.

Elgin St.

Lyndhurst Ter.

8

Pedder St.

Ice House St.

Robinson Rd.

Peel St.

Shelley St.

Old Bailey St.

Caine Rd.

D'Aguilar St.

Wyndham St.

Duddell St.

Lower Alber.

Conduit Rd.

Mosque St.

Wyndham St.

Arbuthnot Rd.

Lower

Albert
Rd.

Lower Alber.

N

Upper

Albert Rd.

Albany Rd.

20

21

KEY

Ⓜ Metro Stops

Bonham Strand East
and West, **12**

Central Market, **9**

Chater Garden, **7**

City Hall complex, **4**

Des Voeux Road
West, **13**

Exchange Square, **3**

Government
House, **20**

HMS *Tamar*, **5**

Hollywood Road, **15**

Hong Kong Park, **18**

Jardine House, **2**

The Landmark, **8**

Man Mo Temple, **16**

Peak Tram, **22**

Queen's Road
West, **14**

St. John's
Cathedral, **19**

Star Ferry, **1**

Statue Square, **6**

Upper Lascar Row/
Cat Street, **17**

Victoria Peak, **23**

Western Market, **11**

Wing Lok Street, **10**

Zoological and
Botanical
Gardens, **21**

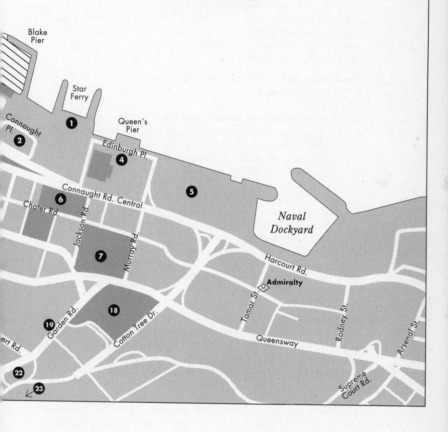

Victoria Harbour

Blake
Pier

Star
Ferry

1

Queen's
Pier

Connaught
Pl.

2

Edinburgh Pl.

4

5

Connaught Rd. Central

6

Chater Rd.

Jackson Rd.

Murray Rd.

Naval
Dockyard

7

Harcourt Rd.

Admiralty

Tamar St.

Rodney St.

Arsenal St.

18

19

Garden Rd.

Cotton Tree Dr.

Queensway

ert Rd.

22

23

Supreme
Court Rd.

From Central to the Peak

Most of the important colonial buildings of the Victorian era are in this area. Walking around this part of Central can be tricky because of a series of elevated highways. However, there are pedestrian tunnels and overpasses. With a little patience and a good map, you should not have too much trouble finding your way about on foot.

Sights to See

American Library. This is the place to go for current and back issues of American magazines and books. Microfilm editions of the *New York Times* are also available. Materials cannot be checked out, but you can make photocopies for a small charge. It is next to impossible to get information about the library by telephone, so the best thing to do is to simply arrive. ⊠ *American Consulate, 26 Garden Rd., Central,* ☎ *2523–9011.* ⊙ *Weekdays 10–6.*

⑳ Government House. This handsome white house is the official residence of the governor. It was constructed in 1891. ⊠ *Upper Albert Rd.*

OFF THE
BEATEN PATH

HONG KONG MUSEUM OF MEDICAL SCIENCES – This new museum, tucked away in an Edwardian-style building behind a small park in Mid-Levels, is worth the climb through tiny backstreets for anyone interested in Chinese medicine's history in Hong Kong. Exhibitions show comparisons of how Chinese and Western medicines are used, examples of Chinese medicines of both animal and herbal origin, and a traditional Chinese medical practitioner's equipment, as well as several rooms devoted to Western medical subjects. To get there from Hollywood Road, follow Ladder St. behind Man Mo Temple, south, uphill to Square St., which veers right, then left to Caine Lane. Follow a circular path about 300 feet, upward, around Caine Lane Garden, a park with colorful stucco structures, until you reach #2. ⊠ *2 Caine La., Mid-Levels, Hong Kong,* ☎ *2549-5123,* 𝔽𝔸𝕏 *2559-9458.* ✉ *HK$10.* ⊙ *Tues.–Sat. 10 am–5 pm, Sun. 1 pm–5 pm.*

✋ ⑱ Hong Kong Park. A 25-acre marvel in the heart of Central, this park is composed of lakes, gardens, sports areas, a rain forest aviary with 500 species of birds, and a greenhouse filled with 200 species of tropical and arid-region plants. The park also contains **Flagstaff House,** the former official residence of the commander of the British forces and the city's oldest colonial building (built in 1846). The house is now the *Museum of Tea Ware,* and it holds displays on everything connected with the art of serving tea from the 7th century onward. The core collection, which includes Yi Xing tea ware (famous tea sets from Jiangsu Province, China), was donated by Dr. K. S. Lo, who wanted the public to share his appreciation for tea. ⊠ *Cotton Tree Dr.,* ☎ *2869–0690.* ✉ *Free.* ⊙ *Thurs.–Tues. 10–5.*

㉒ Peak Tram. Housed in the Lower Peak Tram Terminus is the world's steepest funicular railway. It passes five intermediate stations en route to the upper terminal, 1,805 feet above sea level. The railway was opened in 1880 to transport people to the top of ☞ **Victoria Peak,** the highest hill overlooking Hong Kong Harbour. Before the tram, the only way to get to the top was to walk or take a bumpy ride up the steep steps in a sedan chair. The tram has two 72-seat cars that are hauled up the hill by cables attached to electric motors. A free shuttle bus to and from the Peak Tram leaves from next to City Hall, at Edinburgh Place. ⊠ *Between Garden Rd. and Cotton Tree Dr.* ✉ *HK$14 one-way, HK$21 round-trip.* ⊙ *Daily 7 AM–midnight. Trams run every 10–15 min.*

⑲ St. John's Cathedral. An Anglican (Episcopal) church completed in 1849, the cathedral was built with Canton bricks in the shape of a cross. It serves as a good example of both Victorian-Gothic and Norman architecture. ⊠ *Garden Rd.* ⊙ *Daily 9–5. Sun. services open to the public.*

㉓ Victoria Peak. The Chinese name for Victoria Peak is Tai Ping Shan (Mountain of Great Peace). It might also be called Mountain of Great Views, for the panorama is breathtaking. On clear days you can see across the islands to the People's Republic of China. The area is a popular picnic spot, filled with beautiful walking paths that circle the peak. A lookout pavilion just below the summit was once part of a former governor's residence. The original gardens and country walks remain and are open to the public. The new Peak Galleria shopping mall has a wide selection of restaurants and boutiques selling souvenirs, clothes, and gifts.

As an alternative to taking the ☞ **Peak Tram** down the hillside, you can catch Bus 15 or a cab to Central. This will take you on a trip as beautiful as the one on the tram, through the steep roads of the residential areas of Mid-Levels.

Yan Yuen Shek. Also known as Lover's Rock, this is a shrine that women visit every day, burning joss sticks and making offerings in search of a husband. The 6th, 16th, and 26th days of each lunar month are the most popular times. During the Maidens Festival, held in August, fortune-tellers set up shop for the lovelorn. A visit here is best combined with a visit to the ☞ **Zoological and Botanical Gardens.** Leave the Gardens by the upper exit, east of the aviaries. Cross Garden Road and take the left fork (Magazine Gap Road) at the traffic circle. Take a sharp left into Bowen Road, a pleasant street that is closed to traffic and has an almost rural feeling. From there, Lover's Rock is a 20- to 30-minute walk. To get back to town, walk to the Wong Nai Chung Gap Road traffic circle at the end of Bowen Road, where you can catch Bus 15 or 15B to the Peak or Bus 6 or 61 back to Exchange Square, or take a taxi.

㉑ Zoological and Botanical Gardens. A visit here is a delightful way to escape the city's traffic and crowds. In the early morning, the spectacle of people practicing *t'ai chi ch'uan* (the ancient art of shadowboxing) is an interesting sight. The quiet pathways are lined with semitropical trees, shrubs, and flowers. The zoo has jaguars and gorillas, and this has been a source of friction between the government and animal rights groups, but last year the cages were expanded to give the animals a better simulation of their natural habitat. There is a less controversial aviary with more than 300 species of birds, including flocks of cranes and pink flamingos. ⊠ *Upper Albert Rd., opposite Government House,* ☎ *2530–0155.* ▨ *Free.* ⊙ *Daily 6:30 AM–7 PM.*

Wanchai

Whoever expects to discover the raunchy world of old Wanchai may be disappointed. Wanchai still has its nocturnal charms (☞ Chapter 5), but the Wanchai of Richard Mason's novel, *The World of Suzie Wong,* seems a bit faded now. Wanchai has always been a magnet for sailors on shore leave. Today it's a bit more tourist-oriented and expensive, but topless bars are still in business, and sailors from all nations and military patrols are still on the streets when ships are in the harbor. The old Luk Kwok Hotel, better known as the Suzie Wong Hotel, has been replaced with a large modern hotel, but the novel's famous **Lock-**

hart Road, with its restaurants and seedy bars, British pubs, and tailors' shops, is still worth a stroll.

Wanchai was once one of the five "wan," areas that the British set aside for Chinese residences. Today, in addition to the old section with its bars and massage parlors, it is a mixture of office buildings, restaurants, apartment buildings, and shops.

Sights to See

Numbers in the margin correspond to points of interest the Wanchai, Causeway Bay, Happy Valley, and North Point map.

❸ Arts Centre and Academy for Performing Arts. These two adjacent buildings serve as the venue for the heart of Hong Kong's cultural activities. They have excellent facilities for both exhibitions and performing arts. You can get information on the busy schedule of activities—ranging from dance performances and classical music recitals by local and visiting artists to productions staged by visiting dance troupes and theater companies—from local newspapers or the ticket reservations office. The Academy for Performing Arts was financed with horse-racing profits donated by the Royal Hong Kong Jockey Club. While you're at the Arts Centre, visit the **Pao Gallery** (4th–5th floors), which hosts international and local exhibitions, and try the excellent restaurant. ✉ *2 Harbour Rd., Academy,* ☎ *2582–0256.* ✇ *Free.* ☺ *Daily 10–8.*

❽ Cargo Handling Basin. East of the Wanchai Ferry Pier, where you catch a ferry to Kowloon, you can watch the unloading of boats bringing cargo ashore from ships anchored in the harbor. ✉ *Hung Hing Rd. near Wanchai Stadium.*

❻ Central Plaza. On Harbour Road past Chinese Arts and Crafts you'll find Central Plaza, an office complex completed in 1992 and worth noting simply because, at 78 stories, it is the tallest building in Asia and the fourth-tallest building in the world.

Hennessy Road. Roughly following the line of the original harbor frontage is one of the better shopping streets and another good place for browsing.

❺ Hong Kong Convention and Exhibition Centre. The Centre opened in 1988 as one of the largest and best-equipped meeting facilities in the world. It is the venue for annual international trade fairs, regional conferences, and hundreds of local events. It is adjoined by an office tower, a block of service apartments, and two hotels: the Grand Hyatt and the New World Harbour View. ✉ *Seafront Rd.*

❷ Hopewell Centre. At 66 stories, this is Hong Kong's third tallest building. Circular in plan with a slapdash aesthetic, it's known to detractors as the "Stone Cigar." That criticism aside, the view atop the building from the Revolving 66 restaurant (☎ *2862–6166*) is splendid. Even if you don't plan to eat here, you may want to ride the exterior "glass-bullet" elevator. ✉ *183 Queen's Rd E.*

Luard Road. With cross streets Hennessy, Lockhart, and Jaffe roads, the heart of Old Wanchai is here. At night the area is alive with multicolor neon signs and lively trade at bars, pubs, massage parlors, and restaurants.

❼ Museum of Chinese Historical Relics. Housed in the **Causeway Centre** building, the collection covers 1,000 years of Chinese history and culture, with all types of art and crafts on display. ✉ *26 Harbour Rd.,* ☎ *2827–4692.* ✇ *HK$5.* ☺ *Weekdays 10–6, Sat. 1–6. Closed Jan.*

1, Chinese New Year, Oct. 1 (Chinese National Day), and during setting up of new exhibitions.

❶ Queen's Road East. If you head east along this busy shopping street, you'll pass rice and food shops and stores selling rattan and traditional furniture, paper lanterns, and Chinese calligraphic materials.

Tai Wong Temple. Along on the right of Queen's Road East, heading east, you can see this temple's altar from the street and smell the scent of smoldering joss sticks.

Wanchai Road. A busy market area selling a variety of foods, clothing, and household goods, it's a good place for browsing, especially along the narrow side alleyways. To the left are several small lanes leading to **Johnston Road** and more tram lines. There are a number of traditional shops here, including some selling household pets.

Wanchai Sports Grounds. To the east of Causeway Centre at Tonnochy Road, the grounds here opened in 1979 to provide world-class facilities for competitive sports. It has a soccer field, running track, swimming pool, and an indoor games hall.

Causeway Bay, Happy Valley, and North Point

Causeway Bay, one of Hong Kong's best shopping areas, also has a wide range of restaurants and a few sightseeing attractions. Much of the district can be easily reached from Central by the tram, which runs along Hennessy Road, or by the MTR to Causeway Bay Station. If you come by taxi, a good starting point is the Excelsior Hotel (⊠ 281 Gloucester Rd.), which overlooks the harbor.

The area east of Victoria Park (☞ *below*) offers very little for first-time visitors. **North Point** and **Quarry Bay** are both undeniably the "real" Hong Kong, which means tenements and factories. From Causeway Bay you can take the tram for a couple of miles through this area—perhaps the best way to get a feel for the environment. The principal attraction in **Shaukiwan** is **Taikoo Shing,** a massive city-within-a-city. Some years ago this was barren, reclaimed land. Today, it's a middle-class housing estate with a shopping complex, Cityplaza I & II.

Sights to See

⑮ Aw Boon Haw (Tiger Balm) Gardens. Built in 1935 with profits from sales of a popular menthol balm, the gardens were the pet project of two Chinese brothers, who also built a mansion here. Eight acres of hillside are pocked and covered with grottoes and pavilions filled with garishly painted statues and models of Chinese gods, mythical animals, and scenes depicting fables and parables. It's great fun to explore, especially for children. Be forewarned: Some of the scenes of Taoist and Buddhist mythology are decidedly gruesome. There is also an ornate seven-story pagoda containing Buddhist relics and the ashes of monks and nuns. ⊠ *Tai Hang Rd., Happy Valley.* ⛱ *Free.* ☯ *Daily 9:30–4.*

⑯ Happy Valley Race Track. Every Wednesday night and one afternoon each weekend from September to mid-June, you can bet on horses here. Although it was completed in 1841, modern additions include a huge outdoor video screen for close-ups, slow motion, and instant replays. It is for members only, but you can obtain a special visitor's admission if you have been in Hong Kong for less than three weeks and are over 18. Your passport with the tourist visa stamp is required as proof. ⊠ *Royal Hong Kong Jockey Club, 2 Sports Rd., Happy Valley,* ☎ *2966–8111 or 2966–8364.* ⛱ *HK$50 for entrance badge.*

Wanchai, Causeway Bay, Happy Valley, and North Point

0   330 yards

0   300 meters

KC

KEY

⟨M⟩ Metro Stops

Victoria Harbour

Wanchai
Ferry Pier

Hung Hing Rd.

Seafront Rd.

5

*Wanchai
Stadium*

Harbour Rd.

3 **4**

6 **7**

Harbour Dr.

Gloucester Rd.

Stewart Rd.

Tonnochy Rd.

Marsh Rd.

Bowlinton Rd.

Canal Rd. West

Fenwick St.

Luard Rd.

Jaffe Rd.

O'Brien Rd.

Lockhart Rd.

Fleming Rd.

Wanchai Rd.

Hennessey Rd.

⟨M⟩ **Wanchai**

Admiralty

Thomson Rd.

1

Queen's Rd. East

Johnston Rd.

*Morrison
Hill*

Spring Garden Ln.

Cross St.

Wanchai Rd.

2

Queen's Rd. East

Academy for Performing Arts, **4**

Arts Centre, **3**

Aw Boon Haw (Tiger Balm) Gardens, **15**

Cargo Handling Basin, **8**

Central Plaza, **6**

Happy Valley Race Track, **16**

Hong Kong Convention and Exhibition Centre, **5**

Hopewell Centre, **2**

Kwun Yum Temple, **14**

Museum of Chinese Historical Relics, **7**

Noonday Gun, **10**

Queen's Road East, **1**

Royal Hong Kong Yacht Club, **9**

Sampans, **11**

Tin Hau Temple, **13**

Victoria Park, **12**

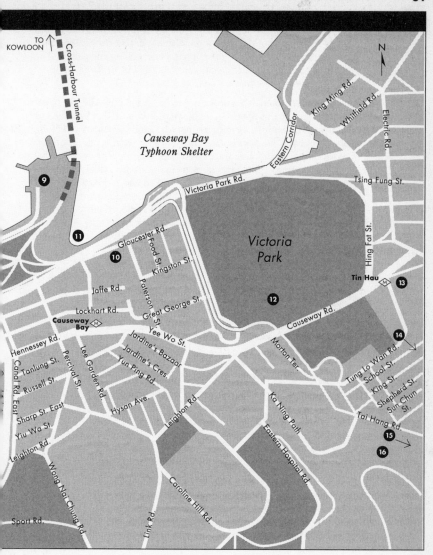

TO
KOWLOON
Cross-Harbour Tunnel

Causeway Bay
Typhoon Shelter

9

11

10

Victoria Park Rd.

Gloucester Rd.

Food St.

Kingston St.

Jaffe Rd.

Lockhart Rd.

Causeway Bay

Hennessey Rd.

Paterson St.

Great George St.

Yee Wo St.

Jardine's Bazaar

Jardine's Cres.

Yun Ping Rd.

Canal Rd. East

Tanlung St.

Russell St.

Sharp St. East

Yiu Wa St.

Leighton Rd.

Percival St.

Lee Garden Rd.

Hysan Ave.

Leighton Rd.

Wong Nai Chung Rd.

Sport Rd.

Link Rd.

Caroline Hill Rd.

Eastern Hospital Rd.

Ka Ning Path

Morton Ter.

Causeway Rd.

Victoria
Park

12

Eastern Corridor

King Ming Rd.

Whitfield Rd.

Electric Rd.

Tsing Fung St.

Hing Fat St.

Tin Hau

13

14

Tung Lo Wan Rd.

School St.

King St.

Shepherd St.

Sun Chun St.

Tai Hang Rd.

15

16

N

⓮ Kwun Yum Temple. Dedicated to the goddess of mercy, a house of worship has stood on this site for 200 years, but the current one is in a heavily renovated building and is mostly new, dating from 1986. Constructed on top of a huge boulder, it has a high ceiling and gallery. The temple is very popular with local believers. ✉ *Lin Fa Kung St. W.* ☉ *Daily 9 am until nightfall.*

Law Uk Folk Museum. It's worth a trip to the end of the MTR line (Chai Wan stop) to see this museum, a 200-year-old house that belonged to a family of Hakkas, the farming people who originally inhabited Hong Kong Island and the peninsula all the way into what is now southern Guangdong province. Decorated as a period house, the museum displays rural furniture and farm implements. A photo exhibition shows you what bustling industrial Chai Wan looked like in the 1930s, when it was a peaceful bay inhabited only by fishermen and squatters. ✉ *14 Kut Shing St., 1 block from Chai Wan MTR station. Outside the station, turn left, then follow Kut Shing St. as it turns to the right.* ☎ *2896–7006.* ✆ *Free.* ☉ *Tues.–Sat. 10 AM–1 PM and 2 PM–6 PM., Sun. and public holidays 1 PM–6 PM.*

⓾ Noonday Gun. "In Hong Kong they strike a gong and fire off a noonday gun," wrote Noel Coward in his song, "Mad Dogs and Englishmen." They still fire that gun at noon each day in a small enclosure overlooking the Yacht Club Basin and Typhoon Shelter, opposite the **Excelsior Hotel** and World Trade Centre. The tradition was started by Jardine Matheson and Co., the great hong (trading company) that gave James Clavell inspiration for his novels *Taipan* and *Noble House.* Jardine would fire a salute each time one of its ships arrived safely in the harbor. It is said that this angered the local governor, who ordered the company to use a gun instead of a cannon, and to fire it only as a noon-time signal. The gun itself, with brass work polished bright, is a 3-pound Hotchkiss dating from 1901. Signs in English point the way to an unlikely looking doorway beside the Excelsior, which opens to the long underground tunnel you must take to get to the viewing area.

NEED A
BREAK?

On weekends from spring through fall it is pleasant to have coffee or lunch in the first-floor coffee shop of the **Excelsior Hotel,** which overlooks the Yacht Club, and gaze at yachts docked in the harbor. The South China Sea Race to Manila, the Philippines, is held every two years at Easter. The **Royal Hong Kong Yacht Club** (☎ 2832–2817) organizes ferry charters to view the racers start. The next race takes place in spring 1998.

⑨ Royal Hong Kong Yacht Club. The club is a place worth a visit, but it's not open to the public, so try to find a local resident who is a member, or who knows one, to give you guest privileges. If you belong to a yacht club at home, you may have reciprocal guest privileges. Once inside you are surrounded by glass-fronted cabinets containing silver prize trophies and a delightfully old-fashioned bar with magnificent views of the harbor. The menu in the members' restaurant is excellent. On weekends the place hums with activity, especially when there are races being held, a common event from spring through fall. ✉ *Off Hung Hing Rd.,* ☎ *2832–2817.*

⑪ Sampans. At the western end of the Causeway Bay Typhoone Shelter is a boat basin that used to house a community of sampan (tiny bottom boats) dwellers. As the number of fishing families who live in their boats has dwindled, the basin has filled with pleasure craft. You can still see a few sampans amidst the sleek sailboats and restored junks.

⑬ Tin Hau Temple. On a street of the same name off Causeway Road, behind Park Cinema on the southeast side of **Victoria Park,** the temple is one of several in Hong Kong similarly named and dedicated to the goddess of the sea. Its decorative roof and old stone walls are noteworthy. The date of construction is unknown, but the temple bell was made in 1747.

⑫ Victoria Park. Beautifully landscaped with trees, shrubs, flowers, and lawns, this park has an aviary and recreational facilities for swimming, lawn bowling, tennis, roller-skating, and even go-cart racing. The Lantern Carnival is held here in mid-autumn, with the trees a mass of colored lights. Just before Chinese New Year (late-January–early February), the park hosts a huge flower market. Here, too, you will find early-morning practitioners of t'ai chi ch'uan. ⊠ *Gloucester Rd.*

The South Side

To explore the south, take a city bus or taxi from Central, and stop at the following points of interest along the way. If you have less time, take a four-hour organized bus tour, but it will show you only a few highlights.

Sights to See

Numbers in the margin correspond to points of interest on the South Side of Hong Kong Island map.

② Aberdeen. Named after an English lord, not the Scottish city, Aberdeen got its start as a refuge for pirates some 200 years ago. The name "Hong Kong" (again, "Fragrant Harbour" in Cantonese) was first used for this area where incense was produced. The British later applied it to the entire island. After World War II, Aberdeen became fairly commercial as the Tanka (boat people) attracted tourists to their floating restaurants. These people continue to live on houseboats and are as picturesque to the occasional visitor as their economic conditions are depressing. Some visitors regret the fact that many of these boat people are turning to factory work, but drab as that work may be, it's a definite improvement over their old way of life.

You can still see much of traditional Aberdeen, such as the **Aberdeen Cemetery** (⊠ Aberdeen Main Rd.), with its enormous gravestones and its glorious view of the bay, and side streets where you can find outdoor barbers at work and many dim-sum restaurants. In the harbor, along with floating restaurants, there are some 3,000 junks and sampans, and you will undoubtedly be asked on board for a ride through the harbor. Use one of the licensed operators, which depart on 20-minute tours daily from 8 AM to 6 PM from the main Aberdeen seawall opposite Aberdeen Centre. Groups can bargain—a trip for 4 to 6 people should cost from HK$100 to HK$150. Individual tickets are HK$40.

Also in Aberdeen is a famous **Tin Hau Temple,** whose ancient, original bell and drum are still used at its opening and closing each day. Currently in a state of decline, this is one of several shrines to the goddess of the sea celebrated in the Tin Hau Festival in April and May, when hundreds of boats converge along the shore.

Apleichau (or Duck's Tongue) Island. To get here you can take a bus across the bridge or arrive by sampan. The island has a boat-building yard where junks, yachts, and sampans are constructed, almost all without formal plans. Look to your right when crossing the bridge for a superb view of the harbor and its countless junks. Vehicles are not allowed to stop on the bridge, so you'll have to walk back if you'd like to take a picture.

On your left is a view of boats belonging to members of the Marina Club and the slightly less exclusive Aberdeen Boat Club, as well as the famous floating Jumbo Restaurant. A quiet, unspoiled area just a decade ago, Apleichau is now bursting at the seams with development, both public housing and a number of gleaming new private residential buildings and shopping malls.

Deep Water Bay. On Island Road, just to the east of Ocean Park, Water World, and Middle Kingdom, the bay was the setting for the film *Love Is a Many-Splendored Thing,* and its deep coves are still beautiful. It has become a millionaire's paradise, home to Hong Kong's richest man, Li Ka-shing, a very private property tycoon.

Fung Ping Shan Museum. This museum contains an excellent collection of Chinese antiquities (ceramics and bronzes, some dating from 3,000 BC, fine paintings, lacquerware, and carvings in jade, stone, and wood). The museum also has the world's largest collection of Nestorian crosses of the Yuan Dynasty (1280–1368). Additionally, it has superb pieces from pre-Christian periods: ritual vessels, decorative mirrors, and painted pottery. This museum is a bit out of the way, but it is a must for the curious and the true Chinese art lover. ⊠ *94 Bonham Rd.,* ☎ *2859–2114.* ▧ *Free.* ☺ *Mon.–Sat. 9:30–6. Closed major holidays.*

❶ **Hong Kong University.** Established in 1911, the university has a total of almost 10,000 undergraduate and graduate students. Most of its buildings are spread along Bonham Road.

Housing Developments. Around the western end of the island, you come to two huge housing developments: privately owned **Pok Fu Lam,** and government-sponsored **Wah Fu Estate.** Both overlook Lamma Island and are full of shops, recreational facilities, and banks. They are typical of Hong Kong's approach to mass housing.

🖑 ❸ **Ocean Park, Water World, and Middle Kingdom.** These three attractions, east of Aberdeen, were built by the Royal Hong Kong Jockey Club. Ocean Park is on 170 acres of land overlooking the sea and is one of the world's largest oceanariums. It attracts daily crowds. On the "lowland" side are gardens, parks, and a children's zoo. A cable car, providing spectacular views of the entire south coast, can take you to the "headland" side and to Ocean Theatre, the world's largest marine mammal theater, where dolphins and a killer whale perform. There are seats for 4,000 people. There are also various rides including a mammoth roller coaster. The adjacent, 65-acre Water World is an aquatic fun park with slides, rapids, pools, and a wave cove. Middle Kingdom is a theme park depicting architecture, arts, crafts, and industry through 3,000 years of Chinese history. The complex has cultural shows, souvenir shops, and restaurants. ⊠ *Wong Chuk Hang Rd.;* ☎ *2873–8888 (Ocean Park),* ☎ *2870–0268 (Middle Kingdom),* ☎ *2555-6055 (Water World).* ▧ *Ocean Park and Middle Kingdom: HK$130;* ☺ *Daily 10 AM–6 PM.* ▧ *Water World:* ▧ *HK$60;* ☺ *June–Oct. daily 10 AM–6 PM.*

❹ **Repulse Bay,** named after the British warship HMS *Repulse* (not, as some local wags say, after the pollution of its waters). The famed Repulse Bay Hotel was demolished in 1982 and has been replaced with a luxury residential building, but replicas of its Repulse Bay Verandah Restaurant and Bamboo Bar were opened in 1986 and are run by the same people who operated the original hotel. To indulge in an experience of colonial pampering, treat yourself to British high tea, served

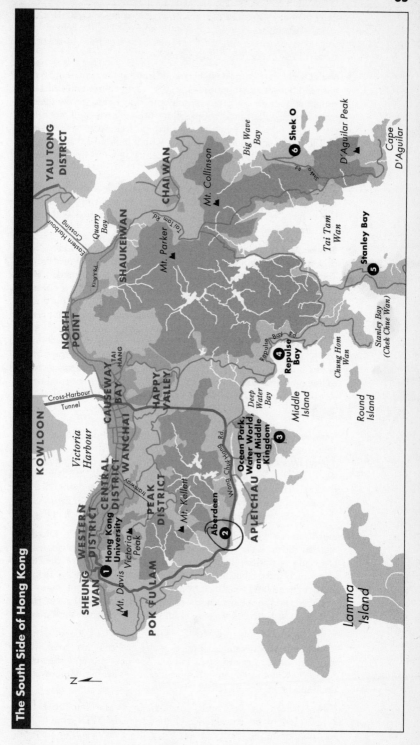

The South Side of Hong Kong

daily from 3 PM to 5:30 PM. The hotel gained notoriety in December 1941 when invading Japanese clambered over the hills behind it and entered its gardens, which were being used as headquarters by the British. After a brief battle, the British surrendered.

⑥ Shek O. The easternmost village on the south side of the island is filled with old houses, great mansions, a superb golf course and club, a few simple restaurants, a pretty beach, and fine views. Leave the little town square, full of small shops selling inflatable toys and other beach essentials, and take the curving path across a footbridge to the "island" of **Tai Tau Chau,** really a large rock with a lookout for scanning the South China Sea. Little more than a century ago, this open water was ruled by pirates.

You can hike through **Shek O Country Park** in less than two hours. Look here for birds that are hard to find in Hong Kong, such as Kentish plovers, reef egrets, and black-headed gulls, as well as the colorful rufus-backed shrike and the bulbul.

⑤ Stanley Bay. It became notorious as the home of the largest Hong Kong prisoner-of-war camps run by the Japanese during World War II. Today, Stanley is known for its picturesque beaches and its market, where casual clothing is sold at wholesale prices. Hong Kong has dozens of shops offering similar bargains, but it's more fun to shop for them in the countrified atmosphere around Stanley. You can also find ceramics, paintings, and books. Past the market, on Stanley Main Street, a strip of restaurants and pubs faces the bay. On the other side of the bay is a Tin Hau temple, just beyond land that is being cleared for a public housing estate, which will give low-income residents a chance to live on prime waterfront property.

KOWLOON

Kowloon peninsula juts down from mainland China, directly across Victoria Harbour from Central. Legend has it that Kowloon was named by a Chinese emperor who fled here during the Sung Dynasty (960–1279). He counted eight hills on the peninsula and called them the Eight Dragons—so the account goes—but a servant reminded him that an emperor is also considered a dragon, and so the emperor called the region Gau-lung (nine dragons), which became Kowloon in English.

Kowloon is the site of most of Hong Kong's hotels. In the Old Tsim Sha Tsui district is the Victorian-era clock tower of the old Kowloon–Canton Railway station, the new Hong Kong Cultural Centre, the Peninsula Hotel, and the bustling Nathan Road area. The Tsim Sha Tsui East district lies on land reclaimed from the harbor and contains many luxury hotels and shopping centers, the Space Museum, and a waterfront esplanade. It is here that you will find the new railroad station.

In the 1930s, people took the Star Ferry from Hong Kong Island to Kowloon to stay overnight at the ever-elegant Peninsula Hotel, which was next door to the railroad station. The next morning they could board the Kowloon–Canton Railway trains for Peking, Moscow, London, and other Western cities.

Today visitors can take a taxi through the Cross-Harbour Tunnel from Causeway Bay or Central to Kowloon or ride the MTR from Central to Kowloon in minutes. The Star Ferry, however, is still unquestionably the most exciting way to cross the harbor.

Sights to See

Numbers in the margin correspond to points of interest on the Kowloon Peninsula map.

⑬ Bird Market. On Hong Lok Street, two blocks from Nathan Road, at the Mong Kok MTR stop, you'll find the famous market where old-timers sell antique cages and porcelain, along with, of course, little brown songbirds and colorful talking parrots. Stroll around and listen to the cacophony of birdcalls mingled with the chirp of grasshoppers that will be the birds' dinner. The Bird Market was supposed to have been demolished to make way for developers by now, but a "stay of execution" has been granted for another year or two. See it now, because it's hard to say exactly how much longer it will be there.

❷ Hong Kong Cultural Centre. This stark, architecturally controversial building has tiled walls inside and out, sloped roofs, and no windows—an irony, since the view is superb, the building being situated on the city's one part of reclaimed harbor-front land that already juts out so far it is unlikely to see any further reclamation and development. It houses a concert hall and two theaters. ⊠ *10 Salisbury Rd.,* ☎ *2734–2010.*

❺ Hong Kong Museum of Art. Formerly housed in the City Hall, the new museum now occupies its own building behind the ☞ **Hong Kong Space Museum.** The exterior is unexciting, but inside are five floors of well-designed galleries. One is devoted to historic photographs, prints, and artifacts of Hong Kong, Macau, and other parts of the Pearl River delta. Other galleries feature Chinese antiquities and fine art and visiting exhibitions. ⊠ *10 Salisbury Rd.,* ☎ *2734–2167.* ▨ *HK$10.* ⊙ *Mon.–Wed., Fri., Sat. 10–6; Sun. and holidays 1–6.*

NEED A BREAK? The **Regent** is among Hong Kong's finest luxury hotels. Its lobby has windows offering panoramic views of the harbor, making it the perfect place for a sunset cocktail. ⊠ *18 Salisbury Rd., Tsim Sha Tsui,* ☎ *2721–1211.*

Hong Kong Museum of History. The museum covers a broad expanse of the past with life-size dioramas depicting prehistoric scenes, the original fishing village, a 19th-century street, the Japanese occupation, and modern Hong Kong—all complete with sounds and smells. There is also a multiscreen slide show. ⊠ *Haiphong Rd.,* ☎ *2367–1124.* ▨ *HK$10.* ⊙ *Mon.–Thurs. and Sat. 10–6, Sun. and holidays 1–6.*

⊙ ❼ Hong Kong Science Museum. It houses more than 500 scientific and technological exhibits that emphasize interactive participation, including an energy machine, a miniature submarine, and the DC3 that launched Cathay Pacific airlines. The buildings look like giant Lego blocks. ⊠ *2 Science Museum Rd., corner of Cheong Wan Rd. and Chatham Rd.* ☎ *2732–3232.* ▨ *HK$25.* ⊙ *Tues.–Fri. 1–9, weekends and holidays 10–9.*

⊙ ❹ Hong Kong Space Museum. Across from the Peninsula Hotel, the dome-shaped museum houses one of the most advanced planetariums in Asia. It also contains the Hall of Solar Science, whose solar telescope permits visitors a close look at the sun; Exhibition Hall, which houses several exhibits at a time on topics such as outerspace and astronomy; and a Space Theatre, with Omnimax movies on space travel, sports, and natural wonders. Children under 6 are not admitted. ⊠ *10 Salisbury Rd.,* ☎ *2734–2722.* ▨ *HK$10.* ⊙ *Mon. and Wed.–Fri. 1–9, weekends and holidays 10–9. 7 shows daily, first at 2:30, last at 8:30.*

⑪ Kansu Street Jade Market. The daily jade market carries everything from fake jade pendants to precious carvings. If you don't know much about jade, take along someone who does, or you may pay a lot more than you should. The best time to visit is from 10 AM to noon. ⊠ *Kansu St., off Nathan Rd.*

⑨ Kowloon Park. The former site of the Whitfield Military Barracks is today a restful, green oasis, with a Chinese garden with a lotus pond, streams, a lake, and an aviary with a colorful collection of rare birds. The Jamia Masjid and Islamic Centre is on the south end of the park, near the Haiphong Road entrance. This is Hong Kong's principal mosque. Built in 1984, it has four minarets, decorative arches, and a marble dome. ⊠ *Just off Nathan Rd.*

⑧ Nathan Road. The "Golden Mile" runs north for several miles and is filled with hotels and shops of every description. To the left and right are mazes of narrow streets lined with even more shops crammed with every possible type of merchandise.

❸ Peninsula Hotel. You'll notice this sumptuous hotel with a fleet of Rolls-Royce taxis and doormen in white uniforms outside. The huge colon-naded lobby has charm, grandeur, celebrities (though with the opening of the Regent Hotel, no longer a monopoly on them), string quartets, and a high tea that is the perfect way to rest your shopping feet in style. (High tea is served daily 3–6:30 in the lobby at HK$113 per person; 3–5 in the Verandah Restaurant at HK$135 per person.) ⊠ *Salisbury Rd.,* ☎ *2366–6251.*

❶ Star Ferry Pier. This is a convenient starting place for any tour of Kowloon. Here you will also find the bus terminal, with traffic going to all parts of Kowloon and the New Territories. As you face the bus station, Ocean Terminal—where luxury cruise ships berth—is on your left. Inside this terminal, and in the adjacent Harbour City, miles of air-conditioned shopping arcades are filled with hundreds of shops.

To the right of Star Ferry is **Victoria Clock Tower,** all that is left of the Kowloon–Canton Railway Station, which once stood on this site. The new station, for travel within China, is a mile to the east. Nearby, a pleasant waterside walkway continues to the Hung Hom area. At night it offers a splendid view of Hong Kong's lights.

OFF THE
BEATEN PATH

HAN DYNASTY BURIAL VAULT – It's worth a visit to the 1,600-year-old vault at Lei Cheng Uk Museum, in Sham Shui Po, Kowloon. The four bar-rel-vaulted brick chambers form a cross around a domed vault. The fu-nerary objects are typical of the tombs of the Han Dynasty (AD 25–220). It was discovered in 1955 during excavations for a huge housing estate that now surrounds it. ⊠ *41 Tonkin St., Lei Cheng Uk Resettlement Es-tate. Take Bus 2 from Kowloon Star Ferry terminal to Tonkin St., or MTR to Cheung Sha Wan Station.* ☎ *Free.* ☉ *Mon.–Wed., Fri., and Sat. 10–1 and 2–6; Sun. 1–6.*

⑭ Sung Dynasty Village. You'll go back in history hundreds of years when you visit this village northwest of Kowloon city. Take the MTR line (the one that is red on maps) to the Mei Foo station. From here it is a short walk along Lai Wan and Mei Lai roads. The village re-creates the life of a Sung Dynasty village 1,000 years ago. There are faithful replicas of houses, shops, restaurants, and temples of the period. Ob-serve craftspeople at work and other dressed in period costume. Visit on your own, or take an organized tour, which can be arranged through your hotel tour desk. ⊠ *Sung Dynasty Village,* ☎ *2744–1022.* ☎ *HK$120.* ☉ *Mon.–Sun. 10–8.*

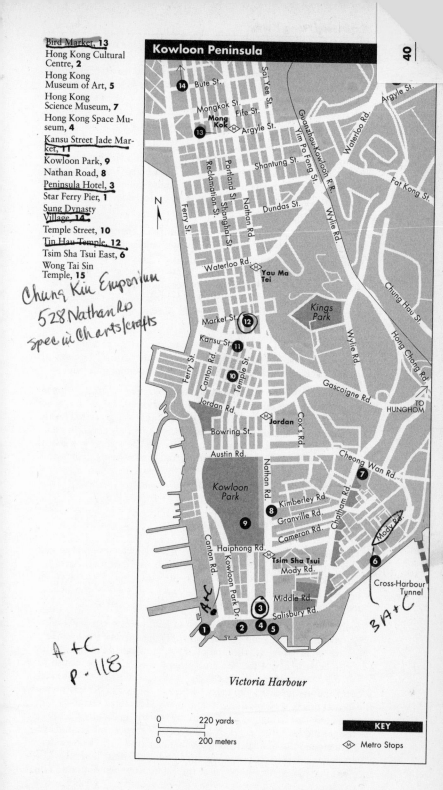

Bird Market, 13
Hong Kong Cultural Centre, 2
Hong Kong Museum of Art, 5
Hong Kong Science Museum, 7
Hong Kong Space Museum, 4
Kansu Street Jade Market, 11
Kowloon Park, 9
Nathan Road, 8
Peninsula Hotel, 3
Star Ferry Pier, 1
Sung Dynasty Village, 14
Temple Street, 10
Tin Hau Temple, 12
Tsim Sha Tsui East, 6
Wong Tai Sin Temple, 15

Chung Kiu Emporium
528 Nathan Rd
spec in Charts/crafts

Kowloon Peninsula

40

Bute St.
Mongkok St. Fife St.
Mong Kok
Argyle St.
Sai Yee St.
Argyle St.
Waterloo Rd.
Fat Kong St.
Guanzhou-Kowloon R.R.
Shantung St.
Portland St.
Reclamation St.
Shanghai St.
Nathan Rd.
Dundas St.
Yim Po Fong St.
Wylie Rd.
Ferry St.
Waterloo Rd.
Yau Ma Tei
Kings Park
Chung Hau St.
Market St.
Kansu St.
Temple St.
Wylie Rd.
Hong Chong Rd.
Jordan Rd.
Gascoigne Rd.
TO HUNGHOM
Bowring St.
Jordan
Cox's Rd.
Austin Rd.
Cheong Wan Rd.
Kowloon Park
Nathan Rd.
Kimberley Rd.
Granville Rd.
Cameron Rd.
Chatham Rd.
Mody Rd.
Haiphong Rd.
Tsim Sha Tsui
Mody Rd.
Cross-Harbour Tunnel
Middle Rd.
Canton Rd.
Kowloon Park Dr.
Salisbury Rd.

A+C
3 A+C

A+C
p. 118

Victoria Harbour

0   220 yards
0   200 meters

⑩ Temple Street. Go north on Nathan Road three blocks to Jordan Road, and make a left and a right onto Temple Street, the heart of a busy shopping area. Tiny streets to your right are ideal for wandering and people-watching. By day you'll find market stalls with plenty of kitsch and a few worthwhile clothing bargains, but the best time to visit is after 8 PM, when the streets become an open-air market filled with street doctors offering cures for almost any complaint, fortune-tellers, and, on most nights, Chinese opera.

Shanghai Street and **Canton Road** are also worth a visit for their colorful shops and stalls selling everything from herbal remedies to jade and ivory. **Ning Po Street** is known for its shops selling paper kites and the colorful paper and bamboo models of worldly possessions that are burned at Chinese funerals.

Paperkites Ning Po St.

⑫ Tin Hau Temple. This is a colorful sight, with its curved tile roofs designed to deter evil spirits. One of Kowloon's oldest temples, it is filled with incense and crowds of worshipers. You'll probably be encouraged to have a try with the fortune sticks, known as chim sticks. Each stick is numbered, and you shake them in a cardboard tube until one falls out. A fortune-teller asks you your date of birth and makes predictions from the stick based on numerology. ⊠ *Market St., 1 block north of Kansu St.* ☉ *Daily 7 AM–5:30 PM.*

⑥ Tsim Sha Tsui East. East on Salisbury Road, this area is part of the land reclamation that has transformed the entire district into a galaxy of luxury hotels, restaurants, and entertainment and shopping complexes.

⑮ Wong Tai Sin Temple. Have your fortune told here—a large, colorful compound with a Buddhist shrine dedicated to a shepherd boy who was said to have had magic healing powers. Take the green MTR line to Wong Tai Sin; the temple is directly opposite the station. In addition to the main altar, the pavilions, and the arcade—where you'll find soothsayers and palm readers happy to interpret Wong Tai Sin's predictions for a small fee—there are two lovely Chinese gardens and a Confucian Hall. ☎ *2807–6177.* ✉ *Small donation expected.* ☉ *Daily 7 AM–5:30 PM.*

THE NEW TERRITORIES

The visitor who has explored Hong Kong and Kowloon should go one step farther and spend at least a day in the New Territories. Here you can look across the border into the People's Republic of China, enjoy panoramas of forested mountainsides, and visit some of the ancient temples and clan houses of the area.

Only about 15 miles (25 kilometers) of land lie between Kowloon's waterfront and the People's Republic of China—hence the New Territories' appellation as "the land between." It is called the New Territories because it was the last area of land claimed by the British in extending their Hong Kong colony. Although most of the original farmland has given way to urban development just as densely populated as much of Hong Kong Island, you will be surprised at the village flavor that has remained in many areas, with small "wet-markets" (the ground beneath them is always wet) selling fresh produce and live chickens and fish in small fishing towns along the water. The New Territories also has vast areas of country park, including Tai Po Kou, a forest that has wild monkeys, near the Tai Po Kowloon–Canton Railway stop.

The easiest way to see the region is by taking a tour organized by the Hong Kong Tourist Association (HKTA). The six-hour Land Between tour takes you to the Chuk Lam Shim Yuen (Bamboo Forest Monastery); Hong Kong's tallest mountain, Fanling; the Luen Wo market; the Chinese border town of Luk Keng; the Plover Cove Country Park; Tai Po; and Chinese University. It leaves Monday through Saturday (except holidays) and costs $365. The Heritage Tour goes to Sam Tung Uk, a restored 18th-century walled village; buildings along the Ping Shan Heritage Trail, some of which date back to the 12th century; and other restored homes and ancestral halls from the era when the New Territories was the sleepiest tip of southern China. These tours last a half day and run on Monday, Wednesday, Friday, and Saturday, and cost $295. A full day tour on Monday costs $480. *Book through your hotel tour desk or an HKTA Information Centre. For information,* ☎ *2807–6543 on weekdays, 2807–6177 on Sun. and holidays.*

To explore the area on your own, rent a self- or a chauffeur-driven car for a day. There are also nine Kowloon–Canton Railway stations between Kowloon and the Lo Wu Station on the Chinese border; you can get off at any one of them. (You will need a visa to enter China at Lo Wu.) A leaflet from the Kowloon–Canton Railway Corporation outlines main attractions in the areas near railroad stations. Pick one up at the railroad station or any HKTA office. *For information,* ☎ *2356–4488. First-class fare to Sheung Shui, the stop before the border: HK$16.*

Sights to See

Numbers in the margin correspond to points of interest on the New Territories and the Outer Islands map.

⑯ Amah Rock. From the perch of the ☞ Temple of Ten Thousand Buddhas you can see the famous rock. Amah means "nurse" in Chinese, and the rock, which resembles a woman with a child on her back, is popular with female worshipers.

⑩ Chinese University. The Art Gallery, in the university's Institute of Chinese Studies building, is well worth a visit. It has large exhibits of paintings and calligraphy from the Ming period to modern times. There are also important collections of bronze seals, carved jade flowers, and ceramics from South China. Take the KCR to University Station and then take a campus bus or taxi. ⊠ *12 Miles Tai Po Rd., Shatin, New Territories,* ☎ *2609–7416.* 🎫 *Free.* ☉ *Mon.–Sat. 10–4:30, Sun. and holidays 12:30–4:30. Closed between exhibitions and on major holidays.*

NEED A BREAK?

Across from the Chinese University campus is the popular **Yucca de Lac Restaurant,** in Ma Liu Shiu village on Tai Po Road, which has outdoor dining facilities with a pleasant view of the university, nestled in green hills along Tolo Harbour. ☎ *2691–1630. C Daily 11 AM–11 PM. MC, V.*

---

❷ Ching Chung Koon Taoist Temple. This huge temple, near the town of Tuen Mun, has room after room of altars, all filled with the heady scent of incense burning in bronze holders. On one side of the main entrance is a cast-iron bell with a circumference of about 5 feet. All large monasteries in ancient China had such bells, which were rung at daybreak to wake the monks and nuns for a day of work in the rice fields. On the other side of the entrance is a huge drum that was used to call the workers back in the evenings. Inside are rooms with walls of small pictures of the departed. Their relatives pay the temple to have these photos displayed, so they can see them as they pray. The temple also includes a retirement home, built from donations, which provides a quiet and serene atmosphere for the elderly. The grounds are beautiful, with plants and flowers, hundreds of dwarf shrubs, ornamental fish ponds, and pagodas.

❶ Chuk Lam Sim Yuen. "The Bamboo Forest Monastery" is one of Hong Kong's most impressive monasteries. It has three large statues of Buddha. Large crowds of worshipers on festival days prove its continuing importance to the Chinese.

❽ Fanling. This town combines the serene atmosphere of the Royal Hong Kong Golf Club with the chaos of rapid growth. The nearby **Luen Wo Market** is a traditional Chinese market, well worth visiting. You might find snakes for sale here in the winter months, and you're sure to see whole dried chickens hanging on prominent display.

❻ Kam Tin Walled Village. A regular stop on most tours and accessible on Bus 51, the village was built in the 1600s as a fortified village belonging to the Tang clan. There are actually six walled villages around Kam Tin, but **Kat Hing Wai** is the most popular. The original walls are intact, with guardhouses on the four corners and arrow slits for fighting off attackers. The image of antiquity is somewhat spoiled now by the modern homes and their TV antennas looming over the ancient fortifications. Directly inside the main gate, a narrow street is lined with shops selling souvenirs and mass-produced oil paintings.

❺ Lau Fau Shan. A village famous for its fish market, here you will find people selling freshly caught fish, dried fish, salted fish, and shellfish. Make your selection, then take it to one of the village's many restaurants, and have it cooked to order. This is the oyster capital of Hong Kong, but don't eat them raw. Hepatitis is a serious problem in the territory.

❼ Lok Ma Chau. The attraction here is a hillside view of vast fields and the Sham Chun River winding through them. Across the river, barely a mile away, is the People's Republic of China. Unless you plan a tour into China, this is as close as you will get. Elderly "models" here demand HK$1 before you can photograph them.

❹ Miu Fat Buddhist Monastery. On Castle Peak Road near Tuen Mun, this is a popular place for a vegetarian lunch. The monastery itself is ornate, with large, carved-stone animals guarding the front. Farther on is the village of Yuen Long, now completely redeveloped as an industrial and residential complex.

❸ Sai Kung Peninsula. The area here consists mostly of park land. **Clearwater Bay Road**, past Kai Tak Airport, will take you into forested areas and land that is only partially developed, with Spanish-style villas overlooking the sea. Take the MTR to Choi Hung and then Bus 92, 96R or Minibus 1 to Sai Kung Town, or take a taxi along Clearwater Bay Road. Stroll along the waterfront and you'll see some of the most unusual marine life ever—in tanks, outside restaurants. If you choose to eat in one of the seafood restaurants, note once again that physicians caution against eating raw shellfish here because of hepatitis outbreaks.

Rent a *kaido* (pronounced guy-doe; one of the small boats run by private operators) for about HK$130 round-trip to cruise around the harbor, stopping at tiny **Yim Tin Tsai Island**, which has a rustic Catholic mission church built in 1890. **Sai Kung Country Park** has one of Hong Kong's most spectacular hiking trails, through majestic hills overlooking the water (☞ Hiking *in* Chapter 6).

❹ Shatin. Whether you enter Shatin by road or rail, you will be amazed to find this metropolis in the middle of the New Territories. Considered one of the "new towns," Shatin underwent a population explosion that took it from a town of 30,000 to one of more than a half million in 10 years. It is home to the **Shatin Racecourse,** Hong Kong's largest. Nearby is the huge **Jubilee Sports Centre,** a vast complex of tracks and training fields designed to give Hong Kong's athletes space to train under professional, full-time coaches for international competition. Shatin is also home of **New Town Plaza,** the most extensive shopping complex in the New Territories.

⑰ Tai Mo Shan. To the west of the ☞ **Temple of Ten Thousand Buddhas** is Hong Kong's highest peak, rising 3,230 feet above sea level.

⑨ Tai Po. Translated, Tai Po means "shopping place" in English and every visitor here discovers that the town more than lives up to its name. In the heart of the region's breadbasket, Tai Po has long been a trading and meeting place for local farmers and fishermen. It is now being developed as an industrial center, with new housing and highways everywhere you look. It has a fine traditional market stretching along several blocks, with most of the action taking place outdoors. Adjacent to the market is the 100-year-old Man Mo Temple.

⑫ Tai Po Kau Nature Reserve. To get here, take a bus from the Tai Po KCR stop or take Bus 70 from Nathan Road at Jordan. You can follow well-marked trails through the reserve's rain-forest vegetation and along its small meandering river. Look for exotic species of trees, many of which are labeled, including the joss stick tree, believed by some to be the tree that gave Hong Kong its name, which means "Fragrant Harbour." A "talking post" at the entrance to the forest plays recordings of the various birdsongs you are likely to hear as you wander along, such as that of the rufus turtledove and the greater necklaced laughing thrush. Be aware, however, that there are also less-friendly species there—snakes, porcupines, civet cats, scorpions, and some rather fierce-looking monkeys. The reserve is as safe as any wooded area, but you are advised to wear sturdy hiking boots and not to try to get too close to the monkeys.

⑮ Temple of Ten Thousand Buddhas. You have to climb some 500 steps to reach this temple, nestled among the foothills of Shatin, but a visit is worth every step. Inside the main temple are nearly 13,000 gilded ceramic statues of Buddha, all virtually identical. They were made by Shanghai craftsmen and donated by worshipers.

⑪ Tolo Harbour and Tap Mun Island. About a 15-minute walk from the ☞ **Chinese University** along Tai Po Road is the Ma Liu Shui ferry pier, the starting point for a ferry tour of the harbour and Tap Mun Island. The ferry makes many stops, and if you take the 8:30 AM trip, you'll have time to hike around Tap Mun Island. Visit the New Fisherman's Village on the southern tip of the island, populated mostly with Hakka fisherwomen. About half a mile north, near the western shore, is the ancient village of Tap Mun, where you'll see old women playing mahjongg. **Tin Hau Temple** is less than a quarter of a mile north of the village. This huge structure, dedicated to Tin Hau, the goddess of the sea, is one of the oldest temples in Hong Kong; it sits at the top of a flight of steps that lead down into the water of the harbor. Inside are old model junks and, of course, a veiled figure of the goddess herself. Go to the eastern side of the island to see the Tap Mun Cave and some of the best-kept beaches in the territory. *Call the HKTA information hot line for ferry schedule,* ☎ 2807–6177.

❸ Tuen Mun. With a population of almost a half million, this is one of Hong Kong's "new towns"—independent, small cities created to take the spillover of population from the crowded areas of Kowloon and

The New Territories and the Outer Islands

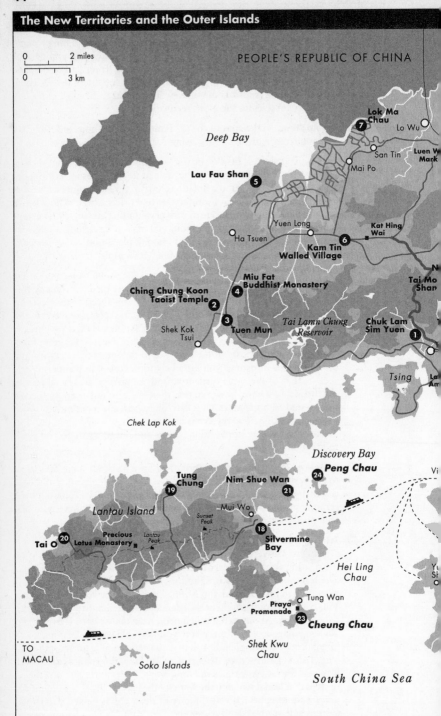

PEOPLE'S REPUBLIC OF CHINA

0   2 miles
0   3 km

Deep Bay

Lok Ma Chau **7**

Lo Wu

San Tin

Luen Wo Mark

Mai Po

Lau Fau Shan 5

Yuen Long

Ha Tsuen

Kat Hing Wai

Kam Tin Walled Village **6**

Miu Fat Buddhist Monastery **4**

Ching Chung Koon Taoist Temple **2**

Shek Kok Tsui

3 **Tuen Mun**

Tai Lam Chung Reservoir

Chuk Lam Sim Yuen **1**

Tai Mo Shan

Tsing

Chek Lap Kok

Tung Chung

19

Lantau Island

Sunset Peak

Lantau Peak

Nim Shue Wan

21

Mui Wo

18

Silvermine Bay

Discovery Bay

Peng Chau **24**

Vi

Tai O **20**

Precious Lotus Monastery

Hei Ling Chau

Tung Wan

Praya Promenade

23 **Cheung Chau**

Yu Sh

TO MACAU

Soko Islands

Shek Kwu Chau

South China Sea

N

Crooked Island

Sheung
Shai

Fanling 8

Wu Kau
Lang

Grass
island

Plover Cove
Reservoir

Tolo Channel

Tai Po

Kam Shan 9

Pan
Chung

**Tolo Harbour and
Tap Mun Island** 11

**Chinese
University** 10

**Tai Po Kau
ature Reserve** 12

Chek
Keng

THE NEW TERRITORIES

17

Amah Rock 16

**Temple of Ten
housand Buddhas**

15 14 **Shatin**

Sai Kung

suen Wan

**Sai Kung
Peninsula** 13

**Chi Kok
usement
Park**

Sung Dynasty Village

Ho Chung

Kau Sai
Chau

High Island

Port Shelter

Basalt
Island

KOWLOON

Kowloon
Bay

Yau Tong

ctoria *Victoria
Harbour*

Junk Bay

Tai Wan
Tau

HONG KONG

Tei Tong
Tsui

*Tung Lung
Chau*

ng
ue Wan

Sok Kwu Wan

Stanley

22 **Lamma
Island**

Stanley
Peninsula

Po Toi
Islands

KEY	
▨▨▨	Hong Kong Metro
——	Rail Lines
⛴	**Ferry Lines**

Hong Kong Island. They provide both industrial areas and living accommodations for the workers and their families. Other new towns are Tsuen Wan, Yuen Long, **Shatin**, Tai Po, Fanling, and Junk Bay. These seven towns now house more than 40% of Hong Kong's population.

THE OUTER ISLANDS

Looking out the airplane window on the approach to Kai Tak Airport on a fine day, you will see clusters of small islands dotting the South China Sea. Fishing fleets trawl slowly through the blue waters. Tiny sampans scamper from one outcrop to another, ignoring the junks, ocean liners, and cargo ships steaming in and out of Hong Kong Harbour. Look closer and you will see sandy coves, long strands of fine yellow sand washed by gentle surf, and countless tiny village settlements clinging to rocky bay shores and small sandbars.

These outer islands are the "Other Hong Kong," the unspoiled natural beauty that is as much a part of Hong Kong as Kowloon's crowded tenements or Hong Kong Island's concrete canyons. Unfortunately, most visitors are caught up in the frantic urban experience and miss the opportunity to escape to this side of the territory. Try to go on a weekday; on weekends, Hong Kongers flock to them and pack the ferries.

In addition to Hong Kong Island and the mainland sections of Kowloon and the New Territories, there are 235 islands under the control of the British—until 1997. Most of them are uninhabited. Others are gradually being developed, but at nowhere near the pace of the main urban areas. A number of the outlying islands have been turned over to Vietnamese refugee camps and are off-limits unless you have special permission. But the four that are most accessible by ferry—Lantau, Lamma, Cheung Chau, and Peng Chau—have become popular residential areas and welcome visitors. The largest, Lantau, is bigger than Hong Kong Island; the smallest is just a few square feet of rock.

You can reach the islands by scheduled ferry services operated by the Hong Kong and Yaumati Ferry Company. The ferries are easy to recognize by the large HKF letters painted on their funnels. Leave from the Outlying Districts Services Pier, Central, on the land reclamation area behind Exchange Square. Ferry schedules are available at the information office on the pier, or contact the Hong Kong and Yaumati Ferry Co.(☎ 2542–3081, inquiries hot line 2525–1108). Round-trip fares vary from HK$15 to HK$50.

Lantau

The island of Lantau lies due west of Hong Kong. At 55 square miles (143 square kilometers), it is almost twice the size of Hong Kong Island. For now, that is until development increases, Lantau's population is only 20,000, compared with Hong Kong Island's 1.5 million. Visitors with historical interests will find many surprises on Lantau. The imperial hold on the islands of the South China Sea was tenuous, but at one time Lantau was the temporary home for an emperor of the Sung Dynasty. That was in 1277, when 10-year-old Emperor Ti Cheng and his small retinue set up camp just behind modern Silvermine Bay's beaches. They were fleeing the Mongol forces of Kublai Khan. The young emperor died on Lantau, and the Sung Dynasty was crushed the following year, leaving no traces of the island's brief moment of imperial glory.

There are traces, however, of Sung Dynasty communities of the 13th century, including their kilns and burial sites. Many excavations on the island show evidence of even earlier settlements, some dating from Neolithic times.

Sights to See

㉑ Nim Shue Wan. For quiet and solitude, visit the **Trappist Monastery** on Eastern Lantau. Drink the fresh milk produced by a small dairy herd owned by the monks. Although the monastery can be reached by bus from Silvermine Bay, it's easier to take a small passenger ferry, or *kaido,* between Peng Chau Island and Nim Shue Wan. Hike through this old fishing village—where you might see grandchildren of fishermen talking on their cellular phones—and the unspoiled woods and hills beyond to the monastery. (Note: This is a nearly 90-minute walk, and there are no buses from Nim Shue Wan.) You can also get to Nim Shue Wan from Discovery Bay. Take the ferry to this pristine suburban development from the **Star Ferry pier** (☎ 2987–7351 for schedule). From the Discovery Bay ferry pier, turn left and walk to Nim Shue Wan, then head to the monastery. On the way you will see beaches that would be beautiful except for the astounding amount of trash that has been thrown there or washed ashore. You can spend the night in the monastery's simple accommodations, but you must make reservations well in advance. ⊠ *Grand Master, Trappist Haven, Lantau Island, Box 5, Peng Chau, Hong Kong,* ☎ *2987–6286.*

⑱ Silvermine Bay. The ferry will take you to this area, which is being developed as a commuter's suburb of Hong Kong Island. You can rent bicycles in front of the Silvermine Beach Hotel for riding around the village, still surrounded by picturesque terraced fields. The island is very mountainous, however, so for a tour of the outlying villages, plan to hike (☞ Hiking *in* Chapter 6) or take a bus. The island's private bus services link the main ferry town, **Mui Wo** on Silvermine Bay, with **Tung Chung,** which has a Sung Dynasty fort; ☞ **Tai O,** an ancient fishing village; and **Po-Lin (Precious Lotus) Monastery.**

⑳ Tai O. Divided into two parts connected by a rope-drawn ferry, the village still has many stilt houses along the water and fishing shanties. Visit the local temple, dedicated to Kuanti, the god of war, and taste local catches at the seafood restaurants. In the mountainous interior of the island you will find a tea plantation with a horseback-riding camp and a monastery, which has the world's tallest outdoor bronze statue of Buddha—it is more than 100 feet high and weighs 275½ tons. The monastery, gaudy and exuberantly commercial, is also famous for the vegetarian meals served in the temple refectory. Nearby are the Lantau Tea Gardens, where there are horses for hire and a poorly kept roller-skating rink with skate rentals.

⑲ Tung Chung. If you visit here, walk out to the bay, where you will see Chek Lap Kok Island, site of a proposed multibillion-dollar airport. The entire island, mountains and all, has been leveled to build the airport, strategically scheduled to open in 1998. Construction is underway on bridges that will eventually connect Lantau with the New Territories and a tunnel that will connect it to Hong Kong Island. The MTR is planning to build a subway route in this vicinity, and high-rise buildings are sure to follow. Enjoy the view of the Pa Mei farming village, just beyond the bay. It won't be there much longer. You can also visit the ancient Sung Dynasty fort, which was evacuated by the Qing dynasty army in 1898 when the New Territories was leased to Britain. It is now an elementary school.

LANTAU LODGING

Lantau is well worth a full day's visit, even two. The best overnight accommodations are at the ⓣ **Silvermine Beach Hotel** (☎ 2984–8295,

FAX 2984–1907), which has doubles starting at HK$693 on weekdays, HK$989 on weekends (price includes a 15% service charge and tax) or the smaller ⛺ **Mui Wo Inn** (☎ 2984–7225) where doubles start at HK$320 on weekdays, HK$550 on weekends. Visitors may also stay overnight at a tea plantation or at the Precious Lotus Monastery. The HKTA has an information sheet on these and other accommodations available on Lantau.

Lamma Island

For a glimpse of what rural China must have been like in past centuries, wander across **Lamma Island,** which faces the fishing port of Aberdeen on Hong Kong Island's south side. (The ferry from Central to Yung Shue Wan or Sok Kwu Wan takes about 40 minutes.) Here you'll see farmers, shielded from the sun by black-fringed straw hats, tending their vegetables, while fishermen gather shellfish, much as their ancestors did before them. Lamma is also home to a bohemian contingent of expats, some of whom look as though they're in a time warp of their own, in 1968 or so. But there are just as many lawyers, journalists, and bankers who have come to escape the high rents of Hong Kong Island and spend their weekends relaxing on an island that has the feel of a casual beach community. Ignore the power station and cement factory and seek out the small bays along narrow paths that offer changing views of the ocean and Hong Kong Island.

Allow time to stop for a meal at either of Lamma's two ferry villages—**Sok Kwu Wan** and ☞ **Yung Shue Wan.** In both villages, lines of inviting open-air harborside restaurants, some with amazingly diverse wine lists, offer feasts of freshness that put many restaurants on Hong Kong Island to shame. In particular, try Lancombe for Cantonese in Sok Kwu Wan or the trendy, inexpensive Deli Lamma in Yung Shue Wan. **Yung Shue Wan,** the larger of the ferry villages, is a treat if you have shopping, or just browsing, on your mind. The ever-present smell of fish markets hovers around you as you wander into places that sell interesting pottery and baskets. **Silk Road Bazaar** (✉ 76 Main St., ☎ 2982–1200), a tiny stall, sells a striking selection of amber jewelry. It's only open on weekends, but appointments are available if you decide to visit on a weekday. About midway between Sok Kwu Wan and Yung Shue Wan is **Hung Shing Ye** beach, which is sometimes swimmable. (Don't go in if you see plastic bags and other refuse floating on the water.)

LODGING

You can spend the night on the beach at the ⛺ **Concerto Inn** (☎ 2982–1668, FAX 2982–0022). Of its 12 rooms, some have a good view, and the inn has a garden café as well. Rooms start at HK$680 with service charge and tax, but there is a 30% discount on weekdays.

Cheung Chau

Cheung Chau, Hong Kong's most crowded outlying island, has a population of about 22,000 people, most of them living on the sandbar that connects the dumbbell-shape island's two hilly tips. There's a Mediterranean flavor here that has attracted artists and writers from around the world, some of whom have created an expatriate artists' colony here. The entry into Cheung Chau's harbor, through lines of gaily bannered fishing boats, is an exhilarating experience. Also colorful is the island's annual springtime **Bun Festival,** one of Hong Kong's most popular community galas. Held at the 200-year-old **Pak Tai Temple,** dedicated to the protector of fishermen, the festival originated in the 18th century as appeasement for the spirits of those killed by pirates who were thought to wreak plagues upon the village. There is also history on Cheung Chau—pirate caves and ancient rock carvings, located along the waterfront, just below the Warwick Hotel.

Throughout the year, small sampans provide ferry service from Hong Kong Island to beaches on Cheung Chau—beaches that are virtually deserted and have beautiful, clear water.

Dining out is a joy on Cheung Chau, which lies southwest of Lantau, about one hour from Central by ferry. A favorite of almost all Western visitors, it has dozens of good open-air cafés on either side of its crowded sandbar township—both on the **Praya Promenade** along the waterfront and overlooking the main public beach at **Tung Wan.**

LODGING

You can stay on the island in reasonable comfort at the ⛱ **Cheung Chau Warwick Hotel** (☎ 2981–0081, ⅢX 2981–9174) on East Bay at Tung Wan Beach. Rooms start at HK$820.

Peng Chau

㉔ The tiniest of Hong Kong's four major islands, **Peng Chau** was once home for a few farmers, fishermen, and a fireworks factory. Although the factory is now closed and the villagers have built three-story weekend retreats for Hong Kong's city folks, the community feeling remains. Peng Chau doesn't have the lively café scene found on Lamma, but **The Forest** (✉ 38C Wing Hing St., ☎ 2983–8837) is a popular watering hole among locals, with American home-style cooking and live music several nights a week. The village shopping district is known for its unpretentious little stores selling locally made porcelain at remarkably low prices. **Ming Lei Fong** (✉ 10 Wing On St., ☎ 2987–7423), open on Sunday, has Chinese elm-wood furniture, jewelry, and antique porcelain. **Elaine Gallery** (✉ 26 Wing Hing St., ☎ 2983–0235) sells watercolors of Hong Kong and Nepalese handicrafts.

Stand on the Peng Chau ferry quay and watch the kaido for Lantau's Trappist monastery sputter toward dark green hills. Choose your fresh shellfish from baskets held aloft by local fishermen bobbing in boats below the quay, and take it back to a café to be cooked. Then breathe in that stirring ambience of Hong Kong's islands—a mix of salt air, shrimp paste, and dried fish, combined with a strong dose of local pride and a sense of independence that has been lost in urban Hong Kong.

Other Islands

The adventurous visitor can try the more out-of-the way islands, not quite as easy to reach but all the more rewarding for their remoteness. Besides Tap Mun and Yim Tin Tsai in the New Territories, here are two other favorites:

Minuscule **Ping Chau,** not to be confused with Peng Chau, is 1 square mile of land lying in the far northeast of the New Territories, close to the coast of China. It is almost deserted now, but it has a checkered history. Guns and opium were smuggled out of China through Ping Chau, and during the Cultural Revolution many mainlanders swam through shark-infested waters in hopes of reaching Ping Chau and the freedom of Hong Kong. The island's largest village, **Sha Tau,** is something of a ghost town, with many cottages boarded up, but here and there you'll find old farming families eager to take you in, maybe even for the night.

A large part of the island is country park, with footpaths overgrown with orchids, wild mint, and morning glory. Look for the strange rock formations at either end of the island. At the southern end are two huge rocks known as the **Drum Rocks** or **Watchman's Tower Rocks.** At the northern end is a chunk of land that has broken away from the island. The Chinese say this represents the head of a dragon.

You must be prepared to stay for the night when you go, as the ferry runs only on weekends, departing Saturday and returning Sunday. Bring camping gear, or accept the invitation of villagers to spend the night. Take the ferry from Ma Liu Shui near the University KCR stop. It departs on Saturday at 11:15 AM and returns Sunday at 1:10 PM. Call the HKTA hot line at 2807–6177 for an update on the ferry schedule before you go.

The three **Po Toi** islands—barren little fishing islands, virtually unchanged since medieval times—are situated at the extreme southeast of Hong Kong's waters. Only Po Toi Island itself is inhabited, with a population of less than 100. Go there for spectacular strolling and fine seafood restaurants. Walk uphill past primitive dwellings, many of them deserted, to the Tin Hau temple. Walk east, through the hamlet of Wan Tsai, past banana and papaya groves, to Po Toi's famous **rock carvings.** The geometric patterns in these rocks are believed to have been carved during the local Bronze Age, about 2,500 years ago. Getting to the island will take some planning. The most convenient way to go to the Po Toi islands is by junk. For a rental call Simpson Marina (☎ 2555-7349; ☞ Junking *in* Chapter 4). Ferries depart from Aberdeen on Tuesday, Thursday, and Saturday at 9 AM, and return from Po Toi at 10:30 AM, so you have to stay overnight if you want to explore the island. On Sundays and holidays, you can get a morning ferry (10 or 11:30 AM) from St. Stephen's Beach in Stanley, and return the same day at 3 or 4 PM. You can make the necessary reservations by calling 2554-4059, but you'll need the help of someone who speaks Cantonese, because no one answering the phone will speak English.

3 Dining

By Jack Moore
and Sue
Marshall

ANYWHERE YOU GO IN HONG KONG, in any direction you'd care to look, you're liable to see a restaurant sign. Establishments that sell prepared food are as old as Chinese culture itself, and the fact that most local people live in small apartments and have little space for home entertaining means that restaurants are usually the chosen venues for special occasions and family get-togethers. Nowhere in the world is cooking more varied than in this city, where Cantonese cuisine (long regarded by Chinese gourmands as the most intricate and sophisticated in Asia) is joined by delights from not only other parts of China, but also virtually every other culinary region on earth. Whether it's French, German, Italian, Portuguese, Japanese, Korean, Indian, Indonesian, Thai, or specialty American food, or exotic fare from places such as Burma, Mexico, Holland, the Caribbean, Switzerland, Sri Lanka, or the Philippines, the traditional, deeply rooted Chinese love of good food flourishes.

Be advised, however, that Hong Kong's extraordinary culinary vitality is offset by some of Asia's worst restaurants. Don't expect just any old neighborhood restaurant to turn out dreamy dishes.

Gastronomically speaking, the words "Chinese cuisine" don't mean much more than do "European cuisine." The largest country in the world has dozens of different cooking styles, though only five are prominent in Hong Kong. These are as follows:

Cantonese. As 94% of the population comes from Guangdong (Canton) Province, this is the most popular style by far. This is fortunate, because the semitropical province has the largest selection of fruits, vegetables, and meats. The Cantonese ideal is to bring out the natural taste of ingredients by cooking them quickly at very high temperatures. This creates *wok chi,* a fleeting energy that requires food to be served immediately and eaten on the spot. If it is properly prepared, you will never taste fresher food. Says international gourmet William Mark: "Only Cantonese chefs understand simplicity, purity, and variety." Menus are enormous.

Shanghai. Shanghai is a city of immigrants, not unlike New York and Hong Kong, and its cosmopolitan population has several different culinary styles. Lying at the confluence of several rivers on the South China Sea, the city has especially good seafood. Shanghai crabs (actually from Suzhou) are winter favorites. Many dishes are fried in sesame oil or soy sauce, and can be a bit greasy—no one can forget the famous "squirrel fish," so-called because the oil-based sauce poured over the fish sizzles or "chatters" like a squirrel. This dish also originated in Suzhou, but is featured in Shanghai restaurants.

Peking. Of course Peking duck is a favorite, and nowhere is it better than in Hong Kong. It was originally an Imperial Mongolian dish, and is usually served in two (or three) courses. This is a northern "noodle" rather than a rice culture. Peking noodles, along with Mongolian barbecue and onion cakes, are inevitably ordered.

Szechuan. The spiciest Chinese food (also known as Sichuan) is now a favorite around the world. Rice, bamboo, wheat, river fish, shellfish, chicken, and pork dishes all have plenty of salt, anise, fennel seed, chili, and coriander. Ingredients are simmered, smoked, stirred, and steamed. The effect is an integrated flavor—the opposite of Cantonese food, where each ingredient has its own taste.

Chiu Chow. Coming from near Canton, the Chiu Chow people have a gutsy, hearty cuisine, which has never caught on in the West. It begins with "Iron Buddha" tea and moves on to thick shark's-fin soup, soya goose, whelk (tiny snails), bird's nest, and irresistible steamed lobsters served with tangerine jam.

A few more hints:

Dim-sum restaurants serve tasty Chinese hors d'oeuvres and must be tried at lunch (or a bit earlier, to avoid crowds). The staff push trolleys around calling out the names of dishes, and you point to what you want. Some, such as congealed blood and giblets, are esoteric, but others, such as steamed pork buns or spring rolls, are readily acceptable to most diners. Always check prices of things labeled "market price." Anything from a typhoon to heavy traffic can determine the cost. Ask for the exact price for your party's meal rather than for a *catty,* a unit in the Chinese weight system equal to about 1.1 pounds.

Ironically, however, many visitors and residents tend to indulge in other Asian food styles, as so many are available in Hong Kong—particularly Thai, Vietnamese, and Japanese. The city's cosmopolitan population and tendency to see eating out as a hobby (to be indulged in virtually every evening) explains the sheer weight of restaurants, as well as the incredible collection of cuisines on offer—and variation in quality. For someone starting off with Thai food for the first time, a visit to Thai Delicacy in Wanchai would give a good introduction to the spicy dishes of that country. For the more experienced a visit to Wyndham Street Thai in Central will show how modern Thai can be interpreted. Likewise, for those wishing to experiment with Vietnamese without spending oodles, try Saigon Beach in Wanchai—an unusual and tiny hole in the wall. For something more upmarket in Vietnamese food you could do no better than Indochine in Central. For reasonably priced Japanese food, the streamlined environs of Tokio Joe in Central are a good start, but for the full works (and a workout for your wallet) Imasa at the Peninsula will provide exceptional food as perfectly presented as a painting.

Tips are expected at most restaurants, even if there is already a service charge on the bill. In more traditional Chinese restaurants, tips are not expected. However, it is customary to leave small change.

Reservations are always a good idea; we note only when they're essential or when they are not accepted. Unless otherwise noted, the restaurants listed are open daily for lunch and dinner. We mention dress only when men are required to wear a jacket or a jacket and tie.

CATEGORY	COST*
$$$$	over HK$500 (US$64)
$$$	HK$300–HK$500 (US$38–US$64)
$$	HK$100–HK$300 (US$13–US$38)
$	under HK$100 (US$13)

per person, not including 10% service charge

HONG KONG ISLAND

Central

One of the busiest sections of the city, Central is a madhouse at lunchtime when hungry office workers crowd the streets and eateries. Most restaurants provide set lunches and service that will see most diners in and out in an hour and are generally good value. Otherwise evening dining is either super smart or a quick bite followed by many drinks, specifically in an area called Lan Kwai Fong. The variety and the quality of dining has improved over the years and there's now much to choose from in Central.

Asian
CANTONESE

$$ ★ **✕ Yung Kee.** For more than half a century, this massive (five floors hold some 5,000 guests), multistory eatery (you're taken upstairs in a lift by a woman wielding a mobile phone, organizing your table) has been serving very good Cantonese food amid riotous, writhing-golden-dragon decor. Convenient to hotels and business in Central, the restaurant attracts a varied clientele—from office workers to visiting celebrities—all of whom receive the same cheerful, high-energy service. Roast goose is a specialty, the skin beautifully crisp. Seafood fanciers should try sautéed fillet of pomfret with chili and black bean sauce, or one of the many—expensive—shark-fin soups. ⊠ 32–40 Wellington St., ☎ 2522–1624. AE, DC, MC, V.

$ **✕ Luk Yu Tea House.** Food takes a backseat to atmosphere in this unofficial historical monument—Luk Yu is a living museum with extraordinary character. It has been in business for more than 60 years and as such lets you catch a rare glimpse of old colonial Hong Kong, but from the Chinese (not British) perspective. The decor, including handsome carved wooden doors, hardwood paneling, marble facings, and, unfortunately, spittoons (noisily used by the clientele), is definitely worth seeing. The morning dim sum is popular with Chinese businesspeople, though the fare is no more than standard Cantonese. Reservations are impossible unless you speak Cantonese. ⊠ 24–26 Stanley St., ☎ 2523–5464. No credit cards.

INDIAN

$$–$$$ **✕ Ashoka.** The authenticity of the food in this restaurant, just above the Central business district, has made it a favorite of the local Indian community. Tasteful Indian art and plenty of pillows are reflected in mirrors that provide a much-needed illusion of space. The restaurant offers a large menu of spiced Mogul dishes. A local favorite is chicken *tikka* soaked in a spicy marinade and barbecued in a clay oven, and you shouldn't miss stuffed tomato (not on the menu but available by request) filled with a complex mixture of raisins, rice, and lamb in a mild curry sauce. ⊠ 57–59 Wyndham St., ☎ 2524–9623. AE, DC, V. Closed Sun. for lunch. No lunch Sun.

$$ ★ **✕ Mughal Room.** You can get anything from a bargain set lunch to a full banquet at one of the best Indian restaurants in town, and it's still good on the value-for-money stakes, too. The Mughlai cuisine, specializing in clay-oven cookery, is given a written introduction at the start of the menu. Each page bears an illustration and short history on one of the Mughals, the ancient rulers of India, and offers mainly Indian, but also some other Asian, dishes. Select from the *bismillah* (appetizers)—the chicken, lamb, or vegetarian samosas are fabulous, but save space: The main servings are huge. The Tandoori *sabzi* are tomatoes and capsicum stuffed with mildly spiced cottage cheese and vegetable mash and then baked. The staff wear Bathan (a tribe from Pakistan) dress complete with curl-toed slippers of a past era and caps sporting a flag symbolizing bravery. The tasteful, muted decor is stylish, making it one of the posher curry houses on this strip. ⊠ Carfield Commercial Bldg., 75–77 Wyndham St., 1st Floor, ☎ 2524–0107. AE, DC, MC, V.

$$ **✕ Tandoor Restaurant.** This upstairs eatery, one of the most distinguished in town for Indian food, is exotically decorated with mirrors, Indian paintings, colorful cloth hangings, and musical instruments. A glass-fronted kitchen allows you to watch the chef at work on one of the

100 or so dishes from which to choose, but don't miss tandoor (clay oven) specialties, roast lamb *sagwalla* (covered with tasty spinach), and lamb *rogan josh,* swimming in Kashmiri spices. There are no fewer than 14 kinds of Indian bread on the menu, all worth tasting. ⊠ *On Hing Bldg., 1–9 On Hing Terr., 3rd Floor,* ☎ *2845–2299. Reservations essential. AE, DC, V.*

$ ✕ **Spice Island Gourmet Club.** Specializing in Indian and Nepalese food, this popular eatery is called a "club" because there is no back door, disqualifying it for a restaurant license. Spice Island requires diners to "join" (it's free) and get a membership card before being properly qualified to sample one of the best Indian buffets in the city. Different buffets at lunch and dinner offer a variety of Indian chicken, lamb, and seafood dishes. Basic decor is enlivened by interesting old Victorian lithographs. The club is in the old district, just west of the business core. ⊠ *63 Wellington St.,* ☎ *2522–8706. MC, V. Closed Sun.*

JAPANESE

$$$ ✕ **Benkay Restaurant.** Light-tone wood and many panels and decorative screens create an elegant Japanese atmosphere in this Central venue. Those who aren't already familiar with Japanese food may require a little expert help from the staff to decipher the menu. For a delightful culinary overview, try one of the set *kaiseki* meals, in which 10 or more tiny portions of fried, steamed, or raw delicacies are served. For sheer entertainment, order a *teppanyaki* meal, prepared before your eyes on a hot griddle. There's also a good sushi selection as well as *shabu-shabu* (a Japanese delicacy of thin strips of beef swished in boiling water). Try the grilled codfish and eel from the Kyoto-style à la carte menu. ⊠ *1 Gloucester Tower, The Landmark,* ☎ *2521–3344. AE, DC, MC, V.*

$ ✕ **Tokio Joe.** This casual but classy Japanese joint serves up basic fare with some finesse. Accompanied by funky world music, there's a rush at most lunchtimes, when the feeling is bustling and businesslike, but there's also a sushi bar where you can sit for a quick snack. The attention that has been paid to design elements makes the atmosphere fun—place mats depict elegant watercolors of a variety of sushi servings; there's a contraption for dispensing Japanese chili pepper that can take some figuring out; and beautiful ceramic pots line the walls. For example, the *unaju don,* or fried eel with rice, comes in a lacquer box complete with assorted pickles in little bowls. The hot, tender flesh is tasty and fresh, and you can watch the chefs at work on all their orders in a central bar area. ⊠ *16 Lan Kwai Fong,* ☎ *2525–1889. Reservations essential. AE, DC, MC, V.*

SRI LANKAN

$ ✕ **Club Lanka.** This is top-quality bottom-end dining in Hong Kong, the best value other than indigenous Cantonese. Here they serve a meat buffet and a vegetarian buffet with a handful of well-cooked selections accompanied by rice and roti. The majority of the curries are mild, but very tasty. Vegetarians can choose from winter-melon curry, Mysore dhal, spinach curry, eggplant curry, mixed-vegetable curry accompanied by Gothamba roti, two types of rice and three of chutney (coconut, tamarind, and onion and chili). Bitter-gourd *sambol* (a kind of fried salad) is especially delicious. However, the low-key atmosphere may be too much so for those who expect more from their dining spot. ⊠ *17 Hollywood Rd.,* ☎ *2526–6559. MC, V.*

THAI

$$$ ✕ **Wyndham Street Thai.** Nothing will have prepared you for this Thai experience, so throw out all past memories. You are greeted at the front door by a beautifully spotlit golden Buddha, beyond which

Dining

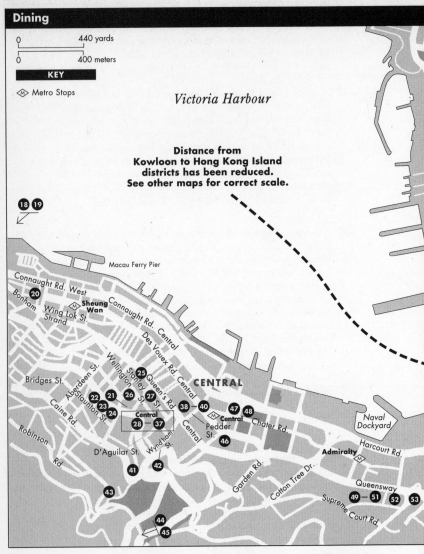

0 |———| 440 yards
0 |———| 400 meters

KEY

Ⓜ Metro Stops

Victoria Harbour

**Distance from
Kowloon to Hong Kong Island
districts has been reduced.
See other maps for correct scale.**

American Peking
Restaurant, **54**
Ashoka, **34**
Au Trou Normand, **4**
Bali Restaurant, **1**
Benkay
Restaurant, **46**
Bentley's Seafood
Restaurant and Oys-
ter Bar, **47**
Black Sheep, **68**
Bodhi
Vegetarian, **6**

Cafe Deco Bar
and Grill, **45**
Camargue Club, **25**
Casa Lisboa, **23**
Chinese
Restaurant, **16**
Chiu Chow
Garden, **61**
Club Lanka, **30**
The Continental, **62**
Dan Ryan's, **49**
Delaney's, **57**
Deli Lama, **18**
Dynasty, **59**

Felix, **10**
Gaddi's, **12**
Grappa's, **50**
Great Shanghai
Restaurant, **5**
Grissini, **59**
Hugo's, **15**
Indochine 1929, **38**
Imasa, **11**
Isshin, **63**
Jimmy's
Kitchen, **13, 32**
JW's California
Grill, **52**

La Brasserie, **8**
Lai Ching Heen, **17**
Lancombe, **19**
Le Tire Bouchon, **24**
Lucy's, **64**
Luk Yu Tea House, **27**
M at the Fringe, **42**
Mozart Stub'n, **41**
Mughal Room, **37**
Nepal, **22**

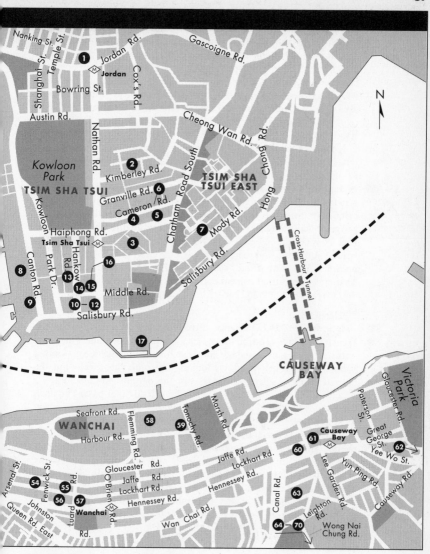

One Harbour Road, **59**
Papillon, **21**
Peak Cafe, **44**
Pierrot, **48**
Post '97, **39**
Ricos, **43**
Sagano Restaurant, **7**
Saigon Beach, **55**
San Francisco Steak House, **9**
Shek O Thai-Chinese Place, **70**
Spice Island Gourmet Club, **26**

Stanley's French Restaurant, **65**
Stanley's Oriental, **66**
Supatra's Thai Gourmet, **29**
Szechuan Lau, **60**
Tables 88, **67**
Tandoor Restaurant, **33**
Thai Delicacy, **56**
Three-Five Korean Restaurant, **14**
Tiger's, **53**
Tokio Joe, **35**
Tutto Bene, **2**

Va Bene, **28**
Valentino Ristorante Italiano, **3**
The Verandah, **69**
The Viceroy, **58**
Wyndham Street Thai, **36**
Yung Kee, **31**
Zen, **51**
Zona Rosa, **40**

a curved, blazing pink wall leads you inside to equally shocking lime green walls. The rest of the decor is austere in comparison: black leather chairs and stark white tablecloths, but the whole effect is successful. The menu consists of strikingly new interpretations of traditional Thai dishes. Try crispy fish with pork cubes in lime juice, or crab, bean sprouts, coriander, sweet basil, lemongrass, peanuts, and fish sauce wrapped in betel nut leaves—a revelation. Another favorite is stir-fried asparagus with chili jam, snow peas, and shiitake mushrooms. Skip ox tongue unless you're into strange textures and tastes. Desserts are sticky and sweet: Sample lotus seeds with taro or sweetened rice artfully tied in a bamboo leaf. Ask your waiter for help with the wine list, which is decidedly exotic and includes many Australian vintages. ⊠ *38 Wyndham St.,* ☏ *2869–6216. AE, DC, MC, V.*

$$–$$$ ✕ **Supatra's Thai Gourmet.** This trendy establishment has developed a devoted local clientele. In Central's fashionable Lan Kwai Fung restaurant district, it has a chic boat-shape bar downstairs where you can get ice-cold Singha beer from Bangkok, and an upstairs dining room with views of the passing pedestrian parade. The menu is limited but strictly authentic, and there are seven Thai chefs in the kitchen at dinnertime. Try light but spicy seafood salad, rich and tangy curries, and Thai-style, deep-fried fish cakes (the least rubbery in Hong Kong). ⊠ *46 D'Aguilar St.,* ☏ *2522–5073. AE, MC, V.*

VIETNAMESE

$$$ ✕ **Indochine 1929.** The name directly evokes the period when the
★   French were in possession of what is modern-day Vietnam. The mood of the 1930s is gloriously, but subtly summoned by the decor—potted palms, huge French windows looking out onto the street—but the true atmospheric effect is from the old photographs and memorabilia decorating the walls from Vietnam's French colonial past. The chef, who regularly visits both North and South Vietnam to discover new dishes, has created a contemporary version of Vietnamese cuisine—a kind of cross between the cooking styles of Saigon and Southern California. The deep-fried soft-shell crabs are to die for. Try the mildly spicy shredded chicken salad for a fresh, zesty appetizer and move on to the Hanoi fish—a famous Vietnamese dish served with thin, white noodles that is still cooking when it is served on one of the attractive pottery platters. The busy, chatty atmosphere, peopled by a smart, casual crowd, is comfortable and relaxed. ⊠ *California Tower, Lan Kwai Fong, 2nd Floor,* ☏ *2869–7399. AE, MC, V.*

European

AUSTRIAN

$$–$$$ ✕ **Mozart Stub'n.** To get to this local gourmet hideaway, either take a
★   taxi or toil up a long hill on foot—many believe the haul is worth it. The "stub'n" in the name of the restaurant translates as "farmhouse kitchen," and it's furnished accordingly, with high-backed chairs and solid wood tables. Much of the service is provided by the affable owner, who adds a pleasant personal touch. After an appetizer of cold cuts (bacon, salami, and smoked meats, with a taste of schnapps) you might try more of the authentic Austrian cuisine, such as lentil soup with chunks of bacon and sausage. Boiled beef comes in thick slices with creamed spinach and apple horseradish. And for dessert, homemade Viennese *Apfelstrudel* is a must, as are the succulent soufflés. ⊠ *8 Glenealy,* ☏ *2522–1763. Reservations essential. MC, V. Closed Sun.*

CONTINENTAL

$$$$ ✕ **M at the Fringe.** This unique spot above the Fringe Club sets itself
★ apart with original, quirky decor and a truly superior menu that
changes seasonally and mixes Continental with Middle Eastern cuisine. It's hard to choose from among dishes whose descriptions on the
menu are as mouthwatering as the meal itself. For starters, the phyllo
package with avocado, feta, and pine nuts has a nicely spicy hot red
sauce that gives the dish a lift without overdoing it. The pigeon (pigeon is very popular locally) is served warm with a Neapolitan walnut salad. It's a toss-up between lightly smoked salmon brushed with
hazelnut oil or the oven-baked, pure whitefish cod with a tangy crust
of capers, lime, and pepper on sweet-potato-and-polenta puree. Soups
and appetizers are always interesting, and desserts are sublime— especially the orange soufflé with chocolate-chip ice cream or the ginger crème brûlée. Round it all off with Turkish coffee served from a
tiny Turkish coffeepot and Turkish delight. Lunch is a bargain. ⊠ *South
Block, 2 Lower Albert Rd., 1st Floor,* ☎ *2877–4000. Reservations essential. AE, MC, V.*

$$$ ✕ **Camargue Club.** Although named after the French region famous
★ for its horses, the food here is more Continental than Provençal. One
of the most pleasant features of this elevated eatery is the casual and
unpretentious charm of the room, the staff, and the food itself. A
handwritten menu changes seasonally—you can get wild boar and veni-
son in winter. Camargue is becoming known among the Chinese pop-
ulation for fried pâté de foie gras, a particular delicacy here. Duck breast
in orange and clove sauce is beyond wonderful. Despite a lack of overt
decor, small touches such as the open kitchen and wine rack along one
wall create a cozy and intimate atmosphere—that's probably why it's
busy every night of the week. ⊠ *Regent Centre, 88 Queen's Rd., 24th
Floor,* ☎ *2525–7997. Reservations essential. AE, DC, MC, V.*

$$ ✕ **Jimmy's Kitchen.** Probably the most famous—and still one of the
best—of the territory's restaurants, this institution first opened for busi-
ness in 1928. It has been catering to a deeply devoted Hong Kong clientele in one location or another (currently there are two) ever since. Nicely
decorated, it has comfortable booths, dark woodwork, lattice partitions, and brass work on the walls. The food is as charmingly old-fashioned as the place itself: Where else in Hong Kong can you find corned
beef and cabbage? Other European specialties, including borscht,
Stroganoff, goulash, and bangers and mash, are accompanied by the
restaurant's traditional pickled onions. Their rhubarb tart is a must
for dessert. Unfortunately, the Kowloon branch, on Ashley Road, does
not uphold the standards of the Wyndham Street location. ⊠ *South
China Bldg., 1 Wyndham St.,* ☎ *2526–5293. Lunch reservations essential. AE, DC, MC, V.*

$–$$ ✕ **Post '97.** With its image as a hip coffeehouse/nightspot and gath-
ering point for the local intelligentsia, people sometimes forget just how
good the food is here—and it won't break the bank. The menu features delicious pastas, salads, and sandwiches; there's a chalkboard of
daily specials; and soups and desserts are almost always worthwhile.
Post '97 has a 24-hour menu on weekends and is great for breakfast.
Service is fun and funky. ⊠ *9 Lan Kwai Fong,* ☎ *2810–9333. DC,
MC, V.*

ENGLISH

$$$ ✕ **Bentley's Seafood Restaurant and Oyster Bar.** One flight down
★ from the Prince's Building office and shopping complex is an exact copy
of a well-known, swank London restaurant, the elegance and decorum
of which in turn replicate the feeling of an exclusive English club. In
season, Bentley's even serves English oysters from Colchester—as well

as oysters from many other places in the world—served raw or cooked either at the oyster bar or at your table. Choose from among oysters Imperial with champagne sauce, oysters Bentley with tomato and curry sauces, and oysters Kilpatrick with tomato, chili, and bacon. Seafood here is some of the best in town, grilled simply with lemon and butter. The house fish pie represents the best of classic English cooking. ⊠ *Prince's Bldg., 10 Chater Sq. (enter off Statue Sq.),* ☎ *2868–0881. Lunch reservations essential. Jacket and tie. AE, DC, MC. Closed Sun.*

FRENCH

$$$$ ✕ **Papillon.** Down a dead-end alley in the heart of Central, this inti-
 ★   mate restaurant, reminiscent of a small bistro in the south of France, is frequently suggested as Hong Kong's most romantic dinner location. Settle in for an evening at Papillon, celebrated for its informal atmosphere, by trying a drink invented here, the refreshing Parrot, a mix of Calvados with cider, ginger ale, and Amaretto. As you sip your aperitif you can observe the Parisian black-and-white prints, the bar hung with glasses, wines and spirits on show, and an unpretentious cheese board. The traditional French onion soup and authentic salmon tartare with salmon caviar are good starters. As entrées, the tuna steak with aioli and grilled vegetables is a light main dish, accompanied by endive gratin. For a memorable dessert order the soufflé ahead—try lemon and Grand Marnier. The light, fluffy concoction is served with custard, and virtually the same ingredients are used for the crème brûlée. Ask the manager to recommend food for you and he'll match wines by the glass, too. ⊠ *8 Wo On La.,* ☎ *2526–5965. AE, DC, MC, V.*

$$$ ✕ **Pierrot.** A ceramic version of the famed French clown welcomes you to this theatrical restaurant. Windows, framed with ornate plum-and-gold drapes, look onto the quintessential Hong Kong Harbour panorama. Pierrot's management often invites visiting European chefs to prepare their specialties as part of food promotions. Both lunch and dinner menus are small but feature exquisitely crafted dishes such as ravioli of scampi with white curry sauce—to be enjoyed with a selection from one of the most extensive and best-chosen wine lists in this part of the world. Service is flawless, and the bar offers a variety of caviars. ⊠ *Mandarin Oriental Hotel, 5 Connaught Rd.,* ☎ *2522–0111. Reservations essential. Jacket and tie. AE, DC, MC, V. No lunch weekends.*

$$–$$$ ✕ **Le Tire Bouchon.** Something of a Hong Kong secret, this bistro is hidden on a steep hill on Old Bailey Street. Decor is French without being stuffy (comfortable chairs, lots of wood), and the menu, while small, includes treasures such as sautéed chicken livers with raspberry vinegar and walnuts, and homemade goose-liver pâté with Armagnac. Consider also chicken in cranberry sauce, calf's liver in red-wine sauce, and beef tenderloin with pears and Saigon cinnamon. There's a variety of reasonably priced French wines from which to choose. ⊠ *6–9 Old Bailey St.,* ☎ *2523–5459. MC, V. Closed Sun.*

ITALIAN

$$$ ✕ **Va Bene.** This small, trendy Northern Italian restaurant is a classy
 ★   combination of sleek Los Angeles decor and friendly, capable service. An inventive menu includes melt-in-your-mouth risotto with shrimp and orange, a wide selection of pasta dishes, and daily specials. Homemade breads are served with pesto and other freshly-made dips, and there is great tiramisù. ⊠ *58–62 D'Aguilar St., Lan Kwai Fong,* ☎ *2845–5577. AE, DC, MC, V.*

\$\$–\$\$\$ ✕ **Zona Rosa.** Hong Kong's newest Mexican restaurant is hot stuff—
★   and that's not just the mole sauce. A Mexican chef, Roberto Arteago,
a spice specialist, created the menu that's as fine as the two-level interior stacked full of Mexican memorabilia. For starters try chicken
tostadas, quesadillas *surtidas* (three Mexican turnovers with sausage
and potatoes, mozarrella and feta cheese, mushrooms and green salsa)
and *sopa de lima* (chicken and lime soup). For a main course, chili
poblano relleno, a green chili stuffed with beef, ham, and various
fruits all covered with a walnut sauce, is successful. Sea bass and game
hen are also good. If you're a fan of flan, don't go home without trying Zona Rosa's version, ever so subtly flavored with coconut. ✉ *1
Lan Kwai Fong, 2nd Floor,* ☎ *2801–5885. AE, DC, MC, V.*

Admiralty

Since this is essentially an office area and a series of large shopping
malls, much of the food offered meets the lunch demands of office workers and shoppers. However, with a major cinema and several good restaurants in the Pacific Place mall and in the area, the public is well-served
making it a destination at night.

Asian

\$\$\$ ✕ **Zen.** This upscale nouveau Cantonese restaurant is under the same
ownership as the ultra-chic London eateries of the same name. Thin-
sliced pig's ears is one of the unusual specialties here, and Peking duck
is delicious (give advance notice if you want to try it). The more standard Cantonese dishes are quite delicately prepared and presented. Service is flawless, and the decor contemporary, with dramatic hanging
lights and a central waterfall. ✉ *The Mall, Pacific Place One, 88
Queensway,* ☎ *2845–4555. AE, DC, MC, V.*

\$\$\$ ✕ **Tiger's.** If you happen to be shopping in the Pacific Place mall and
need some food, this is a good bet. Sit inside facing away from the shopping atrium and you can escape reality with the mad decor here. Selections include seafood, vegetarian, curry, tandoori, and rice and
noodles, with each dish identified by its country of origin. The *banh
cuon* (traditional homemade Vietnamese steamed ravioli) is exquisite,
with crispy, mouthwatering pork and mushroom filling contrasting with
a delicate, translucent wrapper. *Pao phak gap hed hom* (stir-fried fresh
broccoli and Chinese mushrooms with homemade oyster sauce) is
equally tasty. ✉ *Basement, Pacific Place in the Admiralty complex, 88
Queensway,* ☎ *2537–4682. AE, DC, MC, V.*

North American

\$\$ ✕ **Dan Ryan's.** A popular bar, there is often only standing space here,
★   so book ahead for a table. Aside from beer, the menu offers a smat-
tering of international dishes, pasta and the like, but Dan Ryan's reputation in town is for great burgers and soups served up in bread bowls.
Simple, rib-sticking stuff, but sometimes that's all you want, and Dan
Ryan's provides it without fuss or formality. ✉ *114 Pacific Place, 88
Queensway.* ☎ *2845–4600. Reservations essential. AE, DC, MC, V.*

\$\$–\$\$\$ ✕ **JW's California Grill.** This is that rare uptown hotel restaurant that
achieves a relaxed feeling. Sleek-looking yet supercomfortable seating
islands around the perimeter of the dining room are widely spaced for
privacy. A very attentive wait staff (they guarantee getting you fed, wa-
tered, and back out the door quickly, if you ask) serves dishes from

chef Barry Schneider's eclectic menu of fresh California cuisine. Of particular note are honey-glazed lamb chops and stir-fried lobster and prawns. Pasta here is also excellent, as is the extensive list of American wines. ⊠ *Marriott Hotel, Pacific Place,* ☎ *2841–3899. AE, DC, MC, V.*

European
ITALIAN

$$–$$$ ✕ **Grappa's.** Don't let the mall location mislead you—Grappa's serves
★   superb Italian food. Once inside you can turn your back on the mall and let the kindly staff look after you. The endless selection of pasta dishes can make you ponder your best bet for a long while, but nothing will be disappointing. Excellent coffee and a range of bottled beers means that Grappa's is also a good spot for a quick pick-me-up or a place to rendezvous after shopping. ⊠ *132 Pacific Place, 88 Queensway,* ☎ *2868–0086. AE, DC, MC, V.*

Midlevels

Heavily residential, Midlevels is strangely devoid of much in the way of dining spots, with a few rare—but generally favorable—exceptions. The advent of the Midlevels escalator seems to have invigorated the area, with commuters enticed up hill into new neighborhood haunts by the promise of something casual, as opposed to the more glitzy offerings down the hill.

Asian
NEPALI

$$ ✕ **Nepal.** If you're feeling adventurous, but not quite up to an assault
★   on Everest, you can stimulate your imagination with a Yaktail or Yeti Foot cocktail in this tiny Nepali restaurant. The small space, with traditional wooden carvings and Gurkha daggers that make up the light fixtures, resonates with Indian music. Nepali cuisine differs from Indian because of its ingredients, and the ones used here are freshly flown in from Nepal. Like Chinese medicine, these ingredients, called *timor,* can have benefits (other than filling a hungry stomach), but overall the result is lighter curry dishes than those of traditional Indian food. For starters try the *momocha,* delicious dumplings (either lamb, chicken, pork, or vegetable) that you can order steamed or fried. *Boghote sadeko* is a lip-smacking combination of grapefruit and coriander. Or opt for *hanta tareko,* thin slices of eggplant grilled with Nepali herbs, neither greasy nor slushy, as eggplant can often be. *Khasi kadai* is a lamb dish with herbs and spices cooked in a *kadai,* or Nepalese wok. *Ramtora* is okra in butter-based curry and *luiche rana paribar* is "forest" chicken cooked the way the Nepalese royal family likes it. Served on a hot plate with hot lemon segments, the dish is wonderfully tender and tangy with slivers of vegetables. Wash it down with specially imported Nepali beer. ⊠ *14 Staunton St.,* ☎ *2521–9108. Reservations essential. AE, DC, MC, V.*

European
PORTUGUESE

$$–$$$ ✕ **Casa Lisboa.** A mini waterfall blends with the fado music in the back-
★   ground, paintings line the yellow walls, and ivy and bottles with eruptions of melted candle wax all add to the atmosphere. Replete with checkered tablecloths and painted pottery plates, the dimly lit space is serviced by a professional but low-key staff. Choosing a starter from the ones offered is a challenge, with anything from Portuguese cheese and ham to snails with chili, garlic, and mushrooms available. Opt for the grilled sardines and you won't be disappointed. Typically the menu features lots of codfish and chorizo options. The scallops with chorizo

are served on a small wooden box with a plate that stays hot just long enough for you to cook the seafood, turning the scallops over yourself. The codfish soup is a divine broth with chunks of the flaked fish and slivers of garlic and coriander. There's an amusing set of special effects for the flambéed dish of king prawns, and remember to ask for the mashed potato *ze do pipa,* a fabulous mash with cheese, fish, and olives. All wines on the list are Portuguese (except for the champagne). ⊠ *20 Staunton St.,* ☎ *2869–9361. Reservations essential. AE, DC, MC, V.*

SPANISH

$$$ ✕ **Ricos.** A Spanish tapas bar, this is one of only a few restaurants this far up the hill. The selection of food is traditional and generally satisfying, but what gives Ricos an edge are the wooden fittings and charming casual atmosphere. People here always seem to be having a good time, and couples find it romantic. Its intimate feel has won the hearts of many a Midlevels resident. If you go up the Midlevels escalator, go as far as Conduit Road, get off and turn left. Ricos is just six doors down. ⊠ *44 Robinson Rd.,* ☎ *2840–0937. Reservations essential. AE, DC, MC, V.*

The Peak

Whether you take the tram or a taxi, on a clear day, even the views en route will justify the trip to the highest spot to dine in Hong Kong. The view is spectacular, but if there are low clouds you won't see a thing, although you can hear the city below you. There's a small selection of restaurants, but two compete for the number-one position. For the view, stick with Cafe Deco, but old-timers stay loyal to the Peak Cafe.

Asian

PAN-ASIAN

$$$ ✕ **Cafe Deco Bar and Grill.** If you're in Hong Kong on a clear day, take the Peak tram up to the top to dine at this spiffy, double-decker restaurant overlooking the city. Views *are* stunning. The decor is art deco to the hilt—you can spend an age wandering around looking at authentic period fittings. The menu includes a global range of choices: Chinese, Indian (there's a tandoor in the kitchen), Italian, Mexican, and Thai dishes, with dishes using ancho chilis or combining striped sea bass with fennel and pancetta. There is also an extremely reasonable wine list. Eat in the dining room, at the oyster bar, or in the ice cream parlor. The location is a favorite with visitors and residents alike. ⊠ *The Peak Galleria, 1st Level, 118 Peak Rd.,* ☎ *2849–5111. AE, DC, MC, V.*

$$–$$$ ✕ **Peak Cafe.** You won't get speedy service here, but the food is worth
★ the wait. The atmospheric colonial-style café opposite the top terminus of the Peak tram has been taken over by a Californian restaurateur who has renovated it while maintaining its original appeal. Now it has air-conditioning in the main room, where the open kitchen includes a tandoor. On the terrace, marble-top café tables sit under a thick bower of trees and afford views of the Lamma Channel. The menu includes plenty of tasty appetizers (try smoked salmon in pesto), as well as sandwiches, soups, Indian dishes, and such Asian favorites as Hainan chicken and Thai smoked duck. ⊠ *121 Peak Rd.,* ☎ *2819–7868. Reservations essential for sea-view tables. AE, DC, MC, V.*

Wanchai

At lunchtime, Wanchai is just another jumble of people and not a particularly invigorating shopping area. But at night, Wanchai comes into its own. In Hong Kong Island's primary nightlife destination, fluorescent lights stretch endlessly along the roads jam-packed with taxis and people out for what will inevitably be a long night. Dining options are extreme—from fail-safe five-star hotel luxury to street-level eateries that are authentic and welcoming, with fine food.

Asian

CANTONESE

$$$–$$$$ ✕ **Dynasty.** Of the two entrances to this hotel restaurant, one takes you past a beautiful, two-floor chandelier to typically subdued Cantonese decor—beige tones, mirrors, unobtrusive fixtures. The beautiful crockery design, especially commissioned for the Hong Kong hotels (the New World hotel in Kowloon, the New World Harbour View hotel in Wanchai—both with a well-respected Dynasty restaurant) combines an art-deco feel with a Buddhist aesthetic. Palm trees and live traditional Chinese music provide a total contrast to the modernity on display outside the windows: neon signs advocating you buy Epson or Hitachi, and the Wanchai car ferry, lit up at night, traversing the harbor. Sections on the menu are devoted to soups, chicken, pigeon, duck, and beef. If you really want to push the boat out, try the braised imperial bird's nest with bamboo mushrooms and pigeon at HK$1,300. Definitely try the roast suckling pig—thin skins on top of tiny buns, although the melon balls served with this dish may present you with a real chopstick challenge. ⊠ *New World Harbour View, 1 Harbour Rd., ☎ 2802–8888. Reservations essential. AE, DC, MC, V.*

$$$ ✕ **One Harbour Road.** One of five dining options set in the opulent Grand Hyatt, this top-end Cantonese restaurant has typically muted cream decor but with added extras—a glass roof for a view of the stars at night and a two-tier layout that adds to the open feel. In the 1930s, after Shanghai's economic boom faded, many of its citizens came to Hong Kong to set up homes. One Harbour Road's design emulates the elegant, art deco–style of that period—you are even deposited in the restaurant by a circular brass elevator. The food is classic hotel Cantonese—it's very fresh and beautifully presented, but the delicate flavors of this authentic regional food can often seem bland. If you go for dim sum you can try many delicate and delicious little packages such as deep-fried taro or vegetable shrimp rolls. Also try the sauteed scallops with vegetables and sweetened walnuts. Ask for a single serving of lotus-leaf rice (in a large serving, the fragrance of the leaves can be lost on the rice inside). A selection of sauces, from XO sauce (made from preserved scallops and chili) to mustard and soy sauces mean you can perk up your dish if you so wish. For desserts, the unappealingly named deep-fried savory bean curd and the baked puff pastry filled with mashed red bean will convert you to both bean curd and red bean if you dare to order them. ⊠ *Grand Hyatt, 1 Harbour Rd., 7th and 8th Floors, ☎ 2588–1234, ext 7338. Reservations essential. AE, DC, MC, V.*

PAN-ASIAN

$$–$$$ ✕ **The Viceroy.** Mottled golden walls with murals, low-key music, and
★   a calming space with a harbor view make the Viceroy a good choice for an evening meal. In the summer, be sure to book ahead for a table on the veranda where you will feel the thrill of the Hong Kong skyline—huge neon lights and all. The menu is pan-Asian, primarily Indian with Thai and Indonesian dishes. *Kai hor bai teoy* (white-meat chicken in succulent parcels of pandanus leaves) is a favorite. The *kung kra borg* (juicy prawns wrapped in rice sheets with sweet and sour sauce) are superb. Even the humble samosas are royally presented, just two on a plate, virtually Japanese in presentation, with tamarind sauce. For a sticky dessert combine *gulab jamun* (balls of deep-fried milk pastry

soaked in sugar syrup and served warm) with a glass of Cointreau, a perfect accompaniment for this dish. E *Sun Hung Kai Centre, 30 Harbour Rd., 2nd Floor, P 2827–7777. Lunch reservations essential. AE, DC, MC, V.*

PEKINESE

$ ✕ **American Peking Restaurant.** Pekinese cuisine is made up of hearty, stick-to-the-ribs dishes suitable for the chilly climate of northern China (modern-day Beijing). An overdecorated restaurant full of red and gold fixtures, the American Peking has been a gastronomic amenity in Hong Kong for more than 40 years. Favorites here include hot-and-sour soup, fried and steamed dumplings, and delicious hot pots in winter. Also try the excellent beggar's chicken (so called because it's cooked in clay and lotus leaves), minced pigeon, and, of course, Peking duck. Every meal starts with complimentary peanuts and sliced cucumber in vinegar—for practicing your chopstick skills. (Don't confuse this with the American Cafe, which has branches all over town and is merely a fast-food chain.) ✉ *20 Lockhart Rd.,* ☎ *2527–7277 or 2527–7770. Weekend reservations essential. No credit cards.*

THAI

$ ✕ **Thai Delicacy.** This is a perennial favorite with lovers of inexpensive Thai, although there's little to make Thai Delicacy stand out except for its casual, friendly approach. The food is fine, an extensive menu gives you lots of choices, and little chili symbols are used to indicate the fieriness of each dish. They'll mellow the flavor if you ask. The *tom yung kung* (spicy prawn and coconut soup) is wonderful, as is the papaya salad. The decor incorporates the Thai equivalent of an angel in a variety of poses. Nothing is particularly fancy, but it's the low-key atmosphere, as well as the relatively low price tags that make this such a hub, and the babble of conversation makes for a convivial atmosphere. ✉ *44 Hennessy Rd.,* ☎ *2527–2598. DC, MC, V.*

VIETNAMESE

$ ✕ **Saigon Beach.** An absolute hole in the wall, this tiny place can seat only about 20, so avoid the rush hours unless you don't mind standing. The decor, an amalgam of fishing gear—cheap plastic hung from nets, and the like—folding chairs, and formica tables won't impress anyone. Instead, the extremely authentic Vietnamese fare and the jolly feeling of a little elbow-rubbing with the type of people who know that this is a find more than make up for the not quite prepossessing environs. ✉ *66 Lockhart Rd.,* ☎ *2529–7823. No credit cards.*

European

IRISH

$–$$ ✕ **Delaney's.** There's much more to recommend the authentic bent of this new Irish pub than Guinness on draft. The decor was imported lock, stock, and beer barrel from the Emerald Isle, there's live music by Irish lads, and the very tasty food is well-prepared. Leek and oatmeal soup is thick and satisfying enough to stave off a cold winter. The menu has good vegetarian choices, although there are two hearty—and meaty—Irish stews from which to choose. Very crowded immediately after offices empty for the night, Delaney's is a better option for lunch when things are less frantic: Dinner can be noisy. ✉ *One Capital Place, 18 Luard Rd., 2nd Floor,* ☎ *2804–2880. Reservations essential. AE.*

ITALIAN

$$$$ ✕ **Grissini.** As you enter this second-floor restaurant you'll overlook
★ the magnificent, some say over-the-top, Grand Hyatt lobby. The trompe l'oeil floor makes your eyes boggle and emphasizes the art-

deco-meets-Tuscan-villa feel. The restaurant specializes in Northern Italian cuisine. It's expensive, but you are rewarded with exceptionally fresh and delicate flavors—even the humble tomato and mozzarella salad with olive paste is wonderful. Veal carpaccio is combined with a tuna sauce, salmon carpaccio with cranberries, and beef carpaccio with bulgur wheat and truffle oil. You can choose pastas such as ravioli *zucca tarfufati con ricotta affumicate* (pumpkin in ravioli with truffles and smoked ricotta), fish (panfried fillet of sole with fennel, capers, and black olive paste), or meat (rack of lamb with garlic and thyme). The desserts can be anything from strawberries marinated in balsamic vinegar with a savory mint sorbet to chocolate pistachio truffle with a "dialogue of sauces" to a small, smooth serving of tiramisù. There's a fine Italian wine list to choose from as you gaze through the huge floor-to-ceiling windows—ask for a window table with a view toward Central—but don't leave before trying one of the grappas, served with ceremony from a selection of curvaceous bottles that have nicknames like the UFO. ⊠ *Grand Hyatt, 1 Harbour Rd., Wanchai. 2588-1234. Reservations essential. AE, DC, MC, V.*

Causeway Bay

An absolute phenomenon on a Saturday afternoon, Causeway Bay, host to a series of large Japanese department stores, is one of the city's busiest shopping destinations. Consequently, the density of the population can be overwhelming. There are several pubs in the vicinity, but they are not concentrated in one strip. Likewise, there are several good restaurants, but to the uninitiated, they can be hard to find. Times Square, a huge, modern shopping mall, has four floors in one of its towers devoted to restaurants, nearly all of which offer reliably good food, from Korean to Thai, American and French steak houses, and regional Chinese.

Asian

CHIU CHOW

$$ ✕ **Chiu Chow Garden.** Seafood-based Chiu Chow cuisine originated in the area around Swatow on the China coast and is popular among Chinese gourmets, though little known outside of East Asia. Service in this spacious, well-lit restaurant tends to be slow, and getting a waiter who speaks English is not always easy, but the food is delicious. Try Iron Buddha tea (served in thimble-size cups and packed with caffeine), cold roast goose on a bed of fried blood (far better than it sounds), Fukien abalone in light ginger sauce, and exquisite sautéed shrimp and crabmeat balls served over crispy prawn crackers. There are branches of Chiu Chow Garden in Jardine House and at Vicwood Plaza, on Hong Kong Island. ⊠ *Hennessy Centre, 500 Hennessy Rd.,* ☎ *2577–3391. AE, DC, MC, V.*

JAPANESE

$$$ ✕ **Isshin.** Of the many restaurants in the Times Square dining tower, this is the only Japanese place, and it's interesting as much for the decor as for the food. A basic sushi combination of 10 pieces plus a tuna roll may not be cheap, but each is prepared to perfection. But the best thing about Isshin is the variety of smaller items offered, which could qualify as a rarefied dim-sum menu. Soybean soup with mushrooms has a sharp, full-bodied flavor, and the three pieces of deep-fried bean curd in soup are a rare experience: The crisp batter is garnished with translucent shavings of fish, and the tofu interior melts in your mouth. ⊠ *Times Square, 13th Floor,* ☎ *2506–2220. AE, DC, MC, V.*

$$ ✕ **Szechuan Lau.** Lovers of spicy, garlicky Szechuan food have come
★ to this no-frills-but-comfortable restaurant for many years. The place
is always packed with both locals and visitors, and the noisy chatter
of diners is part of the fun. Popular picks are hot garlic eggplant,
smoked duck, and prawns in hot peppers on a sizzling platter. Small
portions are available and advisable, so that you can taste more dishes.
The staff is accustomed to Western guests. ✉ *466 Lockhart Rd.,* ☎
2891–9027. AE, MC, V.

Repulse Bay

Repulse Bay's beach is one of the longest and cleanest in the territory.
An exhilarating 20-minute bus ride from Central, the Repulse Bay Hotel,
demolished in 1982 and rebuilt as a luxury residential building, has
several quality eateries and shops.

European
ENGLISH

$$$ ✕ **The Verandah.** A great way to pass half a day is to wander in to
this colonial relic and take afternoon tea (on Sundays and public hol-
idays only). Your finger sandwiches, scones, and pastries are accompanied by a choice of Fortnum and Mason blends (orange pekoe,
Darjeeling, Earl Grey, Lapsang Souchong), Verveine tea from "La Ti-
sanerie," or coffee, all in heavy, classic silver service. Alternatively, turn
up for the Sunday brunch (11 AM–2:30 PM) for a full buffet of fruit,
pancakes, and other morning fare. The high ceilings, balustrades,
wooden fixtures, and huge windows hark back to Raffles in Singapore, and the relaxed feel is a welcome relief from the rigors of Hong
Kong's city life. ✉ *109 Repulse Bay Rd.,* ☎ *2812–2722. AE, DC,
MC, V.*

Stanley Village

Asian
PAN-ASIAN

$$–$$$ ✕ **Stanley's Oriental.** Designed like an eastern version of an Old Quar-
ter house in New Orleans, complete with ornate balconies and ceiling
fans, Stanley's Oriental has a menu that marries Eastern and Western
cuisines, matching Cajun and Creole with Thai, Indian, and Japanese.
Try Thai curry or Cajun blackfish. Views of Stanley Bay are an additional pleasure. For a little romance, reserve a table on an upper level
overlooking the water. ✉ *90B Stanley Main St.,* ☎ *2813–9988. AE,
DC, MC, V.*

European
CONTINENTAL

$$ ✕ **Lucy's.** Run by local catering whiz Lucy Humbert, this addition
to the Stanley dining scene is done in brushed yellow paint, rattan
chairs, and bright fabrics on cushions and sofas. The menu may not
be extensive, but quality is high and prices are low. Soups are
always a good start, and try fish cakes or tagliatelle with salmon in
vodka sauce. Each is well-prepared, delicious, and presented with
the little touch that makes you feel like someone cares. ✉ *64 Stan-
ley Main St. (just behind Park 'n' Shop),* ☎ *2813–9055. AE, DC,
MC, V.*

$–$$$ ✕ **Tables 88.** It's worth a visit here just to see if you can make sense
of the abstract wall designs, zebra-skin booths, and avant-garde fur-
niture that would take a forklift to move (the owners gutted the inside
of one of the few remaining historic buildings, a Stanley police station

circa 1854). The menu is vast—an entire page is devoted to the post-dinner cheese selection. The tree-trunk bar is a great place for a quick pick-me-up: After a hot slog around Stanley Market, if you're not in the mood for a meal, you could just pop in for a drink. ⊠ *88 Stanley Village Rd.,* ☎ *2813–6262. AE, DC, MC, V.*

FRENCH

$$–$$$ ✕ **Stanley's French Restaurant.** Enter under the flags (one bearing a
★ Chinese bear, one with the words LIBERTE AND PATRIE emblazoned on it, and you will be transported. Elegant dips and hors d'oeuvres arrive unbidden, and the daily menu chalked up on a board gives you a glimpse of what will be one of your best meals in the territory. One of the dishes you may be treated to is warm scallop salad with balsamico. The extraordinarily delicately fried—and flavored—scallops melt in your mouth. Guinea fowl with salad and pumpkin in a grapefruit and ginger sauce is a superb combination. There's a good selection of New World wines, and you can indulge in cheeses from Cannes and perhaps smoke a cigar. The pink walls, comfy rattan chairs, and plants hanging in brass pots create a nostalgic feel. There is no music—just the sound of people enjoying themselves. Needless to say, the restaurant is full every night of the week. ⊠ *86–88 Stanley Main St.,* ☎ *2813–8873 or 2813–9721. Reservations essential. AE, DC, MC, V.*

Quarry Bay

Hardly a tourist destination, this commercial and residential area has finally been treated to a few neighborhood restaurants to satisfy the needs of the locals with a penchant for exotic foods and businesspeople who want to take out clients without having to go all the way into town. Should you find yourself here after a tram ride, there are now several good eateries to choose from, all found in a quadrangle of streets—Hoi Kwong Street, Hoi Tai Street, Hoi Wan Street, and Tong Chong Street.

Australian

$$ ✕ **The Continental.** The design of this little gem is clean and simple,
★ and it feels airy despite its size. A deli counter is crammed with goodies, and shelves are lined with handmade chutneys and vegetables. The menu is short and changes quarterly. Daily homemade specials—such as carrot or mushroom soups, pasta, grilled polenta stacked with feta, spinach, and roasted peppers, or orange and poppy-seed cake—are all fabulous, as is the coffee. ⊠ *Shop 2A, 2 Hoi Wan St., Ground Floor,* ☎ *2563–2209. AE, MC, V.*

Shek O

Shek O is a long way, but it is a good bet for tourists who don't mind a bit of traveling for an adventurous meal. Once you've undertaken the journey—the longest one possible from Central on Hong Kong Island—you'll be in need of some sustenance. Shek O is tiny, but the little seaside village boasts a few decent open-air restaurants.

Asian
CHINESE-THAI

$ ✕ **Shek O Thai–Chinese Place.** There's nothing particularly outstanding in decor or food here, but the Shek O Thai–Chinese Place is a legend in its own dinner time—it's just such *fun*. People arrive *en masse* on the weekend and sit for hours, despite the relentless summer heat. The curious Thai-Chinese hybrid cuisine means there's plenty of rice, noodles, and fish dishes. The *tom yung kung* (spicy prawn and coconut soup) is always guaranteed to bring color to your cheeks, the green curry is a safe chicken choice, and the honey-fried squid is a must. While it may not be something to write home about, the friendly holiday ambience is a real winner, and you can eat royally without breaking the bank. ⊠ *Main corner of Shek O next to bus stop,* ☎ *2908–4426. Reservations required on weekends. No credit cards.*

International

$$ ✕ **Black Sheep.** This unpretentious, slightly offbeat place was opened by an artist, and it shows. There's a lot of *stuff* on the walls; look for the mounted chair, lamp, and clock. The changing menu—and music—is a mix of African (such as spicy pumpkin and squash soup), vegetarian (savory stuffed eggplant), crowd-pleasers (tasty lamb chops and salmon), and novelty items (vegetarian Mooncake). The place attracts a lot of locals who hang around until there's a free table, so call ahead if you're making a special trip from a distant district. ⊠ *Directions for Shek O location: from Shek O village, turn left at Thai restaurant by small traffic circle; Black Sheep is down road and around corner on right,* ☎ *2809–2021. AE, MC, V.*

KOWLOON

Parts of Kowloon are among the most densely populated areas on the planet, and there's a corresponding abundance of dining opportunities. Many of the hotels, located here for the view of Hong Kong Island (spectacular at night), have excellent restaurants, although they're uniformly expensive. On the street you may have much luck just being adventurous and walking into places on spec, though you take your chances. Some of the best finds are, however, in the back streets, where immigrants from all over Asia have brought with them their Vietnamese, Indonesian, or Thai cooking skills.

Asian
CANTONESE

$$$$ ✕ **Chinese Restaurant.** It takes some nerve to claim to be *the* Chinese restaurant in Hong Kong, but this one gets away with it. A postmodern interior is a new take on the traditional 1920s teahouse, and subdued lighting creates a mellow atmosphere. The talented kitchen staff's innovative Cantonese cooking is what makes the place stand out. The menu changes seasonally, though some oft-ordered items—papaya soup, crispy chicken skin, and stewed goose in brown ginger gravy—are always available and worth tasting. Peking duck here is out of this world, as is braised abalone on a bed of artichoke hearts. ⊠ *Hyatt Regency Hotel, 67 Nathan Rd.,* ☎ *2311–1234. Reservations essential. Jacket and tie. AE, DC, MC, V.*

$$$$ ✕ **Lai Ching Heen.** The name of this truly luxurious Cantonese restaurant means, quite appropriately, "In the Regent, where you'll be very happy." Tucked away in the lower level of the Regent Hotel, the subtly decorated dining room has a stunning view of the Harbour near sea level. Opulent table settings include ivory chopsticks and curved jade spoons. Each patron is welcomed with a complimentary appetizer that represents the yin and yang: Mild slivers of deep-fried fish are dressed with tart vinegar, the contrasting but complementary tastes signifying balance and harmony. Special menus for each month of the Chinese lunar calendar feature fresh steamed seafood dishes and seasonal Chinese fruits and vegetables. The most popular dishes are braised abalone with oyster sauce, deep-fried scallops and pears, and braised shark fins in brown sauce. The food at Lai Ching Heen is some of the most highly regarded by Hong Kong's culinary critics. ⊠ *Regent Hotel, 18 Salisbury Rd.,* ☎ *2721–1211. Reservations essential. Jacket and tie. AE, DC, MC, V.*

CHINESE VEGETARIAN

$$ ✕ **Bodhi Vegetarian.** This small chain of restaurants offers some of the best Chinese vegetarian food in Hong Kong. The diverse selection of dishes will probably be a pleasant surprise to Westerners—even vegetarians. A wide array of vegetables, dozens of varieties of mushrooms, bird's nests, and noodles are often combined with tofu, prepared to suggest meat or fish. Try deep-fried taro (a potato-like vegetable) or stir-fried Chinese vegetables. Buddhist scrolls decorating the walls emphasize the philosophical roots of the menu. No alcohol is served. ⊠ *56 Cameron Rd.,* ☎ *2739–2222. AE, DC, MC, V.*

INDONESIAN

$ ✕ **Bali Restaurant.** This strange little place is a good bet for an inexpensive way to explore the delights of Indonesian cuisine. The traditional dishes—*nasi goreng* (fried rice with egg) and *gado gado* (salad with peanut dressing)—are there, but there's a whole section of noodles and curries. The curries tend to be tempered with coconut milk so they're mild and creamy. Service is pretty much a family affair, and you should wave your arms about for attention if they are all busy chatting. It's rarely completely packed, but cozy and well-worn booths can ensure a bit of privacy (although the lurid red color may not tempt you to stay too long). Off the beaten path and hardly what you'd call posh dining, Bali is nevertheless an interesting option. ⊠ *10 Nanking Rd., Jordan, Tsim Sha Tsui,* ☎ *2780–2902. No credit cards.*

JAPANESE

$$$$ ✕ **Imasa.** Although not designed by Philippe Starck (unlike Felix in the Peninsula's extension) Imasa's design is along similar lines: The warm walnut veneer keeps the tone from becoming too formal, the lines are clean without being rigid. An excellent way to sample the menu is to try the monthly seasonal banquet, or *kaiseki* (around HK$700– HK$1,000). Begin with the cold saki delivered in an elegant glass teapot with delicate glasses. The winter menu starts with an appetizer of grilled lily bulb with sea urchin, deep fried whitefish (which looks like snow), broad beans steamed with sake—all served in teeny portions, but wonderfully exciting. The winter soup is like the commonly known miso but this time with green-color broad-bean curd and a pungent herb (*sansho,* or mountain pepper, also known as Japanese pepper to the rest of the world) plus bamboo and seaweed. Grilled silver cod teriyaki, crab croquette in the shell with sesame sauce, and Kobe beef (often referred to as marbled beef) marinated overnight in miso with Japanese radish salad are all delicious. For the last dish of noodles, try the green-tea buckwheat noodle or the *inaniwa udon* (thin white noodles), both of which arrive in soup. Fresh seasonal ingredients are flown in from Japan and you can ask for table-side preparation of the sushi or tempura dishes. The truly remarkable presentation of the dishes makes each meal unique. ⊠ *The Peninsula, Salisbury Rd., Kowloon,* ☎ *2316–3175. AE, DC, MC, V.*

$$$$ ✕ **Sagano Restaurant.** Impeccable service, a panoramic view of Hong Kong Harbour, a sushi bar with fresh fish imported exclusively from Japan, and a teppanyaki counter where chefs chop and cook on the spot have made this into what is probably the most popular Japanese restaurant in Hong Kong. Kansai cuisine, from the region around Kyoto, is characterized by light sauces and the use of fresh ingredients. Seasonal dishes should always be considered. Save room for the special house dessert, plum sherbet, and sample the liqueured ginger cocktail. ⌧ *Hotel Nikko, 72 Mody Rd.,* ☎ *2739–1111. Reservations essential. AE, DC, MC, V.*

KOREAN

$ ✕ **Three-Five Korean Restaurant.** A genuine treasure, this tiny but impressive eatery is tucked away on a minor Tsim Sha Tsui street. Inside it's sparsely decorated, spotlessly clean, and a trifle cramped; but the food makes up for any of the other shortcomings. Westerners typically order beef, ribs, chicken, or fish barbecues that you cook yourself at the table, but classic dishes such as *gopdol bibim bap* (beef, egg, tofu, and vegetables served over rice sizzling in a hot stone bowl) or *jap chae* (beef or chicken strips and vegetables with rice vermicelli in a delicious, slightly sweet, brown sauce) are delightful. These are accompanied by many small dishes of Korean specialties, such as bean curd, marinated vegetables, dried anchovies, bean sprouts, and the traditional *kimchi* (cabbage preserved in brine, with black beans, red peppers, and a delightful use of garlic). ⌧ *6 Ashley Rd.,* ☎ *2376–2993. No credit cards.*

SHANGHAI

$–$$ ✕ **Great Shanghai Restaurant.** This restaurant isn't esteemed for its decor (which is old and dingy), but it's an excellent spot for culinary adventurers and for those who prefer the bold flavors of Shanghai food to the more delicate flavors of local Cantonese fare. You may not be ready for the sea blubber or braised turtle with sugar candy, but do try one of the boneless eel dishes, Shanghai-style yellow-fish soup, beggar's chicken, or the excellent spiced and soy duck. ⌧ *26 Prat Ave.,* ☎ *2366–8158 or 2366–2683. AE, DC, MC, V.*

European

CONTINENTAL

$$$$ ✕ **Hugo's.** A Kowloon Hyatt showpiece since it opened in 1969, Hugo's manages to be cozy even in the grand space that it occupies. Strolling minstrels and complimentary roses and cigars are some of the extras that make this place a favorite, especially for celebratory dinners. The food is renowned, and for good reason. Lobster bisque and prime rib are superb, with exceptional rack of lamb in onion-and-potato crust with juniper-berry cream and salmon and scallops baked in flaky pastry with mango and spinach attaining an even higher level. Go to Hugo's for romantic candlelight at night or a terrific Sunday brunch. ⌧ *Hyatt Regency Hong Kong, 67 Nathan Rd.,* ☎ *2311–1234. Jacket and tie. AE, DC, MC, V.*

FRENCH

$$$$ ✕ **Felix.** The flagship of the Peninsula Hotel's new extension—designed by Philippe Starck—Felix is perched on the 28th floor just beneath a helipad. At night, views looking over to Hong Kong Island through the floor-to-ceiling glass wall are breathtaking. Every nook and cranny in this ultramodern dining space was touched by the French designer, creating a wonderful and fascinating environment for dining. The food, of course, is just as spectacular. The Hawaiian chef boldly mixes some odd ingredients but the results are as fascinating as they are successful. Peppered foie gras served with ginger payaya and Thai chili broth would make purists faint away at the mere sound such sacrilege, but the challenging combination is a winner. Pernod smoked wild salmon may sound flat on the menu, but the results are also superlative. The entrée of citrus-miso seared wild salmon is cooked to flaky perfection and served on sweet potato with ginger. The lobster and sea scallops includes water chestnuts, the Szechuan peppered grilled filet of beef comes with a heavenly black-truffle herb sauce. Things tend to get busy after 9 PM. ⊠ *Peninsula Hotel, Salisbury Rd., 28th Floor,* ☎ *2366–6251. DC, MC, V.*

$$$$ ✕ **Gaddi's.** The classiest lunch or dinner venue in Hong Kong for the last 40 years—completely refurbished in 1994—Gaddi's reputation is as grand as that of the Peninsula Hotel in which it thrives. With huge chandeliers made in Paris and salvaged from wartime Shanghai, ankle-deep Tai Ping carpets that match the napery, and a priceless Chinese coromandel screen made in 1670 for the emperor's summer palace in Beijing, the decor is sumptuous, to say the least. Service is also superlative. The menu changes frequently, but always offered is the exquisite soufflé, a favorite liberally laced with Grand Marnier. Tasteful live music accompanies a magnificent wine list. ⊠ *Peninsula Hotel, Salisbury Rd.,* ☎ *2366–6251, ext. 3989. Reservations essential. Jacket and tie. AE, DC, MC, V.*

$$$ ✕ **Au Trou Normand.** For 30 years this haven has offered diners a chance
★   to hide away in a typical French farmhouse—not an easy thing to arrange in the middle of bustling Tsim Sha Tsui. Red-checked tablecloths, a dark wood mantlepiece, and candlelight on shiny copper utensils create the atmosphere. At this marvelous retreat, you can be certain you're getting a series of authentic Gallic tastes. Tournedos Rossini is topped with Strasbourg pâté, rack of lamb lies in a tangy Dijon mustard sauce, and chicken in Madeira sauce is a delight. Also among the many selections are long established favorites such as silky mousses, savory terrines, and veal and kidney dishes. ⊠ *6 Carnarvon Rd.,* ☎ *2366–8754. Jacket and tie. AE, DC, MC, V.*

$$–$$$ ✕ **La Brasserie.** What might have been a boring basement coffee shop has here been cleverly changed into a charming French bistro, with lots of plants, etched glass, and framed prints of cartoon chefs engaged in various antics. Live music is supplied by an accordionist, and the chef's daily menu is written on a large mirror that's wheeled to your table. French provincial cooking is the draw, with fresh crabmeat ravioli or salmon marinated in lime and olive oil appetizers and outstanding bouillabaisse using local seafood. Strangely enough, this is one of the better places in town to find California wine. ⊠ *Omni Marco Polo Hotel, Harbour City, Canton Rd.,* ☎ *2736–0888, ext. 113. AE, DC, MC, V.*

ITALIAN

$$–$$$ ✕ **Tutto Bene.** The food here is trattoria in style, that is, geared to light
★   meals but with generous portions. The pizzas are great, and pastas come in a variety of shapes and colors (with squid-ink pappardelle and linguine). Vegetable fritters are fried in unbelievably light batter. One of the best things about this spot, second to the food, is that there are two areas in which to dine alfresco: in front on the terrace, or in back, behind the kitchen in a quaint garden setting. It's hard to find, so here's some help: Walk up Nathan Road away from the Star Ferry and turn right on Granville Road; turn left on Carnarvon Road and walk to the end, where you'll see a brick path leading up a hill—it looks like it's heading into a parking lot. At the top, turn right onto Knutsford Terrace. ⊠ *7 Knutsford Terr.,* ☎ *316–2116. AE, DC, MC, V.*

$$–$$$ ✕ **Valentino Ristorante Italiano.** This romantic hideaway found right in the middle of the otherwise bustling Tsim Sha Tsui district lies behind a marble facade and a doorway flanked by potted cedar trees. Pastel decor includes framed posters of 1920s movie star Valentino. There's a wide variety of pizza and pasta; try fettuccine with scallops. Macau sole grilled in lemon butter and Italian herbs, any of the tempting veal dishes, and the chef's daily specials are also good choices. There is plenty of room between tables—a rare commodity in Hong Kong. ✉ *16 Hanoi Rd.,* ☎ *2721–6449. AE, DC, MC, V.*

North American
CALIFORNIAN

$$–$$$ ✕ **San Francisco Steak House.** For more than 20 years, this mock Barbary Coast eatery has been pleasing both locals and travelers with a combination of casual Bay Area atmosphere—dark paneled walls, red flocked wallpaper, and replicas of Powell Street cable cars—and American fare. The clam chowder is an original Boston recipe, and the cioppino is what you'd expect at Fisherman's Wharf. American Angus steaks are treated with the respect good meat deserves. Also excellent is the Canadian salmon, served as a whole baked baby coho. You can always ask for a burger; they're the best in town. All portions are very generous. ✉ *Harbour City, Canton Rd.,* ☎ *2735–7576. AE, DC, MC, V.*

OUTLYING AREAS

Lamma Island

Relatively easy to get to, Lamma Island is served by ferries from Central's ferry pier approximately once an hour. Yung Shue Wan, where you disembark, has a collection of local seafood restaurants, one or two Western ones, and an odd assortment of shops.

Asian
CANTONESE

$ ✕ **Lancombe.** This Cantonese seafood restaurant is Lamma's best source for no-nonsense food at no-nonsense prices. The huge English/Cantonese menu features seafood, seafood, and more seafood. Try deep-fried squid, garoupa (local fish) in sweet corn sauce, broccoli in garlic, and beef with black beans. Dishes come in three sizes; the small is sufficient for most. Go through the front of the restaurant via the kitchen (don't loiter, they're busy in there!) to the terrace out back, where you'll have a view of the sea and distant Peng Chau Island. ✉ *47 Main St., Yung Shue Wan,* ☎ *2982–0881. No credit cards.*

International

$ ✕ **Deli Lamma.** This trendy but laid-back joint has more style than any other place on Lamma—with a designer bar made from old doors suspended from the ceiling on heavy chains, and backgammon and chess boards painted on long tables along one wall, encouraging lazy afternoons with endless cups of coffee. Choose your fancy from two blackboards that will bear up to seven choices of pasta and "world" food such as Thai fish curry, Mexican chili crêpes, or Mediterranean *tumbet.* Yummy slabs of fresh garlic bread or salad come with your order. Service is low-key, competent, and friendly. ✉ *36 Main St., Ground Floor, Yung Shue Wan,* ☎ *2982–1583. No credit cards.*

4 Lodging

SINCE THE EARLY 1990S HONG KONG'S SUPPLY of hotel rooms has steadily fallen behind the demand for them, a situation which will be particularly problematic in 1997, when many people would like to visit the territory as it passes from British to Chinese rule. Hotels long ago blocked off the weeks around the actual handover on June 30, of course, but there are likely to be many other times when Hong Kong is fully booked—and visitors without proof of accommodation could be refused entry. As things stood at the end of 1996 there were about 33,400 rooms in 86 hotels and hostels, while visitor arrivals for the year were expected to exceed 9.5 million. There are various hotels on the drawing boards and under construction, but none are scheduled to be completed until 1998, and it will take longer to compensate for the loss of such hotels as the Hilton, Victoria, and Lee Gardens, which were torn down in favor of office buildings or converted into apartments.

Hong Kong is certainly not for budget travelers. Most of the hotels provide deluxe or first-class accommodations and facilities, so it is not surprising that so many rooms are in the higher price categories. The best charge close to US$300 and even if you are in a group tour, expect to pay at least US$100 a night for a hotel room of normal international standards. For that price, you probably won't have a prime location, but you will have reliable facilities—bathrooms with hot and cold running water, color TV, radio, telephone, same-day valet laundry service, room service, secretarial service, safe deposit box, refrigerator and minibar, and air-conditioning. Most hotels also have at least one restaurant and bar, a travel and tour-booking desk, and limousine or car rental.

Of course, Hong Kong *is* a business executive's paradise. Most major hotels have business centers that provide secretarial, translation, courier, telex, fax, and printing services—even personal computers. Charges vary from hotel to hotel, but typing should cost HK$40 to HK$60 a page, shorthand work HK$200 to HK$250 per hour, and computer rental HK$150 to HK$250 per hour. Each hotel prints a business tariff list, so check prices before hiring. Many hotels have ballrooms, and most have smaller meeting rooms. For an overview of Hong Kong meeting, convention, and incentive facilities, contact the **Convention and Incentive Department** (✉ Hong Kong Tourist Association, 10/F, Citicorp Centre, 18 Whitfield Rd., North Point, Hong Kong Island, ☎ 2807–6543).

Most hotels also offer special perks to business travelers: Regency Club floors at the Hyatt Regency, the Sheraton Club International, the Six Continents Club at the Furama Kempinski, the Regal Club and Holiday Inn's Executive Club. Typically these executive floors have extra concierge services, complimentary breakfasts and cocktails, and a place where guests can meet with their business contacts. Some hotels have office extras in the rooms; for instance, the Ramada Renaissance has fax machines and modem outlets in all suites and executive floor rooms.

Book your rooms well in advance for a trip to Hong Kong. With fewer hotels and more visitors, rooms will be scarce, especially in June and July as well as during the traditional high seasons of March and September through early December. Where available, we have provided toll-free numbers for making reservations from the United States.

The following hotels are all members of the **Hong Kong Tourist Association,** which publishes a *Hotel Guide,* listing members' rates, services, and facilities. The brochure is published once a year, making it at least one price hike behind the current situation. The HKTA does not arrange hotel reservations. The Hong Kong Hotel Association (HKHA) does, at no extra charge, but only through its reservations office at Kai Tak International Airport, located immediately beyond the Customs area.

Choosing where to stay in Hong Kong depends on the purpose of your visit. Thanks to the two tunnels that run underneath the harbor, the Star Ferry, and the Mass Transit Railway (MTR) subway, it no longer matters whether you stay "Hong Kong–side" or "Kowloon-side": The other side will be only minutes away by MTR.

If you want to avoid the main tourist accommodation areas, there are a few places in the New Territories and outlying islands that provide alternatives, which are also generally less expensive than lodgings on Hong Kong Island or in Kowloon.

Our categories for hotel rates are based on the average price for a double room for two people. All rates are subject to a 10% service charge and a 5% government tax, which is used to fund the activities of the HKTA. Accommodations are listed by three geographical areas—Hong Kong Island, Kowloon, and New Territories and the Outer Islands—alphabetized within each price category.

The 800 numbers listed below are for use in the United States.

CATEGORY	COST*
$$$$	over HK$1,800 (US$230)
$$$	HK$1,200–HK$1,800 (US$155–US$230)
$$	HK$850–HK$1,200 (US$110–US$155)
$	under HK$850 (US$110)

All prices are for a double room, not including 10% service charge and 5% tax.

HONG KONG ISLAND

If you need to be near the city's financial hub, you'll prefer the Central district on Hong Kong Island. Central is as busy as New York City on weekdays, but, except for the Lan Kwai Fong area, it is quiet at night and on weekends. Wanchai, east of Central, was once a sailor's dream of "Suzie Wongs" and booze. It still has plenty of nightlife, but new office high-rises and the Convention and Exhibition Centre now draw businesspeople. Causeway Bay, farther east, is an ideal area for shopping or trying lots of different restaurants. Happy Valley is near the racetrack and Hong Kong Stadium, the territory's largest sports stadium. Hotels have also sprung up farther east along the MTR line in North Point and Taikoo Shing.

Central

$$$$ **Conrad International.** The first Conrad in Asia, this hotel opened in 1990 in a gleaming white oval-shaped tower rising from Pacific Place, an upscale complex on the edge of Central with a multistory mall of shops, theaters, restaurants, and convention space. The rooms, in the top 21 floors of the 61-story building, have dramatic views of the harbor and city. The Brasserie on the Eighth restaurant is very popular for its French fare and views of the park; Nicholini's is one of the city's top spots for Italian cuisine. The hotel also offers four floors of executive rooms, each containing fax machines, modems, and exercise machines, a well-equipped business center, and one of Hong Kong's largest fitness centers. ⌧ *Pacific Place, 88 Queensway,* ☎ *2521–3838 or*

800/445–8667, ℻ *2521–3888. 513 rooms. 4 restaurants, 3 bars, pool, health club, business services. AE, DC, MC, V.*

$$$$ ⌘ **Island Shangri-La.** Like the Conrad, this hotel opened in 1990 in ★ one the taller towers of Pacific Place's complex of shops, offices, restaurants, and cinemas. Built by Shangri-La International, a leading Asian group that also owns the Shangri-La in Kowloon, the hotel has the highest standards of furnishings, decor, and service. The 565 spacious guest rooms, between the 39th and 56th floors, have views of either the Peak or Victoria Harbour. The lobby and lounge share a 25-foot-high picture window, and the atrium in the upper floors has a 14-story mural depicting the Great Wall of China and the mountains around it. The top floor has fantastic views and two marvelous facilities: Cyrano, an intimate music room where guests can hear visiting cabaret artists, and Petrus, an exclusive French restaurant with its own signature wines and the atmosphere of a European club. The Lobster Bar is a clubby, lobby-side retreat that serves seafood for lunch and dinner. The pool and health club on the eighth floor overlook Hong Kong Park. ⌂ *2 Pacific Place, 88 Queensway,* ☎ *2877–3838 or 800/942–5050,* ℻ *2521–8742. 565 rooms. 4 restaurants, 1 lounge, 4 no-smoking floors, pool, barbershop, beauty salon, health club, shops, cinema, business services. AE, DC, MC, V.*

$$$$ ⌘ **J. W. Marriott.** This American-style hotel was the first to open at Pacific Place. A box-shaped building, it has an extravagant glass-walled atrium lobby filled with plants and featuring a cascading waterfall. Rooms have harbor and mountain views and endless amenities, including data ports for modem or fax machines and 50 pay movies on demand. J. W.'s serves popular California cuisine, and flexible function rooms suitable for a variety of events are convenient for business travelers. ⌂ *Pacific Place, 88 Queensway,* ☎ *2810–8366 or 800/228–9290,* ℻ *2845–0737. 575 rooms, 29 suites. 3 restaurants, pool, barbershop, beauty salon, health club, business services. AE, DC, MC, V.*

$$$$ ⌘ **Mandarin Oriental.** Celebrated by travel writers as one of the world's ★ great hotels, the Mandarin Oriental represents Hong Kong's high end, serving the well-heeled and the business elite since 1963. It is a handsome landmark, with balconies off most rooms—although many of them have lost a harbor view as reclamation has moved the hotel back from the waterfront—and an entrance designed to suggest London-elite. The vast lobby, decorated with Asian antiques, has a live band playing in the mezzanine Clipper Lounge early in the evening. Comfortable guest rooms are decorated with antique maps and prints, and a complimentary plate of fresh fruit welcomes you upon arrival. Mah Wah, on the 25th floor, serves Cantonese cuisine in a genteel atmosphere; the Pierrot serves fine French food. Centrally located beside the Star Ferry concourse, the Mandarin is rightfully the hotel of choice for many celebrities and VIPs. ⌂ *5 Connaught Rd.,* ☎ *2522–0111 or 800/526–6566,* ℻ *2810–6190. 489 rooms, 58 suites. 4 restaurants, 3 bars, indoor pool, barbershop, beauty salon, health club, business services. AE, DC, MC, V.*

$$$$ ⌘ **Ritz-Carlton.** Opened in 1993, the Ritz occupies the prime block be-★ tween Chater Road and Connaught Road right next to the Furama Kempinski. Its exterior recalls art deco New York, while the interior has an elegant, refined atmosphere created by European antiques and reproductions mixed with Oriental accents. Everything from Chippendale-style furniture to gilt-frame mirrors is spotless and shining. The large guest rooms, all with marble bath, honor bar, and Colonial-style rosewood furniture, overlook either Victoria Harbour or Chater Garden. The main restaurant, Toscana, serves Northern Italian cuisine. There

are also Chinese and Japanese restaurants; Cossacks, a vodka bar; and a lounge serving breakfast, lunch, and high tea. The new Executive Business Center has Internet and E-mail access as well as computer workstations and color printer hookups. ⊠ *Connaught Rd.,* ☎ *2877–6666 or 800/241–3333,* FAX *2877–6778. 189 rooms, 27 suites. 4 restaurants, bar, 3 no-smoking floors, pool, health club, shops. AE, DC, MC. V.*

$$$ 🏨 **Furama Kempinski.** A facade decorated with scenes from the court of Imperial Peking distinguish this elegant, but businesslike hotel in the heart of Central. (Although the hotel is no longer managed by Germany's Kempinski group, the group continues to handle reservations.) For beautiful views of either Chater Garden and the Peak or City Hall and Victoria Harbour, ask for a room above the 17th floor. The revolving rooftop restaurant and bar offers the ultimate panorama, as well as a spectacular daily lunch and dinner buffet of Chinese, Japanese, and Western dishes. On the ground floor, a bakery sells delicious snacks to famished shoppers. ⊠ *1 Connaught Rd.,* ☎ *2525–5111 or 800/426–3135,* FAX *2845–9339. 474 rooms, 43 suites. 5 restaurants, 2 no-smoking floors, barbershop, beauty salon, health club, shops, business services. AE, DC, MC, V.*

Midlevels

$$ 🏨 **Bishop Lei International House.** Owned and operated by the Catholic diocese, this is the first hotel in this part of the Midlevels residential area. Rooms are what you would expect from a good hostel, and the clientele tends to be church groups, academics, and students. It has a fully equipped business center, a workout room, a rooftop pool, and a restaurant serving Chinese and Western meals. ⊠ *4 Robinson Rd.,* ☎ *2868–0828,* FAX *2868–1551. 207 rooms. Restaurant, pool, exercise room, business services. AE, DC, MC, V.*

$$ 🏨 **Garden View International House.** This attractive hotel on a hill over-
★   looking the botanical gardens, Government House, and the harbor, is about a five-minute drive from Central. It has well-designed rooms that make excellent use of small, irregular shapes and emphasize the picture windows. There is a coffee shop serving European and Asian dishes. Guests can also use the swimming pool and gymnasium in the adjoining YWCA, which owns the hotel. ⊠ *1 MacDonnell Rd.,* ☎ *2877–3737,* FAX *2845–6263. 131 rooms. Coffee shop, pool, business services. AE, DC, MC, V.*

Wanchai

$$$$ 🏨 **Grand Hyatt.** No expense was spared in building this opulent, black-marble-faced hotel, which adjoins the Hong Kong Convention Centre. On the Wanchai waterfront, the facility has fabulous views. The hotel's restaurants are notable: Grissini serves superb Northern Italian food; One Harbour Road could be the most elegant Cantonese garden-style restaurant in town; and Kaetsu specializes in Japanese Edo cuisine. The restaurants are very popular with locals, who also line up to get into JJ's, the nightclub and disco. Art deco touches enhance the marble-clad, greenery-filled lobby and the ballroom, reminiscent of Old World Europe. Seventy percent of the guest rooms have harbor views, while those remaining overlook the pool and garden. The Hyatt and the New World Harbour View share a vast recreation deck on the 11th floor with pools, gardens, a golf driving range, tennis courts, and health club facilities. Suites have compact disc and laser disc players, fax and step machines, and bathroom TV. ⊠ *1 Harbour Rd.,* ☎ *2588– 1234 or 800/233–1234,* FAX *2802–0677. 572 rooms. 4 restaurants, 2 lounges, pool, beauty salon, driving range, 2 tennis courts, nightclub. AE, DC, MC, V.*

$$$ 🏨 **Century.** This 23-story Wanchai hotel, opened in 1992, is ideal for conventioneers—it's a five-minute walk by covered overpass (a lifesaver in steamy summer months) from the convention center and the MTR. Rooms are modern, with wooden furniture painted in pastels. One restaurant and the bar take advantage of the building's corner location, with picture windows looking out on the busy street. There is a health club with an open-air pool, a gymnasium, and a golf driving bay. ✉ *238 Jaffe Rd.,* ☎ *2598–8888,* 𝔽𝔸𝕏 *2598–8866. 486 rooms, 25 suites. 4 restaurants, bar, pool, health club, shops, business services. AE, DC, MC, V.*

$$$ 🏨 **Luk Kwok.** This contemporary hotel-and-office tower designed by Hong Kong's leading architect Remo Riva has replaced the Wanchai landmark of the same name immortalized in Richard Mason's novel, *The World of Suzie Wong.* Luk Kwok's appeal is its proximity to the Convention Centre, the Academy for Performing Arts, and the Arts Centre. Room decor is clean and simple, with contemporary furniture; higher floors afford mountain or city views. It has a good Chinese restaurant but no bar. ✉ *72 Gloucester Rd.,* ☎ *2866–2166,* 𝔽𝔸𝕏 *2866–2622. 198 rooms. 2 restaurants, 2 no-smoking floors, business services. AE, DC, MC, V.*

$$$ 🏨 **New World Harbour View.** Sharing the Convention Centre complex with the Grand Hyatt is this more modest but equally attractive hotel. Guest rooms are moderately sized and have modern decor with plenty of beveled-glass mirrors. Amenities include excellent Chinese and Western restaurants, a cozy bar, and the pools, gardens, driving range, tennis courts, and health-club facilities found on the recreation deck between the two hotels. The free-form pool here is Hong Kong's largest, complete with lagoons and an alfresco dining area. The lobby lounge is a very popular rendezvous for local and visiting businesspeople. ✉ *1 Harbour Rd.,* ☎ *2802–8888 or 800/227–5663,* 𝔽𝔸𝕏 *2802–8833. 862 rooms. 3 restaurants, 2 bars, 215 no-smoking rooms, pool, barbershop, beauty salon, health club, shops, business services. AE, DC, MC, V.*

$$ 🏨 **Harbour View International House.** This waterfront YMCA property offers small, but clean and relatively inexpensive accommodations next to the Convention Centre. The best rooms face the harbor. The hotel provides free shuttle service to Causeway Bay and the Star Ferry. ✉ *4 Harbour Rd.,* ☎ *2802–0111,* 𝔽𝔸𝕏 *2802–9063. 320 rooms. Restaurant. AE, DC, MC, V.*

$$ 🏨 **The Wesley.** Opened in 1992 on the site of the old Soldiers and Sailors Home, this 21-story, moderately (for Hong Kong) priced hotel is a short walk from the Convention Centre, the Academy for Performing Arts, and the MTR. The rooms are small but pleasantly furnished, and the corner "suites" have alcove work areas—very convenient for businesspeople. It has a tram stop outside the door, and Pacific Place is close by, as are the bars of Wanchai. ✉ *22 Hennessy Rd.,* ☎ *2866–6688,* 𝔽𝔸𝕏 *2866–6633. 251 rooms. Restaurant, coffee shop. AE, DC, MC, V.*

$$ 🏨 **Wharney.** Within walking distance of the Convention Centre, this former Ramada Inn, which looks like its neighboring office blocks, is in the heart of Wanchai. Its rates no longer qualify it for the budget-conscious traveler but it is convenient and comfortable, with two restaurants, a health club, and a pub that's popular with locals. ✉ *57–73 Lockhart Rd.,* ☎ *2861–1000,* 𝔽𝔸𝕏 *2865–6023. 335 rooms. 2 restaurants, pub, indoor pool, health club, business services. AE, DC, MC, V.*

80

Lodging

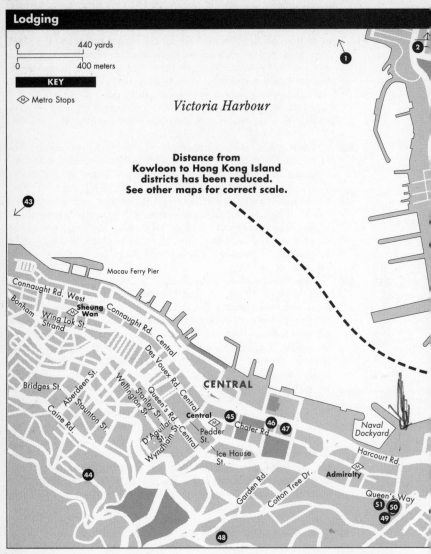

0   440 yards
0   400 meters

KEY

Ⓜ Metro Stops

Victoria Harbour

Distance from Kowloon to Hong Kong Island districts has been reduced. See other maps for correct scale.

Macau Ferry Pier

Connaught Rd. West
Bonham
Wing Lok St.
Strand
Sheung Wan
Connaught Rd. Central
Des Voeux Rd. Central

Bridges St.
Aberdeen St.
Staunton St.
Wellington St.
Stanley St.
Queen's St.
D'Aguilar St.
Wyndham St.
Caine Rd.

CENTRAL

Central
Pedder St.
Ice House St.
Chater Rd.
Garden Rd.
Cotton Tree Dr.

Naval Dockyard
Harcourt Rd.

Admiralty
Queen's Way

Bangkok Royal, **13**
Bishop Lei International House, **44**
Booth Lodge, **5**
BP International House, **11**
Caritas Bianchi Lodge, **6**
Century, **57**

Cheung Chau Warwick, **43**
City Garden, **66**
Concourse, **8**
Conrad International, **49**
The Excelsior, **63**
Furama Kempinski, **47**
Garden View International House, **48**

Gold Coast, **1**
Grand Hyatt, **56**
Grand Plaza, **60**
Grand Stanford Harbour View, **33**
Grand Tower, **7**
Guangdong, **21**
Harbour Plaza, **17**
Harbour View International House, **53**

Holiday Inn Golden Mile, **27**
Holy Carpenter Church Guest House, **15**
Hong Kong Renaissance, **25**
Hongkong, **36**
Hotel Nikko, **34**
Hyatt Regency, **26**
Imperial, **28**
International, **20**

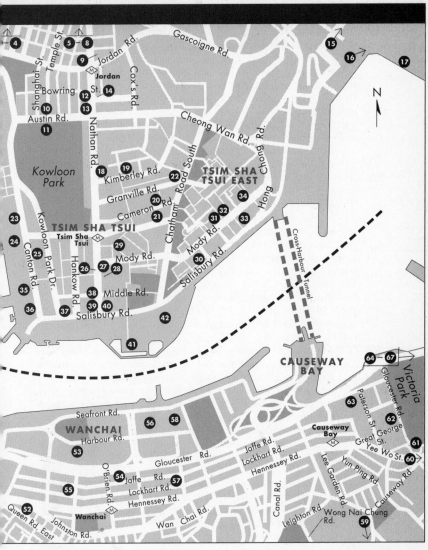

Island Shangri-La, **51**
J.W. Marriot, **50**
Kowloon, **38**
Kowloon Panda, **2**
Kowloon
Shangri-La, **30**
Luk Kwok, **54**
Majestic, **9**
Mandarin Oriental, **45**
Marco Polo, **24**
Miramar, **18**
New Astor, **29**

New Cathay, **61**
Newton, **65**
New World, **42**
New World Harbour
View, **58**
Park Lane, **62**
Pearl Seaview, **10**
Peninsula, **39**
Prince, **23**
Prudential, **14**
Ramada Hotel
Kowloon, **22**

Regal Airport, **16**
Regal Hongkong
Hotel, **64**
Regal Kowloon, **32**
Regal Riverside, **3**
The Regent, **41**
Richmond, **59**
Ritz-Carlton, **46**
Royal Garden, **31**
Royal Pacific, **35**
Royal Park, **4**

Salisbury YMCA, **37**
Shamrock, **12**
Sheraton Hong Kong
Hotel and Towers, **40**
South China, **67**
The Wesley, **52**
Wharney, **55**
Windsor, **19**

Causeway Bay

$$$$ ⊞ **Park Lane.** This elegant hotel, with an imposing facade reminiscent of London's Knightsbridge area, overlooks Victoria Park and backs onto one of Hong Kong Island's busiest shopping, entertainment, and business areas. All rooms have luxurious marble bathrooms, elegant hand-crafted furniture, and marvelous views of the harbor and/or Victoria Park. The rooftop restaurant serves Continental cuisine, while at ground level there's a spacious coffee shop and a new bar that serves pasta buffets at lunchtime. ⊠ *310 Gloucester Rd.,* ☎ *2890–3355,* ℻ *2576–7853. 790 rooms, 25 suites. 3 restaurants, 2 lounges, 4 no-smoking floors, beauty salon, health club, shops, business services. AE, DC, MC, V.*

$$$$ ⊞ **Regal Hongkong Hotel.** Opened in 1993, the slightly over-the-top opulence of the decor in this 33-story hotel leans toward European, with masses of marble and a dramatic lobby with high windows, Louis XIV furniture, and a huge mural depicting a scene from the Mediter-ranean. Gilded elevators lead to nicely appointed guest rooms with maple-inlay furniture crafted by local artisans, walls and carpets in muted earth tones, and brightly colored bedspreads. Bathrooms are spacious, with triangular tubs. There are three no-smoking and four executive floors. The dining areas are sumptuous, especially the top-floor Mediter-ranean restaurant, with great views of Victoria Park. ⊠ *88 Yee Wo St.,* ☎ *2890–6633, or 800/222–8888,* ℻ *2881–0777. 425 rooms. 4 restaurants, bar, 3 no-smoking floors, pool, health club, shops, dance club, business services. AE, DC, MC, V.*

$$$ ⊞ **The Excelsior.** In Causeway Bay, looking out on the Royal Hong Kong
★   Yacht Club, the Excelsior is one of the city's most popular hotels. It is a veteran that readily adapts to the changing demands of the group and business markets. Only its upper floors now boast harbor views, but the location is ideal for shopping and dining. Spend evenings feast-ing at Cammino (Italian) or listening to live jazz in the basement Dick-ens Bar, recently refurbished as a sports bar. Enjoy TOTT, the top-floor, split-level restaurant-cum-bar-cum-nightclub, with a niche brandy bar, sushi bars, an open tandoori kitchen, and glass-enclosed private rooms. Rooms are decorated in shades of terra-cotta and purple, and many (80%) have harbor views. The fitness-conscious will appreciate rooftop tennis courts and a jogging track in adjacent Victoria Park. Of course, business travelers are well provided for. ⊠ *281 Gloucester Rd.,* ☎ *2894–8888,* ℻ *2895–6459. 875 rooms, 22 suites. 4 restaurants, 5 no-smoking floors, barbershop, beauty salon, shops, business services. AE, DC, MC, V.*

$$ ⊞ **New Cathay.** A Chinese-managed hotel close to Victoria Park, this fairly basic hotel is favored by Asian tour groups and westerners on a budget. Rooms are very small but have the basic necessities of air-con-ditioning, TV, tea- and coffeemakers. It has a good coffee shop and a large seafood restaurant. ⊠ *17 Tung Lo Wan Rd.,* ☎ *2577–8211,* ℻ *2576–9365, 225 rooms. Restaurant, coffee shop. AE, DC, MC, V.*

Happy Valley

$$ ⊞ **Richmond.** The simple rooms here are spare but functional. Don't expect much space, however; this is Hong Kong, after all. The hotel boasts a good Cantonese restaurant. It's also near the Happy Valley racetrack, convenient for horse-racing fans, but it's at least 5 to 10 min-utes by taxi to the shopping area of Causeway Bay. ⊠ *1A Wang Tak St.,* ☎ *2574–9922,* ℻ *2838–1622. 108 rooms, 3 suites. 2 restaurants, pool, fitness center, business services. AE, DC, MC, V.*

Quarry Bay

$$$ 🏨 **Grand Plaza.** This hotel, part of a large residential-commercial-entertainment complex, is a little out-of-the-way, but it's connected to a subway station and has enough space for a vast recreational club, with a huge pool, squash courts, a billiard room, a gymnasium, an aerobics hall, a putting green, and a jogging track. There are evening barbecues on the garden terrace, an upmarket coffee shop, a disco, and extensive shopping in the adjoining Jusco Department Store. ⊠ *2 Kornhill Rd.,* ☎ *2886–0011,* ℻ *2886–1738. 306 rooms, 42 suites. 2 restaurants, indoor pool, putting green, health club, squash, shops, billiards, dance club, business services. AE, DC, MC, V.*

North Point

$$ 🏨 **City Garden.** Although not as close to the subway as its brochure suggests, this hotel has the advantage of being easily accessible to the Eastern Corridor, which links Causeway Bay to Taikoo Shing and the Eastern Harbour Crossing. Rooms are basic and rather small. The hotel caters to Asian tour groups and offers a good Cantonese restaurant and such recreational facilities as a pool, sauna, and fitness center. ⊠ *9 City Garden Rd.,* ☎ *2887–2888,* ℻ *2887–1111. 615 rooms, 2 restaurants, pool, health club, business services. AE, DC, MC, V.*

$$ 🏨 **Newton.** In a boxy high-rise that is functional yet relatively featureless, this hotel's advantages are that it's close to an MTR station and it has a pleasant bar/restaurant, with live entertainment. Rooms are small but adequate. ⊠ *218 Electric Rd.,* ☎ *2807–2333,* ℻ *2807–1221. 362 rooms. Restaurant, bar, pool, sauna, business services. AE, DC, MC, V.*

$$ 🏨 **South China.** Managed by a mainland Chinese company, naturally attracting groups from mainland China, this is a small, functional hotel, with a large Chinese restaurant and bar. It is some distance from the subway. ⊠ *67 Java Rd.,* ☎ *2503–1168,* ℻ *2512–8698. 204 rooms. Restaurant, bar. AE, DC, MC, V.*

KOWLOON

Most of the hotels in Hong Kong are on the Kowloon peninsula, which includes "Old" Tsim Sha Tsui, Tsim Sha Tsui East, Harbour City, and the districts north of Tsim Sha Tsui to the border of the New Territories. The fabled "Golden Mile" of shopping on Nathan Road runs through "Old" Tsim Sha Tsui. Backstreets are filled with restaurants, stores, and hotels.

Tsim Sha Tsui East is a grid of modern office blocks (many with restaurants or nightclubs) and luxury hotels. This area has been created on land reclaimed from the harbor in the last decade, so none of the hotels is very old.

There are three luxury hotels (owned and managed by the Marco Polo Group) in Harbour City on the western side of the Tsim Sha Tsui promontory. This area next to the Star Ferry is one of Asia's largest air-conditioned shopping and commercial complexes.

Northern Kowloon contains more of the older, smaller, moderately priced hotels. Most are on or very near to Nathan Road and are probably the best bets for economy-minded visitors. Excellent bus service and the MTR make it possible to return to the center of "Old" Tsim Sha Tsui quickly.

$$$$ ☷ **Harbour Plaza.** Opened in summer 1995, this 20-story, glass-clad hotel can well claim unique harbor views—it is the first hotel in the recently developed Hung Hom area, between the railroad terminus and the airport. It can be reached by ferry from Central in 20 minutes, with sailings every 15 minutes. The hotel has buses shuttling all day to and from the airport—about 15 minutes away—and it's about five minutes from the station where trains leave for China. The hotel sports a spacious, well-designed atrium lobby with good harbor views from lounges on two levels. For dining it has a Japanese *robatayaki* barbecue, a Cantonese restaurant, a Western grill, and a fun pub called the Pit Stop, which features actual racing cars. For recreation there's a large scenic rooftop pool as well as a fitness center and a health spa. For executives, the Harbour Club on the top two floors has all of the usual business services. ⊠ *20 Tak Fung St., Hung Hom, Kowloon,* ☎ *2621–3188,* FAX *2621–3318. 418 rooms. 5 restaurants, 2 bars, deli, pool, beauty salon, health club, shops, business services. AE, DC, MC, V.*

$$$$ ☷ **Hong Kong Renaissance.** The luxurious lobby of this 19-story building is decorated with Louis XVI–style leather furniture and thick area rugs and has a barrel-vaulted ceiling. Guest rooms are tastefully decorated, and the best (and more expensive) of them have harbor views. The Bostonian restaurant has a great selection of American seafood dishes, and Capriccio is one of the most elegant Italian dining rooms in the city. All suites and rooms on Renaissance Club executive floors have fax machines and computer modem outlets. ⊠ *8 Peking Rd., Tsim Sha Tsui,* ☎ *2375–1133 or 800/854–7854,* FAX *2375–6611. 474 rooms, 27 suites. 5 restaurants, no-smoking floor, barbershop, beauty salon, pool, health club, shops, business services. AE, DC, MC, V.*

$$$$ ☷ **Hotel Nikko.** Part of the Japanese Nikko chain, this luxury harborfront hotel is at the far end of Tsim Sha Tsui East. Guest rooms are attractively decorated in gray and almond tones and have contemporary furnishings. Sagano, the hotel's Japanese restaurant, is reputed to be the most popular in Hong Kong, and the French Les Célébrités has a grand Belle Epoque design and atmosphere. ⊠ *72 Mody Rd., Tsim Sha Tsui East,* ☎ *2739–1111 or 800/862–9354,* FAX *2311–3122. 442 rooms, 19 suites. 4 restaurants, pool, barbershop, beauty salon, health club, shops, business services. AE, DC, MC, V.*

$$$$ ☷ **Hyatt Regency.** Major renovations over the past two years have given
★   the Hyatt a glamorous new look, with a white facade and upgraded ground-floor shopping arcade. On the second floor is a dramatic marble and teak lobby, which leads to the spacious coffee shop. The hotel has a gallery of Oriental antiques and an award-winning Chinese restaurant. Gourmets will also want to sample the classic Continental fare at Hugo's. The hotel is five minutes away from the Star Ferry, and next door to an MTR station. ⊠ *67 Nathan Rd., Tsim Sha Tsui,* ☎ *2311–1234 or 800/233–1234,* FAX *2739–8701. 706 rooms, 17 suites. 4 restaurants, 95 no-smoking rooms, barbershop, beauty salon, shops, business services. AE, DC, MC, V.*

$$$$ ☷ **Kowloon Shangri-La.** Billed as one of the top 10 hotels in the world,
★   this waterfront hotel, owned and managed by Shangri-La International, caters to the international business traveler. Twenty-one stories above the lobby—dominated by a tapestry depicting Shangri-La—is the executive floor, with 24-hour business and concierge services, personalized stationery, and complimentary breakfast and cocktails. The modern, pastel rooms are large by Hong Kong standards. A variety of in-house restaurants serving Japanese, Chinese, French, and American cuisines, lounges, a bar, and a nightclub offer a range of live entertainment, including string quartets and harp and piano music. Views are of Victoria Harbour or the city. The owners' attention to detail;

the expert, loyal staff; and the regular fine-tuning of facilities make this a hotel with a lot of repeat business. ⊠ *64 Mody Rd., Tsim Sha Tsui East,* ☎ *2721–2111 or 800/942–5050,* FAX *2723–8686. 689 rooms, 29 suites. 5 restaurants, bar, no-smoking floor, pool, barbershop, health club, shops, nightclub, business services. AE, DC, MC, V.*

$$$$ 🖬 **Peninsula.** The "Pen," the grand old lady of Hong Kong hotels, was
★ built in 1928, when travelers from London took many weeks (and many trunks) to reach Hong Kong by boat and then by train. This is the ultimate in colonial elegance. The Pen's taste and Old World style is in evidence everywhere: a columned and gilt-corniced lobby, a fleet of Rolls-Royces, spacious bedrooms, attentive room valets, and luxurious bath accessories. Gaddi's, the hotel's French restaurant, is one of Hong Kong's most distinguished gourmet institutions. In 1994 the Pen added a 30-story tower, reclaiming the view of Victoria Harbour stolen by the construction of the Cultural Centre across the street. The 132 spacious new guest rooms and suites are decorated in the same classic European style of the Pen's other rooms. Rich deep blue, gold, and ivory fabrics and Chinese prints provide a subtle Oriental accent. The tower also includes a new business center, banquet and meeting facilities, a sundeck, a health club, a swimming pool (with massive columns and a retractable glass screen for year-round use), and a rooftop restaurant, Felix, designed by superstar French architect Philippe Starck. There are even two helipads, making access to the rest of the territory a snap. ⊠ *Salisbury Rd., Tsim Sha Tsui,* ☎ *2366–6251,* FAX *2722–4170. 246 rooms, 54 suites. 6 restaurants, pool, barbershop, beauty salon, health club, shops, business services, helipad. AE, DC, MC, V.*

$$$$ 🖬 **The Regent.** This elegantly modern hotel on the southernmost tip
★ of Tsim Sha Tsui offers luxurious guest rooms and spectacular harbor views from the very edge of the waterfront. The restaurants and cocktail lounge share this view, from windows that rise 40 feet above the polished granite floor. The Lai Ching Heen restaurant has some of the best Cantonese dishes in Hong Kong; The Steak House is one of the most exclusive grills; while local society gathers in the new Club Shanghai, which recaptures the atmosphere as well as the look of a Shanghai nightclub in the 1920s and '30s. A wide range of features, such as displays of Oriental art, a health spa with masseur, an oversize outdoor pool, and a computer system that stores information about guests' preferences, will appeal to those who want nothing but the best. ⊠ *18 Salisbury Rd., Tsim Sha Tsui,* ☎ *2721–1211 or 800/545–4000,* FAX *2739–4546. 508 rooms, 94 suites. 5 restaurants, pool, barbershop, beauty salon, health club, shops, business services. AE, DC, MC, V.*

$$$$ 🖬 **Sheraton Hong Kong Hotel and Towers.** This Sheraton, with a trademark four-floor atrium lobby, is across the street from the Space Museum at the southern end of the fabled Golden Mile. Guest rooms are done in soft pastels and contemporary furniture and offer a choice of harbor, city, or courtyard views. Make sure you visit the rooftop pool and terrace via the exterior glass elevator, as well as the Grandstand Grill—one of the best in town—and Someplace Else, an art deco café popular as a happy hour hangout. Fitness facilities are state-of-the-art. ⊠ *20 Nathan Rd., Tsim Sha Tsui,* ☎ *2369–1111 or 800/334–8484,* FAX *2739–8707. 806 rooms, 26 suites. 9 restaurants, 2 no-smoking floors, pool, barbershop, beauty salon, health club, shops, business services. AE, DC, MC, V.*

$$$ 🖬 **Grand Stanford Harbour View.** At the eastern end of Tsim Sha Tsui East, this luxury hotel (formerly a Holiday Inn Crowne Plaza) has an unobstructed harbor view from more than half its rooms. The hotel is well known locally for its restaurants, including Mistral, which serves Italian cuisine, and the French-style Belvedere, but particularly for Tiffany's New York Bar, which celebrates the Roaring 20's with an-

tique furniture, Tiffany glass ceilings, and American entertainment. Taxis or Tsim Sha Tsui East ferries provide more convenient transportation than the MTR or Star Ferry, on the other side of the peninsula. The large guest rooms, done in warm earth tones, have finely crafted wood furniture. The hotel has extensive recreational facilities including two golf driving nets on the roof. ⊠ *70 Mody Rd., Tsim Sha Tsui East,* ☏ *2721–5161 or 800/465–4329,* ℻ *2369–5672. 574 rooms, 18 suites. 4 restaurants, pool, beauty salon, driving range, health club, shops, business services. AE, DC, MC, V.*

$$$ 🏨 **Grand Tower.** Owing to its location in one of the most traditional parts of town, this hotel gives tourists a sense of the real Hong Kong. Bird Street (where many Chinese walk and talk, together with their caged birds) and the Women's Market are a short walk away, as is the Mongkok MTR. Rooms are clean and functional. ⊠ *627–641 Nathan Rd., Mongkok,* ☏ *2789–0011,* ℻ *2789–0945. 536 rooms, 13 suites. 4 restaurants, barbershop, beauty salon, shops, business services. AE, DC, MC, V.*

$$$ 🏨 **Guangdong.** This mainland Chinese–managed hotel is popular among Southeast Asian and Chinese visitors. Comfortable rooms, with beige walls and nondescript French furniture, look out on the street below, which is usually bustling with shoppers and patrons of the many local restaurants and bars. There are no bars or live entertainment in-house, but you don't have to travel far to find evening activities. The best views are on or above the ninth floor. The Canton Court restaurant serves only mediocre Cantonese cuisine. ⊠ *18 Prat Ave., Tsim Sha Tsui,* ☏ *2739–3311,* ℻ *2721–1137. 234 rooms, 11 suites. 2 restaurants, shops, business services. AE, DC, MC, V.*

$$$ 🏨 **Holiday Inn Golden Mile.** On the Golden Mile of Nathan Road, the hub of Kowloon's business and shopping area, this business-style hotel has been a popular choice since it opened in 1975. Rooms here are comfortably large and furnished in attractive floral designs. Public areas are always busy, with local businesspeople meeting in the newly converted Baron's Table, where you can enjoy informal dining, entertainment, and views of Nathan Road, or the new, contemporary Cafe Vienna, with similar views. ⊠ *50 Nathan Rd., Tsim Sha Tsui,* ☏ *2369–3111 or 800/465–4329,* ℻ *2369–8016. 591 rooms (100 no-smoking), 9 suites. 5 restaurants, pool, barbershop, beauty salon, health club, shops, business services. AE, DC, MC, V.*

$$$ 🏨 **Hongkong.** This member of Marco Polo hotels, formerly known as
★   Omni hotels, has resumed its original name. It stands next to the Star Ferry on the western side of Tsim Sha Tsui, with sister hotels Marco Polo and Prince (formerly Omni Marco Polo and Omni Prince), in the wharfside Harbour City complex, which also houses offices, shopping malls, cinemas, restaurants, and such pop culture centers as Hard Rock Cafe and Planet Hollywood. The Hongkong is especially popular with business travelers because of its excellent reputation for efficiency. It is also noted for its first-class Taipan Grill and the Gripps bar, with close-up, sixth-floor views of the harbor, and live entertainment at night. Rooms here are pleasant but plain, which is a problem only if you're assigned one without an ocean view. Old Tsim Sha Tsui is just a short walk away. ⊠ *Harbour City, Tsim Sha Tsui,* ☏ *2736– 0088 or 800/843–6664,* ℻ *2736–0011. 665 rooms, 84 suites. 7 restaurants, bar, no-smoking floor, pool, barbershop, beauty salon, shops, business services. AE, DC, MC, V.*

$$$ 🏨 **Kowloon.** A shimmering mirrored exterior and a chrome, glass, and
★   marble lobby reflect the Kowloon's high efficiency and high-tech amenities. Rooms are incredibly compact, similar to what you would find in a Japanese business hotel, but each has an interactive telecenter with a multisystem TV that provides information on shopping, events,

flights, and your bill, and interfaces with personal fax machines for printouts. Other modern conveniences include video games and a voice message system. The location, on the southern tip of Nathan Road's Golden Mile, puts you just minutes away from the Star Ferry and next door to the MTR. You have a choice of restaurants and can also use the facilities of the Peninsula hotel across the street. ✉ *19–21 Nathan Rd., Tsim Sha Tsui,* ☎ *2369–8698,* FAX *2739–9811. 704 rooms, 34 suites. 3 restaurants, 192 no-smoking rooms (4 no-smoking floors), barbershop, beauty salon, shops, business services. AE, DC, MC, V.*

$$$ 🏨 **Marco Polo.** The specialty restaurant here is La Brasserie, a charming French bistro, with lots of plants, etched glass, and framed prints of cartoon chefs engaged in various antics. Rooms here lack the harbor views of the Hongkong, but guests appreciate the convenience to the shops, entertainment spots, and other hotels of the Harbour City complex. Guests here can use the pool at the Hongkong. ✉ *Harbour City, Tsim Sha Tsui,* ☎ *2736–0888 or 800/843–6664,* FAX *2736– 0022. 384 rooms, 56 suites. 3 restaurants, no-smoking floor, barbershop, shops, business services. AE, DC, MC, V.*

$$$ 🏨 **Miramar.** At the top of the Golden Mile, across the street from Kowloon Park, the Miramar has a vast lobby with a dramatic stained-glass ceiling, several opulent banquet rooms, and a convention center. Guest rooms are exceptionally large and are done in muted tones and light wood. The restaurants, serving Chinese and Western food, are as popular with locals as with tourists so they both have a "down-home" atmosphere. The hotel is close to an MTR station and convenient for transport to the airport. ✉ *130 Nathan Rd., Tsim Sha Tsui,* ☎ *2368– 1111,* FAX *2369–1788. 550 rooms. 4 restaurants, pool, barbershop, beauty salon, health club, shops, business services. AE, DC, MC, V.*

$$$ 🏨 **New World.** This hotel, with beautifully landscaped gardens and terraces, is part of a huge shopping complex on the southeast tip of Tsim Sha Tsui. The decor is pleasantly postmodern, with contemporary furniture throughout. It has a good selection of restaurants and evening entertainment, including the Panorama restaurant, one of Hong Kong's great hidden delights, and Catwalk, one of the area's most popular discos. ✉ *22 Salisbury Rd., Tsim Sha Tsui,* ☎ *2369–4111 or 800/227– 5663,* FAX *2369–9387. 550 rooms. 6 restaurants, no-smoking floor, pool, barbershop, beauty salon, health club, dance club, business services. AE, DC, MC, V.*

$$$ 🏨 **Prince.** Like its neighbors in the Harbour City complex (the Hongkong and Marco Polo) the Prince is very convenient. It is close to the China Hong Kong Terminal for ferries to ports in the Pearl River Delta and boats to Shanghai, Shantou, and Xiamen, as well as buses to Guangzhou and Shenzhen. The shops and restaurants of Tsim Sha Tsui are just a short walk away. Most rooms overlook expansive Kowloon Park, while some of the suites have views of Victoria Harbour. The Spice Market restaurant serves the cuisines of China, Japan, Thailand, and India. Guests here can use the pool at the Hongkong. ✉ *Harbour City, Tsim Sha Tsui,* ☎ *2736–1888 or 800/843–6664,* FAX *2736–0066. 345 rooms, 51 suites. 4 restaurants, no-smoking floor, shops, business services. AE, DC, MC, V.*

$$$ 🏨 **Regal Airport.** A three-minute stroll through an air-conditioned walkway leads you from this Regal to the customs area of the airport. It's the perfect place to stay if you're moving on quickly or have air-port-related business. The best rooms face the airport, as does the Five Continents restaurant, where you get excellent international meals and marvelous picture-window views. All rooms are fully sound-proofed. There is a half-price day-use discount for transit passengers. ✉ *30 Sa Po Rd.,* ☎ *2718–0333 or 800/222–8888,* FAX *2718–4111.*

400 rooms, 20 suites. 3 restaurants, 3 no-smoking floors, pool, barbershop, beauty salon, shops, business services. AE, DC, MC, V.

$$$ ☰ **Regal Kowloon.** When this hotel opened a decade ago, it was the first done in the French style in Hong Kong. The lobby has an impressive tapestry, and Louis XVI–style furniture graces one of the lounges and the guest rooms. Rooms are decorated in peach and green with chintz bedspreads and curtains. Le Restaurant de France has a gorgeous dining room with French Regency decor and a menu based on that of Maxim de Paris. ⊠ *71 Mody Rd., Tsim Sha Tsui East, ☎ 2722–1818 or 800/222–8888, FAX 2369–6950. 600 rooms, 33 suites. 5 restaurants, no-smoking rooms, barbershop, beauty salon, health club, shops, business services. AE, DC, MC, V.*

$$$ ☰ **Royal Garden.** This hotel is named for its elegant garden atrium, which rises from the ground floor to the roof. Glass-sided elevators, live classical music, trailing greenery, and trickling streams give the Royal Garden a serene atmosphere. Guest-room doors are soundproofed, and rooms are Oriental in style. For a contrast, head to the basement disco, which is a Victorian-style pub until 9 PM. Guests especially appreciate Sabatini's, sister to the famous Roman restaurant, and a state-of-the-art rooftop health club with indoor-outdoor pool and spa services. ⊠ *69 Mody Rd., Tsim Sha Tsui East, ☎ 2721–5215, FAX 2369–9976. 377 rooms, 45 suites. 6 restaurants, pub, no-smoking floor, indoor-outdoor pool, barbershop, beauty salon, spa, health club, shops, business services. AE, DC, MC, V.*

$$ ☰ **BP International House.** Built by the Boy Scouts Association, this new hotel provides excellent value. It is on the northern edge of Tsim Sha Tsui, next to Kowloon Park and close to the MTR. A portrait of BP himself—Baron Robert Baden-Powell, founder of the Boy Scouts—hangs in the spacious lobby. The rooms are small and hostel-like, but equipped with multichannel TV and telephones. In addition to restaurants and other standard facilities, the hotel contains one of the biggest health clubs in town. ⊠ *8 Austin Rd, Kowloon, ☎ 2376–1111, FAX 2376–1333. 536 rooms. 2 restaurants, health club, business services. AE, DC, MC, V.*

$$ ☰ **Concourse.** One of Hong Kong's nicer budget hotels, the Concourse was opened in 1991 by the China Travel Service in Mongkok, and it is reasonably close to public transportation and an active nightlife scene. There is a Chinese restaurant, a Korean restaurant, and a karaoke lounge named Cheers. ⊠ *20 Lai Chi Kok Rd., ☎ 2397–6683, FAX 2381–3768. 435 rooms, 5 suites. 2 restaurants, coffee shop. AE, DC, MC, V.*

$$ ☰ **Imperial.** This relatively small but comfortable hotel lacks its own bars, lounges, restaurants, and live entertainment, unlike most hotels in the territory; however, its location on the Golden Mile of Nathan Road means you don't have to walk far for any product or service. In fact, in the basement is the popular Mad Dogs pub, frequented by many local expats. The MTR and Star Ferry are only a short walk away. There are also limited business services. ⊠ *30 Nathan Rd., Tsim Sha Tsui, ☎ 2366–2201, FAX 2311–2360. 209 rooms, 6 suites. Pub (no restaurant). AE, DC, MC, V.*

$$ ☰ **Majestic.** This hotel opened in 1992 on the site of the old Majestic Cinema on upper Nathan Road. It's managed by the Furama Kempinski, so standards are higher than the price range suggests. Sparsely furnished rooms have contemporary furniture, and all suites are equipped with fax machines. There is an elegant bar and a superior Western restaurant. In the same complex are two cinemas, shops, and several Chinese restaurants. ⊠ *348 Nathan Rd., ☎ 2781–1333, FAX 2781–1773. 387 rooms. Restaurant, bar, no-smoking floor, shops, cinema, business services. AE, DC, MC, V.*

In case you want to see the world.

At American Express, we're here to make your journey a smooth one. So we have over 1,700 travel service locations in over 120 countries ready to help. What else would you expect from the world's largest travel agency?

do more®

http://www.americanexpress.com/travel

Travel

In case you want to be welcomed there.

We're here to see that you're always welcomed at establishments everywhere. That's why millions of people carry the American Express® Card – for peace of mind, confidence, and security, around the world or just around the corner.

do more®

Cards

In case you're running low.

We're here to help with more than 118,000 Express Cash locations around the world. In order to enroll, just call American Express before you start your vacation.

do more

Express Cash

And just in case.

We're here with American Express® Travelers Cheques and Cheques *for Two®*. They're the safest way to carry money on your vacation and the surest way to get a refund, practically anywhere, anytime.

Another way we help you...

do more®

Travelers Cheques

$$ ⚏ **New Astor.** This small, inviting, triangle-shaped hotel is on a busy corner of Old Tsim Sha Tsui across the road from the MTR. Rooms are decorated in blue and white and have standard dark-wood furniture. Guests tend to be groups from China and the more affluent backpackers. ⊠ *11 Carnarvon Rd., Tsim Sha Tsui,* ☎ *2366–7261,* FAX *2722–7122. 151 rooms, 2 suites. Restaurant, shop. AE, DC, MC, V.*

$$ ⚏ **Pearl Seaview.** Unfortunately, reclamation of the harbor front and new construction has taken away most of this hotel's sea view, but it has compensatory features. It's convenient to the Yaumati MTR and is on Shanghai Street, where traditional Hong Kong still holds out, with shops selling handmade kitchenware, temple offerings, and wedding dresses. Guest rooms are very small but the basement restaurant has bargain-priced buffets. The hotel attracts a lot of tour groups from Europe and Asia. ⊠ *262 Shanghai St., Yau Ma Tei, Kowloon,* ☎ *2782–0882,* FAX *2388–1803. 253 rooms. Brasserie restaurant, bar, lounge. AE, DC, MC, V.*

$$ ⚏ **Prudential.** Rising from a busy corner in upper Nathan Road, with an MTR station underneath, this hotel is a great find for travelers on a modest budget. Rooms are spacious and offer interesting city views. It shares a building with a lively shopping mall and has its own pool, sauna, and gym. ⊠ *222 Nathan Rd.,* ☎ *2311–8222,* FAX *2367–6537. 434 rooms. Coffee shop, lounge, pool, sauna, shops, business services. AE, DC, MC, V.*

$$ ⚏ **Ramada Hotel Kowloon.** This modern hotel is relatively small and tries to appeal to travelers with a home-away-from-home ambience. A fireplace in the lobby and comfortably furnished rooms with natural wood throughout create a cozy atmosphere. It has two pleasant restaurants, serving Japanese and American meals. ⊠ *73–75 Chatham Rd., south Tsim Sha Tsui,* ☎ *2311–1100 or 800/854–7854,* FAX *2311–6000. 205 rooms, 1 suite. 2 restaurants, shop, business services. AE, DC, MC, V.*

$$ ⚏ **Royal Pacific.** Right on the Tsim Sha Tsui waterfront, this hotel is part of the China Hong Kong City complex, which includes the terminal for ferries to China. Rooms are small but attractively furnished and equipped for tea and coffee making. Among its assortment of restaurants is one serving excellent Swiss food. ⊠ *33 Canton Rd., Kowloon,* ☎ *2736–1188,* FAX *2736–1212. 675 rooms. 3 restaurants, 2 bars, beauty salon, nightclub, business services. AE, DC, MC, V.*

$$ ⚏ **Windsor.** This smart little hotel offers clean, functional accommodations just east of the Nathan Road Golden Mile of shopping and entertainment. It has a coffee shop–cum–bar, but no other facilities. ⊠ *39–43A Kimberley Rd., Tsim Sha Tsui,* ☎ *2739–5665,* FAX *2311–5101. 166 rooms. 2 restaurants, business services. AE, DC, MC, V.*

$ ⚏ **Bangkok Royal.** Just off Nathan Road and steps away from the Jordan MTR, this hotel has rooms that are sparse and somewhat down-at-the-heels, but clean. There are no bars, lounges, or live entertainment, but there is a good Thai restaurant off the lobby, and you are within walking distance of the restaurants and entertainment of Nathan Road. ⊠ *2 Pilkem St., Yau Ma Tei,* ☎ *2735–9181,* FAX *2730–2209. 70 rooms. 2 restaurants. AE, DC, MC, V.*

$ ⚏ **Booth Lodge.** This pleasant contemporary retreat, built in 1985 near the Jade Market, is operated by the Salvation Army. But don't be turned off—the facilities are not of the donated kind. In fact, everything is clean, bright, and new, from crisply painted walls to starched sheets on the double beds. The lobby is a study in minimalism and has an officelike atmosphere, but the Booth is a good value. ⊠ *11 Wing Sing La., Yau Ma Tei,* ☎ *2771–9266,* FAX *2385–1140. 53 rooms. Restaurant. AE, MC, V.*

$ ⌘ **Caritas Bianchi Lodge.** This clean and friendly lodge, done in simple modern decor, is close to the Jade Market and the nightly Temple Street Market. ⌧ *4 Cliff Rd., Yau Ma Tei,* ☎ *2388–1111,* ℻ *2770–6669. 90 rooms, 2 suites. Restaurant. AE, DC, MC, V.*

$ ⌘ **Holy Carpenter Church Guest House.** In the center of the discount shopping and industrial district of Hunghom, this small, 17-year-old hostel is close to the airport and train station. It is most attractive to budget travelers who are able to book at least a month in advance and just want a place to sleep. ⌧ *1 Dyer Ave., Hunghom,* ☎ *2362–0301,* ℻ *2362–2193. 14 rooms. MC, V.*

$ ⌘ **International.** This hotel provides the basics. A bright orange lobby helps prepare you for the pink and orange color scheme of the rooms, the best of which face Cameron Road and have balconies from which to view the bright lights and active nightlife of Tsim Sha Tsui. ⌧ *33 Cameron Rd.,* ☎ *2366–3381,* ℻ *2369–5381. 91 rooms, 2 suites. Restaurant. MC, V.*

$ ⌘ **Salisbury YMCA.** The most popular of Hong Kong's Ys, the Salisbury occupies a huge, sterile-looking block. Although the rooms are decorated circa 1960, the location is convenient to the Star Ferry and is a few minutes walk from the MTR. The Airbus stops across the street. The restaurants serve good, cheap food and the shops are bargain-priced. ⌧ *41 Salisbury Rd., Tsim Sha Tsui,* ☎ *2369–2211,* ℻ *2739–9315. 380 rooms. 3 restaurants, pool, health club, squash. AE, DC, MC, V.*

$ ⌘ **Shamrock.** With rooms that are more spacious than elegant and an atmosphere best described as old-fashioned, this hotel is still a good bargain. It is just north of Kowloon Park and steps away from the Jordan MTR. ⌧ *223 Nathan Rd., Yau Ma Tei,* ☎ *2735–2271,* ℻ *2736–7354. 148 rooms. Restaurant. AE, DC, MC, V.*

THE NEW TERRITORIES AND THE OUTER ISLANDS

Tsuen Wan's 1,026-room Kowloon Panda has helped alleviate the shortage of first-class accommodations in the fast-developing New Territories and has been welcomed by visitors involved in manufacturing here. Accommodations are still limited on the outlying islands, although some of them (such as Cheung Chau) have a booming business in rooms to rent, with agents displaying photographs of available rentals on placards that line the waterfront opposite the ferry pier.

The New Territories

$$$ ⌘ **Gold Coast.** Opened in 1994, this is Hong Kong's first conference resort. It consists of a vast complex on the western harbor front of Kowloon, served by special ferries from Central, 30 minutes away. There are also shuttle buses to the MTR and airport. The hotel has extravagant decor with acres of marble, miles of wrought iron balustrades, a grand ballroom, and palm-court atriums. The resort has a large marina, a water sports area, tennis courts, pitch-and-putt golf, an all-service spa, and even an archery range. It has gained a reputation among conference organizers for facilities that can accommodate up to 1,200 people. It is also the only hotel in Hong Kong with assault equipment for Outward Bound courses. ⌧ *1 Castle Peak Rd., Tuen Mun, New Territories,* ☎ *2452–8888,* ℻ *2440–7368. 443 rooms. 4 restaurants, 3 bars, pool, beauty salon, spa, 2 tennis courts, health club, squash, specific water sports info, business services. AE, DC, MC, V.*

$$ 🏨 **Kowloon Panda.** This massive hotel was the first of its size in the western New Territories. Close to the MTR in bustling Tsuen Wan, it offers a pool, a health club, business and meeting facilities, and a variety of restaurants. The decor is reminiscent of hotels in Tokyo's Ginza district, with lots of open-plan lounges and very contemporary rooms, some with harbor views. There is also a department store on the premises. ⊠ *3 Tsuen Wan St., Tsuen Wan,* ☎ *2409–1111,* 𝔽𝔸𝕏 *2409– 1818. 1,026 rooms. 4 restaurants, 2 bars, no-smoking floor, pool, health club, shop, business services. AE, DC, MC, V.*

$$ 🏨 **Regal Riverside.** In one of the territory's new towns, this large, modern hotel overlooks the Shing Mun River in the foothills of Shatin. Rooms, which have harbor and garden views, are done in pastel colors and have contemporary furniture. The Riverside has Hong Kong's largest hotel disco and a health club that's home to Hong Kong's only float capsule, purported to soothe away the day's pressures. Be prepared to spend at least 20 minutes getting to the Kowloon shopping district. ⊠ *Tai Chung Kiu Rd., Shatin,* ☎ *2649–7878 or 800/222– 8888,* 𝔽𝔸𝕏 *2637–4748. 786 rooms, 44 suites. 3 restaurants, no-smoking floor, pool, barbershop, beauty salon, health club, shops, nightclub, business services. AE, DC, MC, V.*

$$ 🏨 **Royal Park.** This hotel adjoins the shops, restaurants, cinemas, and train station of Shatin's Town Plaza. Rooms are basic, but they are clean and pleasant. ⊠ *8 Pak Hok Ting St., Shatin,* ☎ *2601–2111,* 𝔽𝔸𝕏 *2601– 3666. 448 rooms. 3 restaurants, pool, health club, business services. AE, DC, MC, V.*

Cheung Chau Island

$ 🏨 **Cheung Chau Warwick.** This eight-story hotel overlooks Tung Wan Beach. The tennis court, beach, and swimming pool, and the fact that there are no cars on this island, only an hour by ferry from Hong Kong Island, has made this a popular getaway for Hong Kong families. ⊠ *East Bay, Cheung Chau,* ☎ *2981–0081,* 𝔽𝔸𝕏 *2981–9174. 70 rooms. 2 restaurants, pool, tennis court. AE, DC, MC, V.*

5 Nightlife and the Arts

NIGHTLIFE

Hong Kong is a 24 hour city. When the sun sets, the pace doesn't stop—it just continues in a more carefree style. There are night markets, a zillion restaurants (from five-star to hole-in-the-wall places), sophisticated piano bars, elegant lounges, superstrobed discos, cozy bars, smoky jazz dens, topless bars and hostess clubs, marble massage parlors, cabarets, and, of course, the karaoke (video sing-along) bars, oh so popular with locals.

All premises licensed to serve alcohol are subject to stringent fire, safety, and sanitary controls. True clubs, as distinct from public premises, are less strictly controlled, and wise visitors should think twice before succumbing to the city's raunchier hideaways. If you stumble into one, check out cover and hostess charges *before* you get too comfortable. Pay for each round of drinks as it's served (by cash rather than credit card), and never sign any blank checks. As in every tourist destination, the art of the tourist rip-off is well-practiced. To be safest, visit spots that are sign-carrying members of the Hong Kong Tourist Association (HKTA). You can pick up its free membership listing (including approved restaurants and nightspots) at any HKTA Information Office.

Take note, too, of Hong Kong's laws. You need to be over 18 to be served alcohol. Drugs, obscene publications, and unlicensed gambling are ostensibly illegal. There is some consumer protection, but the generally helpful police, many of whom speak English, expect every visitor to know the meaning of *caveat emptor* (buyer beware!).

Following is a checklist of some suggested drinking and dancing spots (with telephone numbers where reservations are possible or wise). Many of Hong Kong's smarter nightspots are in hotels.

Fast-paced, competitive Hong Kong is a world of change where buildings seem to vanish overnight and new fads emerge weekly. Don't be surprised if our listing includes some spots that have changed their decor or name or have closed down since these words were set in type.

Cabaret and Nightclubs

The biggest and best old-fashioned nightclub-restaurants are Chinese, where the cuisine is Cantonese, as are most of the singers. Big-name local balladeers and "Cantopop" stars make guest appearances. Though modest by Las Vegas standards, the shows can be entertaining, as at the massive **Ocean City Restaurant & Night Club** (⊠ New World Centre, Tsim Sha Tsui, ☎ 2369–9688).

Ocean Centre's **Ocean Palace Restaurant & Night Club** (⊠ Harbour City, Canton Rd., Tsim Sha Tsui, ☎ 2730–7111) is a favorite for Hong Kong family and wedding parties.

Check out the **Golden Crown** (⊠ 94 Nathan Rd., ☎ 2366–6291) nightclub-restaurant. Here locals and tourists dine and dance the night away.

Club 97 (⊠ 8–11 Lan Kwai Fong St., Central, ☎ 2810–9333) is a small, glitzy, often crowded nightclub for gatherings of the "beautiful people." It is open from 9 PM to 4 AM or later, as long as there are customers. The club charges HK$97 (appropriately) nightly entrance fee.

Cocktail and Piano Bars

Sophisticated and elegant cocktail bars are the norm at all luxury hotels. You'll find live music (usually Filipino trios with a female singer, occasionally international acts) in a gleaming decor, and some have a small dance floor. Hong Kong's happy hours run typically from late afternoon to early evening, with two drinks for the price of one.

High-altitude harbor-gazing is the main attraction at the Island Shangri-La's 56th-floor **Cyrano** music lounge (⊠ 2 Pacific Place, 88 Queensway, Hong Kong, ☎ 2820–8591). The Peninsula's **Felix Bar** (⊠ Salisbury Rd., Tsim Sha Tsui, ☎ 2366–6251) has a great view. Go up in the bubble elevator and try to get the Sheraton's **Sky Lounge** (⊠ 20 Nathan Rd., Tsim Sha Tsui, 18th Floor, ☎ 2369–1111) at sunset and you won't be disappointed. At the Excelsior's **Talk of the Town** (⊠ 281 Gloucester Rd., Causeway Bay, ☎ 2894–8888) you'll be greeted by a 270° vista of Hong Kong Harbour.

Marvelous harbor views are also part of the appeal of **Gripps** (⊠ Harbour City, Tsim Sha Tsui, ☎ 2736–0088), the nightspot in the Omni Hongkong Hotel; it has ocean liner–level views of the harbor, and a central bar modeled on a high-class London pub. There is entertainment nightly by visiting pianists and other artists. The unique glass roof as well as the harbor scenery are attractions found at the New World Harbour View's **Oasis Bar** (⊠ 1 Harbour Rd., Wanchai, ☎ 2802–8888).

Feeling pampered is your pleasure at The Peninsula's **The Bar** or its club-like **Verandah** (⊠ Salisbury Rd., Tsim Sha Tsui, ☎ 2366–6251). The socially aware go to the Peninsula's lobby; sit to the right of the Peninsula's entrance to be where the cream of society traditionally lounges. The Mandarin Oriental's mezzanine **Clipper Lounge** (⊠ 5 Connaught Rd., Central, ☎ 2522–0111) is perfect for a relaxing drink after a long day of shopping or touring. The **Regent's two lobby lounges** (⊠ 18 Salisbury Rd., Tsim Sha Tsui, ☎ 2721–1211) are places to see and be seen. Be ready to chat about the fashion industry with the parade of Armani-clad and Chanel-scented men and women.

Pubs

Pubs can be found in all areas of Hong Kong. Some places are dives but may serve cheap drinks, while others are more upper-class and, of course, charge more. Live music is often provided by a local band and most pubs offer snacks.

Off-duty Central business folk flock to the pirate-galleon **Galley One** at Jardine House (⊠ In front of Star Ferry Terminal, Central, ☎ 2526–3061) for pub grub, which includes a delicious and reasonably priced lunch buffet.

Central's oak-beamed, British-managed **Bull & Bear** is in Hutchison House, on Lambeth Walk (⊠ 10 Harcourt Rd., ☎ 2526–1953). This place draws all types—a large share of whom are English expats—serves standard pub fare, and is known to get a little rowdy on weekends.

The latest trend to enter the territory is Irish-theme pubs. The interiors of the two branches of **Delaney's** (⊠ G/F, Multifield Plaza, 3 Prat Ave., Kowloon, ☎ 2301–3980; ⊠ 2/F One Capital Place, 18 Luard Rd., Wanchai, ☎ 2804–2880) were "made in Ireland" and shipped to Hong Kong, where they seem totally authentic, in furnishings and atmosphere. There's Guinness and Delaney's ale (a specialty microbrew) on tap, private corner "snugs," and a menu of Irish specialties. It's not cheap except for happy hours, when both pubs are usually packed.

In Wanchai, pub-hopping is practiced by the fit and less fastidious. **The Horse & Groom** (⊠ 161 Lockhart Rd., ☎ 2507–2517) is down-at-the-heels, but certainly a true pub. its neighboring **Old China Hand Tavern** (104 Lockhart Rd., ☎ 2527–9174) has been here since time immemorial and decor suffers accordingly, but it makes for authentic pub atmosphere. A relatively new drinking hole is **BB's Bar and Brasserie** (⊠ 114–120 Lockhart Rd., ☎ 2529–7702), which can be rather fashionable. **Dali's** (⊠ G/F, 76 Jaffe Rd., ☎ 2528–3113) attracts the district's suited business types. **Ridgeway's** (⊠ 1/F, Empire Land Commercial Bldg., 81–85 Lockhart Rd., ☎ 2866–6608) has pool tables. **The Flying Pig** (⊠ 2/F, Empire Land Commercial Bldg., 81–85 Lockhart Rd., ☎ 2865–3730) has amusing and original decor. For a reasonable hotel drinking hole, the Excelsior Hotel's **Dickens Bar** (⊠ 281 Gloucester Rd., ☎ 2894–8888), provides live music (most nights) and jazz sessions on Sunday afternoon.

Alternatively, if it's not too hot, you can sit at an outdoor table at Causeway Bay's **King's Arms** (⊠ Sunning Plaza, Sunning Rd., ☎ 2895–6557), one of Hong Kong's few city-center "beer gardens." The convivial outdoor area is a great place to meet other visitors to the colony.

A favorite bar in this part of town is **The Jump** (⊠ 463 Lockhart Rd., Wanchai, ☎ 2832–9007). Formerly China Jump (the name change was political), this pub has the bartenders flaring (tossing bottles) to concoct some strange brews—consider the FBI, a combination of ice cream and vodka. Beware the dentist's chair, however, unless you like to sip your margaritas upside down.

Over in Tsim Sha Tsui, a diverse, happy crowd frequents the Aussie-style **Kangaroo Pub** (⊠ 35 Haiphong Rd., ☎ 2376–0083), which has good pub food and interesting views of Kowloon Park.

Rick's Cafe (⊠ 4 Hart Ave., Tsim Sha Tsui, ☎ 2367–2939), a local hangout, is a restaurant-pub decorated à la *Casablanca,* with potted palms, ceiling fans, and posters of Bogie and Bergman (there's also a branch on Lockhart Road in Wanchai). **Grammy's Lounge** (⊠ 2A Hart Ave., ☎ 2368–3833) features Filipino-led sing-alongs and attracts a rowdy crowd. **Ned Kelly's Last Stand** (⊠ 11A Ashley Rd., Tsim Sha Tsui, ☎ 2376–0562) is an institution with Aussie-style beer and grub and loud and fun live jazz in the evening. For Central's Lan Kwai Fong area *see* For Singles *below.*

A trendy place to be in Tsim Sha Tsui is an out of the way strip called Knutsford Terrace, where a new breed of bars and restaurants have recently made their home. Tropical rhythms can be found at the Caribbean-inspired **Bahama Mama's** (⊠ 4–5 Knutsford Terr., ☎ 2368–2121) where there's world music. You wouldn't think that **Chasers** (⊠ G/F Shop 2, Knutsford Terr., ☎ 2367–9487), fitted with genuine English antiques, including chairs, lamps, and prints, would be as groovy as it is. Young locals love it.

Wine Bars

Western stockbrokers and financial types unwind in Central's **Brown's Wine Bar** (⊠ 2/F Tower 2, Exchange Sq., ☎ 2523–7003). It has excellent British food and a splendid bar.

For an intimate encounter, try **Le Tire Bouchon** (⊠ 9 Old Bailey St., Central, ☎ 2523–5459), which dispenses tasty bistro meals and fine wines by the glass.

Fenton's Wine Bar (⊠ Evergreen Plaza Hotel, 33 Hennessy Rd., Wanchai, ☎ 2866–9111) attracts a lot of suits; it's open from noon to midnight.

A cozy ambience describes tiny, classy **Juliette's** (⊠ 6 Hoi Ping Rd., Causeway Bay, ☎ 2822–5460), where chuppie (Hong Kong's Chinese yuppies) couples and just-left-work corporate types can be found.

Pacific Wine Cellars (⊠ Basement, Seibu, Pacific Place, 88 Queensway, Admiralty, ☎ 2971–3897) is tucked away behind tall shelves of vintage wines in Seibu's magnificent basement floor grocery store. Mainly suits and shoppers discover this joint.

Afrikan Cafe and Wine Bar (⊠ 7 Glenealy, Central, ☎ 2868–9299) has wine happy hours and regular wine promotions. Well-heeled travelers and, bearing its Central location, the inevitable business types, frequent this bar.

Pomeroys (⊠ Pacific Place, Level 3, The Mall, ☎ 2523–4772; 1–9 On Hing Terr., Central, ☎ 2810–1162) is a congenial place, if rather noisy, where crowds gather—especially at happy hour.

Jazz and Folk Clubs

Since 1989, jazz lovers have enjoyed great performances at the **Jazz Club** (⊠ 34 D'Aguilar St., Central, ☎ 2845–8477). Recently revamped, the club boasts a wide selection of local jazz, R&B, and soul talent as well as top-notch international acts every month, including harmonica player extraordinaire Carey Bell, and bluesmen Georgie Fame and Joe Louis Walker.

Ned Kelly's Last Stand (☞ Pubs, *above*) is an Aussie-managed home for pub grub and Dixieland, courtesy of Ken Bennett's Kowloon Honkers. Get here early, before 10 PM, to get a comfortable seat.

Sunday afternoon sessions at the Excelsior Hotel's **Dickens Bar** (☞ Pubs, *above*) are always worth checking out, as is the resident band. Wednesday-night gigs are definitely worth stopping by for at the **Godown** bar-restaurant, in the basement of the Furama Kempinski Hotel (⊠ 1 Connaught Rd., ☎ 2524–2088).

Wanchai's unpretentious alternative to the topless bar scene is **The Wanch** (⊠ 54 Jaffe Rd., ☎ 2861–1621), known for its live local folk and rock performances. The interesting Hong Kong–theme decoration (remember *Love is a Many Splendored Thing*?) is also worth a visit.

There are many rousing evenings when Filipinos take on American country-and-western music in **Bar City** (⊠ New World Centre, Tsim Sha Tsui, ☎ 2369–8571). It is particularly popular with young locals.

Hardy's Folk Club (⊠ 35 D'Aguilar St., Central, ☎ 2522–4448) is another Hong Kong rarity—there's an open stage for anyone to get up and give it a go. Several steps away from karaoke, there's usually a guitarist who takes requests, but singers vary from the talented amateur to the self-conscious Western transient bellower, to dismal, one-drink-too-many wailers—can be amusing. It can be amusing or awful.

Discos

At the discos in Hong Kong, young people with money to spend prance about in the latest fashions (both the fashions and the dancing can be worrying). Whether it's thigh-high PVC boots, neon-color tops, or life-preserver-type jackets, if the clothes are in the windows of hip shops, the young guns are wearing them. Cover charges are high by American standards; entrance to the smarter spots can be HK$100 or more (much more on the eves of major public holidays), although this usually entitles you to two drinks. If discos aren't your taste, and dance parties are, look out for posters in Lan Kwai Fong and Wanchai, which scream of the latest international DJ (usually very well-known) arriving in town to play for one night only. Some bars and restaurants also hold weekly or monthly club nights and music ranges from funk and jazz to house and easy listening.

The perennial favorite nightspot is **JJs** (⊠ Grand Hyatt, 1 Harbour Rd., Hong Kong, ☎ 2588–1234), the Grand Hyatt's entertainment center. It contains a disco, a nightclub, and a pizza lounge with a pool table and dartboard, but it is remembered most for its flashy disco lights, good house band, and the wall-to-wall suits and their escorts.

The **Catwalk** in the New World Hotel (⊠ 22 Salisbury Rd., Tsim Sha Tsui, ☎ 2369–4111) has a disco, live band, and karaoke lounges. The interesting decor has antler chandeliers hanging from the ceiling and cat prints on the floor.

Japanese tourists gravitate to the Park Lane Hotel's **Starlight** (⊠ 310 Gloucester Rd., Causeway Bay, ☎ 2890–3355). Some tourists check out the Japanese high-tech **Zodiac** disco, known for its Cantopop, in the New World Centre's Bar City drinking complex (⊠ Salisbury Rd., Tsim Sha Tsui, ☎ 2369–8571). One ticket admits you to the City's three operations.

Joe Bananas (⊠ 23 Luard Rd., Wanchai, ☎ 2529–1811) is a legend in its own drinking time. This disco-cum-bar strictly excludes the military and people dressed too casually—no shorts, sneakers, or T-shirts. This is a yuppie favorite and there's frequently a line to get in. The evening starts with friends meeting up for drinks—the cocktails are lethal, by the way—but later in the night the tables are pushed aside and the dancers have their way.

The dance floor at **The Big Apple Pub and Disco** (⊠ Basement, 20 Luard Rd., Wanchai, ☎ 2529–3461) gets going in the wee hours of the morning—and keeps going. There is a sleaze factor involved with this joint, but it's one of the best places to dance and is a favorite among the clubbers and dance-party crowd who wander out into the morning air at 8 AM to finally go home to their beds. **Neptune Disco II** (⊠ 98–108 Jaffe Rd., Wanchai, ☎ 2865–2238) is late night dancing for the dance-till-you-drop set. It starts late and ends later.

Topless Bars

With a few exceptions, most topless bars are scruffy dives. A beer may seem reasonably priced, at around HK$25, but the "champagne" the women drink is not. Charges for conversational companionship can also be an unexpected extra charge.

Bottoms Up (⊠ 14 Hankow Rd., Tsim Sha Tsui, ☎ 2721–4509) was immortalized by its use in the James Bond film *The Man with the Golden Gun*. Cozy circular bar counters are tended by topless women. This place is so respectable that visiting couples are welcomed.

Over in Wanchai, once known as "The World of Suzie Wong," the friendliest faces are those of off-duty Filipina amahs either working or lounging around the dance floors of spots such as the **San Francisco Bar** (⊠ 129 Lockhart Rd., ☎ 2527–0468) and **Club Mermaid** (⊠ 96 Lockhart Rd., ☎ 2529–2113).

A popular cluster of Wanchai haunts is to be found on and off Wanchai's **Fenwick Street**—stick your nose in An-An, Crossroads, Club Mikado, and, of course, the Suzie Wong Club.

Other bars, with or without door charges, in Wanchai or Old Tsim Sha Tsui (on the side roads off Nathan Rd.) warrant sober assessment by potential visitors. Avoid the so-called "fishball" stalls farther out in Kowloon, unless you are a Cantonese-speaking anthropologist who likes working in the dark. Ditto for massage parlors.

Hostess Clubs

These are clubs in name only. Hong Kong's better ones are multimillion-dollar operations with hundreds of presentable hostess-companions of many races. Computerized time clocks on each table tabulate companionship charges in timed units—the costs are clearly detailed on table cards, as are standard drink tabs. The clubs' dance floors are often larger than a disco's, and they have one or more live bands and a scheduled lineup of singers. They also have dozens of fancily furnished private rooms—with partitioned lounges and the ubiquitous karaoke setup—that are often palatially comfortable. Local and visiting businessmen adore these rooms—and the multilingual hostesses. Business is so good that the clubs are willing to allow visitors *not* to ask for companionship. The better clubs are on par with music lounges in deluxe hotels, though they cost a little more. Their happy hours start in the afternoon, when many have a sort of tea-dance ambience, and continue through to mid-evening. Peak hours are 10 PM–4 AM.

Club BBoss is the grandest and most boisterous, in Tsim Sha Tsui East's Mandarin Plaza (☎ 2369–2883). Executives, mostly locals, entertain in this oddly named club, tended by a staff of more than 1,000. If one's VIP room is too far from the entrance, one can hire an electrified vintage Rolls Royce and purr around an indoor roadway. Be warned that this is tycoon territory, where a bottle of brandy can cost HK$18,000. Along the harbor, in New World Centre, are **Club Cabaret** (☎ 2369–8431) and **Club Deluxe** (☎ 2721–0277), both luxurious dance lounges.

As its name implies, **Club Kokusai** (✉ 81 Nathan Rd., Tsim Sha Tsui, ☎ 2367–6969) appeals to visitors from the land of the rising yen. As in other clubs, karaoke dominates here.

Mandarin Palace (✉ 24 Marsh Rd., ☎ 2575–6551) is a comfortable grand Wanchai nightclub where clients can indulge their singing aspirations in karaoke duets with the hostesses until the wee hours.

For Singles

Hong Kong is full of single people, possibly because of the transient nature of the town or because their hardworking lifestyle leaves them no time for relationships. Either way, there's a rampant singles scene with people out looking for that special someone or that special someone just for tonight. Taking yourself off to any of the major bar and club areas will guarantee sheer numbers; the rest is, as they say, up to you.

Many Westerners and chuppies choose to meet in crowded comfort in the Lan Kwai Fong area, a hillside section around Central's D'Aguilar Street. It contains many appetizing bistros, wine bars, and ethnic cafés.

Singles mix happily at **California** (✉ 24–26 Lan Kwai Fong St., Central, ☎ 2521–1345), a laid-back American-style restaurant for all ages. It has a late-night disco most nights.

The tiny bar area of **La Dolce Vita** (✉ G/F, 9 Lan Kwai Fong St., Central, ☎ 2810–8698), underneath sister restaurant Post 97, often spills out onto the pavement. With sleek decor, this is a place to be seen and the cliques tend to be a tad pretentious. Cheery Western crowds gather at Scottish-Victorian pub **Mad Dogs** (⊠ Century Square, 1 D'Aguilar St., Central, ☎ 2810–1000), also in the Lan Kwai Fong area, and in Tsim Sha Tsui near the Sheraton Hotel.

Schnurrbart (⊠ Winner Bldg., D'Aguilar St., Central, ☎ 2523–4700) is a friendly German pub. For a low-key evening, try **Hardy's Folk Bar** (⊠ 35 D'Aguilar St., ☎ 2522–4448). One place where the arts-minded can mingle is the **Fringe Club** (⊠ 2 Lower Albert Rd., Central, ☎ 2521–7251), housed in a historic redbrick building that also incorporates the members-only Foreign Correspondents Club. The Fringe Club is home to Hong Kong's alternative arts scene. Another drinking favorite for the casual is **Club 64** (⊠ 12–14 Wing Wah Lane, Central, ☎ 2523–2801), where a cheap drink in a small and old, but cozy setting can be had.

Solo businessmen can always find someone to talk to at hotel bars, frequented by both locals and expatriates. The Hyatt's **Chin Chin** or **Nathan's** (⊠ 67 Nathan Rd., Tsim Sha Tsui, ☎ 2311–1234), the Ritz Carlton's **Cossack's Bar,** and the **Chinnery** in the Mandarin Oriental all have their appeal.

THE ARTS

The best daily calendar of cultural events is the Life section of the *Hong Kong Standard*. You can also read reviews in its weekend *Hong Kong Life* magazine. The other English-language newspaper, the *South China Morning Post,* also lists events. Highlights of weekly happenings are listed in the *TV Times,* which comes out on Thursday, and in *HK Magazine,* a free newspaper distributed each Friday to many restaurants, stores, and bars.

City Hall (⊠ By Star Ferry, Hong Kong Island, ☎ 2921–2840) has posters and huge bulletin boards listing events and ticket availability. Tickets for cultural events held in government centers can be purchased in booths found on the ground floor by the main entrance. **URBTIX** outlets are the easiest place to purchase tickets for most general performances. There are branches at City Hall and the Hong Kong Arts Centre (☎ 2734–9009 for bookings and information). The free monthly *City News* newspaper also lists events and is available at City Hall.

Performance Halls

Hong Kong Island
City Hall (⊠ Edinburgh Pl., by Star Ferry, Central, ☎ 2921–2840). Classical music, theatrical performances, films, and art exhibitions are presented at this complex's large auditorium, recital hall, and theater.
Hong Kong Arts Centre (⊠ 2 Harbour Rd., Wanchai, ☎ 2582–0200). Here you will find several floors of auditoriums, rehearsal halls, and recital rooms that welcome local and visiting groups to perform. Some of the best independent and classic films and documentaries are shown, often with themes that focus on a particular country, period or on a well-known director.
Hong Kong Fringe Club (⊠ 2 Lower Albert Rd., Central, ☎ 2521–7251). This locally run club hosts some of Hong Kong's most innovative visiting and local entertainment and art exhibitions. Shows range from the blatantly amateur to the dazzlingly professional. It also has good jazz, avant-garde drama, and many other events.
Queen Elizabeth Stadium (⊠ 18 Oi Kwan Rd., Wanchai, ☎ 2591–1346). Although this is basically a sports stadium, with a seating ca-

pacity of 3,500 it is also frequently the venue for presentations of ballet and orchestral and pop concerts.

Hong Kong Stadium (⊠ Happy Valley, ☎ 2839–7300). This new stadium is Hong Kong's largest (seating 40,000) and most impressive, with grandstands half-enclosed by giant shells. It is used for major sports events, in particular the beefy Rugby Sevens as well as, occasionally, rock concerts.

Hong Kong Academy for Performing Arts (⊠ 1 Gloucester Rd., Wanchai, ☎ 2584–8500). This arts school has two major theaters each seating 1,600 people, plus a 200-seat studio theater and 500-seat outdoor theater. Performances include local and international theater, modern and classical dance, plus music concerts.

Kowloon

Hong Kong Coliseum (⊠ Hunghom Railway Station, Hunghom, ☎ 2355–7234). This stadium has the capacity to seat more than 12,000 and presents everything from basketball to ballet, skating polar bears to international pop stars.

Hong Kong Cultural Centre (⊠ Salisbury Rd., ☎ 2734–2009). This venue for shows and conferences contains the Grand Theatre, which seats 1,750, and a concert hall, which accommodates 2,100. The center is used by visiting and local artists, whose performances range from opera to ballet to orchestral music.

Academic Community Hall (⊠ 224 Waterloo Rd., ☎ 2339–5182). This modern auditorium belongs to Baptist College and usually hosts pop concerts. It also offers dance and symphony concerts. Few big names book here, but there's plenty of local talent to check out.

The New Territories

Tsuen Wan Town Hall (⊠ Tsuen Wan, ☎ 2414–0144; take the MTR to Tsuen Wan Station). Although it's off the beaten track, this auditorium has a constant stream of both local and international performers. Groups include everything from the Warsaw Philharmonic to troupes of Chinese acrobats. It has a seating capacity of 1,424 and probably the best acoustics of all the performance halls in the colony.

Shatin Town Hall (⊠ New Town Plaza, Shatin, ☎ 2694–2511). This impressive building, attached to an enormous shopping arcade, is a five-minute walk from the KCR station at Shatin. It hosts cultural events including dance, drama, and concert performances.

Festivals and Special Events

There's a veritable festival season in Hong Kong from January to April each year when the Fringe, Arts, Food, and Film festivals are held back-to-back. Then there are a few more smaller festivals throughout the year. The festivals showcase diverse local and international shows and performers. Often, a group of artists get together a few works, sponsorship is granted, and before you know it, it's proclaimed a festival. Following are the regular cultural festivals—but don't be surprised if a festival turns up that's not on the list.

Hong Kong Fringe Festival (Jan.). Often scooping up top-notch performers from the Edinburgh Fringe in the United Kingdom, the Hong Kong Fringe Festival hosts an assorted heap of international and local drama, dance, music, and light entertainment. The quality can be patchy, but that's part of the fun, and tickets for shows are usually relatively cheap.

Hong Kong Arts Festival (Feb.–Mar.). For many, this festival is the cultural highlight of the year. It embraces four weeks of world-class music and drama from around the globe. Many acts sell out way in advance. Information abroad can be obtained through Cathay Pacific Airways offices or the HKTA. In Hong Kong, City Hall has all the schedules up on boards so you can see what's sold out.

Hong Kong Food Festival (Mar.). This festival, with two weeks of food, glorious food, is designed to give tourists a sampling of the territory's diverse culinary options. The festival holds a smorgasbord of events including cooking classes with world-renowned chefs, tours of famous restaurants and tea houses, and an amusing waiters' race in downtown Central. Brochures and more information are available at the HKTA.

Hong Kong International Film Festival (Apr.). Two weeks of films and documentaries representing virtually every country in the world certainly give Hong Kong film fans a good run for their money. There is neither commercial interest specifically involved nor a competition, and the festival frequently focuses on hot-spots in global cinema, as well as special sections on restored Mandarin classics, commendable locally made films, and many other Asian productions. It's difficult to get tickets for evening performances, but seats at daytime shows, beginning around noon, are usually available (☏ URBTIX at 2734–9009 for information). Brochures are available at City Hall and other Urban Council and Regional Council outlets.

Chinese Opera Fortnight (Sept.). For two weeks, traditional Cantonese, Peking, Soochow, Chekiang, and Chiu Chow opera is presented in City Hall Theatre, Concert Hall, and Ko Shan Theatre.

Festival of Asian Arts (Oct.–Nov.). Perhaps Asia's major cultural festival, this event showcases more than 150 artistic events (dance, music, and theater) from as far afield as Australia, Bhutan, Hawaii, and Mongolia. It is staged not only in concert halls but also at playgrounds throughout the territory. It is held biennially in even-numbered years and will next occur in 1998.

Performing-Arts Ensembles

Regular performances are held by several permanent arts ensembles in the territory. Some survive with government support, others are subsidized by private organizations.

Hong Kong Philharmonic Orchestra (☏ 2721–2320). More than 100 artists from Hong Kong, the United States, and Europe perform everything from classical to avant-garde to contemporary music by Chinese composers. Soloists have included Ashkenazy, Firkusny, and Maureen Forrester. Performances are usually held Friday and Saturday at 8 PM in City Hall or in recital halls in the New Territories (☏ 2721–2030 for ticket information).

Hong Kong Chinese Orchestra (☏ 2853–2622). Created in 1977 by the Urban Council, this group performs only Chinese works. The orchestra consists of strings, plucked instruments, wind, and percussion. Each work is specially arranged and orchestrated for each occasion (☏ 2853–2622 for further information).

Chinese Opera

Cantonese Opera. There are 10 Cantonese opera troupes in Hong Kong, as well as many amateur singing groups. These groups perform "street opera," as in the Shanghai Street Night Market on Sunday, while others perform at temple fairs, in City Hall, or in playgrounds under the auspices of the Urban Council (☏ 2867–5125). Visitors unfamiliar with the form are sometimes alienated by the strange sounds of this highly complex and extremely sophisticated art form. Every gesture has its own meaning; in fact, there are 50 different gestures for the hand alone. Props attached to the costumes are similarly intricate and are used in exceptional ways. For example, the principal female will often wear 5-foot-long pheasant tails attached to the headdress. Anger is shown by dropping the head and shaking it in a circular fashion so the feathers move in a perfect circle. Surprise is shown by "nodding the feathers." One can also "dance with the feathers" to show a mixture of anger and determination. The orchestral instruments punctuate the singing. It is best to have a local friend translate the gestures, since the stories are so complex that they make Wagner or Verdi librettos seem almost simplistic.

Peking Opera. A highly stylized musical performance, this type of opera employs higher-pitched voices than Cantonese opera. This is an older opera form and more respected for its classical traditions. Several troupes visit Hong Kong from the People's Republic of China each year, and their meticulous training is well regarded. They perform in City Hall or at special temple ceremonies. Call 2867–5125 for further information.

Dance

Hong Kong Dance Company (☎ 2853–2642). The Urban Council created the Hong Kong Dance Company in 1981 to promote the art of Chinese dance and to present newly choreographed work on Chinese historical themes. They give about three performances a month throughout the territory and have appeared at the Commonwealth Arts Festival in Australia. The 30-odd members are experts in folk and classical dance.

Hong Kong Ballet (☎ 2573–7398). This is Hong Kong's first professional ballet company and vocational ballet school. It is Western-oriented, both classical and contemporary, with the dancers performing at schools, auditoriums, and various festivals.

City Contemporary Dance Company (☎ 2326–8597). This group, dedicated to contemporary dance, offers innovative programs inspired by Hong Kong themes. Performances are usually held at the Hong Kong Arts Centre (☞ *above*).

Drama

Chung Ying Theatre Company (☎ 2521–6628). A professional company of Chinese actors performs plays (most of them original) mainly in Cantonese. Regular guest performers include English mime artist Peta Lily.

Fringe Club (☎ 2521–7251). An enormous amount of alternative theater, ranging from one-person shows to full dramatic performances, is presented at this club, the only one of its kind to offer facilities to amateur drama, music, and dance groups. Short-run contemporary plays by American and English writers are also presented as well as shows by independent local groups. It is an ideal starting point for anyone interested in seeing how the less established arts groups are getting along.

Zuni Icosahedron (☎ 2893–8419). The best-known avant-garde group puts on new drama and dance in Cantonese and English at various locations.

6 Outdoor Activities and Sports

AS YOU MIGHT EXPECT IN THE hometown of Jackie Chan, Hong Kong is a place where high-octane activity never seems to stop, whether it's on the stock exchange floor, in the gym, or in the racing stands. You won't find much baseball or American-style football, but you can join the men and women doing ta'i chi in the public parks (if you care to get up at 6 AM), and of course, if you've ever dreamed of studying martial arts, here is the place to start. Hong Kong residents are partial to hiking in the mountains and sailing into the more remote stretches of the South China Sea, beyond Victoria Harbour. Golf and tennis are widely available. And if you happen to be in town for horse racing season, don't miss the spectacle. Whether you want to keep active while in Hong Kong or just cheer on the sidelines, here is a guide to participatory and spectator sports.

PARTICIPANT SPORTS

Hong Kong has long been known as a club-oriented city, and whether you're into golf, sailing, squash, or tennis, you'll find that the best facilities are available at members-only clubs. However, in many cases reciprocal privileges are available with clubs outside of Hong Kong. Check with your club before you leave for Hong Kong to see if it has an arrangement with one there. If it does, you'll need to take along your membership card, a letter of introduction, and, often, your passport when you visit the affiliated establishment in Hong Kong. Call when you arrive to book facilities, or ask your hotel concierge to make arrangements.

Golf

Three Hong Kong golf clubs allow visitors with reciprocal privileges from a club at home to play their courses.

The **Clearwater Bay Golf and Country Club,** in the New Territories, has five outdoor and two indoor tennis courts, three indoor squash courts, and two indoor badminton courts, as well as an outdoor pool, a health spa, and an 18-hole golf course. Together with the Hong Kong Tourist Association (HKTA), the club sponsors a Sports and Recreation Tour, allowing visitors to tour the facilities and play golf. ⊠ *Clearwater Bay Rd., Saikung Peninsula,* ☎ *2719–1595, booking office 2335–3885 (HKTA tour,* ☎ *2801–7177).* ▨ *Greens fees: HK$1,200 for 18 holes. Tour cost: HK$380, plus greens fees. Cart, club, and shoe rentals available; no lessons.*

The **Discovery Bay Golf Club** on Lantau Island has an 18-hole course that is open to visitors on weekdays. ☎ 2987–7271 or 2987–7273. *Take the ferry from Star Ferry Pier in Central.* ▨ *Greens fees HK$1,200, club rental HK$150, golf-cart rental HK$170, and shoe rental HK$50. Lessons: HK$500–HK$600 per hr.*

The **Royal Hong Kong Golf Club** allows visitors to play on its three 18-hole courses at Fanling, New Territories. ⊠ *Fanling,* ☎ *2670–1211 for bookings, 2670–0647 for club rentals (HK$250).* ▨ *Greens fees: HK$1,400 for 18 holes. Deep Water Bay,* ☎ *2812–7070. Weekdays only.* ▨ *Greens fees: HK$450 for 18 holes. Lessons at both locations for nonmembers on weekdays only; HK$250–HK$400 per half hour, HK$290–HK$1,270 for 18-hole coaching, depending on pro.*

The **Tuen Mun Golf Centre** is a new public center with 100 golf driving bays and a practice green. ⊠ *Lung Mun Rd., Tuen Mun,* ☎ 2466–

2600. ☎ HK$10 per bay, HK$10 per club, and HK$10 per hour per 30 balls. ⊘ Tues., Wed., and Fri.–Sun. 8 am–10 pm, Mon. and Thurs. 1 pm–10 pm.

Hiking

Hong Kong's well-kept and reasonably well-marked hiking trails, never more than a few hours away from civilization, are one of its best-kept secrets. While visitors are busy shopping, the colony's residents are hitting the trails to escape the bustle and noise. A day's hike (or two days if you're prepared to camp out) takes a bit of planning, but it's well worth the effort. You see the best of Hong Kong, looking out over the expanse of islands from the low, rugged mountains, and discover exotic birds and shrubbery in the wild bushland, as you meander through rolling hillsides and highland plateaus. You feel farther than you really are from the buildings below, which seem almost insignificant from this perspective.

Don't, however, expect to find the wilderness wholly unspoiled. Few upland areas are able to escape for more than a few years at a time Hong Kong's relentless plague of hill fires. Some of these are caused by dried-out vegetation, others by small graveside fires set by locals to clear the land around ancestors' eternal resting spots. You may run into a knee-high charcoal forest of scorched grass and saplings. In more frequented areas, a layer of metal cans, heat-twisted plastic water bottles, and other rubbish lies bared and staring through the blackened stems. Partly because of these fires, most of Hong Kong's forests, except for a few spots in the New Territories, support no obvious wildlife other than birds—and mosquitoes. Bring along repellent.

Gear

In addition to insect repellent, you'll need sturdy shoes or boots, a small knapsack, sunblock, a hat or sunglasses, and a supply of water and food. If you hike the Hong Kong Trail, there is one stretch of urban development where you can stop and replenish your groceries. Wear layered clothing—the weather in the hills tends to be very warm during the day and colder toward nightfall. If you're planning to camp, carry a sleeping bag and tent. You can buy better camping equipment in the United States or in the United Kingdom, but in a pinch, you can buy backpacks, sleeping bags, and clothes at the **Great Outdoor Clothing Company** (⊠ Silvercord Bldg., 30 Canton Rd., Tsim Sha Tsui, ☎ 2730–9009). Inexpensive hiking boots can be bought at any of the dozens of small shops on Fa Yuen Street in Mongkok, Kowloon.

Before you go, pick up trail maps at the Government Publications Centre (⊠ Pacific Place, Government Office, Ground Floor, 66 Queensway, Admiralty, ☎ 2537–1910). Ask for the blueprints of the trails and the Countryside Series maps. The HM20C series is handsome four-color maps, but it's not very reliable.

Main Routes

You can hike through any of the territory's country parks and around any of the accessible outlying islands, but the following are the three most popular hiking trails.

Hong Kong Trail, the most practical for first-time trailblazers, wends for approximately 30 miles over Hong Kong Island from **Victoria Peak** to the beach community of **Shek O.** The full hike takes two days. The trail offers a panoramic view of the island with all of its history and splendor, and passes through some dense forest untouched by development or fires. Follow the map to the starting point on the Peak (you can get there by tram or taxi), and take the trail down through **Pok Fu Lam.** Toward the end of the first day you'll reach **Wang Nai Cheung Gap,** where a road connects Happy Valley to the south side of the island. You can buy food at the grocery market at Parkview Apartments here and continue your hike, or take a bus or taxi back to your hotel. On the second day, hike through **Tai Tam Country Park,** then climb **Dragons Back Ridge** toward the northeastern part of the island. From here the trail takes you down to the unspoiled rural village at **Big Wave Bay.** Between here and Shek O you'll see lavish estates. From **Shek O,** you can take a bus or taxi home.

The **Lantau Trail** is the toughest—three days if you follow the entire trail—but you can break off at a number of points. You can even retreat to a monastery to rest your feet. A long, arduous day's walk will take you from **Silvermine Bay,** which you reach by ferry from Central (☞ Outer Islands *in* Chapter 2), to the **Po Lin Monastery.** You'll walk over Sunset Peak, then down and up again to the top of **Lantau Peak,** Hong Kong's second-highest mountain. From here you drop straight down to the monastery. You can stay here for the night, either in the monastery dorms or the Lantau Tea Gardens cottages, or take a bus back to Silvermine Bay.

Begin your second day from the monastery. (Take the bus there if you returned to Silvermine Bay.) On this branch of the trail, you hike to the picturesque fishing village of **Tai O.** The scenery along this walk, past the Shek Pik Reservoir, is quite spectacular. From the monastery, make your way through the highland meadows of **South Lantau Park,** then turn north. You'll pass a number of small monasteries before dropping down to Tai O. From the village, you might want to turn back. If you're going to camp and continue on the trail, be sure to bring a three-day supply of water, and be prepared to spend the night in complete wilderness. The trail from Tai O follows the remote West Coast of Lantau to **Fan Lau,** site of an old fort and one of Hong Kong's mysterious prehistoric circles of stones. Return to Silvermine Bay on the path alongside the catchment channels, where water from the mountains flows down.

McLehose Trail, a splendidly isolated 60-mile path through the New Territories (a 4–5 day hike), starts at **Tsak Yue Wu,** beyond Sai Kung, and circles the **High Island Reservoir** before breaking north. Climb through **Sai Kung Country Park** to a steep section of the trail, up the mountain **Ma On Shan.** Then turn south, for a high ridge walk through **Ma On Shan Country Park.** From here you walk west along the ridges of eight mountains, also known as the "eight dragons" that gave Kowloon its name. (The last emperor of the Sung Dynasty is thought to have named the peninsula "nine dragons," after these eight peaks, plus himself, the ninth.) You may see wild monkeys on the trail near Eagles Nest. After you cross Tai Po Road the path follows along ridge tops toward **Tai Mo Mountain,** 3,161 feet above sea level. This is the tallest mountain in Hong Kong and sometimes gets snow at the top. Continuing west, the trail drops gradually to **Tai Lam reservoir,** to **Tuen Mun,** where you can catch public transportation.

The **Wilson Trail,** opened last year, runs 78 kilometers (48 miles) from Stanley Gap on Hong Kong Island to Nam Chung in the northeastern New Territories. You have to cross the harbor by MTR at Quarry Bay to complete the entire walk. The trail has been laid out with steps paved with stone and footbridges at steep sections and across streams. Clearly marked with signs and information boards, this popular walk is divided into 10 sections. You can take just one or two, since the whole trail takes about 31 hours to traverse. It begins at Stanley Gap Road on the southern end of Hong Kong Island, and it takes you through rugged peaks that offer a panoramic view of Repulse Bay and nearby Round and Middle islands. This first part, Section 1, is only for the very fit. Much of the trail requires walking up steep mountain grades. For an easier walk, try Section 7, which takes you along a greenery-filled fairly level path, that winds past the eastern shore of the Sing Mun Reservoir in the New Territories and then descends to Tai Po, where there is a sweeping view of Tolo Harbour. Other sections will take you through the monkey forest at the Kowloon Hill Fitness Trail (Section 5), mountains, and charming Chinese villages.

Jogging

The best stretch of land for jogging is Bowen Road. It's a five-mile run back and forth on a wooded street that is closed to vehicular traffic. The recently resurrected **Hong Kong Running Club** is open to all levels of ability, including those training for marathons, and meets every Sunday morning at 7 from April to December. There is no charge to visitors, though there is a small fee (HK$150) to cover printed handouts of articles on running safety, nutrition, and other concerns. Dr. Bill Andress, who runs the club, recommends shorter runs in the oppressively hot summer months, and cautions against starting a running program at that time if you aren't accustomed to the steam-bath weather. ⌧ *Meet in front of Adventist Hospital, 40 Stubbs Rd., Happy Valley, ☎ 2574–6211, ext. 888 (ask for director of health).*

Victoria Park at Causeway Bay also has an official jogging track.

Kung Fu

The **Martial Arts School** (⌧ 446 Hennessey Rd., Causeway Bay, ☎ 2891–1044) of master Luk Chi Fu, uses the "white crane" system of internal-strength training. This method is one of the schools of chi kung or noi kung, the names for internal-strength kung fu, as opposed to the more violent type seen in the movies. This gentler version is said to be the forerunner of yoga. The principles of "white crane" kung fu are attributed to a Tibetan monk from the Ming Dynasty who, while watching a crane fight a monkey, observed that in spite of the monkey's obvious physical advantages, the crane was able to win the dual. The bird accomplished this through a series of graceful movements that enabled him to avoid the monkey's punches; when the monkey's attention wandered, the crane struck the killing blow with its beak. The technique relies on quick thinking, controlled breathing, and an instant grasp of the situation at hand. At the advanced level, a student can absorb blows and use spears and knives as if they were an extension of his or her body. Now run by the master's son, Luk Chung Mau, the school is open to visitors who are in Hong Kong for a few weeks.

You can also study the Lion Dance, kick-boxing, and uses of weaponry at the **South China Athletic Association** (⌧ Caroline Hill Rd., Causeway Bay, ☎ 2665–0834). Other schools offer courses that last from 10 days to a few months. For information contact C.S. Tang at the **Hong Kong Chinese Martial Arts Association** (☎ 2798–2763).

Parachuting

If you're already a fan, or are feeling brave, the **Hong Kong Parachuting Club** holds weekend courses at Sai Kung, where you can jump from a fixed-wing aircraft to the airfield. Caution: Before you leave home, make sure your health insurance policy covers you for injuries incurred abroad. ☎ 2834–4391 or 2488–5447. ✉ HK$3,400 for course and parachute rental.

Skating

There is a first-class ice-skating rink at **Cityplaza II** on Hong Kong Island. ☎ 2885–4697. ✉ HK$50 per person weekdays, HK$60 per person weekends. All sessions are 2 hrs.

The **Festival Walk,** scheduled to open this year in Yau Yat Tsuen, adjacent to the Kowloon Tong train station, is an entertainment complex with the largest ice-skating rink in Hong Kong. Call the HKTA 2807–6177 for further information and an opening date.

Social and Health Clubs

The following **social clubs** have reciprocal facilities. The **Hong Kong Jockey Club** offers free entry to the members enclosure during racing season, but not use of club recreational facilities. Visitors with reciprocal privileges at the **Royal Hong Kong Golf Club** are allowed 14 free rounds of golf each year. Other clubs with reciprocal policies are the **Royal Hong Kong Yacht Club, Hong Kong Cricket Club, Kowloon Cricket Club, Hong Kong Football Club, Hong Kong Country Club, Kowloon Club, Hong Kong Club,** and **Ladies' Recreation Club.**

Health clubs are another matter. Most require membership. Two exceptions, where you pay by the day, are the women-only **Philip Wain** (✉ Parklane Sq., 5th Floor, Kimberley Rd., Tsim Sha Tsui, ☎ 2736–8888; ✉ Caroline Centre, 4th Floor, 28 Yun Ping Rd., Causeway Bay, ☎ 2882–7880) and the **Tom Turk Fitness Club** (✉ Citibank Tower, Citibank Plaza, 3 Garden Rd., 3rd Floor, Central, ☎ 2521–4541; ✉ International House, 8 Austin Rd., Tsim Sha Tsui, ☎ 2736–7188.). The majority of first-class hotels have health clubs on their premises. Many clubs around the world operate affiliate facilities in Hong Kong, so ask at your club before you visit.

Squash

Squash is very much a club activity in Hong Kong. However, there are public courts at the **Harbour Road Indoor Games Hall** (✉ 27 Harbour Rd., Wanchai, ☎ 2827–9684), **Hong Kong Squash Centre** (✉ Cotton Tree Dr. across from Peak Tram Terminal, Central, ☎ 2521–5072), and **Victoria Park** (✉ Hing Fat St., Causeway Bay, ☎ 2570–6186), and **Laichikok Park** (✉ Lai Wan Rd., Kowloon, ☎ 2745–2796). Bookings can be made up to 10 days in advance; book as early as possible. Bring a passport for identification. The Hong Kong Urban Council runs many public squash courts in the territory and provides a central booking service (☎ 2521–5072). Most courts are open from 7 AM to 10 or 11 PM and cost HK$46–HK$50 for 45 minutes. The Urban Council Information Line (☎ 2868–0000) can answer questions about locations of courts.

Tennis

If you want to play tennis, you will probably have to get someone who is a member of a private club to take you or have reciprocal privileges through your home club. Although there are a limited number of public tennis courts, they are usually completely booked far in advance. To book a public tennis court you will need identification such as a passport. The following are courts open to the public: **Victoria Park** (✉ Causeway Bay, ☎ 2570–6186), 14 courts; **Bowen Road Courts** (✉

Bowen Rd., Happy Valley, ☎ 2528–2983), 4 courts; **Hong Kong Tennis Centre** (⊠ Wongneichong Gap, Happy Valley, ☎ 2574–9122), 17 courts; and **Kowloon Tsai Park** (⊠ Kowloon Tong, ☎ 2336–7878), 8 courts. Most courts are open from 6 or 7 AM to 10 or 11 PM and cost HK$34 in the daytime and HK$46 in the evenings. The Urban Council Information Line (☎ 2868–0000) can answer questions about other locations. Further information is available through the Hong Kong Tennis Association (⊠ Sports House, Room 1021, 1 Stadium Path, So Kon Po, Causeway Bay, Hong Kong, ☎ 2504–8266).

Water Sports

Junking

Junking—dining on the water aboard large junks that have been converted to pleasure craft—is unique to Hong Kong. This leisure activity has become so popular in the colony that there is now a fairly large junk-building industry that produces highly varnished, plushly appointed, air-conditioned junks up to 80 feet long.

These floating rumpus rooms serve a purpose, especially for citizens living on Hong Kong Island who suffer from "rock fever" and need to escape through a day on the water. Because so much drinking takes place, the junks are also known as "gin-junks," commanded by "weekend admirals." They also serve as platforms for swimmers and waterskiers. If anyone so much as breathes an invitation for junking, grab it. You can also rent a junk. One established junk charter operator is **Simpson Marine Ltd.** (⊠ Aberdeen Marina Tower, 8 Shun Wan Rd., Aberdeen, ☎ 2555–7349), whose junks, with crew, can hold 35–45 people. Costs start at HK$2,200 for an eight-hour day trip or four-hour night trip during the week, and HK$4,500 on summer weekends. The price goes up on holidays. Other charter outfits recommended by the HKTA are **Jubilee International Tour Centre** (⊠ Man Yee Bldg., 60 Des Voeux Rd., Room 302–303, Central, ☎ 2530–0530), and the **Boatique** (⊠ Aberdeen Marina Club, Shop 10–11, Ground Floor, Aberdeen Marina Bldg., 8 Shum Wan Rd., Aberdeen, ☎ 2555–9355). The pilot will take you to your choice of the following outer islands: Cheung Chau, Lamma, Lantau, Po Toi, or the islands in Sai Kung Harbour.

Sailing

To go sailing you must belong to a yacht club that has reciprocal privileges with one in Hong Kong. Contact the **Royal Hong Kong Yacht Club** (☎ 2832–2817) to make arrangements. Sometimes members need crews for weekend races, so experienced sailors can go to the club and check the "crew wanted" board in the Course Room.

Scuba Diving

A number of clubs offer scuba diving trips, but it is usually difficult to join them unless you are introduced by a friend who is a member. However, **Bunn's Divers Institute** (⊠ 188 Wanchai Rd., Wanchai, ☎ 2893–7899) offers outings for qualified divers to such areas as Sai Kung. The cost of a day trip runs HK$480 if you bring your own equipment and HK$800 if you need to rent gear. You must bring or rent a tank ($70 each; you'll need one each for morning and afternoon). If you're going to be in town a while, **Mandarin Divers** (⊠ Aberdeen Marina Tower, 8 Shun Wan Rd., Aberdeen, ☎ 2554–7110) offers two-week open-water training for a cost of HK$4,500, including boat rental, equipment, and certification (medical certificate required).

Swimming

Swimming is extremely popular with the locals, which means that most beaches are packed on summer weekends and public holidays.

The more popular beaches, such as Repulse Bay, are busy day and night throughout the summer (☞ Beaches, *below*). Pollution is a problem in Hong Kong waters, however, so don't swim if a red flag—indicating either pollution or an approaching storm—is hoisted, or if you see trash floating on the water. Shortly after the Mid-Autumn Festival in September, local people stop using the beaches. This is a good time for visitors to enjoy them, especially since the weather is warm year-round. Public swimming pools are filled to capacity in summer and closed in winter. Most visitors use the pools in their hotels.

Waterskiing

To rent a speedboat, equipment, and the services of a driver, contact the **Waterski Club** (✉ At the pier at Deep Water Bay Beach, ☎ 2812–0391) or ask your hotel front desk for names and numbers of other outfitters. The cost is usually about HK$520 per hour.

Windsurfing

The popularity of this sport was on the decline until Hong Kong's native daughter Lee Lai-shan sailed off with the gold medal in the 1996 Summer Olympics. Now, windsurfing centers at **Stanley Beach** on Hong Kong Island and **Tun Wan Beach** on Cheung Chau Island will gladly start you on the path to Olympic glory with lessons (approximately HK$250 for four hours spread over two days) and board rentals (HK$55 per hour). Other beaches that have stands where you can rent boards are the small beach opposite the main beach at **Shek O**, Hong Kong Island; **Tolo Harbour,** near Taipo in New Territories; and **Sha Ha Beach,** in front of the Surf Hotel at Sai Kung, also in the New Territories. For further information, call the **Windsurfing Association of Hong Kong** (✉ Sports House, 1 Stadium Path, Room 1101, So Kon To, Causeway Bay, ☎ 2504–8255).

SPECTATOR SPORTS

Cricket Fighting

The ancient Chinese sport of cricket fighting (that's cricket as in insect, not as in the sport) is hidden from visitors, so ask for directions from a local friend. If you see someone wandering in a market, carrying a washtub, and softly calling, *"Tau, chi choot,"* ("Come to see the crickets fight") follow him.

Horse Racing and Gambling

Horse racing is the nearest thing in Hong Kong to a national sport. It is a multimillion-dollar-a-year business, employing thousands of people and drawing crowds that are almost crazed in their eagerness to rid themselves of their hard-earned money.

The Sport of Kings is run under a monopoly by the Royal Hong Kong Jockey Club, one of the most politically powerful entities in the territory. Profits go to charity and community organizations. The season runs from September or October through May. Some 65 races are held at two race courses—**Happy Valley** on Hong Kong Island and **Shatin** in the New Territories. Shatin's racecourse is only a few years old and is one of the most modern in the world. Both courses have huge video screens at the finish line so that gamblers can see what is happening each foot of the way.

Races are run at one track on Wednesday night and at one or the other on either Saturday or Sunday. Even if you're not a gambler, it's worth going just to see the crowds. You can view races from the Members'

Stand at both tracks by showing your passport and paying HK$50 for a badge.

In a place where gambling has developed into a mania, it may come as a surprise to learn that most forms of gambling are forbidden. Excluding the stock market, which is by far the territory's biggest single gambling event, the only legalized forms of gambling are horse racing and the lottery. Nearby Macau is another story—there you can get your fill of casino gambling (☞ Chapter 8).

Rugby

One weekend every spring, Hong Kong hosts the international tournament of Sevens-a-Side teams at the Hong Kong Stadium, and the whole town goes rugby mad. In 1997, The Sevens World Cup will be held in Hong Kong on March 21–23. To avoid camping outside the stadium all night to buy tickets, you can purchase them in advance from an overseas agent. For a list of agents, contact Beth Coalter at the **Hong Kong Rugby Football Union** (⌧ Sports House, 1 Stadium Path, Room 2003, So Kon Po, Causeway Bay, ☎ 2504–8300, ⅢFAX 2576–7237).

BEACHES

Few tourists think of Hong Kong as a place for swimming or sunbathing. Yet Hong Kong has hundreds of beaches, about 30 of which are "gazetted"—cleaned and maintained by the government, with services that include lifeguards, floats, and swimming-zone safety markers. The scenery is breathtaking, and the beach is a fine place to while away a sunny day, but we wouldn't advise that you plan to spend the whole day in the water because of pollution problems. For this reason, we've restricted our recommendations to the beaches that offer a variety of activities as alternatives to swimming. Some beaches are periodically closed because of severe pollution. Check with the HKTA before taking the plunge. If the red flag is hoisted at a beach, stay out of the water; it indicates pollution or an approaching storm. The red flag is often flying at Big Wave Bay (on Hong Kong Island, south side) because of the rough surf. Check with the HKTA or listen to announcements on radio or TV before heading out there.

Almost all the beaches can be reached by public transportation, but knowing which bus to catch and where to get off can be difficult. Most bus drivers have neither the time nor the ability to give instructions in English. Pick up bus maps at the HKTA information booths before you start out. Or you can take a taxi all the way to any of the beaches on Hong Kong Island and still have change for lunch! Beaches on outlying islands are reached by Hong Kong Ferry from Central and are often a short walk from the pier.

Hong Kong Island

At **Deep Water Bay** the action starts at dawn every morning, all year long, when members of the Polar Bear Club go for a dip. The beach is packed in summer, when there are lifeguards, swimming rafts, and safety-zone markers, plus a police reporting center. Barbecue pits, showers, and rest rooms are open year-round. A taxi from Central will take about 20 minutes. ⌧ *By public transport, take Bus 6A from Exchange Square Bus Terminus. For a scenic route, take Bus 70 from Exchange Square to Aberdeen and change to Bus 73, which passes the beach en route to Stanley.*

Repulse Bay is Hong Kong's answer to Coney Island. It has changing rooms, showers, toilets, swimming rafts, swimming safety-zone markers, and playgrounds. There are also several Chinese restaurants, and kiosks serving light refreshments. The beach has an interesting building at one end resembling a Chinese temple, with large statues of Tin Hau, goddess of the sea, and Kwun Yum, goddess of mercy. Small rowboats are available for rent at the beach. ⊠ *Take Bus 6, 6A, 64, 260, or 262 from Exchange Square, or Bus 73 from Aberdeen. Most of the drivers on this route speak English and can tell you when to get off.*

Stanley Main, a wide sweep of beach, is popular with the Hobie Cat crowd and has a refreshment kiosk, swimming rafts, changing rooms, showers, and toilets, plus a nearby market. ⊠ *Take a taxi from Central or Bus 6, 6A, or 260 from Exchange Square, or Bus 73 from Aberdeen.*

Turtle Cove, isolated but picturesque, has lifeguards and rafts in summer, barbecue pits, a refreshment kiosk, changing rooms, showers, and toilets. ⊠ *From Central take the MTR to Sai Wan Ho and change to Bus 14; get off on Tai Tam Rd. after passing the dam of Tai Tuk Reservoir.*

Shek O is almost Mediterranean in aspect. A fine, wide beach with nearby shops and restaurants, it has refreshment kiosks, barbecue pits, lifeguards, swimming rafts, playgrounds, changing rooms, showers, and toilets. This is one of the few beaches directly accessible by bus. ⊠ *Take the MTR from Central to Shau Ki Wan (there is a bus from Central to Shau Ki Wan, but it takes hours), then Bus 9 to the end of the line.*

Big Wave Bay, Hong Kong's only surfing beach, often lives up to its name and is frequently closed for swimming because of high surf. When the red flag goes up, signaling dangerous waves, get out of the water. The beach has kiosks, barbecue pits, a playground, changing rooms, showers, and toilets. ⊠ *From Shau Ki Wan take Bus 9 to the parking lot at Big Wave Bay Rd.; you have to walk for about 20 min, down several hills, to get to the beach.*

The New Territories

Expansive Sai Kung Peninsula has some of the most beautiful beaches, and many are easily reached by public transportation. Here are the three most popular beaches in Sai Kung:

Silverstrand is always crowded on summer weekends. Although a little rocky in spots, it has good, soft sand and all the facilities, including changing rooms, showers, and toilets. ⊠ *MTR to Choi Hung, then Bus 92 or taxi.*

Pak Sha Chau is a gem of a beach, with brilliant golden sand. It's on a grassy island near Sai Kung Town and can only be reached by sampan. (Go to a pier and look for sampans. A driver will probably approach you. You must negotiate a fee, but expect to pay about HK$100.) Amenities include barbecue pits and toilets. ⊠ *Take MTR to Choi Hung, then Bus 92 to Saikung.*

Sha Ha's waters are sometimes dirty, but because it is rather shallow far out from shore, it's ideal for beginning windsurfers. You can take lessons or rent a board at the Kent Windsurfing Centre. Facilities include refreshment kiosks, a coffee shop, and a Chinese restaurant in the adjacent Surf Hotel. ⊠ *Take MTR to Choi Hung, then Bus 92 to the end of the line at Saikung, and walk or take a taxi for about a mile.*

The Outer Islands

If you want to make a longer day of it, take a morning ferry to Lamma, Lantau, or Cheung Chau. One option is to combine the beach trip with a sightseeing tour of the island.

Hung Shing Ye, on Lamma Island, is very popular with local young people. There are no swimming rafts, but there are showers, toilets, changing rooms, barbecue pits, and a kiosk. ✉ *Take the ferry from Central to Yung Shue Wan and then walk over a low hill.*

Lo So Shing, also on Lamma Island and popular with local families, is an easy hike on a paved path from the fishing village of Sok Kwu Wan. Facilities include a kiosk, barbecue pits, swimming rafts, changing rooms, showers, and toilets. ✉ *Take a ferry from Central to Sok Kwu Wan and then walk for 20–30 min.*

Cheung Sha is a very popular beach located only a short taxi or bus ride from Silvermine Bay ferry pier. It has a sandy beach a mile long and is excellent for swimming. All the standard facilities are available. ✉ *Take the ferry from Central to Silvermine Bay. Buses meet the ferry every half hr on weekdays; on Sun. and holidays buses leave when full, which will not take long on a sunny day.*

Tung Wan is the main beach on Cheung Chau Island, and the wide sweep of golden sand is hardly visible on weekends because it's so crowded with sunbathers. At one end is the Warwick Hotel. There are plenty of restaurants along the beach for refreshments, seafood, and shade. The standard amenities are available. ✉ *Take the ferry from Central to Cheung Chau ferry pier and walk 5 min through the village to the beach.*

7 Shopping

SINCE THE 1980S, RAPIDLY RISING RETAIL RENTS have put a damper on the megabargains for which Hong Kong was once known. Although retail prices here are still well below those of many Asian and European cities, you will probably find that clothes, computers, and many electronic items cost about the same as or slightly more than they do in the United States. This is not to say that you won't find some good values, and, of course, a wide range of unique items. Many shopping aficionados still swear by Hong Kong, and they return year after year for such items as Chinese antiques, Chinese porcelain, pearls, watches, silk sheets and kimonos, tailor-made suits, and designer clothes found in off-the-beaten-path outlets. Cameras and eyeglasses can also be bargains, partly because lenses are ground in the region. A rule of thumb: Tiffany's, Dior, Waterford, and the other designer boutiques with branches all over the world will probably not offer bargains. Stick to local shops (choose those with the HKTA membership sticker in their window for consumer protection) and to items made in Hong Kong or other parts of Asia.

Shopping Tips

Hong Kong lost most of its third-world bazaar atmosphere years ago. Few of the outdoor market sellers will bargain with you now. In the electronic shops in Tsim Sha Tsui, however, salesmen will frequently drop the list price slightly, by about five percent. Nor is it uncommon for jewelers in the mid-price range to offer you a discount of 10 to 20 percent if you look at a few items and seem moderately interested. Be wary if a salesperson tries to drop the price much lower, however. You might go home to find you've purchased an inferior or defective item.

Major Shopping Areas

Hong Kong Island

WESTERN DISTRICT

From the edge of Central to Kennedy Town (take the MTR to Sheung Wan or the tram to Western Market) is **Western District,** one of the oldest and most typically Chinese areas of Hong Kong. Here you can find craftsmen making mah-jongg tiles, opera costumes, fans, and chops (seals carved in stone with engraved initials); Chinese medicine shops selling ginseng, snake musk, shark fins, and powdered lizards; rice shops and rattan-furniture dealers; and cobblers, tinkers, and tailors. Here, too, you will find alleyways in which merchants have set up small stalls filled with knickknacks and curios.

Also in Western, opposite Central Market, is the huge **Chinese Merchandise Emporium** with a vast display of reasonably priced goods, from luggage to antiques, made in China. Next to the Emporium, on **Pottinger Street,** are stalls selling every kind of button, bow, zipper, and sewing gadget. Cloth Alley, or Wing On Street, is nearby and so is Wellington Street, where you'll find a variety of picture framers, mah-jongg makers, and small boutiques. Going west, don't miss **Man Wa Lane,** where you can buy your personal Chinese chop. In this area you will also find Western's two largest department stores: Sincere and Wing On.

Nearby is the Victorian redbrick structure of **Western Market.** Built in 1906 as a produce market, it is now similar to London's Covent Garden. The first two floors are filled with shops selling crafts, toys, jewelry, collectibles, and fabrics. The top floor has the Mythical China and Family Kitchen restaurants, open for lunch and dinner.

The streets behind Western Market are some of the best places to soak up some of Hong Kong's traditional Chinese atmosphere. **Wing Lok Street** and **Bonham Strand West** are excellent browsing areas, with their herbal shops, snake gall-bladder wine shops—visit She Wong Yuen, (⊠ 89–93 Bonham Strand) for a taste—and shops selling rice, tea, and Chinese medicines. Heading uphill, don't miss the stalls selling bric-a-brac on **Ladder Street,** which angles down from Queen's Road in Central to Hollywood and Caine roads. **Hollywood Road** is the place to look for Chinese antiques and collectibles.

CENTRAL DISTRICT

The financial and business center of Hong Kong, **Central** offers an extraordinary mixture of boutiques, department stores, hotel shopping arcades, and narrow lanes full of vendors selling inexpensive clothing and knockoffs of designer goods.

Lane Crawford, east of the Chinese Merchandise Emporium, is Hong Kong's most luxurious department store. Central is also home to a branch of Chinese Arts & Crafts, which carries small collections of upscale clothing, linen, silk, jewelry, and art objects. Other exclusive shops can be found in Central's major business and shopping complexes, including the **Landmark Central Building, Prince's Building, Nine Queen's Road, Swire House,** and **Pacific Place,** and in hotel shopping arcades, such as those of the **Mandarin Oriental** and **Furama Kempinski** hotels.

You can hunt for bargains on clothing, shoes, woolens, handbags, and accessories in the stalls that fill **Li Yuen streets East and West** (⊠ Between Queen's Rd. and Des Voeux Rd.). **Wyndham** and **On Lan** streets have several good embroidery and linen shops, and **D'Aguilar Street** is filled with flower stalls.

WANCHAI DISTRICT

More famous for its "Suzie Wong" nighttime meanderings than for daytime shopping, **Wanchai** still has some interesting spots for the curious or adventurous shopper. Tattoos, for instance, are available on **Lockhart Road,** and traditional Chinese bamboo birdcages on **Johnston Road.** Wandering through the lanes between Johnston Road and Queen's Road East, with their vegetable and fruit markets, you can find dozens of stalls selling buttons and bows and inexpensive clothes. In tiny **Spring Garden Lane,** you will also find several small factory outlets. **Queen's Road East** (near its junction with Queensway) is famous for shops that make blackwood and rosewood furniture and camphor-wood chests. There are more furniture shops on **Wanchai Road,** off Queen's Road East.

HAPPY VALLEY

Happy Valley is a good area to shop for shoes. Follow **Wong Nai Chung Road** around the eastern edge of the racecourse to **Leighton Road.** At the intersection of these two roads you will find several shops that make shoes, boots, and handbags to order, at reasonable prices. The nearby **Leighton Centre** has several fashionable boutiques, toy shops, and accessory shops, but prices are higher here than they are in nearby Causeway Bay.

CAUSEWAY BAY

Four large Japanese department stores dominate **Causeway Bay**: Mitsukoshi, Jumbo Sogo, Daimaru, and Matsuzakaya. Times Square is a megamall with 12 floors of shopping, from the high-end Lane Crawford to run-of-the-mill moderate boutique chains. The main branch of the China Products Company chain is here, as is the Windsor House branch of Lane Crawford. **Hennessy Road** is filled with shops selling jewelry, watches, stereos, cameras, and electronic goods, and parallel **Lockhart Road** has several good shoe stores. The **Excelsior Hotel Shopping Centre** features a wide range of art, gift, and souvenir shops. **Vogue Alley** has boutiques where you can see the best work of Hong Kong's own fashion designers. The street called **Jardine's Bazaar,** a traditional favorite for inexpensive clothing, has strictly bottom-of-the-barrel merchandise now, but turn into the alley off the street to experience a bustling "wet market," (so called because the vendors are perpetually hosing down their produce) where Chinese housewives shop for fresh produce and chickens that are slaughtered on the spot.

EASTERN DISTRICT

The **Eastern District,** which includes North Point, Quarry Bay, and Shauki-wan, is more of a residential and restaurant area than an exciting shopping area. The best shopping is found in Quarry Bay's huge **City-plaza I & II** complex, which houses Hong Kong's largest department store, UNY, as well as hundreds of shops, ice-skating and roller-skating rinks, gardens, and restaurants.

STANLEY MARKET

The most popular shopping area on the south side of the island is **Stan-ley Market.** It's not quite the bargain mecca it used to be, but if you comb through the stalls, you can still find some good buys in sportswear and casual clothing. It's also a good place to shop for handicrafts, gifts, curios, and linens. The area around the **Main Street** section of the market has a trendy, artsy ambience. On the way to Stanley Market, stop at **Repulse Bay's** antiques-filled shopping arcade. Nearby, on Beach Road, is the **Lido Bazaar,** a series of stalls selling souvenirs, curios, jewelry, and clothing.

Kowloon

TSIM SHA TSUI DISTRICT

Tsim Sha Tsui, known for its "Golden Mile" of shopping along **Nathan Road,** is justifiably popular with tourists for its hundreds of stereo, camera, jewelry, cosmetic, fashion, and souvenir shops. Branching off Nathan Road are narrow streets lined with shops crowded with every possible type of merchandise. Explore **Granville Road,** with its embroidery and porcelain shops and clothing factory outlets (not as plentiful as they were a few years ago, but worth a look for serious bargain-hunters), and **Mody Road,** with its souvenir-shop alleys. Tsim Sha Tsui also has the Yue Hwa Chinese Products Emporium, the Japanese Isetan department store, the huge upscale World of Joyce mall, and three large and well-stocked branches of Chinese Arts & Crafts. Two of Hong Kong's largest shopping complexes—the multistory maze of the **New World Shopping Centre** and the vast, air-conditioned **Harbour City**—are found here. And the new **Tsim Sha Tsui East** area provides a host of other complexes.

Travel east of Tsim Sha Tsui to **Hunghom,** the center of Hong Kong's jewelry and textile-manufacturing industries, for a tremendous selection of designer and factory-outlet bargains. Many are found on **Man Yue Street.**

Shopping Centers

Hong Kong Island

The **Admiralty** (⌧ Queensway, Central, MTR: Admiralty) complex comprises a large selection of shops, clustered in four shopping centers:

Shopping

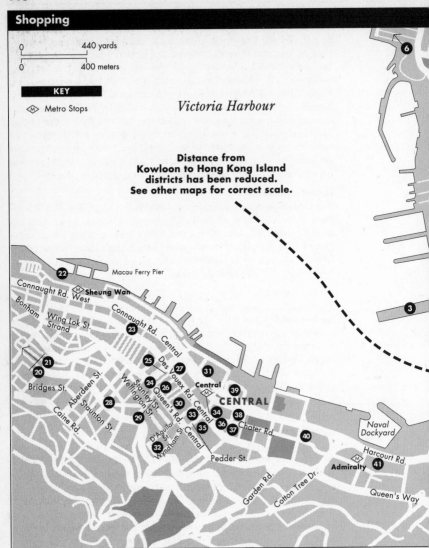

0 ————— 440 yards
0 ————— 400 meters

KEY

⬦ Metro Stops

Victoria Harbour

**Distance from
Kowloon to Hong Kong Island
districts has been reduced.
See other maps for correct scale.**

Macau Ferry Pier

Connaught Rd. West

Sheung Wan

Connaught Rd. Central

Bonham

Wing Lok St.

Strand

Bridges St.

Aberdeen St.

Staunton St.

Caine Rd.

Des Voeux Rd.

Wellington St.

Stanley St.

Queen's St.

Central

CENTRAL

Chater Rd.

D'Aguilar St.

Wyndham St. Central

Pedder St.

Garden Rd.

Cotton Tree Dr.

*Naval
Dockyard*

Harcourt Rd.

Admiralty

Queen's Way

Admiralty, **41**

Alexandra House, **36**

Burlington House, **17**

China Products Company, **46**

Chinese Arts & Crafts, **4**

Chinese Merchandise Emporium, **24**

Chung Kiu Chinese Products Emporium, **5**

Cityplaza I & II, **47**

Dragon Seed, **30**

Eastern Dreams, **28**

Excelsior Hotel Shopping Centre, **44**

Exchange Square, **31**

Flower Market, **8**

Harbour City, **1**

Hollywood Road, **20**

Hung Kei Mansion, **25**

Hutchison House, **40**

Hyatt Regency Shopping Arcade, **12**

Isetan, **15**

Jade Market, **7**

Jardine House, **39**

Jumbo Sogo, **43**

Kowloon City Market, **19**

Ladder Street, **21**

Laichikok, **6**

The Landmark, **35**

Lane Crawford, **29**

Lido Bazaar, **50**

Li Yuen Streets East and West, **26**

Man Cheung Building, **32**

Mandarin Oriental, **38**

Matsuzakaya, **45**

Mirador Mansion, **11**

Mitsukoshi, **42**

New World Shopping Centre, **16**

Ocean Centre, **2**

Ocean Terminal, **3**

Pedder Building, **33**

Peninsula Hotel, **14**

Prince's Building, **37**

Shui Hing, **13**

Shun Tak Centre, **22**

Sincere, **23**

Stanley Village Market, **49**

Swire House, **34**

Temple Street, **10**

Times Square, **48**

Wing On Plaza, **27**

Yaohan, **18**

Yue Hwa Chinese Products Emporium, **9**

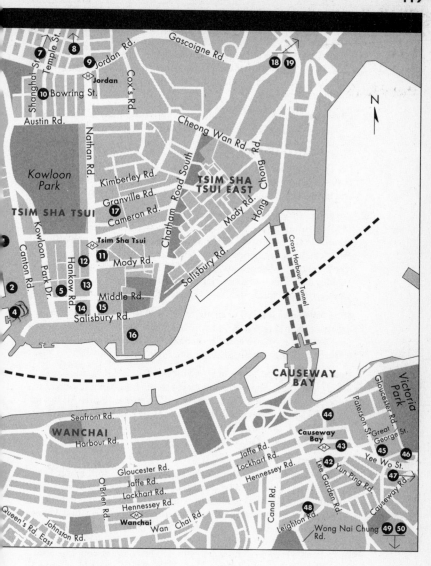

7 Temple St. **8**

9 Jordan Rd.

Shanghai St.

10 Bowring St.

Jordan

Cox's Rd.

Austin Rd.

Gascoigne Rd.

18 **19**

N

Cheong Wan Rd.

Nathan Rd.

Kowloon Park

Kimberley Rd.

TSIM SHA TSUI EAST

Granville Rd.

17 Cameron Rd.

Chatham Road South

Hong Chong Rd.

Mody Rd.

TSIM SHA TSUI

Kowloon Park Dr.

Tsim Sha Tsui

Salisbury Rd.

Canton Rd.

12 **11** Mody Rd.

Hankow Rd.

2

5 **13**

Middle Rd.

4 **14** **15**

Salisbury Rd.

16

Cross Harbour Tunnel

CAUSEWAY BAY

Victoria Park

Seafront Rd.

WANCHAI

Harbour Rd.

44

Gloucester Rd.

Paterson St.

Great George St.

Causeway Bay

43

45 **46**

Jaffe Rd.

Yee Wo St.

Lockhart Rd.

Gloucester Rd.

42

47

Jaffe Rd.

Hennessey Rd.

Yun Ping Rd.

O'Brien Rd.

Lockhart Rd.

Canal Rd.

Lee Garden Rd.

Causeway Rd.

Hennessey Rd.

Wanchai

Wan Chai Rd.

48

Queen's Rd. East

Johnston Rd.

Leighton Rd.

Wong Nai Chung Rd.

49 **50**

Queensway Plaza, United Centre, Pacific Place, and Admiralty Centre. They are connected to one another by elevated covered walkways. Two are really visiting: **Admiralty Centre** has reasonably priced optical shops and men's tailors. In **Pacific Place,** with four floors of upscale shops and restaurants, the Seibu (☎ 2877–3627) department store includes upmarket products and a vast, varied food department in the basement.

Cityplaza I & II (⊠ 1111 Kings Rd., Taikoo Shing, MTR: Taikoo Shing), one of Hong Kong's busiest shopping centers, is popular with families owing to its ice-skating rink, bowling alley, and weekly cultural shows. Many shops carry children's clothing, with labels such as Les Enfants, Crocodile, Peter Pan, and Crystal. The selection of more than 400 shops includes plenty of clothing stores for men and women and a number of toy stores.

The multistory **Landmark** (⊠ Des Voeux Rd. and Pedder St., Central, MTR: Central) is one of Central's most prestigious shopping sites and is home to **Celine, Loewe, D'Urban, Gucci, Joyce, Hermès of Paris,** and other chichi designer boutiques. There are also art galleries and fine jewelry shops. A pedestrian bridge links the Landmark with shopping arcades at the Swire House, Jardine House, Prince's Building, Mandarin Oriental Hotel, and Nine Queen's Road.

Shun Tak Centre (⊠ 200 Connaught Rd., MTR: Sheung Wan). Emerging from the MTR you'll find yourself at the Shun Tak Centre Shopping Arcade (at Macau Ferry Terminal), where a selection of boutiques features clothing, handbags, toys, and novelties.

Times Square (⊠ 1 Matheson St., Causeway Bay, MTR: Causeway Bay) is a gleaming new complex that packs most of Hong Kong's best-known stores, including **Lane Crawford,** into 12 frenzied floors. An indoor atrium has floor shows with everything from heavy-metal music to fashion shows to local movie-star appearances. There is also a cinema complex and a dozen or so eateries.

Kowloon
Harbour City (⊠ Canton Rd., Tsim Sha Tsui, next to the Star Ferry Terminal; MTR or Star Ferry to Tsim Sha Tsui) is Hong Kong's, and one of the world's, largest shopping complexes; if you can't find it here, it probably doesn't exist. Harbour City houses **Ocean Terminal, Ocean Centre, Ocean Galleries,** and the **Hong Kong Omni Hotel.** At last count there were some 50 restaurants and 600 shops, including 36 shoe stores, and 31 jewelry and watch stores. The complex contains a vast Toys 'R Us (⊠ Ocean Terminal, ☎ 2730–9462) and a large branch of Britain's **Marks & Spencer** (⊠ Ocean Centre, ☎ 2926–3318). Farther north on **Canton Road** are two more shopping centers—the **China Ferry Terminal,** a mall including the pier where ferries take off for various destinations in China, and **China Hong Kong City,** an arcade of shops and restaurants.

New World Shopping Centre (⊠ 18 Salisbury Rd., Tsim Sha Tsui; MTR: Tsim Sha Tsui, then walk to Salisbury Rd.). A harbor-front shopping center (next to the New World Hotel), the New World has four floors of fashion and leather boutiques, jewelry shops, restaurants, optical shops, tailors, stereo stores, arts and crafts shops, and the Japanese **Tokyu** Department Store. The **Regent Hotel Shopping Arcade** (⊠ Salisbury Rd., Tsim Sha Tsui), featuring mostly designer boutiques, can be reached through the Centre.

Tsim Sha Tsui East. You can take a minibus from the Kowloon Star Ferry, or board the Hovercraft ferry at Central Star Pier, to get to Tsim Sha

It helps to be pushy in airports.

Introducing the revolutionary new TransPorter™ from American Tourister® It's the first suitcase you can push around without a fight. TransPorter's™ exclusive four-wheel design lets you push it in front of you with almost no effort–the wheels take the weight. Or pull it on two wheels if you choose. You can even stack on other bags and use it like a luggage cart.

Stable 4-wheel design.

TransPorter™ is designed like a dresser, with built-in shelves to organize your belongings. Or collapse the shelves and pack it like a traditional suitcase. Inside, there's a suiter feature to help keep suits and dresses from wrinkling. When push comes to shove, you can't beat a TransPorter™ For more information on how you can be this pushy, call 1-800-542-1300.

Shelves collapse on command.

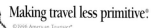

American Tourister

Making travel less primitive®

Your passport around the world.

- Worldwide access
- Operators who speak your language
- Monthly itemized billing

MCI Calling Card

415 555 1234 2244
J.D. SMITH

Use your MCI Card® and these access numbers for an easy way to call when traveling worldwide.

Bahrain†	800-002
Brunei	800-011
China(CC)†	108-12
(Available from most major cities)	
For a Mandarin-speaking operator	108-17
Cyprus♦†	080-90000
Egypt(CC)♦†	355-5770
Federated States of Micronesia	624
Fiji	004-890-1002
Guam(CC)†	950-1022
Hong Kong(CC)†	800-1121
India(CC)†	000-127
(Available from most major cities)	
Indonesia(CC)♦†	001-801-11
Iran✛	(Special Phones Only)
Israel(CC)†	177-150-2727
Japan(CC)♦†	
To call U.S. using KDD ■	0039-121
To call U.S. using IDC ■	0066-55-121
Jordan	18-800-001
Korea(CC)†	
To call using KT ■	009-14
To call using DACOM ■	0039-12

Phone Booths✛	Press Red Button 03, then✱
Military Bases	550-2255
Kuwait†	800-MCI (800-624)
Lebanon(CC)✛	600-624
Macao†	0800-131
Malaysia(CC)♦†	800-0012
Philippines(CC)♦†	
To call using PLDT ■	105-14
To call using PHILCOM■	1026-12
For a Tagalog-speaking operator	105-15
Qatar★	0800-012-77
Saipan (CC)✛†	950-1022
Saudi Arabia (CC)†	1-800-11
Singapore†	8000-112-112
Sri Lanka	(within Colombo) 440100
	(outside of Colombo) 01-440100
Syria	0800
Taiwan(CC)♦†	0080-13-4567
Thailand★†	001-999-1-2001
United Arab Emirates♦	800-111
Vietnam●	1201-1022

To sign up for the MCI Card, dial the access number of the country you are in and ask to speak with a customer service representative.

http://www.mci.com

Tsui East, an area of hotels, shops, and offices east of Chatham Road. There are 15 different shopping plazas clustered in this area, including Wing On Plaza, Tsim Sha Tsui Centre, Empire Centre, Houston Centre, South Seas Centre, and Energy Plaza. Prices are reasonable and the atmosphere is lively.

Department Stores

Chinese

The various Chinese-product stores give shoppers some of the most unusual and spectacular buys in Hong Kong—sometimes at better prices than in China. Whether you are looking for pearls, gold, jade, silk jackets, fur hats, Chinese stationery, or just a pair of chopsticks, you cannot go wrong with these stores. Most are open seven days a week but are crowded on Saturdays, Sunday sale days, and during weekday lunchtimes. These shopkeepers are expert at packing, shipping, and mailing goods abroad, but are not so talented in the finer art of pleasant service.

Chinese Arts & Crafts (⊠ Prince's Bldg., Central; Pacific Place, Admiralty; 26 Harbour Rd., Wanchai; Star House, Silvercord Centre; and 233 Nathan Rd., Tsim Sha Tsui; ☎ 2827–6667 for information). This chain is particularly good for silk-embroidered clothing, jewelry, carpets, and art objects, although prices may be a bit higher than at other stores.
Chinese Merchandise Emporium (⊠ 92–104 Queen's Rd., Central, ☎ 2524–1051) serves a bustling local clientele. The fabric, toy, and stationery departments are particularly good here.
China Products Company (⊠ 19–31 Yee Wo St., Causeway Bay, next to Victoria Park, ☎ 2890–8321; ⊠ 54 Nathan Rd., Tsim Sha Tsui, ☎ 2739–3839) offers a fairly wide and good-quality selection of goods, including household items.
Chung Kiu Chinese Products Emporium (⊠ 528–532 Nathan Rd., Yau Ma Tei, ☎ 2780–2351) specializes in arts and crafts but also has a good selection of traditional Chinese clothing and fine silk lingerie.
Yue Hwa Chinese Products Emporium (⊠ 143–161 Nathan Rd., Tsim Sha Tsui, ☎ 2739–3888; ⊠ 54–64 Nathan Rd., Tsim Sha Tsui, ☎ 2368–9165; ⊠ 301–309 Nathan Rd., Yau Ma Tei, ☎ 2384–0084) carries a broad selection of Chinese goods and has a popular medicine counter.

Japanese

Japanese department stores are very popular in Hong Kong. Stock in these stores includes more upscale Western items than Japanese products, but if you're looking for Japanese cosmetics, inventive gift departments, and exotic food halls, these stores—especially Jumbo Sogo in Causeway Bay and Seibu in Pacific Place—are terrific. Japanese department stores in Causeway Bay include: **Daimaru** (⊠ Great George St., Causeway Bay, ☎ 2576–7321), **Matsuzakaya** (⊠ Causeway Bay Store, 6–20 Paterson St., ☎ 2890–6622), **Mitsukoshi** (⊠ 500 Hennessy Rd., ☎ 2576–5222), and **Jumbo Sogo** (⊠ East Point Centre, 555 Hennessy Rd., ☎ 2833–8338). In Taikoo Shing, try **UNY** (⊠ Cityplaza II, 18 Taikoo Shing Rd., ☎ 2885–0331). At Admiralty, go to **Seibu** (⊠ The Mall, Pacific Place, Admiralty, ☎ 2877–3627). On the Kowloon side, **Isetan** (⊠ Sheraton Hong Kong Hotel, 20 Nathan Rd., Tsim Sha Tsui, ☎ 2369–0111) is packed with boutiques carrying Hunting World, Swatch, Dunhill, and Dior. In the New World Centre is **Tokyu Department Store** (⊠ 24 Salisbury Rd., Tsim Sha Tsui, ☎ 2722–0102). Out of the way, but worth the trip for its food department, is **Yaohan** (⊠ Whampoa Gardens, Hung Hom, ☎ 2766–0338; ⊠ New

Town Plaza, 18 Sha Tin Centre Rd., New Territories, ☎ 2697–9338).
You can reach Whampoa Gardens by bus from the Star Ferry terminal in Tsim Sha Tsui. To get to New Town Plaza, take the KCR to Shatin.
The shopping center is right above the station.

Western

Of the department stores that stock large selections of Western goods
at fixed prices, the oldest and largest chains are **Wing On** (main branch:
✉ 211 Des Voeux Rd., Central, ☎ 2852–1888; 12 other branches),
Sincere (✉ 173 Des Voeux Rd., Central, ☎ 2544–2688; ✉ 75–83 Argyle St., Mongkok, Kowloon, ☎ 2394–8233), and **Shui Hing** (✉ 23
Nathan Rd., Tsim Sha Tsui, ☎ 2721–1495). **Lane Crawford** is the most
prestigious department store of all, with prices to match. Special sales
here can be exhausting because everyone pushes and shoves to find bargains. The store at **One Pacific Place** (✉ 88 Queensway, Admiralty, ☎
2845–1838) is the best. Branches are in Windsor House, Causeway
Bay; Times Square, and Pacific Place on the Hong Kong side; and Ocean
Terminal in Tsim Sha Tsui, Kowloon.

The **Dragon Seed** department store has two branches (✉ 39 Queen's
Rd., Central, ☎ 2524–2016; ✉ New World Centre, 18–24 Salisbury
Rd., Tsim Sha Tsui, ☎ 2721–3980). The branch at Queen's Road has
a wide range of classic European clothing and shoes. The New World
Centre store has men's and women's clothing departments and a gift
shop.

Some of these department stores hold Sunday sales, and all hold seasonal sales. But stay clear of these unless you have great stamina.

Markets, Bazaars, and Alleys

In Hong Kong, each district has an Urban Council–run market that
sells fresh fruit, vegetables, meat, seafood, and live chickens (know in
advance that some slaughtering of fowl takes place). Surrounding the
markets are small stores that sell every imaginable kitchen and bathroom appliance, as well as clothes, and even electronic goods. Around
heavy pedestrian areas, you'll find illegal hawkers with a wide variety
of cheap goods, but the buyer should beware—constantly on the lookout for the police, the vendors may literally run off with their goods.
Get out of the way when they do so! In summer, they can be often found
in Tsim Sha Tsui in front of the Hyatt, around Granville and Mody
roads, and at the Star Ferry terminal. The street bazaars and markets
give you some of the best of Hong Kong shopping—good bargains,
exciting atmosphere, and a fascinating setting. The once-famous Cat
Street, the curio haunt in Upper Lascar Row, running behind the Central and Western districts, has fallen to office development. But there
are still plenty of other alleys and streets filled with bazaars.

The Flower Market. Found, appropriately enough, on Flower Street near
the Prince Edward MTR station, this collection of street stalls offers
cut flowers and potted plants, with a few outlets specializing in plastic plants and silk flowers.

Jade Market (✉ Kansu St., off Nathan Rd., Yau Ma Tei). Jade in every
form, color, shape, and size is on display in the Jade Market. The market is full of traders carrying out intriguing deals and keen-witted sellers trying to lure tourists. Some trinkets are reasonably priced, but unless
you know a lot about jade, don't be tempted into buying expensive
items.

Kowloon City Market (Take Bus 5, 5C, or 1A from Star Ferry in
Kowloon and get off opposite the airport), near the airport, is a fa-

vorite with local bargain hunters because of its huge array of clothes, porcelain, household goods, and electrical gadgets.

Lido Bazaar (⊠ Beach Rd., Repulse Bay). This bazaar is a series of small stalls selling souvenirs, costume jewelry, bags, belts, and some clothing.

Li Yuen Streets East and West (⊠ Between Queen's and Des Voeux Rds., Central). This area offers some of the best bargains in fashions, with or without famous brand names. Many of the shops also sell trendy jewelry and accessories. You can also find traditional Chinese quilted jackets. Bags of every variety, many in designer styles, are particularly good buys here. Watch out for pickpockets in these crowded lanes.

Stanley Village Market (Bus 6, 6A, or 260 from the Central Bus Terminus). This is a popular haunt for Western residents and tourists looking for designer sportswear, washable silk, and cashmere sweaters at factory outlet prices and in Western sizes. **China Town** (⊠ 8A Stanley Main St.), has jeans and casual shirts by the familiar GAP, Banana Republic, and Eddie Bauer, with almost everything selling for no more than HK$100. **Stanley Silk and Linen** (⊠ 74C Stanley New St.) has silk jackets, shirts, ties, blouses, and trousers, with a wider selection of men's clothes than most of Hong Kong's discount silk shops. **Allan Janny Ltd.** (⊠ 17 Stanley New St.) has antique furniture and porcelain ware. Stanley Market is also a good place to buy linens. **Tong's Sheets and Linen Co.** (⊠ 55–57 Stanley St.) has sheets, tablecloths, and brocade pillow covers, as well as silk kimonos and pajamas. Jewelry-mad Hong Kong's "gold rush" has begun to invade Stanley Market, too. Pearls, gemstones, and gold jewelry can be found at **Sam's Art & Jewellery** (⊠ 48 Stanley Main St.). The market is at its most enjoyable on weekdays when it's less crowded.

Temple Street. This Kowloon street (near the Jordan MTR station) becomes an open-air market at night, filled with a colorful collection of clothes, handbags, electrical goods, gadgets, and all sorts of household items. By the light of lamps strung up between stalls, hawkers try to catch the eye of shoppers by flinging clothes up from their stalls; Cantonese opera competes with pop music, and there's the constant chatter of vendors' cries and shoppers' bargaining. The market stretches for almost a mile and is one of Hong Kong's liveliest nighttime shopping experiences.

Clothing and Shoes

Tailor-Made Clothing

Along with Hong Kong's multitude of ready-to-wear clothing shops, you can still find Chinese tailors to make suits, dresses, and evening gowns. Unfortunately, many of the next generation in tailors' families are leaving the business, so don't wait too long to visit their shops. Here are some helpful dos and don'ts.

For a suit, overcoat, or jacket, give the tailor plenty of time—at least three to five days, and allow for a minimum of two proper fittings plus a final one for finishing touches. Shirts can be done in a day, but you will get better quality if you allow more time. Some shirtmakers like to give one fitting.

Tailors in hotels or other major shopping centers may be more expensive, but they are conveniently located and will be more accustomed to Western styles and fittings.

Have a good idea of what you want before you go to the tailor. Often the best method is to take a suit you want copied. Go through the details carefully, and make sure they are listed on the order form, together with a swatch of the material ordered (the swatch is essential). When you pay a deposit (which should not be more than 50% of the final cost) make sure the receipt includes all relevant details: the date of delivery, the description of the material, and any special requirements. All tailors keep records of clients' measurements, so satisfied customers can make repeat orders by mail or telephone. Keep a copy of the original measurements in case you need to change them.

There are a number of reputable and long-established tailors in Hong Kong.

Sam's (⌷ Burlington House, 94 Nathan Rd., Kowloon, ☎ 2721–8375), for men and women, has been patronized by members of the British Forces since 1957; one of the company's regular customers is the King of Belgium.

Shanghai Tang Department Store (⌷ 12 Pedder St., ☎ 2525–7333), on the ground floor of the Pedder Building, is the current retro rage in Hong Kong, selling old-fashioned Mandarin suits for men and women. Custom-made suits start around HK$5,000, including fabric from their large selection of Chinese silks. You can also have a cheongsam made for about HK$2,500 to HK$3,500, including fabric. The store also has a line of ready-to-wear Mandarin suits and kimonos in unisex styles, all in the HK$1,500 to HK$2,000 range, and Chinese memorabilia, including novelty watches depicting dim sum dishes.

FOR MEN

Ascot Chang (⌷ Prince's Bldg., Central, ☎ 2523–3663; Peninsula Hotel, Tsim Sha Tsui, ☎ 2366–2398; Regent Hotel, Tsim Sha Tsui, ☎ 2367–8319) has specialized in making shirts for men since 1949. Clients have included George Bush and Andy Williams. **H. Baromon Ltd.** (⌷ Swire House, Connaught Rd., Central, ☎ 2523–6845) has been making suits for the territory's business barons for more than 40 years. **A-Man Hing Cheong Co., Ltd.** (⌷ Mandarin Oriental Hotel, Central, ☎ 2522–3336) is known for European-cut suits and custom shirts and has its own list of distinguished clients. **W. W. Chan & Sons** (⌷ Burlington House, 92–94 Nathan Rd., Tsim Sha Tsui, ☎ 2366–9738) is known for top-quality classic cuts and has bolts and bolts of fine European fabrics from which to choose. Chan will make alterations for the lifetime of the suit, which should be about 20 years. Chan tailors also travel to the United States several times a year to fill orders for their customers. If you have a suit made here and leave your address, they will let you know when they plan to be in town. A more modestly priced tailor, recommended by locals, is **Tom Li at Leading Company** (⌷ Hyatt Regency Shopping Arcade, Nathan Rd., Tsim Sha Tsui, ☎ 2366–2737), who makes stylish suits for men and women.

FOR WOMEN

You will find that tailors do their best work on tailored suits, coats, and dresses, and do not do as well with more fluid styles or knit fabrics. Tailors are the place to order a traditional Chinese cheongsam. You can bring in something you want copied, or find a style in one of the tailor's catalogs. You can also bring in a photograph from a magazine or, if you're skilled with pencil and paper and sure of what you want, bring in a sketch.

A good tailor has a wide selection of fabrics, but you can also bring in your own. Visit the Chinese Arts & Crafts branches for beautiful Chinese brocades. **Western Market** (⌷ Des Voeux Rd., Sheung Wan) has fabrics on the second floor. One detail frequently overlooked is buttons. Your tailor will probably offer you buttons made of the suit fabric at no extra charge, but if you prefer to select your own, you'll find a dazzling array of buttons in jade, mother-of-pearl, brass, and more ordinary materials at **Wu Sim Ming** (☎ 2543–6328), the small tailor shop on the ground floor of Western Market.

Irene Fashions (⊠ Burlington House, 92–94 Nathan Rd., Tsim Sha Tsui, ☎ 2367–5588) is the women's division of W. W. Chan. **Mode Elegante** (⊠ Peninsula Hotel, Tsim Sha Tsui, ☎ 2366–8153) has become known for high-fashion suits for the executive woman. Local expats like **Bobby's Fashions** (⊠ Mirador Mansion, 5 Carnarvon Rd., Tsim Sha Tsui, ☎ 2724–2615).

Women's Designer Clothing

You need just glance around the streets of Central to see that Hong Kong is one of the world's capitals of chic. Most of the best-known European retail names have stores in Hong Kong, and the territory is starting to produce some interesting, often very trendy, designers of its own.

Some of the leading stores are **Gianni Versace** (⊠ Peninsula Hotel, Tsim Sha Tsui, ☎ 2721–5851; ⊠ The Landmark, Central, ☎ 2522–0399; ⊠ The Mall, Pacific Place, Central, ☎ 2522–8329), **Joyce Boutique** (⊠ The Landmark, Central, ☎ 2523–5236; ⊠ Galleria, 9 Queen's Rd., Central, ☎ 2810–1120; ⊠ The Regent Hotel, Tsim Sha Tsui, ☎ 2368–7649), **Issey Miyake** (⊠ Kowloon Hotel, Nathan Rd., Tsim Sha Tsui, ☎ 2723–8386), **Celine Boutique** (⊠ The Landmark, Central, ☎ 2525–1281; ⊠ Peninsula Hotel, Tsim Sha Tsui, ☎ 2722–0762), **Chanel Boutique** (⊠ Prince's Bldg., Central, ☎ 2810–0978; ⊠ Peninsula Hotel, Tsim Sha Tsui, ☎ 2368–6879), **Jil Sander** (⊠ Alexandra House, Central, ☎ 2869–9121; ⊠ Regent Hotel, Tsim Sha Tsui, ☎ 2368–2332), **Giorgio Armani** (⊠ Alexandra House, Central, ☎ 2530–1998; **Emporio Armani** at New World Tower, 16 Queen's Rd., Central, ☎ 2524–4407), **Christian Dior** (⊠ St. George's Bldg., 2 Ice House St., Central, ☎ 2537–1079), **Gucci** (⊠ The Landmark, Central, ☎ 2524–4492; ⊠ Sogo, East Point Centre, 555 Hennessy Rd., Causeway Bay, ☎ 2893–4276; ⊠ Pacific Place, Admiralty, ☎ 2869–4886; ⊠ Peninsula Hotel, Tsim Sha Tsui, ☎ 2311–5008), **Hermès of Paris** (⊠ Galleria, 9 Queen's Rd., Central, ☎ 2525–5900; ⊠ Peninsula Hotel, Tsim Sha Tsui, ☎ 2723–1556), **Loewe** (⊠ The Landmark, Central, ☎ 2522–0996), **Prada** (⊠ Alexandra House, Central, ☎ 2522–2989), and **Nina Ricci** (⊠ Peninsula Hotel, Tsim Sha Tsui, ☎ 2311–5922; ⊠ Regent Hotel, Tsim Sha Tsui, ☎ 2721–4869).

For upscale women's wear, Central and five-star hotels are the best places to look. Remember that most major hotels have a shopping arcade. You can also try **Pavlova** (⊠ Swire House, Central, ☎ 2522–1773; ⊠ Ocean Centre, Tsim Sha Tsui, ☎ 2736–0926), **Diane Freis** (⊠ Prince's Bldg., Central, ☎ 2810–0378; ⊠ The Mall, Pacific Place, Central, ☎ 2810–9069; ⊠ Ocean Galleries, Harbour City, Tsim Sha Tsui, ☎ 2730–3790; ⊠ Regent Hotel, Tsim Sha Tsui, ☎ 2311–3903), and **Michel Rene** (⊠ The Landmark, Central, ☎ 2810–5320; ⊠ Excelsior Plaza, Causeway Bay, ☎ 2577–2592).

For innovative, youthful creations, many by Hong Kong's own up-and-coming designers, check out the boutiques that line **Vogue Alley,** which starts at the intersection of Paterson and Kingston streets in Causeway Bay.

Other well-known designers with shops in Hong Kong include **Esprit** (⊠ Prince's Bldg., Central, ☎ 2523–2757; ⊠ The Landmark, Central, ☎ 2845–6687; ⊠ Ocean Galleries, Harbour City, Tsim Sha Tsui, ☎ 2735–6975; about 20 other branches around town), **Benetton** (⊠ The Landmark, Central, ☎ 2522–5861; other branches all over town),

Moschino (⊠ Ocean Terminal, Harbour City, Tsim Sha Tsui, ☎ 2735–9799), and **Naf Naf Boutique** (⊠ Peninsula Hotel, Tsim Sha Tsui, ☎ 2369–5482; ⊠ Ocean Terminal, Harbour City, Tsim Sha Tsui, ☎ 2735–5834). **Giordano** (⊠ 29 Queen's Rd. Central, ☎ 2921–2028; other branches all over town) has very low prices on jeans, shorts, and casual shirts. Consult the HKTA's Shopping Guide, available at HKTA information booths, for complete listings of branches of these stores.

Lingerie
For frothy negligees, try **Private Affair** (⊠ Swire House, Central, ☎ 2596–0402) or **The Intimate Shop** (⊠ Prince's Bldg., Central, ☎ 2801–7850).

Factory Outlets
Hong Kong used to be the factory-outlet center of the world, the place where European and American labels were manufactured and the overruns sold at close-to-wholesale prices. Those days are long gone, but because many manufactured garments from China and other developing countries still come through Hong Kong's duty-free port, you can find samples and overruns in the territory's many outlets. Discounts generally run a mere 20%–30% off retail, but comb through everything, and more often than not you'll be able to bag at least one fabulous bargain. One word of caution, however: check the garment carefully for damage and fading. Outlets do not accept returns. The biggest surprise about outlets is how conveniently located some of the best ones are. If you came to Hong Kong to shop, don't miss the Pedder Building in the heart of Central, and a number of small outlets tucked away in the Lan Kwai Fong area.

PEDDER BUILDING
Just a few feet from a Central MTR exit is the **Pedder Building** (⊠ 12 Pedder St., Central), which contains five floors of small shops. The **Anne Klein Shop** (☎ 2521–2547) is its first full-fledged retail outlet, so don't venture through that particular door if discounts are what you're after. Nevertheless, the Pedder Building is always worth a look, and the number of shops offering discounts of around 30% off retail (and sometimes more) seems to be growing rather than shrinking now, after a couple of years of an upscale trend. The best discount shops there are **Ca Va** (☎ 2537–7174), which has fabulous knitwear, along with suits and designer casual wear; **Labels Plus** (☎ 2521–8811), which has some men's fashions as well as women's daytime separates; **Shopper's World–Safari** (☎ 2523–1950), which has more variety than most outlets and a small upstairs department with men's fashions; **The Silkwear House** (☎ 2877–2373), where blouses with Tahari and Nordstrom labels were going for a song; and **Pretty Way** (☎ 2501–5727), which has low prices on sweaters with labels including Ralph Lauren, J. Crew, and Saks. **Cascal** (☎ 2523–4999) has good prices on leather bags.

The Pedder Building also has a number of linens shops. **Hongkong & Shanghai Lace Co.** (☎ 2522–4408) has sheets, duvet covers, and table linens, as well as a line of children's clothes, at fairly low prices.

LAN KWAI FONG AREA
The small area of Central made up of Lan Kwai Fong and its intersecting streets is another good place to outlet-shop. Ask passersby for directions if you have trouble finding Lan Kwai Fong; it's small and tucked away, but well known to residents because of its nightlife.

Gat (⊠ Cosmos Bldg., 8–11 Lan Kwai Fong, 7th Floor, ☎ 2524–9896; ⊠ Kowloon's Taurus Bldg., 21 A–B Granville Rd., 12th Floor, Tsim

Sha Tsui, ☎ 2722–6287; and ✉ 22 Yee Wo St., Causeway Bay, ☎ 2808–1053) carries Kenar, sometimes at as much as 40% to 50% off United States retail prices. There have been reports, however, of rayon sweaters from Gat coming unraveled, and the store refusing to give refunds or exchanges, so shop carefully. **Whispers** (✉ 9A Grand Progress Bldg., 15–16 Lan Kwai Fong, ☎ 2877–9590) carries career wear and casual clothes by Ann Taylor, Next, Talbot's, and an occasional item designed for Nordstrom, as well as designer ball gowns. **Zeno Fashions** (✉ Man Cheung Bldg., 15–17 Wyndham St., Block B, ☎ 2868–4850) has mostly career wear, from labels such as Ellen Tracy, Emmanuel Ungaro, Episode, Krizia, Banana Republic, and Country Road. **Ricki's** (✉ Cosmos Bldg., 8–11 Lan Kwai Fong, Room 8-11, ☎ 2877–1552) has, from time to time, Emanuel Ungaro, Episode, Donna Karan, Tahari, Jaeger, Ellen Tracy, and Just Cotton. **Pot Pourri** (✉ Wong Chung Ming Commercial Bldg., 16 Wyndham St., 12th Floor, ☎ 2525—1111) has Talbot's, Emanuel Ungaro, and Fenn Wright & Manson. A recent addition is **Italian Dazzlers** (✉ Grand Progress Bldg., 58–62 D'Aguilar St., Room 1A [enter from Lan Kwai Fong St.], ☎ 2868–4798) has Italian bags and belts at a slight discount. In the same room is **Moda Mia** (☎ 2868–2426), which carries most major Italian designers, and a fine selection of men's Italian ties for HK$350.

LAICHIKOK

There are a number of outlets worth visiting within a few blocks of Kowloon's Laichikok MTR station. Despite the dust, the Ah Chow Factory (☞ Ceramics, *below*) has some good buys on decorative porcelain. **Le Baron** (✉ 4th Floor, Flat B Yeung Chung [No. 6] Industrial Bldg., 19 Cheung Shun St., ☎ 2785–0863) has some of the best buys in cashmere in the territory, which makes the trouble of finding it worth it. Almost at the end of Cheung Shun Street, enter through the garage, and use the single elevator on the far right. It's in an office with a sign that says HEYRO DEVELOPMENT CO. LTD. Go into the office, then enter the showroom through the second door on the right. **Rotterdam** (✉ Kee Wah Industrial Bldg., 666 Castle Peak Rd., 12th Floor, ☎ 2741–2586) has women's designer clothes, sometimes at almost-giveaway prices. **Mia Fashion Designs** (✉ Ardour Centre, 680 Castle Peak Rd., Ground Floor, ☎ 2745–9771) is a small store, easy to find compared to other outlets in the area, that carries silk and cotton blouses and lingerie, often with Nordstrom labels, at bargain-basement prices.

OTHER OUTLETS

The **Joyce Warehouse** (✉ Gee Luen Hing Industrial Bldg., 2 Yip Fat St., Wong Chuk Hang [near Aberdeen], ☎ 2814–8313) has taken shopaholic locals by storm. This is the outlet for women's and men's fashions that are sold in the ritzy Joyce Boutiques in Central and Pacific Place, with labels by such major designers as Jil Sander and Giorgio Armani. Prices for each garment are reduced by about 10% each month, so that the longer the piece stays on the rack, the less it costs. The outlet is open Tuesday to Saturday from 10–6 and Sunday 12–6. Take Bus 70 from Exchange Square and get off at the fourth stop after Aberdeen Tunnel, on Wong Chuk Hang Street. From there, turn right onto Nam Long Shan Road, and walk one block to Heung Yip Road. Turn right. It is just a few yards to the outlet, which has large signs pointing the way.

Tsim Sha Tsui is jam-packed with small shops that sell washable silk shirts, blouses, and blazers at minuscule prices. Many of these shops carry lovely silk lingerie and colorful men's boxers. The price is very low but don't expect the underwear to survive more than a dozen washings. Comb through the stores on Haiphong Road across from Kowloon

Park. One that stands out is **Klaxon** (⊠ 188-C Mody Rd., ☎ 2367–9881). On Granville Road, try **Fair Factor** (⊠ 44 Granville Rd.). You will have to comb through many uninteresting items, but you may be rewarded with some real finds—such as items by GAP, Adrienne Vittadini, Villager, and Victoria's Secret, going for a mere HK$50 to HK$100. **Fashions of 7th Avenue** (⊠ Sing Pao Centre, 8 Queen's Rd., 12th Floor, Central, ☎ 2868–4208; ⊠ Shopping Arcade, Convention Plaza, 1 Harbour Rd., Wanchai, ☎ 2824–0619; ⊠ Kaiser Estate, Phase III, Hok Yuen St., Hunghom, Kowloon, ☎ 2764–4655) is known for its casual knit sportswear and classic suits. **Timothy Fashion Co.** (⊠ Kaiser Estate, Phase I, 41 Man Yue St., Hunghom, Kowloon, ☎ 2362–2389) has classic wool sweaters for men and women at good prices. Silk garments for men and women, and lingerie are also a good buy here, but you can find a similar selection in Tsim Sha Tsui, so don't go all the way to Hunghom if these are all you're after. **TSL Jewellery Showroom** (⊠ Summit Bldg., 30 Man Yue St., Hunghom, ☎ 2764–4109; ⊠ Wah Ming Bldg., 34 Wong Chuk Hang Rd., Aberdeen, ☎ 2873–2618) has fairly good prices on diamonds and other precious stones in unique settings, and both locations have an on-premises workshop where you can watch the jewelry being made.

Ask your hotel concierge about the bus to the outlets in Hunghom. Many of the outlets there have branches in Central, so you may decide it's not worth the trip. However, if you're a fan of Hong Kong–based designer Diane Freis, you can find discounts of around 30% on her day-wear concoctions and her elaborate cocktail dresses at the **Diane Freis Factory Outlet** (⊠ Kaiser Estate, Phase I, 41 Man Yue St., Hunghom, ☎ 2362–1760). **Coast 2 Coast Design Warehouse** (⊠ Hing Wai Centre, 7 Tin Wan Praya Rd., Rm. 1904, Aberdeen, ☎ 2870–0191) has clothes, crystal, linens, and ceramics at up to 50% off retail prices.

Furs

It seems bizarre that Hong Kong, with its tropical climate, should have so many fur shops. But fur is a good buy here, with high-quality skins, meticulous tailoring, excellent hand finishing, and competitive prices. Some of the largest and most popular shops are **Siberian Fur Store** (⊠ 29 Des Voeux Rd., Central, ☎ 2522–1380; ⊠ 21 Chatham Rd., Tsim Sha Tsui, ☎ 2366–7039) and **Victoria Fur** (⊠ Tsim Sha Tsui Centre, 66 Mody Rd., Tsim Sha Tsui East, ☎ 2311–0223; ⊠ Ocean Galleries, Harbour City, Canton Rd., Tsim Sha Tsui, ☎ 2735–9898).

Children's Clothing

There are plenty of stores in Hong Kong that sell Western-style, ready-to-wear children's clothing. Among the best are **G2000** (⊠ Manning House, 38 Queen's Rd., Central, ☎ 2522–4449; ⊠ New World Centre, Tsim Sha Tsui, ☎ 2369–0911) and **Crocodile Garments Ltd.** (⊠ The Mall, Pacific Place, Central, ☎ 2524–3172; ⊠ Ocean Terminal, Tsim Sha Tsui, ☎ 2735–5136; and other locations all over town). For traditional English-style smocks and rompers, go to **Baba's** (⊠ Prince's Bldg., Central, ☎ 2523–7212), or Britain's **Mothercare** (⊠ Windsor House, 311 Gloucester Rd., Causeway Bay, ☎ 2882–3468; ⊠ Prince's Bldg., Central, ☎ 2523–5704; ⊠ Ocean Terminal, Tsim Sha Tsui, ☎ 2735–5738) for baby clothing and maternity wear. You can also find fabulous, traditional Chinese-style clothing for tots in two clothing alleys in Central—**Li Yuen streets East and West.**

Shoes

The place to buy shoes in Hong Kong is on **Wong Nai Chung Road,** in Happy Valley, next to the racecourse. Here you will find many shoe shops selling inexpensive, locally made shoes and Japanese-made shoes, as well as copies of European designer shoes, boots, and bags. If you have small feet, these shops can offer excellent buys. If you wear size 8 or larger, you'll probably have trouble finding shoes that fit well. The merchants are also particularly good at making shoes and bags, covered with silk or satin, to match an outfit. If you leave your size chart, you can make future purchases through mail order.

Top-name Italian and other European shoes can be found in the department stores and shopping centers. But don't expect prices for designer shoes to be much less than they are back home.

Custom-made shoes for both men and women are readily and quickly available. Cobblers, even those with names such as **Lee Kee Boot & Shoe Makers** (⌗ 19–21B Hankow Rd., Tsim Sha Tsui, ☎ 2367–1180; men's shoes only), are renowned for their skill in copying specific styles at reasonable prices. **Mayer Shoes** (⌗ Mandarin Oriental Hotel, Central, ☎ 2524–3317) has an excellent range of styles and leathers for men and women. If you like cowboy boots in knee-high calfskin, try the **Kow Hoo Shoe Company** (⌗ Prince's Bldg., First Floor, Central, ☎ 2523–0489). **Maylia Shoe Co.** (⌗ The Peninsula Arcade, Mezzanine Floor, Salisbury Rd., Tsim Sha Tsui, ☎ 2367–1635) has more women's than men's shoes, with lizard-skin shoes starting at around HK$2500, and a wide range of designer handbag copies.

Specialty Stores

Antiques

The first half of 1997 might be a time to pick up bargains in the oldest, finest antiques as merchants seek to clear their inventories. The unofficial word from Hong Kong's antiques dealers is that much of the ancient porcelain, textiles, and specialty furniture will not be available after the Chinese takeover. China has laws against taking items older than 120 years out of the country, and it is expected to apply the same ruling to Hong Kong. To be sure, a great deal is smuggled out of China anyway, but shops dealing with very old pieces expect to lose much of their export business, so these shops will stop handling anything that might be affected by the law. Everyday furniture and pottery are not considered national treasures and will not be affected.

To be sure your purchase is authentic, patronize shops such as **Altfield Gallery** (⌗ Prince's Bldg., Central, ☎ 2537–6370; ⌗ 45 Graham St., Central, ☎ 2524–4867) for furniture, fabrics, and collectibles from all over Asia; **Charlotte Horstmann and Gerald Godfrey** (⌗ Ocean Terminal, Tsim Sha Tsui, ☎ 2735–7167) for wood carvings, bronze ware, and furniture; and **Eileen Kershaw** (⌗ Peninsula Hotel, Tsim Sha Tsui, ☎ 2366–4083) for fine Chinese porcelain and jade carvings.

If you have more curiosity than cash, **Hollywood Road** is a fun place to visit. The street, running from Central to Western, is undeniably the best place for poking about in shops and stalls selling antiques from many Asian countries. Treasures are hidden away among a jumble of old family curio shops, sidewalk junk stalls, slick new display windows, and dilapidated warehouses.

C. L. Ma Antiques (⌗ 43–55 Wyndham St., Central, ☎ 2525–4369) has Ming Dynasty–style reproductions, especially large carved chests and tables made of unlacquered wood. **Eastern Dreams** (⌗ 47A Hollywood Rd., Central, ☎ 2544–2804; ⌗ 4 Shelley St., Central, ☎ 2524–4787) has antique and reproduction furniture, screens, and curios. **Honeychurch Antiques** (⌗ 29 Hollywood Rd., Central, ☎ 2543–2433) is known especially for antique silver jewelry from Southeast Asia,

China, and England. **Yue Po Chai Antique Co.** (✉ 132–136 Hollywood Rd., Central, ☎ 2540–4374) is one of Hollywood Road's oldest shops, and it has a vast and varied stock. **Schoeni Fine Arts** (✉ 27 Hollywood Rd., Central, ☎ 2542–3143) sells Japanese, Chinese, and Thai antiques; Chinese silverware, such as opium boxes; and rare Chinese pottery.

Cat Street (✉ Upper Lascar Row), once famous for its thieves' market of secondhand stolen goods, now has almost as many small antiques shops as Hollywood Road itself, behind the outdoor stalls selling old—or at least old-looking—jewelry, curios, and assorted bits of junk. **Cat Street Galleries** (✉ 38 Lok Ku Rd., Sheung Wan, Western, ☎ 2541–8908) is a mall of shops selling porcelain and furniture on the ground floor. **China Art** (✉ 15 Upper Lascar Row, ☎ 2542–0982) has fine furnishings, mostly from the Suzhou area of China, and offers tours, usually once a month, to its warehouse in southern China.

In the unlikely event that you don't find anything to interest you on Hollywood Road, there are several other fascinating contemporary emporiums worth investigating. **The Banyan Tree** (✉ Prince's Bldg., Central, ☎ 2523–5561; ✉ Repulse Bay Shopping Arcade, Repulse Bay, ☎ 2592–8721; ✉ Ocean Terminal, Harbour City, Tsim Sha Tsui, ☎ 2730–6631) has furniture and bric-a-brac, both old and new, from India and Southeast Asia. You can arrange to visit Banyan Tree's warehouse by calling the office (☎ 2877–8303). You will not receive a discount if you buy from the warehouse, but you will have the chance to see— and buy—pieces that have just arrived. **Tequila Kola** (✉ main showroom at United Centre, Admiralty, ☎ 2520–1611; also at Prince's Bldg., Central, ☎ 2877–3295) has reproductions of antique wrought-iron beds, one-of-a-kind furniture, home accessories, and jewelry from various corners of Asia.

If you know what you are after, keep an eye out for auction announcements in the classified section of the South China *Morning Post.* **Lammert Brothers** (✉ Union Commercial Bldg., 12–16 Lyndhurst Terr., Mezzanine Floor, Central, ☎ 2545–9859) holds regular carpet and antiques sales. **Victoria Auctioneers** (✉ Century Sq., 1–13 D'Aguilar St., 16th Floor, Central, ☎ 2524–7611) has sales of ceramics, paintings, and jewelry.

For antique embroidered pieces, try **Teresa Coleman** (✉ 79 Wyndham St., Central, ☎ 2526–2450). **True Arts & Curios** (✉ 91 Hollywood Rd., tel. 2559–1485) is a cluttered store with good buys in embroidered items (including slippers for bound feet), silver, porcelain, and snuff bottles. **Dynasty Furniture Co.** (✉ 68-A Hollywood Rd., ☎ 2369–6940) has small netsukes skillfully carved out of tagua, a rain-forest nut that looks a lot like ivory. For Japanese dolls, prints, and kimonos, 19th-century export silver, and Chinese blackwood furniture, go to **Nishiki Gallery** (✉ 1 Exchange Sq., Central, ☎ 2845–2551). **Alvin Lo & Co.** (✉ 2 Exchange Sq., Central, ☎ 2524–3395) has porcelain vases and figurines, mostly from the Qing and Ming dynasties, but some date farther back.

Art

At a time when recession has caused most of the high-profile art buyers of Japan and the West to fade into the background, Hong Kong's economic boom has made the city a hot spot for art collecting. The **Pao Gallery at the Arts Centre** (✉ 2 Harbour Rd., Wanchai, ☎ 2582–0200), university affiliated, specializes in contemporary painting and photography. The **Hong Kong Museum of Art** (Salisbury Rd., Tsim Sha Tsui, ☎ 2734–2167), university affiliated, is the place to go for Chinese masters and traveling exhibitions of fine art from around the world. There is also a lively contemporary gallery scene, much of it concentrating on the best work coming out of China and Southeast Asia today, and an **Art Asia Expo** every November (⌧ Hong Kong Convention Centre, Wanchai), when galleries from all over the world arrive with work for sale. The two major **auction houses** from the West have branches in Hong Kong. Call Christie's Swire (⌧ Gloucester Tower, Suite 1107–09, Landmark, Central, ☎ 2521–5396) and Sotheby's (⌧ 2 Exchange Sq., 1st Floor, ☎ 2524–8121) for information about upcoming events.

GALLERIES

Asian Art News, a bimonthly magazine, on sale at the bigger newsstands around town for HK$50, is a good guide to what is happening in galleries around the region. If you're interested in a firsthand view of the new trends in Asian art, plan to spend a day gallery-hopping in Central and the Lan Kwai Fong area.

Alisan Fine Arts Ltd. (⌧ Prince's Bldg., Central, ☎ 2526–1091) was one of the first galleries in Hong Kong to promote Chinese artists living abroad and has a wide range of contemporary art with an East-meets-West flavor.

Galerie La Vong (⌧ 1 Lan Kwai Fong, 13th Floor, Central, ☎ 2869–6863) is the place to see the works of today's leading Vietnamese artists, many of whose creations reveal an intriguing combination of French Impressionist and traditional Chinese influences. Many paintings from the 1960s and 1970s are on newsprint, because canvas was unavailable during the Vietnam War.

Fringe Gallery (⌧ 2 Lower Albert Rd., Central, ☎ 2521–7251) is part of the Fringe Club and is a showcase for young, not-yet-famous Hong Kong artists, both Chinese and expat.

Hanart TZ Gallery (⌧ Old Bank of China Bldg., 2A Des Voeux Rd., 5th Floor, Central, ☎ 2526–9019) shows contemporary Chinese artists from the mainland, Taiwan, Hong Kong, and abroad.

LKF Gallery (⌧ Lan Kwai Fong House, 5–6 Lan Kwai Fong, 1st Floor, Central, ☎ 2524–8976) exhibits a trendy blend of contemporary Eastern and Western abstract art.

Mandarin Oriental Fine Arts Gallery (⌧ Mandarin Oriental Hotel Arcade, Mezzanine Floor, Connaught Rd., Central, ☎ 2825–4822) shows a wide range of late-19th-century to contemporary Western and Chinese art. Antique Chinese pottery is sold here year-round.

Plum Blossoms Gallery (⌧ Coda Plaza, 51 Garden Rd., 17th Floor, Central [across from the Botanical Gardens], ☎ 2521–2189) shows Chinese and Western art, along with antique textiles and Tibetan carpets.

Schoeni Art Gallery (⌧ Coda Plaza, 51 Garden Rd., 18th Floor, Central, ☎ 2869–8802) exhibits a dramatic mix of abstract, realist, and political paintings by contemporary mainland-Chinese artists. Once a year Schoeni hosts a show of European masters.

Wagner Art Gallery (⌧ Lusitano Bldg., 4 Duddell St., 7th Floor, Central, ☎ 2521–7882) is owned by an Australian couple who are making it their mission to introduce the best Australian artists to the territory. From time to time there are also shows of major contemporary names.

Wattis Fine Art (⌧ 20 Hollywood Rd., 2nd Floor, Central, ☎ 2524–5302) specializes in 18th- to 20th-century European paintings and the work of contemporary artists living in Hong Kong, both Chinese and expat.

Zee Stone Gallery (⌧ 3 Exchange Sq., Central, ☎ 2845–4476) displays a combination of contemporary Chinese paintings and antique

Tibetan silver and carpets. Another branch (⌧ Yu Yuet Bldg., 43–55 Wyndham St., Central, ☎ 2810–5895) sells Chinese furniture as well.

FRAMERS

It may be worth having your artwork framed in Hong Kong because prices are much lower than in Europe and the United States. Shops in Central that do excellent work include **Man Fong** (⌧ 1 Lyndhurst Tower, Lyndhurst Terr., ☎ 2522–6923), **Wah Cheong** (⌧ 15 Hollywood Rd., ☎ 2523–1900), and **Po Shu Frame & Glass Co.** (⌧ 255 Queen's Rd. East, Ground Floor, Wanchai, ☎ 2573–7334.

Cameras, Lenses, and Binoculars

Many of Hong Kong's thousands of camera shops are clustered in the Lock Road–lower Nathan Road area of Tsim Sha Tsui, in the back streets of Central, and on Hennessy Road in Causeway Bay. There are two well-known and knowledgeable dealers in Central: **Williams Photo Supply** (⌧ Prince's Bldg., ☎ 2522–8437) and **Photo Scientific Appliances** (⌧ 6 Stanley St., ☎ 2522–1903). If you are interested in buying a number of different items in the shop (most also stock binoculars, calculators, radios, and other electronic gadgets), you should be able to bargain for a good discount.

If in doubt about where to shop for such items, stick to the HKTA-member shops. Pick up the HKTA shopping guide at any of its information centers. All reputable dealers should give you a one-year, worldwide guarantee. Unauthorized dealers, who obtain their camera gear illegally from sources other than the official agent, may not provide a proper guarantee—although you may pick up better bargains in these outlets.

Carpets and Rugs

Regular imports from China, Iran, India, Pakistan, Afghanistan, and Kashmir make carpets and rugs a very good buy in Hong Kong. There are also plenty of carpets made locally. Though prices have increased in recent years, carpets are still cheaper in Hong Kong than they are in Europe and the United States.

For Chinese carpets, branches of **China Products** and **Chinese Arts & Crafts** give the best selection and price range. For locally made carpets, **Tai Ping Carpets** (⌧ Hutchison House, 10 Harcourt Rd., Ground Floor, Central, ☎ 2522–7138; ⌧ Wing On Plaza, 62 Mody Rd., Tsim Sha Tsui East, ☎ 2369–4061) is highly regarded, especially for custom-made rugs and wall-to-wall carpets. The store takes 2½–3 months to make specially ordered carpets; customers can specify color, thickness, and even the direction of the weave. There is a showroom on the ground floor of Hutchinson House. Tai Ping's occasional sales are well worth attending; check the classified section of the South China Morning Post for dates. **Carpet World** (⌧ 46 Morrison Hill Rd., Wanchai, ☎ 2893–0202; ⌧ Ocean Terminal, Harbour City, Tsim Sha Tsui, ☎ 2730–4275) has a wide selection.

On Upper Wyndham Street, in Central, you will find several shops selling Persian, Turkish, Indian, Pakistani, Tibetan, and Afghan rugs—though don't expect miraculously low prices. **Oriental Carpet Trading House** (⌧ 34 Wyndham St., ☎ 2521–6677), **Mir Oriental Carpets** (⌧ 52 Wyndham St., ☎ 2521–5641), and **Tribal Rugs Ltd.** (⌧ Admiralty Centre, 18 Harcourt Rd., 2nd Floor, ☎ 2529–0576) are all reputable dealers. Owing to customs regulations, American citizens are rarely allowed to import Persian rugs into the United States (☞ Customs and Duties *in* the Gold Guide).

Ceramics

Fine English porcelain dinner, tea, and coffee sets are popular buys in Hong Kong. Some of the best finds, including Royal Crown Derby, Royal Doulton, Royal Worcester, Spode, and Wedgwood china, are found at **Craig's** (⊠ St. George's Bldg., 2 Ice House St., Central, ☎ 2522−8726; ⊠ Ocean Terminal, Tsim Sha Tsui, ☎ 2730−8930). Other stores selling top-quality porcelain include **Hunter's** (⊠ Pacific Place Mall, Admiralty, ☎ 2845−4827; ⊠ Ocean Terminal, Tsim Sha Tsui, ☎ 2730−0155; ⊠ Peninsula Hotel, Tsim Sha Tsui, ☎ 2722−1169; Kowloon Hotel, Tsim Sha Tsui, ☎ 2369−0716); **Meissen Shop** (⊠ The Landmark, Central, ☎ 2877−1592), and **Waterford Wedgwood Trading Singapore Ltd.** (⊠ Alexandra House, Chater Rd., Ground Floor, Central, ☎ 2523−8337).

For a full range of ceramic Chinese tableware, visit the various **China Products Company** stores. They also offer fantastic bargains on attractively designed vases, bowls, and table lamps. Inexpensive buys can also be found in the streets of **Tsim Sha Tsui,** the shopping centers of **Tsim Sha Tsui East** and **Harbour City,** the **Kowloon City Market,** and the shops along **Queen's Road East** in Wanchai. Factory outlets are also a good source. Two of the most popular, offering good bargains, are **Overjoy Porcelain** (⊠ 10−18 Chun Pin St., 1st Floor, Kwai Chung, New Territories, ☎ 2487−0615) and **Ah Chow Factory** (⊠ Room 1−3, Hong Kong Industrial Centre, 489−491 Castle Peak Rd., Block B, 7th Floor, Laichikok, ☎ 2745−1511). To reach Overjoy Porcelain, take the MTR to Kwai Hing Station, then a taxi. For Ah Chow, take the MTR to Laichikok Station and follow exit signs to Leighton Textile Building/Tung Chau West.

For antique ceramic items, visit **Yue Po Chai Antique Co.** (⊠ 132−136 Hollywood Rd., Central, next to Man Mo Temple, ☎ 2540−4374). For good reproductions, try **Sheung Yu Ceramic Arts** (⊠ Vita Tower, 29 Wong Chuk Hang Rd., Aberdeen, ☎ 2555−6542). For unusual and very beautiful reproductions of Chinese vases and bowls, try **Mei Ping** (⊠ 55 Wellington St., Central, ☎ 2521−3566).

Chocolates

See's Candies, flown fresh from California daily, are available in their outlets, including the main branch in the Landmark (⊠ 11 Pedder St., Central, ☎ 2523−4977), as well as in Ocean Terminal, Tsim Sha Tsui. **Peninsula Chocolates,** from the hotel of the same name, are sold in the **Lucullus** outlets (⊠ New Henry House [main branch], Ice House St., Central, ☎ 2868−9449) and have an excellent reputation. The **Mandarin Shop** (⊠ Mandarin Oriental Hotel, 5 Connaught Rd., Central, ☎ 2825−4084) has an irresistible selection of chocolate truffles. **Chocolate Boutique** (⊠ Regent Hotel, 18 Salisbury Rd., Room 44 basement arcade, Tsim Sha Tsui, ☎ 2721−1211) makes its own chocolates on the premises.

Computers

All of the big names sell in Hong Kong. If you are going to buy, make sure the machine will work on the voltage in your country; an IBM personal computer sold in Hong Kong works on 220 volts, while the identical machine in the United States works on 110 volts. Servicing is a major concern, too.

The real bargains in computers are the locally made versions of the most popular brands. But be forewarned: Even though the prices are lower than in Europe and the United States, you may have trouble getting your Hong Kong computer past customs on your return.

The following computer stores are members of the HKTA and considered reputable: **Continental Computer Systems** (✉ Hing Tai Commercial Bldg., 114 Wing Lok St., Room 202, Sheung Wan, ☎ 2854–2233); **Expert Computer Store** (✉ Times Square, 1 Matheson St., Causeway Bay, ☎ 2506–3318; ✉ 113 Des Voeux Rd., Central, ☎ 2581–9113); **Mastertech Office Automation** (✉ Star Computer City, Star House, 2nd Floor, 3 Salisbury Rd., Tsim Sha Tsui, ☎ 2736–7263), and **One Take Computer Shop** (✉ New Capital Computer Plaza, 85–95 Un Chau St., Sham Shui Po, ☎ 2728–0045.

Electronic Gimmicks and Gadgets

For those electronic devices that shoppers love to take home, the **Special Interest Electronic Co.** (✉ Hutchison House, 10 Harcourt Rd., Central, ☎ 2526–3648) has hundreds of strange and not-so-strange items crammed into a tiny space.

Furniture and Furnishings

The home-decor market has boomed tremendously in Hong Kong in recent years, and manufacturers of furniture and home furnishings have been quick to increase production. **Design Selection** (✉ 75 Wyndham St., Central, ☎ 2525–8339) has a good selection of Indian fabrics. **The Banyan Tree** and **Tequila Kola** (☞ Antiques, *above*) sell rattan furniture and wrought-iron furniture both old and new, with new selections arriving every month.

Rosewood furniture is a very popular buy in Hong Kong. **Queen's Road East,** in Wanchai, the great furniture retail and manufacturing area, offers everything from full rosewood dining sets in Ming style to furniture in French, English, or Chinese styles. Custom-made orders are accepted in most shops here. **Choy Lee Co. Ltd.** (✉ 1 Queen's Rd. E, ☎ 2527–3709) is the most famous. Other rosewood furniture dealers, such as **Cathay Arts** (✉ Ocean Centre, ☎ 2730–6193), can be found in the Harbour City complex at Tsim Sha Tsui.

A number of old-style shops specialize in the rich-looking blackwood furniture that originated in Southern China at the turn of the century. Chairs, chests, couches, and other pieces can be found at the western end of Hollywood Road, near Man Mo Temple. **Luen Wo Hong** (✉ 88–90 Queen's Rd. East, Wanchai, ☎ 2527–8344) has reproductions of antique blackwood and elm-wood furniture. Queen's Road East and nearby Wanchai Road are also good sources for camphor-wood chests, as is Canton Road in Kowloon.

Luk's Furniture (✉ 52–64 Aberdeen Main Rd., Aberdeen, ☎ 2553–4125) is a bit off the beaten path, but it has two floors of rosewood and lacquer furniture, as well as Korean chests, at warehouse prices. You can place custom orders here.

Reproductions are common, so "antique" furniture should be inspected carefully. Traits of genuinely old pieces are: a mature sheen on the wood, slight gaps at joints as a result of natural drying and shrinking of the wood, signs of former restorations, and signs of gradual wear, especially at leg bottoms. Keep in mind, too, that blackwood, rosewood, and teak must be properly dried, seasoned, and aged to prevent pieces from cracking in climates that are less humid than Hong Kong's. Even in more humid areas, the dryness of winter heating systems can cause harm.

Handicrafts and Curios

The traditional crafts of China include a fascinating range of items: lanterns, temple rubbings, screen paintings, paper cuttings, seal engravings, and wooden birds. The **Welfare Handicrafts Shop** (✉ Jardine

House, Shop 7 basement, 1 Connaught Place, Central, ☎ 2524–3356; ⊠ Salisbury Rd., Tsim Sha Tsui, ☎ 2366–6979), next to the YMCA, stocks a good collection of inexpensive Chinese handicrafts for both adults and children. All profits go to charity. **Mountain Folkcraft** (⊠ 12 Wo On La., Central, ☎ 2525–3199) offers a varied collection of fascinating curios. From Queen's Road Central walk up D'Aguilar Street, past Wellington Street, then turn right onto Wo On Lane. **Kinari** (⊠ Anson House, 61 Wyndham St., Central, ☎ 2869–6827) sells crafts and antiques from all over Southeast Asia. **Banyan Tree** (☞ Antiques, *above*) carries a pricey but attractive selection of items from different Asian countries. For Indonesian silver, crafts, and batiks, visit **Vincent Sum Designs Ltd.** (⊠ 15 Lyndhurst Terr., Central, ☎ 2542–2610).

Jewelry

Jewelry is the most popular item among visitors to Hong Kong. It is not subject to any local tax or duty, so prices are normally much lower than they are in most other places. Turnover is fast, competition fierce, and the selection fantastic.

Famous international jewelers with shops in Hong Kong include **Van Cleef & Arpels** (⊠ The Landmark, Central, ☎ 2522–9677; ⊠ Peninsula Hotel, Tsim Sha Tsui, ☎ 2368–7648; ⊠ Jumbo Sogo, Causeway Bay, ☎ 2574–3619); **Cartier** (⊠ Prince's Bldg., Central, ☎ 2522–2964; ⊠ 1 Pacific Place, Admiralty, ☎ 2523–1852; ⊠ Peninsula Hotel, Tsim Sha Tsui, ☎ 2368–8036); and **Ilias Lalaounis** (⊠ Prince's Bldg., Central, ☎ 2524–3328; ⊠ Regent Hotel, Tsim Sha Tsui, ☎ 2721–2811).

Other opulent and reputable jewelers include **Kevin** (⊠ Holiday Inn, 50 Nathan Rd., Tsim Sha Tsui, ☎ 2367–1041); **Larry Jewelry** (⊠ The Landmark, Central, ☎ 2521–1268; ⊠ Pacific Place, Central, ☎ 2868–3993; ⊠ Ocean Terminal, Harbour City, Tsim Sha Tsui, ☎ 2730–8081); **Chen Brothers Arts Co.** (⊠ Mandarin Hotel, Central, ☎ 2524–7723); **Favourite Jewellers** (⊠ Prince's Bldg., Central, ☎ 2524–5411); **Manchu Gems** (⊠ 402 Asian House, 1 Hennessy Rd., Wanchai, ☎ 2861–0896), **Dabera** (⊠ Admiralty Centre, Central, ☎ 2527–7722); **King Fook** (⊠ 30 Des Voeux Rd., Central, ☎ 2523–5111); and, for loose gemstones, **China Handicrafts & Gem House** (⊠ 25A Mody Rd., Tsim Sha Tsui East, ☎ 2311–9703).

For modern jewelry with an Oriental influence, take a look at the fabulous designs by **Kai-Yin Lo** (⊠ The Mall, Pacific Place, Admiralty, ☎ 2840–0066; ⊠ Mandarin Hotel, Central, ☎ 2524–8238; ⊠ Peninsula Hotel, Tsim Sha Tsui, ☎ 2721–9623). Delicate gold jewelry, a favorite among the Hong Kong Chinese, is available at **Just Gold,** where prices rarely go past HK$5,000 (⊠ 47 Queen's Rd., Central, ☎ 2869–0799; ⊠ 27 Nathan Rd., Tsim Sha Tsui, ☎ 2312–1120; and 14 other branches).

You can find 14- to 18-carat gold Chinese zodiac animals, a unique gift, at the small stores on Pottinger Street, Central, and to your left as you turn onto Queen's Road, Central, from there. **Chan Che Kee** (⊠ 18 Pottinger St., ☎ 2522-6402), has fist-size animals. **Chinese Arts & Crafts** stores have a wide selection of jade, pearls, and gold as well as porcelain, jewelry, and enamelware.

DIAMONDS

As one of the world's largest diamond-trading centers, Hong Kong offers these gems at prices that are at least 10% lower than world-market levels. When buying diamonds, check the "Four C's": color, clarity, carat (size), and cut. Shop only in reputable outlets—those recommended by someone who lives in Hong Kong or listed in the Hong Kong Tourist Association's shopping guide (available in HKTA centers). For information or advice, call the **Diamond Importers Association** (☎ 2523–5497).

Settings for diamonds and other gems will also cost less here than in most Western cities, but check your country's customs regulations, as some countries charge a great deal more for imported set jewelry than for unset gems. Hong Kong law requires all jewelers to indicate on every gold item displayed or offered for sale both the number of carats and the identity of the shop or manufacturer—make sure these marks are present. Also, check the current gold prices, which most stores will have displayed, against the price of the gold item that you are thinking of buying.

PEARLS

Pearls, another good buy, should be checked for color against a white background. Shades include white, silvery white, light pink, darker pink, and cream. Cultured pearls usually have a perfect round shape, semi-baroque pearls have slight imperfections, and baroque pearls are distinctly misshapen. Check for luster, which is never found in synthetics. Freshwater pearls from China, which look like rough grains of rice, are inexpensive and look lovely in several twisted strands.

Jewelry shops with a good selection of pearls include **Trio Pearl** (✉ Peninsula Hotel, Tsim Sha Tsui, ☎ 2367–9171), **Gemsland** (✉ Mandarin Oriental Hotel, Central, ☎ 2525–2729), **Po Kwong** (✉ 82 Queen's Rd., Central, ☎ 2521–4686) and **K. S. Sze & Sons** (✉ Mandarin Oriental Hotel, ☎ 2524–2803), the last of which is known for its fair prices.

JADE

Hong Kong's most famous stone, jade comes not only in green but in shades of purple, orange, yellow, brown, white, and violet. Although you will see "jade" trinkets and figurines everywhere in Hong Kong, high-quality jade is rare and expensive. Translucency and evenness of color and texture determine jade's value. Translucent, deep emerald green Emperor's jade is the most expensive. Be careful not to pay jade prices for green stones, such as aventurine, bowenite, soapstone, serpentine, and Australian jade. Many of the pieces for sale at the Kansu Street **Jade Market** (☞ Markets, Bazaars, and Alleys, *above*) are made of these imposters; but the endless sea of stalls brimming with trinkets of every size, shape, and color make a visit worthwhile. If you are wary of spending any money on Kansu Street, visit **Tsim Sha Tsui's Jade House** (✉ 162 Ocean Terminal, Tsim Sha Tsui, ☎ 2736–1232). **Chow Sang Sang** (✉ 229 Nathan Rd., Tsim Sha Tsui, ☎ 2730–3241, and 17 smaller branches around town) and **Chow Tai Fook** (✉ 29 Queens Rd., Central, ☎ 2523–7128, and 15 branches) are also good places to shop for fine jade.

Kung-Fu Supplies

There are hundreds of kung-fu schools and supply shops in Hong Kong, especially in the areas of Mongkok, Yau Ma Tei, and Wanchai, but often they are hidden away in back streets and up narrow stairways. The most convenient place to buy your drum cymbal, leather boots, sword, whip, double dagger, studded wrist bracelet, Bruce Lee *kempo* gloves, and other kung-fu exotica is **Kung Fu Supplies Co.** (✉ 188 Johnston Rd., Wanchai, ☎ 2891–1912).

Leather

Italian bags, belts, briefcases, and shoes are popular status symbols in Hong Kong, but you'll pay top dollar for them. Locally made leather bags are clearly of inferior quality—the leather isn't as soft, and the smell isn't nearly as luxurious as that of fine European leather. But if you're looking for some bargain-basement buys, check out the locally produced designer copies on Li Yuen streets East and West, in Central, and in other shopping lanes. The leather-garment industry is a growing one, and although most of the production is for export, some good buys can be found in the factory outlets in Hunghom, Kowloon. Medium-quality bags and belts from the local manufacturer Goldlion can be found at **Chinese Arts & Crafts** stores (☞ Department Stores, *above*).

For top-brand international products, visit department stores such as **Lane Crawford, Wing On,** and **Sincere,** and the Japanese stores in Causeway Bay: **Daimaru, Mitsukoshi, Matsuzakaya,** and **Sogo.** All stock designer brands, such as Nina Ricci, Cartier, Lancel, Il Bisonte, Comtesse, Guido Borelli, Caran d'Ache, Franco Pugi, and Christian Dior. You may find the prices higher than they are at home, however.

Linens, Silks, Embroideries
Pure silk shantung, silk and gold brocade, silk velvet, silk damask, and printed silk crepe de Chine are just some of the exquisite materials available in Hong Kong at reasonable prices. The best selections are in the **China Products Emporiums, Chinese Arts & Crafts,** and **Yue Hwa** stores. Ready-to-wear silk garments, from mandarin coats and cheongsams to negligees, dresses, blouses, and slacks are good buys at **Chinese Arts & Crafts**.

Irish linen, Swiss cotton, Thai silk, and Indian, Malay, and Indonesian fabric are among the imported cloths available in Hong Kong. Many of them can be found on **Wing On Lane** in Central. **Vincent Sum Designs** specializes in Indonesian batik; a small selection can also be found in **Mountain Folkcraft** (☞ Handicrafts and Curios, *above*). Thai silk is about the same price in Hong Kong as it is in Bangkok. Fabrics from India are available from **Design Selection** (⊠ 75 Wyndham St., Central, ☎ 2525–8339).

The best buys from China are hand-embroidered and appliquéd linen and cotton. You can find a magnificent range of tablecloths, place mats, napkins, and handkerchiefs in the **China Products Company** and **Chinese Arts & Crafts** stores, and in linen shops in **Stanley Market.** Also, look in the various shops on **Wyndham** and **On Lan streets** in Central. When buying hand-embroidered items, be certain the edges are properly overcast and beware of machine-made versions being passed off as handmade.

Miscellaneous Chinese Gifts
If you are really stuck for a gift idea, think Chinese. Some of the most unusual gifts are often the simplest. How about an embroidered silk kimono, or a pair of chopsticks, in black lacquer and finely painted? Or a Chinese chop, engraved with your friend's name in Chinese? These are available at shops throughout Hong Kong. For chop ideas, take a walk down **Man Wa Lane** in Central (opposite Wing On Dept. Store, 26 Des Voeux Rd.). For those who live in cold climates, wonderful *mien laps* (padded silk jackets) are sold in the alleys of Central or in the various shops featuring Chinese products. Another unusual item for rainy weather—or even as a decorative display—is a hand-painted Chinese umbrella, available very inexpensively at **Chinese Arts & Crafts** and **China Products Company** stores. Chinese tea, packed in colorful traditional tins, can be picked up in the teahouses in **Bonham Strand** and **Wing Lok Street** in Western. A bit more expensive, but a novel idea, are the padded tea baskets with teapot and teacups; or tiered bamboo food baskets, which also make good sewing baskets.

Optical Goods

There are a vast number of optical shops in Hong Kong, and some surprising bargains, too. Soft contact lenses, hard lenses, and frames for glasses go for considerably less than in many other places. All the latest styles and best quality frames are available at leading optical shops at prices generally much lower than in Europe and the United States. **The Optical Shop** (⊠ Main branch: Prince's Bldg., Central, ☎ 2523–8385) is the fanciest and probably the most reliable store and has branches throughout Hong Kong. An eye test using the latest equipment is provided free.

Perfume and Cosmetics

Although aromatic ointments were believed to have been used by the Egyptians more than 5,000 years ago, it was Asia that made the major contributions to the art of perfumery. Today, however, Chinese perfumes are hardly a match for Western fragrances. Scented sandalwood soap is the one exception (the "Maxam" label in Chinese product stores is prettily packaged). Western perfume and cosmetics are expensive in Hong Kong. Up until a few years ago, the territory imposed a substantial cosmetics tax. Even after that was dropped, retailers didn't want to risk lowering their profit margins. You can, however, buy most of your favorite brands from home at department stores such as **Wing On** and **Sincere,** drugstores such as **Manning's** (⊠ Landmark, Central, ☎ 2854–0188; ⊠ Swire House, Central, ☎ 2810–5756; ⊠ 2 Exchange Square, Central, ☎ 2868–1529; ⊠ Queensway Plaza, Admiralty, ☎ 2529–1588; ⊠ Silvercord Bldg., Canton Rd., Tsim Sha Tsui, ☎ 2375–0454; other locations all over town), **Watson's** (⊠ Princes Bldg., Central, ☎ 2522–5153; ⊠ Entertainment Bldg., 30 Queens Rd., Central, ☎ 2868–4388; ⊠ Pacific Place, Admiralty, ☎ 2523–2885; ⊠ Everest Bldg., 241 Nathan Rd., Tsim Sha Tsui, ☎ 2735–5033; other locations around town), and branches of **Fanda Perfume Co. Ltd** (⊠ World Wide House, Pedder St., Central, ☎ 2523–6023; ⊠ 21 Lock Rd., Tsim Sha Tsui, ☎ 2368–3882).

The Body Shop has branches all over Hong Kong, including in the Landmark (☎ 2845–5238), Pacific Place (☎ 2524–2853), and Ocean Centre, Tsim Sha Tsui (☎ 2736–7736). **Red Earth,** an Australian manufacturer of all-natural cosmetics, has convenient branches at Seibu in Pacific Place (☎ 2801–7937) and the Landmark (☎ 2877–6599). For bargain cosmetics, try the basement of the **Island Shopping Centre** in Causeway Bay across from Sogo.

Sporting Goods

Hong Kong is an excellent place to buy sports gear, thanks to high volume and reasonable prices. Tennis players and golfers can find a good range of equipment and clothing in the many outlets of **Marathon Sports** (⊠ Tak Shing House, Theatre La., 20 Des Voeux Rd., Central, ☎ 2810–4521; ⊠ Pacific Place, Admiralty, ☎ 2524–6992; ⊠ Ocean Terminal, Harbour City, Tsim Sha Tsui, ☎ 2730–6160). Water sports enthusiasts will find sailing, waterskiing, surfing, and snorkeling gear (including wet suits) at **Bunns Diving Equipment** (⊠ 188 Wanchai Rd., Wanchai, ☎ 2572–1629). Fishermen can get outfitted at **Po Kee Fishing Tackle Company** (⊠ 6 Hillier St., Central, ☎ 2543–7541; ⊠ Ocean Terminal, Harbour City, Tsim Sha Tsui, ☎ 2730–4562). For a comprehensive range of sports equipment, visit **World Top Sports Goods Ltd.** (⊠ Swire House, Pedder St. entrance, Central, ☎ 2521–3703; ⊠ 9 Carnarvon Rd., Tsim Sha Tsui, ☎ 2721–3188; ⊠ 49 Hankow Rd., Tsim Sha Tsui, ☎ 2376–2937).

Stereo Equipment

Hennessy Road in Causeway Bay has long been the mecca for finding stereo gear, although many small shops on Central's Queen Victoria and Stanley streets and on Tsim Sha Tsui's Nathan Road offer a similar variety of goods. Be sure to compare prices before buying, as they can vary widely. Also make sure that guarantees are applicable in your own country. It helps to know exactly what you want, since most shopkeepers don't have the room or inclination to give you a chance to test and compare sound systems. However, some major manufacturers do have individual showrooms where you can test the equipment before buying. The shopkeeper will be able to direct you. Another tip: Though most of the export gear sold in Hong Kong has fuses or dual wiring that can be used in any country, it pays to double-check.

Tea

Cha (tea) falls into three types: green (unfermented), black (fermented), and oolong (semifermented). Various flavors include jasmine, chrysanthemum, rose, and narcissus. Loong Ching Green Tea and Jasmine Green Tea are among the most popular, and they're often available in attractive tins. These make inexpensive but unusual gifts.

If you wanted to buy a ton of tea, you could probably do so in Hong Kong's most famous tea area—Western District on Hong Kong Island. Walk down Queen's Road West and Des Voeux Road West and you will find dozens of tea merchants and dealers, such as **Cheng Leung Wing** (⊠ 526 Queen's Rd. W, no phone). If you want to enjoy a cup of cha in traditional style, go to the beautiful **Luk Yu Teahouse** (⊠ 24 Stanley St., ☎ 2523–5464), the oldest and most famous of Hong Kong's teahouses, where you can also get dim sum. You can taste teas in a simple atmosphere at **Tea Zen** (⊠ House for Tea Connoisseurs, 290 Queen's Rd., Ground Floor, Central, Sheung Wan, ☎ 2544–1375).

You can buy packages or small tins of Chinese tea in the tea shops of the Western district or at the various Chinese product stores and leading supermarkets, such as Park 'n' Shop.

For more sophisticated tea shopping go to the **Fook Ming Tong Tea Shop** (⊠ Prince's Bldg., Central, ☎ 2521–0337; other branches at Mitsukoshi and Sogo stores in Causeway Bay and Ocean Terminal, Harbour Centre, Tsim Sha Tsui). There you can buy superb teas in beautifully designed tins or invest in some antique clay tea ware.

TVs and VCRs

Color TV systems vary throughout the world, so it's important to be certain the TV set or videocassette recorder you purchase in Hong Kong has a system compatible to the one in your country. Hong Kong, Australia, Great Britain, and most European countries use the PAL system. The United States uses the NTSC system, and France and Russia use the SECAM system. Before you buy, tell the shopkeeper where you will be using your TV or video recorder. In most cases you will be able to get the right model without any problems. The HKTA has a useful brochure called *Shopping Guide to Video Equipment*.

Watches

You will have no trouble finding watches in Hong Kong. Street stalls, department stores, and shops overflow with every variety, style, and brand name, many of them with irresistible gadgets. But remember Hong Kong's remarkable talent for imitation. A super-bargain gold Rolex may have hidden flaws—cheap local mechanisms, for instance, or "gold" that rusts. Stick to officially appointed dealers carrying the manufacturers' signs, if you want to be sure you are getting the real thing. When buying an expensive watch, check the serial number against the manufacturer's guarantee certificate, and ask the salesman to open the case to check the movement serial number. If an expensive band is attached, find out whether it is from the original manufacturer or locally made, as this will dramatically affect the price (originals are much more expensive). You should obtain a detailed receipt, the manufacturer's guarantee, and a worldwide warranty for all items.

For top-of-the-market buys, try **Artland Watch Co. Ltd.** (⊠ Corner of Ice House St. and Des Voeux Rd., Central, ☎ 2523–8872; ⊠ 62A Nathan Rd., Tsim Sha Tsui, ☎ 2366–4508). For less-expensive brands, visit **City Chain** (⊠ 14 branches in Hong Kong, 29 in Kowloon).

Shopping Tours

Shopping for bargains is something of a national sport in Hong Kong and a number of residents have started up small tour operations that visit favorite haunts. **Non-Stop Shoppers** (☎ 2523–3850, FAX 2868–1164) specializes in bargain outlets in out-of-the-way parts of Kowloon and the New Territories. The company charters a bus once a week for a daylong bargain shopping spree. The itinerary, which varies from week to week, takes in outlets for cookware, towels, brass ware, porcelain, Chinese lamps (which can be fitted with American wiring and plugs), furniture, and carpets. Cost is HK$280 per person. Call or fax for current schedule.

Asian Cajun Ltd. (⊠ 12 Scenic Village Dr., 4th Floor, Pokfulam, Hong Kong, ☎ 2817–3687, FAX 2855–9571) offers customized shopping tours for visitors looking for good buys in antiques, art, jewelry, designer clothes, and specialty items. Escorted tours, which visit hard-to-find shops and private dealers, are US$80 per hour, with a three-hour minimum. There is an extra hourly charge for a car and driver.

8 Side Trip to Macau

By Shann
Davies

IF HISTORY BALANCED ITS BOOKS, today no one would be skimming over the 40-mile (64-kilometer) waterway from Hong Kong to Macau or flying into its new international airport. After all, the Portuguese-administered enclave of 9 square miles (23.5 square kilometers) on the South China coast ceased to have any commercial or political significance a century and a half ago.

How and why has it survived? One clue can be found on any of the fast ferries that bring in the majority of visitors. Most of the passengers will be Hong Kong Chinese heading for the casinos, which have provided the territory with much of its revenue since legal gambling was introduced in the 1840s as an attempt to compensate for the loss of entrepôt trade to newly founded Hong Kong.

Also on board might be Jesuit priests and Roman Catholic nuns, both Chinese and European, who run vital, centuries-old charities and tend to one of Asia's oldest and most devout Christian communities. Just as likely, there would be Buddhist priests, who help maintain Macau's firm faith in its Chinese traditions. Then there would be foreign tourists—more than a million per year—textile and toy buyers, British engineers, Swiss chefs, French showgirls, and bar hostesses from Southeast Asia. In their different ways they all prove that there's plenty of life left in the grande dame of the China coast.

The voyage is a pleasant progress between hilly green islands, some a part of Hong Kong, most sparsely populated extensions of China's Zhuhai Special Economic Zone. As it appears on the skyline, Macau jolts the imagination. Hills crowned with a lighthouse and a church spire, a blur of pastel buildings, and tree-lined avenues all confirm that this is a bit of transplanted Iberia, settled in 1557 by the Portuguese as Europe's first outpost in China.

Macau is 90 miles (144 kilometers) south of Canton (now Guangzhou), the traditional port for China's trade with foreign "barbarians." In the 16th century, however, its traders were forbidden by the emperor to deal with Japan, whose shogun had imposed a ban on China trade. The Portuguese saw their chance and soon were making fabulous fortunes from their command of trade between the two Asian countries and Europe. Among the cargoes that passed through Macau were silk, tea, and porcelain from China, silver and lacquerware from Japan, spices and sandalwood from the East Indies, muslin from India, gems from Persia, wild animals and ivory from Africa, foodstuffs from Brazil, and European clocks, telescopes, and cannons.

Macau's golden age came to an abrupt end with the closure of Japan and the loss of Portugal's mercantile power to the Dutch and English. Northern Europeans and Americans sent their India-men and clipper ships to Macau to barter ginseng, furs, woolens, and opium for tea and silk. Their merchants treated the city as their own but, with their rents and customs duties, helped Macau survive. Then, in the mid-19th century, Hong Kong was founded and the merchants moved out, leaving Macau a backwater.

In the early part of this century, Macau was cast by movie producers and novelists as a den of sin, sex, and spies. True, it had casinos, brothels, opium parlors, and secret agents; but, in fact, it was a small, pale shadow of Shanghai and Hong Kong. Today, any traveler in search of wild and wicked Macau will be disappointed, and so will romantics looking for a colonial twilight. As you approach through the ocher waters of the silt-heavy Pearl River estuary, the reality of modern Macau is unavoidable. High-rise apartments and office blocks mask the hillsides, multistory factories cover land reclaimed from the sea, and construction hammers insist that this is no longer a sleepy old town.

The modern prosperity comes from taxes on gambling and the export of textiles, toys, electronics, furniture, luggage, and ceramics. Like Hong Kong, Macau is a duty-free port where anyone can set up a business with minimal taxation or government restrictions. As a result, there is little evidence of city planning, and many of the new skyscrapers are grotesque. However, some building projects have benefited Macau. These include the University of Macau and the racetrack on Taipa Island, a handful of handsome hotels, and a number of superbly restored or re-created historical buildings.

Relations with China have never been better, with ever-increasing two-way trade and joint ventures in Zhongshan, the neighboring Chinese county. Macau's close proximity to China also makes it a popular gateway for excursions across the border. Following the Sino-British agreement to hand Hong Kong back to China in 1997, the Portuguese negotiated the resumption of Chinese sovereignty over Macau, which will take place on December 20, 1999.

Macau has a population of about 450,000, and most live in the 3.5 square miles (9 square kilometers) of the mainland peninsula, with small communities on the mostly rural islands of Taipa and Coloane. About 95% of the inhabitants are Chinese, many of them of long-standing residence. About 7,000 people speak Portuguese as their first language, but only a few come from Portugal; the others are Macanese from old, established Eurasian families. The more transient residents tend to be expatriate Europeans, Americans, and Australians, plus several thousand nightclub hostesses from Thailand and the Philippines. Although Portuguese is the official language, and Cantonese the most widely spoken, English is generally understood in places frequented by tourists.

Pleasures and Pastimes

Casinos

The glamorous images summoned up by the word "casino" should be checked at the door with cameras before you enter the Macau variety. Here you'll find no opulent floor shows, no free drinks, no jet-setters in evening dress, and no suave croupiers. What you do find is no-frills, no-holds-barred, no-questions-asked gambling. Open 24 hours a day, most of the rooms are noisy, smoky, shabby, and in constant use. The gamblers, mostly Hong Kong Chinese, are businesspeople, housewives, servants, factory workers, and students, united in their passion—and what a passion it is! There is almost certainly more money wagered, won, and lost in Macau's casinos than in any others in the world. Sociedade de Turismo e Diversoes de Macau (STDM), the syndicate that has the gambling franchise, admits that the total amount is in excess of HK$100 billion annually. In return for the franchise, STDM is paying the government a premium of HK$1.3 billion (about US$162.5 million) over a 10-year period, plus 26% to 30% of gross income and money to build homes for 2,000 families, provide new passenger ferries, and keep the harbor dredged. The syndicate does not complain, so judge the profits for yourself.

Dining

Although East and West have clashed in many respects, when it came to cooking there was instant rapprochement, and it happened in Macau. By the time the Portuguese arrived, they had learned a lot about the eating habits of countries throughout their new empire. They adopted many of the ingredients grown and used in the Americas and Africa and brought them to China. The Portuguese were the first to introduce China to peanuts, green beans, pineapples, lettuce, sweet potatoes, and shrimp paste, as well as a variety of spices from Africa and India. In China, the Portuguese discovered tea, rhubarb, tangerines, ginger, soy sauce, and the Cantonese art of fast frying to seal in flavor.

Over the centuries a unique Macanese cuisine developed, with dishes adapted from Portugal, Brazil, Mozambique, Goa, Malacca, and, of course, China. Today some ingredients are imported, but most are available, fresh each day, from the bountiful waters south of Macau and the rich farmland just across the China border. One good example of Macanese food is the misleadingly named Portuguese chicken, which would be an exotic alien in Europe. It consists of chunks of chicken baked with potatoes, coconut, tomato, olive oil, curry, olives, and saffron. Extremely popular family dishes include *minchi* (minced pork and diced potatoes panfried with soy), pork baked with tamarind, and duckling cooked in its own blood, all of which are served with rice.

CATEGORY	COST*
$$$	over 150 patacas
$$	70 patacas–150 patacas
$	under 70 patacas

per person including service but excluding wine

Lodging

In the past decade Macau has caught up with neighboring Hong Kong in terms of international first-class accommodations. Some of the world's leading hotel groups are now represented here, in some cases with more resort services than any in the British territory, and always at lower rates. Plus Macau has two *pousadas*, marvelous examples of Portuguese inns with distinctive Macanese characteristics. By and large Macau's hotels depend on Hong Kong residents, who often make plans to visit at the last moment, so business fluctuates with weather conditions and holidays. This means that sizable discounts are usually available for midweek stays. These are best obtained through Hong Kong travel agents or through the hotel itself.

In general, hotels listed in the $$$ category are of the highest international standard, with swimming pools and health clubs, meeting rooms for conferences and parties, fine restaurants, public areas that are design showcases, business centers, and guest rooms with all modern comforts and conveniences. Those in the $$ category are efficient, clean, and comfortable, with air-conditioning, color TV (with English and Chinese programs from Hong Kong as well as the local channel), room service, and restaurants. They cater primarily to gamblers, regular Hong Kong visitors, and budget tour groups. Hotels in the $ category tend to be old and spartan, but they are clean and safe.

CATEGORY	COST*
$$$	800–1,800 patacas
$$	300 patacas–800 patacas
$	under 300 patacas

per room, not including 10% service charge and 5% tax

Serendipity

Like any territory with a long, multicultural past, Macau is packed with interesting things to see and do that overlap one another. This tends to unravel any neatly organized itinerary or program, but makes each visitor's experience unique because he or she will inevitably succumb to the invitation of mysterious courtyards, Baroque churches, colonial squares, imaginative museums, quiet cemeteries, and bustling street markets. Often you'll stumble on some celebration, a religious procession, the opening of a new shop, fireworks displays, or performances by artists in a music or arts festival. Forget your schedule and enjoy the moment.

EXPLORING

Macau divides quite conveniently into eight areas, including Taipa and Coloane Islands to the south, which can be seen separately or back to back.

The Outer Harbour

Numbers in the margin correspond to points of interest on the Macau map.

❶ The history of Portuguese Macau almost came to an end on the site of the **Ferry Terminal** in 1622, when the Dutch fleet landed a large invasion force to capture the rich port. From here the troops attacked Guia and Monte forts, only to be defeated by a ragtag army of Jesuit priests, Portuguese soldiers, and African slaves.

Today this Outer Harbour area is designed to welcome all arrivals. The three-story terminal is attractive and efficient, with different arrival and departure levels containing restaurants, tourist information, a hotel, car rental and travel agencies, a bank and automatic teller machine, duty-free shops, and luggage lockers.

Opposite the terminal is the grandstand of the annual Grand Prix and a reservoir containing a computer-controlled cyberfountain with 292 water jets that play regularly though the day and are lighted after dark.

❷ A short walk from the ferry terminal is the **Jai Alai Casino** and nightclub complex. The Basque sport for which it was built failed to attract enough business, so the complex was converted into one of the busiest gaming places in town.

❸ A center of sporting activity and much else is the **Macau Forum** (✉ Rua Luís Gonzaga Gomes), which includes the Tourism Activities Centre, or TAC. Here there are amphitheaters for the world volleyball championships, roller hockey, and table tennis, as well as for pop concerts and opera.

There are halls for special visiting exhibitions, and, in the basement of the TAC, two wonderful museums. Oldest is the **Grand Prix Museum,** which tells the story of the races that began in 1953. It opened in 1994 and contains some of the cars and motorbikes that have raced here over the years, photos, videos, memorabilia, mock-ups of a pit stop and a rescue operation, plus two simulators, one interactive, in which visitors can experience the sensation of driving in the Grand Prix. ☎ *798–4126, ⊡ 10 patacas, 20 patacas for simulator rides. ☉ Daily 10–6.*

The **Wine Museum,** which opened in 1995, shares the basement of the TAC with the Grand Prix Museum. It illustrates the history of wine making with photographs, maps and paintings, antique wine presses, Portuguese wine fraternity costumes, and 750 different Portuguese

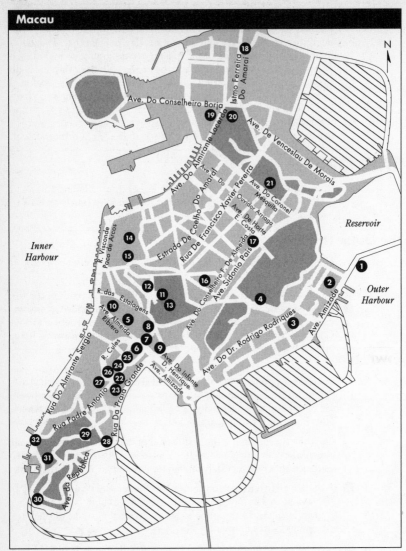

A-Ma Temple, **31**

Avenida Almeida Ribeiro (Sanmalo), **5**

Bela Vista Hotel, **28**

Camões Grotto and Garden (Casa Garden), **14**

Canidrome, **19**

Dom Pedro V, **24**

Ferry Terminal, **1**

Guia Hill, **4**

Jai Alai Casino, **2**

Kun Iam Temple, **21**

Leal Senado, **6**

Lin Fung Miu, **20**

Lou Lim Ioc Garden, **16**

Macau Forum, **3**

Maritime Museum, **32**

Memorial Home of Dr. Sun Yat-sen, **17**

Monte Fort, **13**

Monte Hill, **11**

Old Protestant Cemetery, **15**

Palácio, **23**

Penha Hill, **29**

Portas do Cerco, **18**

Post Office, **9**

Pousada de São Tiago, **30**

Praia Grande, **22**

Rua Cinco do Outubro, **10**

St. Augustine, **25**

St. Lawrence, **27**

St. Paul's, **12**

Santa Casa da Misericordia, **7**

São Domingos, **8**

Seminary of St. Joseph's, **26**

wines. ☎ 798–4108, 🍽 *10 patacas (includes first glass of wine)*. ⊙ *Daily 10–6.*

4 Overlooking the Outer Harbour are the slopes of **Guia Hill,** studded with new homes, a convent, and a hospital. The hill is topped with a fort that dates from the 1630s, the oldest lighthouse on the China coast (built in 1865), and a small white-stone chapel built in 1707. The gate to the fort is open from 7 AM to dusk. Permission from the Macau Marine Department (☎ 573–409) is needed to enter the lighthouse, but the chapel is usually open. Viewed from the fort's platform, the seascape presents a changing panorama, with fishing junks bobbing through the quiet, ocher water, catamaran ferries speeding to ports throughout the Pearl Delta, and white wakes foaming as vessels from Hong Kong arrive and take off like giant waterfowl.

Another kind of aircraft used to appear in the Outer Harbour: the flying clippers of Pan American Airways, which gave Macau a brief, and accidental, place in aviation history. On April 28, 1937, the **Hong Kong Clipper** left Manila on a flight that would inaugurate air service between the west coast of the United States and China. The plane was supposed to land in Hong Kong, but at the last minute the British authorities held back landing permission, in order to gain rights for their own Imperial Airways. The seaplane landed in Macau and was greeted by most of the population before flying on to Hong Kong. The service continued intermittently until the outbreak of war; the Pan Am terminal stood on the site now occupied by the Mandarin Oriental Hotel.

Downtown

For a relatively straightforward introduction to the many-layered and often contradictory character of Macau, stroll the mile or so of the main
5 street, **Avenida Almeida Ribeiro,** generally known by its Chinese name, **Sanmalo.** It begins a short walk from the Lisboa casino-hotel-shopping complex and ends at the floating casino in the inner harbor.

Within this short distance you find colonial Portugal, traditional China, and modern Asia locked in architectural and social embrace. Logically, it is an unworkable misalliance. In Macau it's an enduring marriage of convenience—buildings, institutions, and even lifestyles have survived because enough people wanted them to, not because their preservation was officially decreed. Sanmalo might look and sound casually chaotic, but it works.

Like a European city, the focal point of downtown Macau is the city
6 hall, **Leal Senado** (Loyal Senate), which looks out on **Largo do Senado** (Senate Square), paved with colored tiles in a wave pattern and furnished with benches, plants, and a fountain in the shape of an armillary sphere. Vehicles are banned, and the square is a pedestrian haven. Leal Senado is a superb example of colonial architecture, constructed in the late 18th century to house the senate of leading citizens—who were at the time far more powerful than the governors, who usually served their appointed time and then returned to Portugal. Today the senate, with some elected and some appointed members, acts as the municipal government, with its president holding the same power as a mayor. Inside the building, a beautiful stone staircase leads to wrought-iron gates that open onto a charming garden. The foyer and garden are open during working hours, and there are frequent art and history exhibitions in the foyer and adjoining gallery.

The original national library is also housed within the Leal Senado. A superb copy of the classic Portuguese library in Mafra, it contains possibly the best collection of books in English about China's history, society, economy, and culture. Much was inherited from the British- and American-managed Chinese Customs House. In addition, the library holds rare books from the early days of the Portuguese empire and bound copies of old Macau newspapers. Scholars and others are welcome to browse or study. ⊘ *Mon.–Sat. 1–7.*

⑦ The senate president is by tradition the president of the **Santa Casa da Misericordia** (Holy House of Mercy), the oldest Christian charity on the China coast. Founded in 1569, its headquarters occupy a handsome baroque building on Largo do Senado, and its offices administer homes for the elderly, kitchens for the poor, clinics, and a leprosarium. On the second floor, closed to the public, a reception room contains paintings of benefactress Marta Merop and Macau's first bishop, Dom Belchior, along with the latter's cross and skull.

⑧ At one end of Largo do Senado is **São Domingos,** possibly the most beautiful church in Macau, with a magnificent cream-and-white baroque altar of graceful columns, fine statues, and a forest of candles and flower vases. Built in the 17th century by the Dominicans, it has had a stormy history. In 1644 a Portuguese officer involved in civil strife was murdered at the altar by a mob during mass. In 1707 the church was besieged by the governor's troops when the Dominicans sided with the Pope against the Jesuits in a controversy about whether ancestor worship should be permitted among Chinese Christian converts. After three days, the soldiers broke down the doors and briefly imprisoned the priests.

⑨ The central **Post Office** and telephone exchange, as well as some handsome old commercial buildings with arcades at street level, enclose Largo do Senado. One building has been restored to house the Government Tourist Office, which backs onto the São Domingos produce market. The markets are narrow streets packed with stalls selling fruit and vegetables, as well as wholesale-price clothing from local factories.

Sanmalo has some clothing stores, but the majority of shoppers come here for gold jewelry, watches and clocks, Chinese and Western medicines, brandy, biscuits, and salted fish. Interspersed are banks, lawyers' offices, and the Central Hotel. Now a rather dingy, inexpensive place to stay, the Central used to contain the city's only casinos, where the *fan-tan* (button game) attracted high rollers and the top-floor brothel did a thriving business.

The heart of the old red-light district was **Rua da Felicidade** (Street of Happiness), which runs off Sanmalo. Few brothels have survived the competition from sauna and massage parlors; most have been replaced by budget hotels and restaurants. The area does preserve the atmosphere of a prewar China-coast community, especially in the evening. After sunset, food stalls with stools and tiny tables are set out. Lights blaze from open-front restaurants, laundries, tailor shops, and family living rooms. The pungent smell of cooking pervades the streets, and it seems as if most of Macau's 450,000 people have fled their tiny apartments to eat out, relax, and socialize.

An interesting side street off the main avenue that invites a detour is
⑩ **Rua Cinco de Outubro,** which contains one of the best-looking traditional Chinese medicine shops anywhere. The **Farmacia Tai Ning Tong** has an elaborately carved wood facade and a cavernous interior, its walls lined with huge apothecary jars of medicinal roots, deer horn, and other assorted marvels. In a corner are mortars and pestles for making potions to order. Rua Cinco de Outubro also contains bustling sidewalk

markets packed with bargain-price clothing and electronics, together with a typical working-class Chinese temple.

The Old Citadel

⑪ The most remarkable early buildings in Macau were situated on **Monte Hill.** Built by the Jesuits, they included a fort, a college, and the colle-

⑫ giate church of the Mother of God, commonly known as **St. Paul's.** The church was built between 1602 and 1627 by exiled Japanese Christians and local craftsmen under the direction of the Jesuits, and it was declared the most magnificent in Asia. The college, the first Western-style university in Asia, attracted such scholars as Matteo Ricci and Adam Van Schall, who studied here before going to the court in Peking. A small town of merchants, clerics, and craftsmen grew up around the Monte.

Today this area is the heart of old Macau for visitors and is easily reached from Largo do Senado via Rua da São Domingos. The college was used as army housing until it was destroyed in a disastrous fire in 1835, and the ruins of the fort are now a quiet belvedere. Of the church, only the great stone facade remains, not so much a ruin as a dramatic symbol of Macau. The story of the church can now be better appreciated since the opening in 1996 of a small museum in the crypt that was excavated from beneath what was the high altar. It contains the tomb of the church's founder, a relic of St. Francis Xavier, and the bones of Japanese and Indochinese martyrs.

⑬ **Monte Fort,** on the hill overlooking St. Paul's, was also built by the Jesuits and completed in 1623. In 1622, it was the scene of Macau's most famous battle. The Dutch, jealous of Portugal's power in Asia, invaded the territory, which was protected by a small force of soldiers, African slaves, and priests. As the Dutch closed in on Monte, a lucky cannon shot, fired by one of the priests, hit the enemy's powder supply, and in the ensuing confusion the Dutch were driven back to sea. In 1626, the first full-time governor of Macau evicted the Jesuits from the fort. For the next century and a half it was the residence and office of Macau's governors. The fort's buildings were destroyed in the 1835 fire, but the great walls remain, along with their cannon. Today the fort is a belvedere popular among residents and tourists, housing an information office. It was even used as an auditorium for an open-air performance of *The Barber of Seville* during a recent International Music Festival. A City Museum is being built, partly in the excavated foundations of the fort, with exhibits showing Macau as a crossroads for Europe and China. ✉ *Free.* ⊙ *7 AM to dusk.*

Following Rua de São Paulo from the ruins of Monte Fort, you reach

⑭ **Praça Luis de Camões** and the **Camões Grotto and Garden,** today Macau's most popular public park, frequented from dawn to dusk by people practicing *t'ai chi ch'uan* (shadowboxing), men carrying their caged songbirds for a country walk, young lovers, students, and groups huddled over games of Chinese chess.

The garden was originally the private grounds of the former Camões Museum, now Casa Garden Orient Foundation offices, and in 1785 was used by French cartographer La Perouse for a small observatory aimed at China. The garden was taken over by the city in 1886, when a heroic bronze bust of Camões, Portugal's greatest poet (who is believed to have lived here in 1557), was installed in a rocky alcove. Nearby a wall of stone slabs is inscribed with poems praising Camões and Macau by various contemporary writers. The Orient Foundation restored the 18th-century house, which was once home to the British East India Company. Part of it now serves as a museum for the Camões collection. There is also an art gallery in the basement. ☎ *554–699,* ✉ *Free.* ⊙ *Gardens open dawn–dusk; house open daily 9:30 AM–6 PM.*

⑮ The **Old Protestant Cemetery,** a "corner of some foreign field" for more than 150 Americans and British, is opposite Camões Garden and close to St. Paul's church. It is a tranquil retreat where tombstones recall the troubles and triumphs of Westerners in 19th-century China. Some of the names are familiar: George Chinnery; Captain Henry Churchill, great granduncle of Sir Winston; Joseph Adams, grandson of John Adams, the second U.S. president; Robert Morrison, who translated the Bible into Chinese; opium traders Thomas Beale, Captain John Crockett, and James Innes; Swedish historian Anders Ljungstedt; and American engineer John P. Williams. In addition, there are graves of sailors who were victims of battle, accident, or disease.

Restoration Row

One of the most incredible, and illogical, aspects of Macau is the physical survival of so much of its past, as can be seen, a block or so from the Royal Hotel, on **Avenida do Conselheiro Ferreira de Almeida,** or Restoration Row. Actually it is a row of houses, painted cream and red, built in the 1920s in symmetrical arcadian style, with shady verandas and interior courtyards. The owners of the houses were persuaded to forgo huge profits and sell to the government, which converted the buildings into homes for the Archives, the National Library, the Education Department, a contemporary-art center, and university offices. The exteriors were extensively repaired and the interiors transformed. In the case of the library, the building had to be completely gutted to accommodate the vast collection of old books. The Archives building has space for researchers and a small auditorium.

Leading off Restoration Row, to the north of St Paul's, is **Estrada de Adolfo Loureiro** and the **Lou Lim Ioc Garden,** a classic Chinese garden **⑯** modeled on those of old Soochow. It was built in the 19th century by a wealthy Chinese merchant named Lou. With the decline of the Lou family fortunes early this century, the house was sold and became a school. The garden fell into ruin until it was taken over by the city in 1974 and totally restored. Enclosed by a wall, it is a miniaturized landscape with miniforests of bamboo and flowering bushes, a mountain of sculpted concrete, and a small lake filled with lotus and golden carp. A traditional nine-turn bridge zigzags (to deter evil spirits, which can move only in straight lines) across the lake to a colonial-style pavilion with a wide veranda. This is used for regular exhibitions and Music Festival concerts. ⊙ *Daily dawn–dusk.*

⑰ Not far from Restoration Row, to the west of Guia Hill, is the **Memorial Home of Dr. Sun Yat-sen.** Sun, father of the 1911 Chinese revolution, worked as a physician in Macau from 1892 to 1894, and some of his family stayed here after his death. The memorial home, in strange mock-Moorish style, was built in the mid-1930s. It contains some interesting photographs, books, and souvenirs of Sun and his long years of exile in different parts of the world. ✉ *1 Rua Ferreira do Amaral.* ✉ *Free.* ⊙ *Weekdays (except Tues.) 10 AM–1 PM, weekends 10 AM–1 PM and 3–5 PM.*

On the Doorstep of China

At the northern end of Macau, about 2 miles from the ferry terminal or downtown, **Portas do Cerco** (The Border Gate) marks the traditional **⑱** boundary of Macau. Beyond is the Chinese border town of Gongbei.

The present gate was built in 1870 and bears the arms of Portugal's navy and artillery, along with a quotation from Camões, which reads, in translation: "Honor your country for it looks after you." On either side of the gate is written the date 1849. This commemorates the year when the governor, Ferreira do Amaral (whose statue used to stand outside the Lisboa Hotel), was assassinated by the Chinese. The local warlord planned to invade Macau but a Macanese colonel, Nicolau Mesquita, with 37 men, slipped across the border and captured the Chinese fort. Today the old gate is part of a small park that features large panels of old maps and prints made in blue and white tiles. Modern immigration halls on either side of the park handle a steady flow of vegetable farmers, businesspeople, and tourists who cross the border daily. ⊙ *Daily 7 AM–midnight.*

Close to the Chinese border are two very different attractions. On one **⑲** side is the **Canidrome,** where greyhound races attract an enthusiastic **⑳** following. Across the street from the Canidrome is the **Lin Fung Miu,** or Temple of the Lotus. This superb temple, dedicated to both Buddhist and Taoist deities, was built in 1592 and used for overnight accommodations by mandarins traveling between Macau and Canton. It is famous for its facade of intricate clay bas-reliefs depicting mythological and historical scenes and an interior frieze of colorful writhing dragons. ⊙ *Daily dawn–dusk.*

㉑ **Kun Iam Temple,** on the Avenida do Coronel Mesquita, in the northern suburbs of the city, should not be missed. This Buddhist temple, dedicated to Kun Iam (also known as Kwan Yin), the goddess of mercy, was founded in the 13th century. The present-day buildings are richly endowed with carvings, porcelain figurines, statues, old scrolls, antique furniture, and ritual objects. The temple is best known among Western visitors for the stone table in the courtyard, where, on July 3, 1844, the first Sino-American treaty was signed by the Viceroy of Canton and the United States envoy, Caleb Cushing. The temple has a large number of funeral chapels, where you can see the offerings of paper cars, airplanes, luggage, and money that are burned to accompany the souls of the dead. ⊙ *Daily dawn–dusk.*

Peninsular Macau

The narrow, hilly peninsula stretching from Avenida Almeida Ribeiro to Barra Point and the Pousada de São Tiago is quintessential Macau, very Portuguese and very Chinese, ancient and uncomfortably mod- **㉒** ern, as exemplified on the east side by the **Praia Grande** (and its extension, **Avenida da República.** This graceful, banyan-shaded boulevard was in the past a favorite place where residents would stroll, fish, or play chess on the seawall. Unfortunately the bay is being redeveloped into a business and residential area. The plans promise that two lakes and gardens will compensate for the loss of the old Praia; however for now it's mostly a construction site.

Not part of the construction, although it seems so, is the **Porta de Entendimento** (Gate of Understanding), which rises from an artificial island off Barra Point, and opposite the Pousada de São Tiago. Consisting of 120-foot-high double arches made of concrete clad in polished black marble, the monument was erected in 1993 to illustrate the enduring friendship between Macau and China.

The cargo and fishing wharfs of the **Inner Harbour,** with their traditional Chinese shop houses—ground floors occupied by ship's chandlers, net makers, ironmongers, and shops selling spices and salted fish—are on the west side of the peninsula.

23 Peninsular Macau is one of the oldest districts of the city and contains many places of historic interest, including the pink-and-white **Palácio,** a stately colonial mansion, with deep verandas and a handsome portico, which bears the Portuguese coat of arms. Located on the Praia Grande, it houses the offices of the governor and his cabinet and is Lisbon's seat of power in Macau.

24 A short, steep climb up Rua Central from Senate Square is a dimplestone ramp to St. Augustine's Square, which looks as if it came all of a piece from 19th-century Portugal. On the southwest side of the square is the **Dom Pedro V** theater, the oldest Western theater on the China coast. It was built in 1859 in the style of a European court theater and was in regular use until World War II. After a thorough renovation by the Orient Foundation, it is now in use again as a venue for concerts, plays, and recitals.

25 Facing the Dom Pedro theater is the imposing baroque **St. Augustine** church, which dates from 1814, when it replaced the burned-out 17thcentury original. In the marble-clad high altar is the large statue of Our Lord of Passos that is carried through the streets on the first day of Lent. Among the tombs in the church is that of Maria de Moura, a romantic heroine who in 1710 married the man she loved, even though he had lost an arm when attacked by another of her suitors. She died in childbirth and is buried with her baby and her husband's arm.

26 The **Seminary of St. Joseph's** stands in St. Augustine's Square. It houses a collection of religious art by 17th-century European and Japanese painters. The baroque chapel is now open to the public Thursday–Tuesday 10–4. It is a fine cruciform shape with a dome that helps give it brilliant acoustics, so it is often used for music festival events. Access is via a grand stone staircase.

27 One of the most imposing churches in Macau is that named for **St. Lawrence,** located a short distance from St. Augustine's on a street that, in the last century, was dominated by the luxurious homes of British opium merchants. The church stands in a pleasant garden, shaded by palm trees. It has always been a fashionable place and shows it with elegant wood carving, an ornate baroque altar, and stunning crystal chandeliers. It is used for concerts during the Macau International Music Festival. ⌂ *Free.* ☉ *Daily 10–4.*

28 Perched on the foundations of an old fort, overlooking the Praia Grande is the **Bela Vista Hotel** (☞ Lodging, *below*) a century-old landmark that reopened in 1992 as a luxury inn and restaurant, following restoration by the Mandarin Oriental Hotel Group.

29 Commanding some of the best views of Macau and the surrounding seascapes is **Penha Hill** where you find the courtyard of the **Bishop's Palace** and **Penha Chapel.** The palace is always closed, but the chapel is open daily 10–4. On the site of the original 1622 structure, the present building was constructed in 1935 and is dedicated to Our Lady of Penha, patroness of seafarers.

30 At the far end of the peninsula is **Barra Point,** location of the **Pousada de São Tiago,** a Portuguese inn built into the ruined foundations of a 17th-century fort (☞ Lodging, *below*).

31 At the entrance to the Inner Harbour, below Barra Point, is the **A-Ma Temple,** Macau's oldest and most venerated place of worship. Dating from the early 16th century, this is the most picturesque temple in Macau, with ornate prayer halls and pavilions built among the giant boulders of the waterfront hillside. The rocks are inscribed with red calligraphy telling the story of A-Ma (also known as Tin Hau), the favorite goddess of fishermen, who allegedly saved a humble junk from a storm. One of the many Chinese names for the area was Bay of A-Ma, or A-Ma Gau, and when the Portuguese arrived they adopted it as Macau. ☺ *Daily dawn–dusk. Lion dances held outside the temple 10–10:30 AM Sun. and public holidays.*

32 Barra Point is the logical site for the **Maritime Museum.** This gem of a museum has been a consistent favorite since its doors opened at the end of 1987. It is ideally located on a waterfront site on **Barra Square.** The four-story building resembles a stately ship and is considered one of the foremost maritime museums in Asia. The adjacent dock was restored to provide a pier for a tug, a dragon boat, a sampan, and working replicas of a South China trading junk and a 19th-century, pirate-chasing *lorcha* (wooden sailing ship). Inside the museum are displays of the local fishing industry, models of historic vessels, charts of great voyages by Portuguese and Chinese explorers, a relief model of 17th-century Macau, the story in lantern-show style of the A-Ma Temple, navigational aids such as an original paraffin lamp once used in the Guia lighthouse, and much, much more. The museum also operates 30-minute pleasure junk trips on Saturdays, Sundays, and Mondays. ☎ *307–161.* ✉ *museum, 8 patacas; boat trip, 15 patacas.* ☺ *Wed.–Mon. 10 AM–5:30 PM.*

Taipa Island

Linked to the city by the graceful 1.6-mile Taipa Bridge and the new Friendship Bridge that connects the airport with the terminal and border, Taipa can be reached by bus or taxi. Up until the end of the 19th century, Taipa consisted of two islands that provided a sheltered anchorage where clipper ships and East India–men could load and unload cargoes that were then carried by junks and barges to and from Canton. Gradually the islands were joined by river silt and land reclamation, but Taipa Praia, with its mansions—one of which now houses a museum—offers a reminder of the old days.

Taipa and Coloane, its neighbor, are Macau's New Territories, having been ceded by China only in 1887. Until the building of the Taipa Bridge, both islands led a somnolent existence, interrupted only by occasional pirate raids. Taipa's economy depended on the raising of ducks and the manufacture of firecrackers. The duck farms have given way to apartment blocks while the courtyarded firecracker factories have closed, unable to compete with those in China.

Numbers in the margin correspond to points of interest on the Taipa and Coloane Islands map.

33 The **Taipa Village** is a tight maze of houses and shops in the traditional mold. It is changing, as a result of the island's new prosperity, and now boasts banks, a two-story municipal market, air-conditioned shops, and streets lined with restaurants.

34 On the edge of Taipa Village is a hill crowned by the church of Our Lady of Carmel, which overlooks the **Taipa House Museum.** This finely restored 1920s mansion contains authentic period furniture, decorations, and furnishings that recapture the atmosphere and lifestyle of a middle-class Macanese family in the early part of the century. ✉ *Taipa Praia.* ✉ *Free.* ☺ *Tues.–Sun. 9 AM–1 PM and 3–5 PM.*

35 On the southwestern side of Taipa is the raceway of the **Macau Jockey Club,** 50 acres of reclaimed land with an ultramodern five-story grandstand and track.

154

Chapel of St. Francis Xavier, **41**

Coloane Park, **42**

Hac Sa, **43**

Macau International Airport, **39**

Macau Jockey Club, **35**

Pou Tai Un Temple, **36**

Pousada de Coloane, **40**

Taipa House Museum, **34**

Taipa Village, **33**

United Chinese Cemetery, **38**

University of Macau, **37**

Westin Resort, **44**

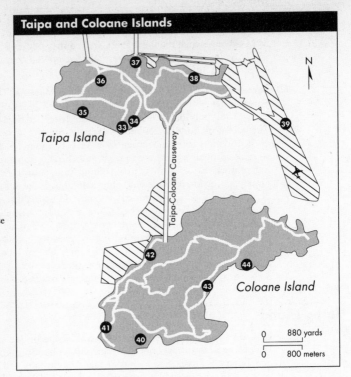

Taipa and Coloane Islands

36 Behind the Hyatt Regency Hotel is the **Pou Tai Un Temple.** It is famed for its vegetarian restaurant (the vegetables are grown in an adjoining garden), and has been embellished with a yellow-tile pavilion and a statue of the Buddhist goddess of mercy.

37 Overlooking the bridges and Macau city is the hilltop **University of Macau.** Compressed into a small area, it nevertheless has spacious lecture halls, sports grounds, and a theater. It offers a wide range of graduate and postgraduate courses.

38 For Buddhists, Taoists, and Confucians, Taipa is a favored last earthly address, in the massive **United Chinese Cemetery,** which covers the cliff on the northeastern coast of the island. It is lavishly decorated with colored tiles and assorted religious images.

39 Built on reclaimed land on the eastern coast of Taipa is the new **Macau International Airport.** The runway occupies a man-made island that stretches between Taipa and Coloane, while the handsome, glass-clad passenger terminal is connected by the gracefully arched Friendship Bridge to the ferry terminal and Chinese border.

Coloane Island

Situated at the end of a 1.6-mile causeway from Taipa is the larger, hillier island of Coloane, where a favorite destination is the attractive 22-room

40 **Pousada de Coloane** (☞ Lodging, *below*). About a 25-minute drive from the city, it is generally considered to be remote, which makes it a popular spot for relaxed holidays. There is a long beach below the pousada, along with casual, open-air restaurants and water sports facilities.

The village of Coloane, with its old tile-roof houses, centers around
④ the **Chapel of St. Francis Xavier.** With its cream-and-white facade and
bell tower, it was built in 1928 to house the reliquary containing an
arm bone of the saint, who died on an island 50 miles south of Macau
while waiting to enter China. Since then the relic has been moved, as
have the remains of Japanese martyrs, although some bones of mar-
tyred Christians from 17th-century Vietnam remain enshrined here. In
the square outside the chapel is a monument surrounded by cannon-
balls commemorating the local defeat of a pirate band in 1910, Macau's
last encounter with old-style pirates.

④ **Coloane Park,** which opened in 1985 on the west coast of the island,
is one of Macau's most interesting natural preserves. Its centerpiece is
a walk-in aviary containing more than 200 species of birds, including
the rare Palawan peacock and the crested white pheasant. Nearby
you'll find a pond with black swans, a playground, the Balichão restaurant, a picnic area, and a nature trail around the hillside. Developed
by the Islands Municipal Council, the park has an impressive collection of exotic trees and shrubs, as well as research laboratories and a
garden of medicinal plants. 🖾 *Free to park, 5 patacas to aviary.* ☺
Tues.–Sun. 10–6.

④ One of the best beaches in Macau is **Hac Sa,** or Black Sands, on
Coloane's east coast. Although an ocher color, thanks to the silt brought
down from the delta by the Pearl River, the water is clean and safe.
The popular **Fernando's** (☞ Dining, *below*) restaurant is a few feet away
from the beach.

④ Built into a bluff overlooking Hac Sa beach, the **Westin Resort** (☞ Lodging, *below*) has rooms with private terraces, two pools, tennis courts,
five-star restaurants, and a championship golf course that spreads
over the hills above the hotel.

DINING

The favorites of Portuguese cuisine are regular menu items. The
beloved *bacalhau* (codfish) is served baked, boiled, grilled, deep-
fried with potato, or stewed with onion, garlic, and eggs. Portuguese
sardines, country soups such as *caldo verde* and *sopa alentejana,* and
dishes of rabbit are on the menus of many restaurants. Sharing the
bill of fare are colonial favorites: from Brazil come *feijoadas,* stews
of beans, pork, spicy sausage, and vegetables; from Mozambique,
African chicken, baked or grilled in fiery *piri-piri* (chilis). In addition, some kitchens prepare baked quail, curried crab, and the
delectable Macau sole that rivals its Dover cousin. And then there
are the giant prawns in spicy sauce—one of Macau's special dining
pleasures.

Not surprisingly, most other restaurants serve Chinese food, predom-
inantly Cantonese and Chiu Chow, but quite a number feature authentic
Japanese, Thai, Korean, Indonesian, and even Burmese meals; still
others serve Italian, Continental, and British fare, along with the inevitable fast-food varieties. Prices are generally very reasonable, and
restaurants are quite similar except at the very top and bottom of the
market.

Wine has traditionally been a real bargain in Macau, and it still sells
very cheaply in the stores. Some restaurants maintain a reasonable mark-
up; others have taken advantage of Hong Kong's ever-increasing price
hikes to raise their own. As a result Portuguese *vinho verde,* a slightly
sparkling new wine, and table reds and whites, such as the Dao family of wines, often cost about 100 patacas. Those restaurants that keep

prices to about half of this are noted below. Except in hotels, beer and spirits—including some powerful Portuguese brandies—are very inexpensive.

All restaurants are open every day of the year except, for some, a few days after Chinese New Year. In most cases there is no afternoon closure for cleaning, and both lunch and dinner tend to be leisurely affairs, with no one urged to finish up and leave. Most people order wine, relax, look at the menu, note what other diners are eating, talk to the waiter, and then make their decision. Dress is informal, and nowhere are jackets and ties required. The Department of Tourism's map brochure, "Eating Out in Macau," is very useful. For price categories, *see* the Dining price chart in Pleasures and Pastimes, *above*.

Macanese-Portuguese

$$$ ✕ **Bela Vista.** Atop a winding staircase in the landmark hotel, this restau-
★ rant has it all—a nostalgically colonial setting, a romantic veranda, a cozy bar, friendly but efficient service, and a superb menu. The last is regularly revamped with a balance between Macanese and Continental. Fish and seafood dishes are particularly good, and desserts—such as the rice pudding with cinnamon—are irresistible. ⊠ *8 Rua do Comendador Kou Neng.* ☎ *965–333. Reservations essential. AE, DC, MC, V.*

$$$ ✕ **Fortaleza.** The setting of this exquisite restaurant would be reason enough to dine here. In the traditional Portuguese inn, Pousada de São Tiago, that was built into a 17th-century fortress, it offers views of the entrance to the Inner Harbour and local Chinese islands. The decor and atmosphere recall the golden age of the Portuguese empire, with crystal lamps, hand-carved mahogany furniture, blue and white wall tiles and plush drapes. The food doesn't let the place down and includes classic Macanese dishes such as quail and spicy prawns as well as Continental fare. ⊠ *Pousada de São Tiago, Av. da República.* ☎ *781–111. AE, DC, MC, V.*

$$$ ✕ **Military Club.** After the club, built in 1870, was beautifully restored to its former colonial elegance, the restaurant was opened to the public. It has a marvelous old-world atmosphere and an extensive menu of Portuguese dishes. Specialties include partridge pie, cold stuffed crab, grilled venison, and a range of egg puddings. ⊠ *795 Av. Praia Grande,* ☎ *714–009. No credit cards.*

$$$ ✕ **O Porto Interior.** The menu at this restaurant, named for its location on the Inner Harbour waterfront, is beautifully presented upmarket Macanese, but it's the design of the place that makes it so special. The architects created an elegant, two-story facade with colonnades and Iberian arches. Inside, the walls are covered with blue and white tiles and intricately carved wooden grilles. Guests enter over a marble bridge. ⊠ *259 Rua Almirante Sergio,* ☎ *967–770. AE, MC, V.*

$$ ✕ **A Galera.** This is an elegant, handsomely decorated restaurant, with blue-and-white-tile wall panels, black-and-white-tile floors, pearl-gray table linen, Wedgwood dishware, a bar with high-back armchairs, and views of the S. Francisco fortress. Try such main dishes as bacalhau *a bras*—cooked in a skillet with rice, olives, egg, and onion— and squid stuffed with spiced meat, any of the rich, homemade soups, and the dessert soufflés. ⊠ *Lisboa Hotel, 3rd Floor of new wing,* ☎ *577–666 ext. 1103. AE, DC, MC, V.*

$$ ✕ **A Lorcha.** This restaurant in a converted shop house near the Mar-
★ itime Museum is believed by many locals to serve the best Portuguese food in town. It is also one of the most attractive dining places, with stone archways, white stucco, and terra-cotta tile floors. Among the most popular dishes are seafood rice, bread-based *açorda* casseroles,

kidney beans, and codfish. Service is first-class, and prices are extremely reasonable. ⊠ *289 Rua do Almirante Sergio,* ☎ *313–193. Reservations essential. MC, V. Closed Tues.*

$$ ✕ **Afonso III.** After some years at the Hyatt Regency (☞ *above*), where he created their Portuguese restaurant, Afonso decided to open his own place and cook food the way his grandmother did. The result is a simple café in the heart of downtown, which is regularly packed with locals. Most choose the specials of the day, which usually include codfish or braised pork and beef stew prepared like nowhere else in Macau. The wine list is equally unusual, and the prices are a real bargain. ⊠ *11A Rua Central,* ☎ *586–272. No credit cards.*

$$ ✕ **Afonso's.** This is one of the most attractively designed restaurants in Macau. It is horseshoe-shape, with Portuguese tiles on the wall, Cantonese tiles on the floor, floral cushions on the rattan chairs, spotless table linen, and dishware made to order in Europe. Picture windows frame the gardens outside, and there is space for musicians when the hotel has promotions such as "April in Portugal." The menu is imaginative and features a good balance of Macanese favorites and Portuguese dishes. ⊠ *Hyatt Regency Hotel, Taipa Island,* ☎ *831–234. AE, DC, MC, V.*

$$ ✕ **Balichão.** This Macanese restaurant has a brilliant location in a spa-
★ cious pavilion in Coloane Park, between a swan lake and an aviary. The decor features birdcages—some with resident birds—brass pots, and rattan furniture. The owner's mother commands the kitchen, where she creates new dishes along with favorites such as casserole of pork and tamarind in *balichão* (the local shrimp paste), curry crab, and chicken Macau. This is also a great place for private parties. ⊠ *Est. Seac Pai Van Granja, Coloane,* ☎ *870–098. AE, DC, MC, V.*

$$ ✕ **Fat Siu Lau.** Dating to 1903, this is the oldest European restaurant in Macau and one that has maintained high standards of food and service. Years ago it looked like an average Chinese café, but now each of its three floors is elegantly furnished and decorated—if a bit kitschy in style. The menu is tried and true. The roast pigeon Fat Siu Lau has made the restaurant famous. Other favorites are African chicken, sardines, and ox breast with herbs. ⊠ *64 Rua da Felicidade,* ☎ *573–580. No credit cards.*

$$ ✕ **Fernando's.** You have to look hard to find this great, country-style
★ Portuguese restaurant located next to Hac Sa beach, because the entrance looks like that of a typical Chinese café (though local cabbies usually know how to find it). There's also an open-sided bar and courtyard in back overlooking a sandy beach. Clams in garlic are the best in town, and the bacalhau is hard to beat. Since the menu is only in Portuguese, you may need the aid of eccentric owner Fernando Gomes, who's always happy to translate and make suggestions. ⊠ *Hac Sa Beach 9, Coloane Island,* ☎ *882–264. No credit cards.*

$$ ✕ **Flamingo.** Designed like a European pavilion, with verandas on three sides, this restaurant is ideally located in the gardens of the Taipa Island Resort. There are no flamingos, but there are some very well-fed ducks in the surrounding pond. At night there is music by a Filipino group in the main room, with Portuguese decor. At all times there is a wonderfully carefree atmosphere. Flamingo has the greatest small crusty cottage loaves in Asia. The menu is varied and reasonable. ⊠ *Taipa Island Resort, Hyatt Regency Hotel,* ☎ *831–234, ext. 1874. AE, DC, MC, V.*

$$ ✕ **Henri's Galley.** Situated on the banyan-lined waterfront, with some tables on the sidewalk, this is a favorite with local residents and visitors from Hong Kong. The decor reflects owner Henri Wong's former career as a ship's steward: a coiled blue-rope pattern on the ceiling, pictures of old ships on the walls, and red and green lights to keep pas-

sengers on an even keel. The food is consistently good, with probably the biggest and best spicy prawns in town, delicious African and Portuguese chicken, Portuguese soups, Macau sole, and fried rice, complete with hot Portuguese sausage. ⊠ *4 Av. da República,* ☎ *556–251. MC, V.*

$$ ✕ **Litoral.** As soon as it opened in late 1995 this Macanese restaurant
★ was a hit with local residents, and it has remained one of the top dining places. The menu has many unusual dishes, and the food is fresh and attractively served by smiling staff at very reasonable prices. Although it occupies a modern, boxy building, it was designed to look like a traditional Portuguese restaurant installed in a Chinese shop house, all to brilliant effect. ⊠ *261 Rua Almirante Sergio,* ☎ *967–878. AE, MC, V.*

$$ ✕ **Montanha Russa.** In the northern suburbs of Macau is a quiet park, built on a hill shaped like a snail shell. It's a great retreat, and the perfect spot for Macau's only real outdoor restaurant, which accounts for its popularity among the people who work nearby. Operated by Filipino residents, it is very much a family-style place, with a daily choice of soups, fish, and meats. Service comes with a smile, and the cost will be a very pleasant surprise. ⊠ *Est. Ferreira de Amaral,* ☎ *302–731. No credit cards.*

$$ ✕ **Pinocchio's.** This was the first Macanese-Portuguese restaurant on Taipa, and it's still one of the best. It began with one room, then grew to fill a large, covered courtyard. Now the owner has expanded again to a neighboring modern block. Favorite dishes are curried crab, baked quail, grilled king prawns, and steamed shrimp. If you order ahead you can have delectable roast lamb or suckling pig. ⊠ *4 Rua do Sol, Taipa Island,* ☎ *327–128 or 327–328. MC, V.*

$$ ✕ **Pousada de Coloane.** This is 20 minutes by car from the city, by Macau standards a long, long way to go for a meal, but many residents and Hong Kong regulars consider it well worth the trip. The setting is fine, with a large open terrace outside the restaurant. When the weather is good, an alfresco lunch overlooking the beach and water is marvelous. For indoor dining, the restaurant is reminiscent of many in Lisbon, with dark-wood panels, colorful tile floors, and folk-art decorations. Service can be rather haphazard, but the food is usually excellent. Among the specialties are feijoadas, grilled sardines, and stuffed squid. ⊠ *Praia de Cheoc Van, Coloane Island,* ☎ *882–143. MC, V.*

$$ ✕ **Praia Grande.** Wonderfully situated on the Praia Grande, this classic Portuguese restaurant was cleverly created from an ordinary corner building. Decor is simple with white arches, terra-cotta floors, and wrought-iron furniture. The menu has such imaginative items as Portuguese dim sum, and the not-so-unusual chocolate cake is terrific too. ⊠ *10A Lobo d'Avila, Praia Grande,* ☎ *973–022. AE, MC, V.*

$$ ✕ **Solmar.** Since most people can remember, the Solmar has been an unofficial club for local Portuguese and Macanese men, who gather here to drink strong coffee and gossip. In 1995 it was given a completely new Portuguese look, with tiled walls, wrought-iron lanterns, and impressionistic pictures. The most popular dishes are the baked Portuguese chicken and spicy African chicken. ⊠ *11 Praia Grande, opposite the Metropole Hotel,* ☎ *574–391. No credit cards.*

$ ✕ **A Casa Macaense.** On the busy Rua Central, this unpretentious place has a family atmosphere and family cooking, with daily specials the price of other restaurants' starters. Wines cost 45 to 60 patacas. The minchi here is probably the best in town. ⊠ *32 Rua Central,* ☎ *937683. No credit cards. Closed Wednesday.*

$ ✕ **Café Luso.** It's easy to pass this modest little restaurant on Rua Central, because it looks like a pizza parlor. It does have the best seafood pizza in Asia, but it also offers a range of Mediterranean dishes such as spicy squid, as well as Portuguese stews. Food and wine are very, very affordable. ⊠ *33B Rua Central.* ☎ *570–413. No credit cards.*

Asian

$$ ✕ **Chiu Chau.** This is probably the best, and certainly the most sumptuous, restaurant in Macau serving the Chiu Chow cuisine of Swatow. Many Hong Kong and Thai Chinese (and therefore many gambling visitors to Macau) are originally from Swatow Province. The food is richer and spicier than Cantonese food, with thick, strong shark's fin soup, chicken in hot *chinjew* sauce, and crabs in chicken sauce. ⊠ *Lisboa Hotel,* ☎ *577–666, ext. 83001. AE, DC, MC, V.*

$$ ✕ **Four Five Six.** Lovers of Shanghainese food flock to this restaurant, where the specialties are lacquered duck, braised eel, and chicken broiled in rice wine, plus steamed crabs during the winter. The atmosphere is generally cheerful, noisy, and welcoming. ⊠ *Lisboa Hotel, mezzanine of new wing,* ☎ *388–404. AE, DC, MC, V.*

$$ ✕ **Korean Restaurant.** This is the place for *bulgogi* (barbecued meat) and *kimchi* (spicy cabbage) as authentic as any in Seoul, made especially agreeable by efficient use of ventilation hoods over the tables. Other traditional dishes to be found here are *sinsollo*, meat grilled on braziers at the table, *japchae*, a tasty cellophane noodle and vegetable concoction, and *gopdol bibimbap*, a feast of rice, vegetables, strips of beef and an egg served sizzling in a stone bowl with a delicious hot sauce. ⊠ *Hotel Presidente, Av. da Amizade,* ☎ *553–888. AE, DC, MC, V.*

$$ ✕ **Long Kei.** One of the oldest and most popular Cantonese restaurants in Macau, Long Kei has a huge menu. Daily specials are printed only in Chinese, so ask the waiter to translate. Like all good Chinese restaurants in this part of the world, it is noisy and apparently chaotic, with no attempt at glamour or sophistication. The focus is the food—few will be disappointed here. Be sure to sample the shrimp toast. ⊠ *7B Largo do Senado,* ☎ *573–970. No credit cards.*

$$ ✕ **Rasa Sayang.** Located in a new residential complex on Taipa, this agreeable restaurant serves a wide variety of dishes from Malaysia, Singapore, and Indonesia. The decor reflects the menu, with batik pictures, lots of potted plants, and summery furniture. ⊠ *Est. Noroeste da Taipa, Ocean Gardens, Plum Court,* ☎ *810–187. AE, MC, V.*

$$ ✕ **Royal Canton.** This large, attractively decorated Cantonese restaurant is very popular with locals and visiting groups, who use it for family parties and celebrations as well as for breakfast and morning dim sum. The menu is extensive and the service friendly and efficient. ⊠ *Royal Hotel,* ☎ *378–633. AE, DC, MC, V.*

LODGING

Characteristically, Macau offers a far more diverse variety of accommodations than other parts of the Far East. Of course it has international hotels, in the three-to-five star range, carrying the names of the world's leading chains and living up to their high standards for guest rooms, restaurants, and recreational facilities. And naturally it has a good choice of budget hotels, owned and managed by Chinese from Macau, Hong Kong, or China. In addition it has hostels and guest houses for real bargain prices. All the lodgings listed below have private baths.

$$$ 🏨 **Bela Vista.** Originally built in the 1880s on a hill overlooking Praia
★ Grande Bay, this landmark hotel has been extensively renovated and upgraded by its new managers, Mandarin Oriental Hotels, and is now a deluxe inn with suites. The Bela Vista veranda has been famous among visitors to Macau for decades, and a marble-floored, open-air terrace

is now available for private parties and barbecues. The clubby bar, with a working fireplace, is a great rendezvous. ⊠ *Rua do Comendador Kou Ho Neng 8,* ☎ *965–333,* FAX *965–588; in Hong Kong,* ☎ *2548–7676. 8 suites. Restaurant, bar. AE, DC, MC, V.*

$$$ ⊞ **Grandeur.** Owned and operated by CTS (Hong Kong), this hotel in the Outer Harbour boasts Macau's first revolving restaurant—which serves Portuguese food and has nightly entertainment. Other restaurants offer Chinese and Italian meals. Rooms are attractively furnished and equipped with a host of gadgets, including hair dryers and tea- and coffeemakers. ⊠ *Rua de Pequim,* ☎ *781–233,* FAX *781–211; in Hong Kong 2857–2846. 350 rooms. 3 restaurants, bar, pool, health club, business center. AE, DC, MC, V.*

$$$ ⊞ **Holiday Inn.** Opened in 1993 and part of the international chain's superior Asia-Pacific brand, this hotel is the latest addition to the rapidly developing Outer Harbour area, minutes from the new Ferry Terminal and within walking distance of the town center. Each of the rooms has contemporary decor and a built-in window seat with a city or sea view. Dining choices include the glass-enclosed restaurant **Frascati,** serving Italian cuisine in an alfresco setting; the **Dragon Court,** for Cantonese specialties; and the **VIP Café,** with its harbor view. At street level is Macau's first sports pub, **Oskar's,** complete with a pool table and video games. ⊠ *Rua de Pequim,* ☎ *783–333,* FAX *782–321; in Hong Kong 2810–9628; in the U.S.,* ☎ *800/465–4329. 450 rooms, 6 suites. 3 restaurants, bar, pool, hot tub, steam room, fitness center, casino. AE, DC, MC, V.*

$$$ ⊞ **Hotel Ritz.** This handsome hotel opposite the Bela Vista commands fine views of Praia Grande Bay and Taipa Island beyond from balconied rooms and the spacious dining terrace. The restaurants serve Chinese and Continental meals. ⊠ *Rua Comendador Kou Ho Neng,* ☎ *339–955,* FAX *317–826; in Hong Kong,* ☎ *2739–6993, 2540–6333, or 2367–3043. 162 rooms and suites. 3 restaurants, bar, 2 indoor pools, sauna, 2 tennis courts, health club, squash, business services. AE, DC, MC, V.*

$$$ ⊞ **Hyatt Regency and Taipa Island Resort.** Rooms here conform to Hyatt
★ Regency's high standards, with modern conveniences and attractive furnishings. The public areas were built in Macau from designs by Dale Keller, and they combine the best of Iberian architecture and Chinese decor. The foyer is a spacious lounge with white arches, masses of potted plants, and fabulous Chinese lacquer panels. Beyond is the coffee shop, an aptly named Greenhouse glass-roof café, a hideaway bar, and **Afonso's** Portuguese restaurant (☞ Dining, *above*). A small casino is off the lobby. The Taipa Resort, which adjoins the hotel, has a complete health spa with various baths and massage and beauty treatments, a running track, a botanical garden, and the marvelous **Flamingo** Macanese veranda restaurant (☞ Dining, *above*). The hotel is close to the racetrack and operates a shuttle-bus service to the wharf and to the Lisboa. It is particularly popular with Hong Kong families. ⊠ *Taipa Island,* ☎ *831–234,* FAX *830–195; in Hong Kong,* ☎ *2559–0168; in the U.S.,* ☎ *800/233–1234; elsewhere Hyatt Hotels Reservations. 365 rooms. 5 restaurants, 2 bars, pool, barbershop, beauty salon, 4 tennis courts, health club, squash, casino. AE, DC, MC, V.*

$$$ ⊞ **Mandarin Oriental.** Built on the site of the old Pan Am seaplane ter-
★ minal, with marvelous views of the Pearl River and islands, this is a beautiful hotel. Its lobby is furnished with reproductions of Portuguese art and antiques, and the **Cafe Girassol** could have been transported from the Algarve. The Italian restaurant, **Mezzaluna,** serves excellent pasta dishes and has a wood-burning pizza oven. The **Bar da Guia** is probably the most elegant drinking spot in town, and the casino is certainly the most exclusive. Recreation facilities overlook the outer har-

bor. The guest rooms have marble bathrooms and teak furniture. ⊠ *Av. da Amizade,* ☎ *567–888,* ⨳ *594–589; in Hong Kong,* ☎ *2881– 1688; in the U.S.,* ☎ *800/526–6566. 438 rooms. 3 restaurants, bar, 2 outdoor pools, beauty salon, massage, sauna, 2 tennis courts, exercise room, squash, casino. AE, DC, MC, V.*

$$$ 🏨 **New Century.** Opened on a site between the university and the Hyatt Regency, this sumptuously appointed hotel has quickly joined the industry leaders. The atrium lobby is breathtaking, and the huge pool terrace offers splendid views of the city and Taipa. Rooms are tastefully furnished, and there is a wide range of dining options, including a wooden deck with Caribbean-style cabanas for parties. The Prince Galaxie is an excellent entertainment center, with a pub, disco and karaoke rooms. ⊠ *Est. Almirante Marques Esparteiro, Taipa Island,* ☎ *831–111,* ⨳ *832–222; in Hong Kong,* ☎ *2581–9863. 599 rooms. 4 restaurants, bar, pub, pool, 2 tennis courts, bowling, health club, squash, dance club. AE, DC, MC, V.*

$$$ 🏨 **Pousada de São Tiago.** This is as much a leading tourist attraction ★ as a place to stay. It is a traditional Portuguese inn that was built, with enormous imagination and dedication, into the ruins of a 17th-century fortress. Ancient trees that had taken over the fort were incorporated into the design, the position of their roots, for example, dictating the shape of the coffee shop and terrace. Furnishings, made to order in Portugal, include mahogany period furniture, blue-and-white-tile walls, and crystal lamps, plus terra-cotta floor tiles from China and carpets woven in Hong Kong. The entrance is the original entry to the fort, and natural springs have been trained to flow down the rocky wall in tile channels on either side of the staircase. Each of the rooms, complete with four-poster beds and marble bathrooms, has a balcony. Book well in advance for weekends and holidays. ⊠ *Av. da República,* ☎ *378–111,* ⨳ *552–170; in Hong Kong,* ☎ *2739–1216. 23 rooms. Restaurant, bar, pool, chapel. AE, DC, MC, V.*

$$$ 🏨 **Royal.** The Royal has an excellent location, with fine views of Guia, the city, and the Inner Harbour. It has a marble-clad lobby with a marble fountain and lounge, and some excellent shops. In the basement are its sports facilities and a karaoke bar. Upstairs are the glass-roof swimming pool and four restaurants: the **Royal Canton** for Chinese food, the Japanese **Ginza,** the Portuguese-Continental **Vasco da Gama,** and a coffee shop. The hotel has shuttle bus service to the casinos. ⊠ *2 Est. da Vitoria,* ☎ *552–222,* ⨳ *563–008; in Hong Kong,* ☎ *2540– 6333. 380 rooms. 3 restaurants, bar, indoor pool, sauna, health club, squash. AE, DC, MC, V.*

$$$ 🏨 **Westin Resort.** This marvelous facility opened in 1993 on a headland overlooking Hac Sa Beach on Coloane Island. Rooms are built around the bluff and have great terraces overlooking the beach and water. The Macau Golf and Country Club (☞ Outdoor Activities and Sports, *below*) has a clubhouse in the building, with the course laid out behind it. ⊠ *Hac Sa Beach, Coloane Island,* ☎ *871–111,* ⨳ *871–122; in Hong Kong,* ☎ *2803–2015; in the U.S.,* ☎ *800/228– 3000. 208 rooms. 4 restaurants, 2 bars, 2 pools, golf course, 8 tennis courts, health club, squash, shops. AE, DC, MC, V.*

$$ 🏨 **Beverly Plaza.** Located in the new suburb behind the Lisboa, this hotel is managed by the China Travel Service, which has offices in the building. The hotel also has a shop with goods at bargain prices. Locals often ship their purchases to relatives in China. The hotel's Chinese restaurant is popular for banquets. ⊠ *Av. Dr. Rodrigo Rodrigues,* ☎ *782–288,* ⨳ *780–684; in Hong Kong,* ☎ *2739–9928. 300 rooms. 2 restaurants, bar. AE, DC, MC, V.*

$$ ⊞ **Guia.** Situated on Guia Hill, this small, unpretentious hotel is an excellent value where guests feel very much at home. Rooms are simple and agreeable, and some have views of the residential area and hills. ✉ *1 Est. Engenheiro Trigo,* ☎ *513–888,* FAX *559–822. 89 rooms. Restaurant, coffee shop, bar, dance club. AE, DC, MC, V.*

$$ ⊞ **Kingsway.** This moderately priced hotel on the Outer Harbour opened in 1992. The rooms are small but equipped with International Direct Dial telephones, minibars, and in-house movies. It has a casino which caters mostly to gambling junketeers from Southeast Asia. ✉ *Rua Luis Gonzaga Gomes,* ☎ *702–888,* FAX *702–828; in Hong Kong, 2571–1886. 410 rooms. 2 restaurants, sauna, casino. AE, DC, MC, V.*

$$ ⊞ **Lisboa.** Rising above a two-story casino, with walls of mustard-color tiles, frilly white window frames, and a roof shaped like a giant roulette wheel, this utterly bizarre building is a local landmark. The main tower of the Lisboa has, for better or worse, become one of the popular symbols of Macau. A second tower wing houses the Crazy Paris Show, the superb **A Galera** restaurant, a children's game room and a billiards hall, plus an ostentatious collection of late Ching Dynasty art objects in the small, lobby-level exhibition area. The original tower has restaurants serving some of Macau's best cuisine of Chiu Chow province, Japan, and Shanghai. Also contained in the complex are a video arcade, a 24-hour coffee shop, a health spa, Macau's first **Pizza Hut,** some very good shops, and a pool terrace. ✉ *Av. da Amizade,* ☎ *377–666,* FAX *567–193; in Hong Kong,* ☎ *2559–1028. 1,050 rooms. 12 restaurants, coffee shop, pizzeria, 3 bars, pool, sauna, bowling, casino, dance club, theater, video games. AE, DC, MC, V.*

$$ ⊞ **Metropole.** This centrally located hotel is managed by the China Travel Service. It has pleasant, comfortable rooms and restaurants serving Chinese and Western food. The hotel is frequented by business travelers and China-bound groups. ✉ *63 Rua da Praia Grande,* ☎ *388–166,* FAX *330–890; in Hong Kong,* ☎ *2540–6333. 109 rooms. Restaurant, coffee shop. AE, DC, MC, V.*

$$ ⊞ **Nam Yue.** This new, China-managed hotel is conveniently close to the ferry terminal, the Jai Alai casino and entertainment complex, and the Yaohan department store. It is a bright, welcoming place, with a popular Chinese restaurant and a coffee shop. ✉ *International Centre, Av. do Dr. Rodrigo Rodrigues,* ☎ *726–288,* FAX *726–726; in Hong Kong,* ☎ *2559–0708. 141 rooms. Restaurant, coffee shop, business services. AE, DC, MC, V.*

$$ ⊞ **New World Emperor.** This 1992 addition to the Outer Harbour district is close to casinos and the wharf and is a smart value. It has a fine Cantonese restaurant and a popular hostess nightclub. ✉ *Rua de Xangai,* ☎ *781–888,* FAX *782–287; in Hong Kong,* ☎ *2724–4622; elsewhere, New World Hotels International. 405 rooms. 2 restaurants, bar, sauna, nightclub. AE, DC, MC, V.*

$$ ⊞ **Pousada de Coloane.** This pousada is a small resort inn that was upgraded in 1993. Among its delights are a huge terrace overlooking a good sandy beach, a pool, and a superb restaurant serving excellent Macanese and Portuguese food. Sunday buffets, held outdoors weather permitting, are popular with locals and tourists alike. There are April in Portugal festivals every year, with star performers flown in. The rooms have balconies and minibars, and roomy bathtubs. This is a place for lazy vacations, and in summer it's usually packed with families from Hong Kong as well as singles who want an inexpensive getaway. ✉ *Praia de Cheoc Van, Coloane Island,* ☎ *882–143,* FAX *882–251; in Hong Kong,* ☎ *2540–8180. 22 rooms. Restaurant, bar, pool. MC, V.*

$$ ▦ **Presidente.** The Presidente has an excellent location and is very popular with visitors from Hong Kong. It has an agreeable lobby lounge, European and Chinese restaurants, the best Korean food in town, and a disco. ⊠ *Av. da Amizade,* ☎ *553–888* ℻ *552–735; in Hong Kong,* ☎ *2857–1533; elsewhere, Utell International reservations offices. 340 rooms. 3 restaurants, sauna, nightclub. AE, DC, MC, V.*

$$ ▦ **Sintra.** A sister hotel of the Lisboa, the Sintra is, in contrast, quiet, with few diversions apart from a sauna and a European restaurant with picture windows and Mediterranean decor. It has a handsome new facade and chic Continental lobby and is ideally located, within easy walking distance of the Lisboa and downtown. ⊠ *Av. Dom Joã, IV,* ☎ *710–111,* ℻ *510–527; in Hong Kong,* ☎ *2546–6944. 236 rooms. 2 restaurants, sauna. AE, DC, MC, V.*

$ ▦ **Central.** In the heart of town, this was once the home of Macau's only legal casino and best brothel. Now it's a budget hotel with clean, basic rooms and an excellent Chinese restaurant. ⊠ *Av. Almeida Ribeiro,* ☎ *378–888,* ℻ *332–275. 160 rooms. Restaurant. AE, MC, V.*

$ ▦ **East Asia.** This attractive small hotel is situated in an interesting old quarter off the main street. It has a restaurant serving Chinese and Western food, and it's close to many good restaurants. ⊠ *1A Rua da Madeira,* ☎ *922–433; in Hong Kong* ☎ *2540–6333,* ℻ *922–430. 98 rooms. Restaurant. AE, MC, V.*

$ ▦ **Grande.** A pre–World War II hotel geared for gamblers who frequent nearby casinos, the Grande has a European atmosphere and good restaurants. ⊠ *146 Av. Almeida Ribeiro,* ☎ *921–111,* ℻ *922–397. 90 rooms. 4 restaurants, nightclub. AE, DC, MC, V.*

$ ▦ **Holiday.** This budget hotel is conveniently close to Monte Fort and St Paul's. ⊠ *36 Est. de Repousa,* ☎ *361-696. 40 rooms. Restaurant, nightclub. AE, MC, V.*

$ ▦ **Hou Kong.** This small hotel is well located in the old Inner Harbour district. ⊠ *1 Trav. das Virtudes,* ☎ *937–555,* ℻ *338–884. 54 rooms. Restaurant. AE, MC, V.*

$ ▦ **Ko Wah.** In a modern building in the Felicidade entertainment district, this guest house is clean and comfortable. ⊠ *71 Rua Felicidade,* ☎ *554–993,* ℻ *502–004; in Hong Kong,* ☎ *2540–8180. 30 rooms. No credit cards.*

$ ▦ **London.** This hotel on the Inner Harbour waterfront is strictly for sleeping, but there are plenty of restaurants nearby. ⊠ *4 Praça Ponte de Horta,* ☎ *937–770. 46 rooms. No credit cards.*

There are some small, old hotels and boardinghouses (referred to as villas) in the $ category. They usually cater to Chinese visitors, so the staff generally speaks little English. However, they are clean and inexpensive, sometimes with private bath and TV. The Department of Tourism and Macau Tourist Information Bureau (MTIB) (☞ *Macau A to Z, below*) can provide details.

NIGHTLIFE

According to old movies and novels about the China coast, Macau was a city of opium dens, wild gambling, international spies, and slinky ladies of the night. It might come as a letdown to some western visitors to find that these days the city's nightlife—apart from the casinos—is dominated by hostess nightclubs, karaoke lounges, and "sauna parlors" that are very much aimed at Asian men. There is, however, other action.

Mona Lisa Theater (Lisboa Hotel). The Crazy Paris Show at the Lisboa was first staged in the late 1970s and has become a popular fixture. The stripper-dancers are professional artists from Europe, Australia, and the Americas, who put on a highly sophisticated and cleverly staged show. They shed their clothes, but there's nothing lewd or exploitative about the performance. In fact, half the audience is likely to be made up of female tourists. The acts are changed completely every few months, but one showstopping act has become a regular. It features a woman, with apparently magical breath control, who does Esther Williams–type routines in a huge tank of water on stage—but, unlike the movie star, she wears no clothes. ✉ *Lisboa Hotel, 2nd Floor, Av. da Amizade,* ☎ *377–666, ext. 1193. Daily shows at 8 and 9:30 PM, with additional show on Sat. at 11 PM.* 💰 *HK$200–250.* ☉ *Tickets available at hotel desks, Hong Kong and Macau ferry terminals, and the theater.*

Discos and Nightclubs

Most nightspots are staffed with hostesses, usually from Thailand or the Philippines, and occasionally from Europe or Russia. The girls drink and dance with customers, who can pay to take them out. Most clubs these days also offer karaoke rooms for private parties, complete with hostesses.

Among the best nightclubs are **China City** (☎ 726–633) in the Jai Alai casino complex, which employs 300 girls in a variety of sensual costumes; **Show Palace** (☎ 727–171), also in the Jai Alai building, where you pay for striptease shows and "table dances" in VIP rooms; the **Tonnochy** (☎ 372–211) in the downtown Si Toi Building that is modeled on a turn-of-the-century Parisian bordello and features elegantly turned-out hostesses, marble statues, and luxurious boudoirs; and the **Skylight** (☎ 553–888) in the Presidente, a glass-roof nightclub with a floor show of European strippers. They have different admissions or minimum charges but all are open 6 PM–4 AM.

Pubs

In the last year or two residents and visitors have welcomed some alternative night entertainment with the opening of music pubs. Especially popular is **Pyretu's,** (✉ 106 Rua Pedro Coutinho, ☎ 581–063), which was created by former Angola residents and offers African music and a bar. Next door is **Talker's Pub** (✉ 102 Rua Pedro Coutinho, ☎ 528–975), with the latest rock on the jukebox.

Casinos

There are nine casinos in Macau: those in the **Lisboa, Mandarin Oriental, Kingsway, Holiday Inn, and Hyatt Regency** hotels, the **Jai Alai Stadium,** the **Jockey Club,** the **Kam Pek,** and the **Palacio de Macau,** usually known as the floating casino. The busiest is the two-story operation in the Lisboa, where the games are roulette, blackjack, baccarat, pacapio, and the Chinese games fan-tan and "big and small." There are also hundreds of slot machines, which the Chinese call "hungry tigers."

There are few limitations to gambling in Macau. No one under 18 is allowed in, although identity cards are not checked. Although there are posted betting limits, high rollers are not discouraged by such things. There are 24-hour money exchanges, and automatic teller machines for drawing cash from Hong Kong banks. Bets are almost always in Hong Kong dollars.

The solid mass of players in the casinos might look rather unsophisticated, but they are as knowledgeable as any gamblers in the world.

They are also more single-minded than most, eschewing alcohol and all but essential nourishment when at the tables. (Small bottles of chicken essence are much in evidence!) And they are extremely superstitious, which leads to gambles that may confuse Westerners.

Baccarat has, in recent years, become a big status game for well-heeled gamblers from Hong Kong, who brag as much about losing a million as about winning one. An admiring, envying crowd usually surrounds the baccarat tables, which occupy their own special corners. Minimum bets are HK$1,000 to HK$30,000. In Macau the player cannot take the bank, and the fixed rules on drawing and standing are complex, making it completely a game of chance.

Big and small is a traditional game in which you bet on combinations of numbers for big or small totals determined by rolled dice. The minimum bet is HK$50.

Blackjack is enormously popular in Macau, and there are frequently dozens of people crowded around the players, often placing side bets. An uninitiated player might feel flattered to have others bet on his skill or luck—until he learns that by Macau rules anyone betting more than the player can call the hand. Otherwise the rules are based on American ones. The dealers, all women, must draw on 16 or less and stand on 17 or more. Minimum bets are HK$100–HK$1,000, depending on the casino. Many of the dealers are rude, surly, and greedy. In the Lisboa they take a cut of any winnings automatically, as a tip, and it's a battle to get it back. Players do, however, have a chance for revenge. No matter how bad a run of luck a dealer is having, she has to sit through her hour's stint.

Fan-tan is an ancient Chinese game that, surprisingly, survived Western competition—surprising because it is so boringly simple. A pile of porcelain buttons is placed on the table, and the croupier removes four at a time until one, two, three, or four are left. Players wager on the result, and some are so experienced that they know the answer long before the game ends.

Pacapio has replaced keno, a game that it in fact resembles. Players choose 4 to 25 numbers from 1 to 80. Winning numbers are chosen by computer and appear, every half hour or so, on screens in the Lisboa and the Jai Alai Stadium.

Pai kao has been a popular Chinese game since the last century. It is played with dominoes and a revolving banker system, which make it all but impossible to understand for novices. Minimum bets are HK$100 or HK$200.

Roulette is based on the European system, with a single zero, but with some American touches. Players buy different-color chips at an American-shape table, and bets are collected, rather than frozen, when the zero appears. It has been steadily losing popularity and is now played only in the Lisboa and Mandarin Oriental casinos. The minimum bet is HK$50.

Slot machines line the walls of all five Western casinos and seem in constant use. The biggest attraction is a "mega-bucks" system with computer links to all casinos and million-dollar payoff possibilities. The record taking to date was HK$13 million.

OUTDOOR ACTIVITIES AND SPORTS

For most regular visitors to Macau, the sporting life means playing the casinos, but there are plenty of other sports, albeit often with gambling on the side. The Macanese are keen on team sports and give creditable performances at soccer and field hockey matches. In addition to traditional annual events such as the Grand Prix motor race, there are also international championships in such sports as volleyball and table tennis. Many events are held in the Macau Forum, and others are held in the new Taipa Stadium that opened in 1996. Participant sports activities have also increased, with some excellent routes for joggers and fitness facilities in hotels.

Dragon-Boat Racing

This newest of international sports derives from the ancient Chinese Dragon Boat Festival during which fishing communities compete, paddling long, shallow boats with dragon heads and tails, in honor of a poet who drowned himself to protest official corruption. At the time, about 2,000 years ago, his friends took to boats and pounded their oars in the water while beating drums to scare away the fish who would have eaten the poet's body. The festival and races have been revived in recent years in many parts of Asia, with teams from Hong Kong, Nagasaki, Singapore, Thailand, Malaysia, and Macau, plus crews from Australia, the United States, Europe, and China's Guangdong Province. The races are held alongside the waterfront, which provides a natural grandstand for spectators. The Dragon Boat Festival takes place on the fifth day of the fifth moon (usually sometime in June) and is attended by a flotilla of fishing junks decorated with silk banners, and fishing families beating drums and setting off firecrackers.

Golf

Opened in 1993, the **Macau Golf and Country Club** is part of the Westin Resort beside Hac Sa Beach. The 18-hole, par-71 course is built into the wooded headland above the hotel, where the clubhouse occupies the upper floors with a pro shop, a pool, sauna and massage rooms, steam baths, and restaurants. The elevator leaves you a few yards from the first tee. ☎ *2803–2002 (in Hong Kong).* ✉ *Greens fees for 18 holes HK$900 weekdays, HK$1,300 weekends and public holidays.*

Greyhound Racing

The dogs are very popular with residents and Hong Kong gamblers, who flock to races in the scenic, open-air **Macau Canidrome,** close to the Chinese border. Most dogs are imported from Australia, with some from Ireland and the United States. The 10,000-seat stadium has rows and rows of betting windows and stalls for food and drink. Multimillion-dollar purses are not unheard of, and special events, such as Irish Nights, are held frequently. ✉ *Av. General Castelo Branco. Races held at 8 PM Tues., Thurs., weekends, and holidays.* ✉ *2 patacas for public stands, 5 patacas for members' stand, 80 patacas for 6-seat box.*

Horse Racing

The **Macau Raceway,** originally built for Asia's first trotting track, is on 3 million square feet of reclaimed land close to the Hyatt Regency Hotel.

Trotting did not catch on with local gamblers, so the Macau Jockey Club was formed and the facility converted, with no expense spared, into a world-class racecourse, with grass and sand tracks, floodlighting, and the most sophisticated, computerized betting system available. The five-story grandstand can accommodate 15,000 people, 6,000 of them in air-conditioned comfort, while members have boxes where five-star meals can be catered. There are several public restaurants, bars, a small casino, and a huge electronic screen to show the odds, winnings, and races in progress. There is racing throughout the year on weekends—usually in the afternoon—and midweek—at night—timed so as not to clash with events at the Hong Kong Jockey Club. The Lisboa Hotel runs free bus service to the race course. For details check with your hotel desk. ✆ *20 patacas.*

Ice Skating

The **Future Bright Amusement Park** is home to Macau's newest ice-skating rink, which accommodates 300 skaters and has a highly qualified training staff. The park also houses a bowling alley, food court, video arcade, and children's playground. ✉ *Praça Luis de Camões,* ☎ *953–399.* ✆ *Weekdays, 25 patacas per hr, Weekends, 35 patacas per hr, including skate rental.*

Motor Racing

The **Macau Grand Prix** takes place on the third or fourth weekend in November. From the beginning of the week, the city is pierced with the sound of supercharged engines testing the 3.8-mile (6-kilometer) Guia Circuit, which follows the city roads along the Outer Harbour to Guia Hill and around the reservoir. The route is as challenging as that of Monaco, with rapid gear changes demanded at the right-angle Statue Corner, the Doña Maria bend, and the Melco hairpin.

The Grand Prix was first staged in 1953, and the standard of performance has now reached world class. Today cars achieve speeds of 140 miles per hour (224 kph) on the straightaways, with the lap record approaching 2 minutes, 20 seconds. The premier event is the Formula Three Championship, with cars brought in from around the world for what is now the official World Cup of Formula Three racing, where winners qualify for Formula One licenses. There are also races for motorcycles and production cars. Many internationally famous drivers have raced here, including the late Ayrton Senna, Michael Schumacher, Damon Hill, Ricardo Patrese, and Keke Rosberg.

Hotel bookings during the Grand Prix should be made well in advance, and the weekend should be avoided by anyone not interested in motor racing. Tickets are available from tourism offices worldwide or from agents in Macau and Hong Kong. Prices vary.

Running

The 26-mile (41.6-kilometer) **Macau International Marathon** has been an annual event since 1980. Held in early December, it offers all comers a challenging course that includes both bridges, the airport, and a circuit of peninsular Macau. If you'd like a shorter challenge, the trails on Coloane are highly recommended. Guia Hill has an exercise trail. For further information, contact the Sports Institute (☎ 580–762).

Stadium Sports

Since the opening of the **Macau Forum,** with its 4,000-seat multipurpose hall, it has been possible to stage a variety of sporting events here. The world table tennis, volleyball, and roller hockey championships have been held here, as have regional basketball, soccer, and badminton matches. Interested visitors should check with their hotel's front-desk staff to find out if something special is on. A new, 20,000-seat Sport Stadium, adjacent to the racetrack on Taipa Island, opened in 1996 with facilities for soccer and track and field contests.

Tennis and Squash

The Hyatt Regency, Mandarin Oriental, New Century, and Westin all have **tennis and squash** courts, for use by guests only. At the Hyatt there is also a tennis coach.

SHOPPING

At first glance, Macau is a poor country cousin to Hong Kong when it comes to shopping. Most stores are small and open to the street, the clerks might be eating snacks at the counter, and the merchandise is likely to be haphazardly arranged. There is also very little for sale here that isn't available in far greater abundance and variety in Hong Kong.

So why shop in Macau? First, the shopping areas are much more compact. Second, sales staff are in general more pleasant and relaxed (although their command of English might not be as good as in Hong Kong). And, most important, many goods are cheaper. Like Hong Kong, Macau is a duty-free port for almost all items. But, unlike the British territory, commercial rents are reasonable and wages low, which reduces the cost of overhead.

Macau's shops are open every day of the year, except for a short holiday after Chinese New Year for family-run businesses. Opening hours vary according to the type of shop, but usually extend into mid-evening. Major credit cards are generally accepted, except on the deepest discounts. Friendly bargaining is expected and is done by asking for the "best price," which produces discounts of 10% or more. Larger discounts on expensive items should be treated with suspicion. Macau has its share of phony antiques, fake name-brand watches, and other rip-offs. Be sure to shop around, check the guarantee on name brands (sometimes fakes come with misspellings), and be sure to get receipts for expensive items.

The major shopping districts of Macau are the main street, Avenida Almeida Ribeiro, commonly known by its Chinese name Sanmalo; Mercadores and its side streets; Cinco de Outubro; and Rua do Campo. One of the pleasures of shopping here is the shop names that reflect Macau's dual heritage, for example, Pastelarias Mei Mun (pastry shops), Relojoaria Tat On (watches and clocks), and Sapatarias João Leong (shoes).

Antiques

The days of discovering treasures from the Ming among the Ching chinoiserie in Macau's **antiques shops** are long gone, but there are still plenty of old and interesting pieces available. Collectors of old porcelain can find some well-preserved bowls and other simple Ming ware once used as ballast in trading ships. Prices for such genuine items run into the hundreds or thousands of dollars. Far cheaper are the ornate vases, stools, and dishware from the late Ching period—China's Victorian era—which are in vogue. This style of pottery is still very popular among the Chinese and a lot of so-called Ching is faithfully reproduced today in China, Hong Kong, and Macau. Many of these copies are excellent and hard to distinguish from their antique cousins.

Over the years, dealers and collectors have made profitable trips to Macau, so it's interesting to ask where new supplies of antiques are coming from. The standard answer used to be "from an old Macau family" that was emigrating or had fallen on hard times. Today there is another explanation: They are brought out of China by legal and illegal immigrants in lieu of capital or foreign currency. Most of these smuggled items are small, but some are rare and precious. Among them are such things as 2,000-year-old bronze money in the shape of knives, later types of coins with holes in the middle, jade *pi* (discs), ivory figurines, and old jewelry. In addition, you can still sometimes find Exportware porcelain, made for the European market in 19th-century China, and old bonds from the early 20th century.

Antique furniture was for many years almost impossible to find, until an English woman from Hong Kong opened **Asian Artefacts** on a side street in Coloane Village. The owner, a collector and connoisseur, has found suppliers in China and other parts of Asia, who keep her shop, and its extension, filled with valuable old tables, screens, chests and wardrobes, as well as some reproduction furniture that looks just like the original. ⊠ *25 Rua dos Negociantes, Coloane.* ☎ *881–022. Closed Wed.*

Other shops that have earned excellent reputations over the years include **Hong Hap** (⊠ 133 Av. Almeida Ribeiro), **Veng Meng** (⊠ 8 Trav. do Pagode), and **Wing Tai** (⊠ 1A Av. Almeida Ribeiro). There are good, reasonably priced reproduction ceramics and furniture on **Rua de São Paulo.**

Clothing

There are many shops in Macau that sell casual and **sports clothes** for men and women at bargain prices. Most are made in Macau and carry brand-name labels. In some cases these are fakes, but more often they are genuine overruns or rejects from local factories that manufacture, under license, garments for **Yves Saint Laurent, Cacharel, Van Heusen, Adidas, Gloria Vanderbilt,** and many others. Name-brand jeans cost about HK$150 and shirts HK$120. There are also padded jackets, sweaters, jogging suits, windbreakers, and a wide range of clothes for children and infants at very low prices. The best shopping areas are on **Rua do Campo** or around **Mercadores.** For the very best bargains you should visit the street markets of **São Domingos** (off Largo do Senado), on **Rua Cinco de Outubro,** and in **Rua da Palha.** There are also a growing number of name-brand boutiques, such as the two-story **Emporio Armani** on the main street. Prices are usually much less than in Hong Kong. Credit cards are accepted at most larger shops.

Crafts

Many traditional **Chinese crafts** are followed in Macau, and the best place to watch the craftspeople at work is along **Tercena** and **Estalagens.** These old streets are lined with three-story shop-houses with openfront workshops on the ground floor (living quarters and offices are above). Some shops produce beautifully carved chests and other furniture made of mahogany, camphor wood, and redwood, some inlaid with marble or mother-of-pearl. Other craftsmen make bamboo birdcages, with tiny porcelain bowls to go in them, family altars, and "lucky" door plaques. Macau also makes lacquer screens, modern and traditional Chinese pottery, and ceremonial items such as lion dance costumes, giant incense coils, and temple offerings.

Department Stores

In 1994, **Yaohan** opened Macau's first major **department store,** a one-stop arena for just about everything you could want, from linen tablecloths to a fully stocked food hall, clothing, jewelry, housewares, shoe repair, a bakery, and several dining options. The liquor store on the premises is a good place to buy Portuguese wine at low prices. Other popular stores are the two branches of **Nam Kwong,** on the main street and next door to the Holiday Inn on Rua Pequim, which specialize in products made in China.

Gold and Jewelry

Macau's **jewelry** shops are not as lavish as those in downtown Hong Kong, but they offer much better prices. Each store displays the current price of gold per *tael* (1.2 troy ounces), which changes from day to day or even hour to hour according to the Hong Kong Gold Exchange. Some counters contain 14- and 18-carat jewelry, such as chains, earrings, pendants, brooches, rings, and bangles. There are also ornaments set with pearls or precious stones, as well as pieces of costume jewelry and fanciful traditional Chinese items. Most important, however, are the counters with 24-carat jewelry and gold in the form of coins and tiny bars, which come with assays from a Swiss bank. Pure gold is very popular with the Chinese as an investment and as a hedge against the vagaries of the stock exchange and currency fluctuations.

Prices for gold items are based on the day's price plus a small percentage profit, so only limited bargaining is possible.

Among the best-known shops are **Chow Sang Sang** (⊠ 58 Av. Almeida Ribeiro), **Pou Fong** (⊠ 91 Av. Almeida Ribeiro), **Sheong Hei** (⊠ 31 Av. Almeida Ribeiro), and **Tai Fung** (⊠ 36 Av. Almeida Ribeiro). Their salespeople speak English and are friendly and helpful.

MACAU A TO Z

Arriving and Departing

By Boat

The Hong Kong–Macau route is among the busiest international waterways in the world, with more than 13.5 million one-way passages a year and over 25 million available seats. The crossing procedure is very efficient, and only on weekends and public holidays, when the Hong Kong gamblers travel en masse, are tickets sometimes hard to get. Of course, services are disrupted when typhoons are in the area.

The majority of ships to Macau leave Hong Kong from the Macau Terminal in the **Shun Tak Centre** (⊠ 200 Connaught Rd.), a 10-minute walk west of Central. In Macau, ships use the modern three-story ferry terminal, which opened in 1994. There is also limited service to and from the China Hong Kong terminal on the Kowloon side of Hong Kong harbor.

Booking offices for all shipping companies, most Macau hotels and travel agents, excursions to China, the Macau Government Tourist Office, and the Macau Tourist Information Bureau (MTIB) are in the Shun Tak Centre.

Information can be hard to obtain over the phone, as the operators don't speak English; it's best to call the MTIB (☎ 2540–8180), whose operators do.

There is a **departure tax** of HK$26 from Hong Kong and 22 patacas from Macau, which is usually included in the price of the ticket.

A fleet of Boeing Jetfoils operated by the **Far East Jetfoil Company** (⊠ Shun Tak Centre, ☎ 2516–1268) provides the most popular service between Hong Kong and Macau. Carrying about 260 passengers, these craft ride comfortably on jet-propelled hulls at 40 knots and make the 40-mile (64-kilometer) trip in about an hour. Beer, soft drinks, and snacks are available on board, as are telephones and Macau's instant lottery tickets. There is no smoking on board. Jetfoils depart every 15 minutes from 7 AM to 8 PM, with less frequent sailings between 8 PM and 7 AM. The top deck of each vessel is first-class. Two new craft, called **Foilcats**, were added to the fleet in 1995. They have three classes and are roomier, if a little less comfortable in bad weather, than the Jetfoils.

Jetfoil fares for first-class are HK$110 on weekdays, HK$120 on weekends and public holidays, and HK$140 on the night service. Lower-deck fares are HK$97 weekdays, HK$108 weekends, and HK$126 at night. Foilcat fares cost about HK$10 more.

The second largest operator is **CTS-Parkview** (⊠ Lai Chi Kok, ☏ 2789–1268), which has a fleet of sleek, spacious catamarans that depart every 30 minutes from Hong Kong and Macau between 8 AM and 5 PM, with additional services in the evening. There are also six services between Kowloon and Macau. The journey takes about an hour. There are three different kinds of catamaran: the 266–303 seat **Turbocats** and **Tri-cats**, which have first-class and economy-class decks; and **Jumbo-cats**, which have one economy-class deck. All have comfortable seats and counters selling drinks and snacks. First-class fares are HK$191 weekdays, HK$208 weekends and holidays, and HK$220 at night. Economy fares are HK$97, HK$108, and HK$120. There are also VIP cabins on the two-deck vessels, which seat six and cost HK$1,180, HK$1,240, and HK$1,320.

There is also catamaran service by **HK Ferries** (⊠ Shun Tak Centre, ☏ 2516–9581) from the China terminal in Kowloon, with eight round-trips a day. Fares are HK$80 weekdays, HK$95 weekends, and HK$110 nights.

TICKETS

Travel agents and most Hong Kong hotels can arrange for tickets. There are also 11 MTR Travel Service computer-booking outlets in Hong Kong that sell tickets up to 28 days in advance for the Jetfoils. They are found in major MTR stations, including Central, Causeway Bay, and Tsim Sha Tsui. You can get your return ticket at the same time, although except for very busy periods it's easy to get it in Macau. If you decide to return earlier than your ticket, you can go standby at the terminal and usually not have to wait long. Jetfoil tickets can also be booked in Hong Kong by phone using credit cards (☏ 2859–6596; AE, DC, V) but must be picked up at least a half hour before the boat leaves. Tickets for CTS-Parkview vessels can be purchased from CTS offices throughout Hong Kong, from the terminals and the Hotel Grandeur in Macau. For information, dial 2789–5421 or 2810–8677 in Hong Kong. Ticket prices include the departure tax.

By Helicopter

Helicopter service is available from the Macau Terminal, with at least nine round-trips daily. The 20-minute flights cost HK$1,206 weekdays, HK$1,310 weekends and holidays from Hong Kong, and HK$1,202 and HK$1,306 from Macau, including taxes. Book through the Shun Tak Centre (☏ 2859–3359) or the terminal in Macau (☏ 572–983).

By Plane

The **Macau International Airport** opened in late 1995 and has established itself as a busy regional hub. The airport itself, built on reclaimed land, is 15–20 minutes by road from downtown Macau and the Chinese border. At press time there were daily flights to and from Beijing, Shanghai, and Taiwan, with regular services from Singapore, Malaysia,

Japan, Korea, Portugal, and Belgium, as well such cities in China as Xiamen, Qingdao, Xi'an, Tianjin, Wuhan, Dalian, and Shenyang. Air Macau is the local carrier. Departure tax for China destinations is 80 patacas, for others it is 130 patacas.

Getting Around

The old parts of town and shopping areas lend themselves to walking. Here the streets are narrow, often under repair, and invariably crowded with vehicles weaving between sidewalk vendors and parked cars. Otherwise transport is varied, convenient, and often fun.

By Bicycle
Rent bicycles for about 10 patacas an hour at shops near the Taipa bus station.

By Bus
Public buses in Macau are cheap—2 patacas within the city limits—and convenient. Services from the terminal are most useful for visitors: the 3A passes the Lisboa, Beverly Plaza, Sintra, and Metropole hotels before proceeding down the main street to the Inner Harbour and the China border; the 28C passes the Lisboa, Guia, and Royal hotels, Lou Lim Ioc Gardens, and Kun Iam Temple en route to the border. All routes are detailed on posts at bus stops. There are several services to Taipa, for 2.50 patacas, and Coloane, for 3.20–4 patacas. The number 1A minibus provides service between the airport, the Lisboa Hotel, and the ferry terminal, costing 3.50 patacas. The other buses in town, which are chartered, are replicas of 1920s London buses and known as Tour Machines. Their depot is at the terminal, and they can be hired for parties of up to nine people, for 200 patacas an hour. They are also often used to transfer groups to and from hotels.

By Hired Car
You can rent mokes, little jeeplike vehicles that are fun and ideal for touring. Drive on the *right* side of the road. International and most national driver's licenses are valid. Rental rates are HK$350 for 24 hours weekdays and HK$380 weekends, plus HK$50 insurance and a HK$1,000 deposit. Hotel packages often include special moke-rental deals. Contact **Happy Mokes,** ☎ 2540–8180 in Hong Kong, 831–212 or 439–393 in Macau). There are also cars for rent, from HK$380 a day for a Cub 4 Pack to HK$2,500 for a Mercedes Benz 230. For details contact Avis Rent-a-Car (☎ 336–789 in Macau, 2541–2011 in Hong Kong).

By Pedicab
Tricycle-drawn, two-seater carriages have been in business as long as there have been bicycles and paved roads in Macau. They cluster at the ferry terminal and near hotels around town, their drivers hustling for customers and usually offering guide services. In the past it was a pleasure to hire a pedicab for the ride downtown, or to take one along the Praia Grande to admire the avenue of ancient trees and the seascape of islands and fishing junks, but the number of construction projects detract from the experience. The city center is not a congenial place for pedicabs, and the hilly districts are impossible. If you decide to take one, you'll have to haggle, but don't pay more than HK$30 for a trip to a nearby hotel.

By Taxi
There are usually plenty of taxis at the terminal, outside hotels, and cruising the streets. All are metered and most are air-conditioned and reasonably comfortable, but cabbies speak little English and probably won't know English or Portuguese names for places. It is highly rec-

ommended that you carry a bilingual map or name card in Chinese.
The base charge is 8 patacas for the first 1,500 meters (about 1 mile),
and 1 pataca for each additional 250 meters. Drivers don't expect more
than small change as a tip. For trips to Taipa there is a 5-pataca surcharge, and to Coloane 10 patacas. Expect to pay about 9–10 patacas for a trip from the terminal to downtown.

Guided Tours

Traditional and customized tours for individuals and groups by bus
or car are easily arranged in Macau, and cover the most ground in the
shortest time.

There are two basic tours available. One covers mainland Macau with
stops at the Chinese border, Kun Iam Temple, St. Paul's, and Penha
Hill. It lasts about 3½ hours. The other typical tour consists of a two-
hour trip to the islands across the bridge to see old Chinese villages,
temples, beaches, the Jockey Club, the University of East Asia, and the
new airport. The tours are available by bus or car at prices that vary
among tour operators.

The most comfortable way to tour is by chauffeur-driven luxury car.
For a maximum of four passengers it costs HK$100 an hour. Regular
taxis can also be rented for touring, although few drivers speak English or know the place well enough to be good guides. Depending on
your bargaining powers, the cost will be HK$100 or more an hour.

Most people book tours with Macau agents while in Hong Kong or
through travel agents before leaving home. If you do it this way, you
will have transport from Hong Kong to Macau arranged for you and
your guide waiting in the arrival hall. There are many licensed tour
operators in Macau. Among those specializing in English-speaking
visitors, and who have offices in Hong Kong, are **Able Tours** (⌗ 5 Trav.
do Pe. Narciso, ☎ 566–939, in Hong Kong; ⌗ 128 Connaught Rd,
☎ 2545–9993); **Estoril Tours** (⌗ Lisboa Hotel, ☎ 710–373, in Hong
Kong; ⌗ Shun Tak Centre, ☎ 2540–8028); **International Tourism** (⌗
9 Trav. do Pe. Narciso, ☎ 975–183, in Hong Kong; ⌗ 60 Wing Lok
St., ☎ 2541–2011); **Macau Tours** (⌗ 35 Av. Dr. Mario Soares, ☎ 710–
003, in Hong Kong; ⌗ 91 Des Voeux Rd, ☎ 2542–2338); and **Sintra Tours** (⌗ Sintra Hotel, ☎ 710–360, in Hong Kong; ⌗ Shun Tak
Centre, ☎ 2540–8028).

Visas

Visas are *not* required for Portuguese citizens or nationals of the United
States, Canada, the United Kingdom, Australia, New Zealand, France,
Germany, Austria, Belgium, the Netherlands, Switzerland, Sweden, Den-
mark, Norway, Finland, Luxembourg, Italy, Greece, Spain, Japan,
Thailand, the Philippines, Malaysia, South Korea, India, Ireland, Singapore, Mexico, and South Africa, for up to 20 days, or Brazil for up
to a six-month stay, or Hong Kong residents for up to 90 days. Other
nationals need visas, available on arrival: 100 patacas for individuals,
200 patacas for family groups and 50 patacas for tour group members.

Important Addresses and Numbers

Visitor Information

In Macau, the **Department of Tourism** offers information, advice, maps,
and brochures about the territory. It has offices at the ferry and airport terminals, open daily 9–6. The main office is in Largo do Senado
(☎ 315–566; ☉ Daily 9–6).

Generally more helpful than the Macau Department of Tourism is the **MTIB** in Hong Kong. It has a wide range of maps, brochures, and up-to-the-minute information on hotels and transportation. The office is in Room 3705 at the Shun Tak Centre (☎ 2540–8180; ⊙ Weekdays 9–5, Sat. 9–1).

In addition, there is a Macau **information desk** in Room 336 of the Shun Tak Centre (☎ 2857–2287; ⊙ Tues.–Sat. 10 AM–1 PM and 2–5 PM), and at Hong Kong's Kai Tak Airport, just outside the Arrivals Hall (☎ 2769–7970; ⊙ Daily, 8 AM–10 PM).

Business visitors to Macau can get trade information from the Macau Trade and Investment Promotion Institute (☎ 378–221).

9 Side Trips to South China

By Shann
Davies

WHEN CHINA OPENED ITS DOORS to foreign visitors in 1979, the response was overwhelming, and it was a rare first-time visitor to Hong Kong who didn't make a brief excursion across the border. Today China is wide open, but still the attraction of a one-day side trip from Hong Kong remains.

Some of the most popular and convenient destinations for both tourists and business travelers are in the Pearl River Delta of Guangdong (Canton) Province. Both geographically and economically, Hong Kong and Macau are intrinsic parts of the delta, one of the richest agricultural regions of China. Here two annual rice crops and a superabundance of vegetables and fruit are produced, while coastal waters yield bountiful catches of fish and seafood.

Ever since the first foreign traders, probably from the Middle East, discovered the vast scope and possibilities of China, merchants have come to the "tradesmen's entrance" in the Pearl River Delta: the port city of Guangzhou (Canton), which was sheltered and close to suppliers from the south and conveniently distant from imperial authorities in the north. As a result, local merchants did not feel bound to obey the imperial ban on trade with Japan, which had been imposed because the government declared that China needed nothing any foreign "barbarian" had to offer. When, in the mid-16th century, Portuguese trading adventurers arrived off the coast and suggested that they act as intermediaries between Guangzhou and the merchants of southern Japan (whose government had similarly banned trade with China), Cantonese businessmen were delighted to accept.

With Guangzhou's approval, the tiny peninsula of Macau was settled by the Portuguese and quickly became a great international port, in time attracting traders from Britain, Europe, and America. By the early 19th century the Macau-based foreigners had gained a virtual monopoly on China's overseas trade.

Opium became the predominant commodity; this angered the Chinese government and, in the mid-19th century, it placed restrictions on the opium trade, provoking the Opium War with Great Britain. Defeated by the British, the Chinese were forced to cede them Hong Kong, which rapidly became the dominant port city of the Pearl Delta.

In the 1980s agreements were signed between the Chinese government and those of Britain and Portugal, with the result that China resumes sovereignty over Hong Kong in 1997 and Macau in 1999. At the same time, investment poured across the borders into China as industrialists and property developers from Hong Kong and Macau transformed the former farmland into booming new economic zones. So history comes full circle, and the future of the two territories is once more bound up with that of South China.

In terms of travel, it has always made sense to treat the delta as a unified destination, and if you're in Hong Kong for at least a week, a Guangdong excursion of one to four days is practically a must to get a feel for the region. If you have less time, a day's excursion will at least give a flavor of the "new" China that is so vividly exemplified by the delta region.

Today Guangdong's cities are thoroughly modernized, in terms of luxury hotels, good restaurants, reasonably reliable transportation, and efficient communications. At the same time they are in transition, with old buildings—however historic—succumbing to glass and steel skyscrapers, streets being dug up for new power lines, and pollution problems growing.

So what of the countryside, the "timeless China" promised in tour brochures? Sadly, a vast majority of the region has been converted to industrial suburbs, dormitory towns, and highways. However, you can still get an idea of what it used to be, with glimpses of rural life off the main roads or in selected villages, which are paid by the tour companies to preserve their traditional appearance and atmosphere.

This all combines to make a delta excursion the opportunity to see China's past, present, and future at one and the same time. Added to that is the chance to experience Cantonese cuisine at its most authentic, and to visit the Shenzhen Bay theme parks that bring Chinese civilization into brilliant if somewhat idealized focus. Best of all, for golfers, the delta is now home to a dozen new courses, which offer overseas visitors the chance to tee off in China.

Pleasures and Pastimes

Dining

When the rest of the world talks of Chinese food they're usually referring to the cuisine of the Cantonese, who comprised the majority of migrants to the Americas, Australia, and Europe in the 19th and early 20th centuries.

Having had to use their ingenuity during centuries of feudal rule to survive on roots, fungi, and every creature found on land and sea, the Cantonese developed what is arguably the most varied and imaginative cooking in the world. The results are to be found at their most authentic in Guangdong, where eating is the favorite activity and restaurants are prime hubs of society. It is possible to have a Cantonese meal for two or four people, but ideally you need twelve or at least eight, so that everyone can share the traditional eight to ten courses.

The table is never empty, from the beginning courses of pickles, peanuts, and cold cuts to the fresh fruit that signals the end of the meal. In between you'll have mounds of steamed green vegetables (known rather vaguely as Chinese cabbage, spinach, and kale), braised or minced pigeon, bean curd that can be steamed or fried, luscious shrimp, mushrooms in countless forms, birds' nest or egg drop soup, fragrant pork or beef, and a large fish steamed in herbs, all accompanied by steamed rice, beer, soft drinks, and tea.

For the adventurous there are also sea cucumbers, duck's feet, fish maw, snake bile, and dishes of dog meat or endangered *pangolin* (spiny anteater). Alternatively you can snack on dim sum, the little baskets of steamed shrimp dumplings, spring rolls, beef balls, and barbecued pork buns.

The restaurants of the Pearl Delta vary in price, decor and atmosphere, but from the alleyway cafe to the banquet hall of a five-star hotel, all offer only the freshest of produce. Prices of course vary accordingly but generally are much lower than in Hong Kong. An eight-course meal in one of the resorts or country towns will cost the equivalent of US$10 per person, including unlimited beer and soft drinks. At top rank Guangzhou hotels the cost is about US$20.

Golf

Because of the rapid industrialization of the Pearl Delta, many of its classically Chinese attractions have vanished. The development of first-class golf courses has given the area a new appeal. The first clubs were built by and for golfers, but their success has given developers visions of big profits from corporate memberships. How many will achieve this remains to be seen, but for now there is a wide choice of clubs that welcome guests as much as they do members.

Lodging

The majority of foreigners making excursions to destinations in the Pearl River Delta are on escorted tours and therefore have no say in the restaurants and hotels they visit. The growing number of independent travelers are usually businesspeople or golfers. They should be aware that, although major hotels meet most international first-class standards, there is a shortage of English-speaking staff, so it's advisable to make reservations through travel agents or hotel offices in Hong Kong. All the hotels listed below have rooms with private baths. The best restaurants are generally found in hotels and resorts (☞ Dining and Lodging sections *below*).

CATEGORY	COST*
$$$	over US$70
$$	US$40–US$70
$	under US$40

Rates are for double occupancy, not including 10% service charge.

EXPLORING

Zhongshan

Numbers in the margin correspond to points of interest on the Pearl River Delta map.

❶ **Zhongshan** is the county across the border from Macau that was known to the first Western visitors as Heungshan ("fragrant mountain"). The name was changed to Chung Shan ("central mountain") in honor of Sun Yat-sen (Chung Shan was his pen name). Zhongshan is the new spelling. The county covers 687 square miles (1,786 square kilometers) of the fertile Pearl River Delta and supports about 1.3 million people, many of whom are wealthy farmers who supply Macau with much of its fresh produce.

With substantial help from overseas Chinese investors, many new industries have been developed in recent years, mostly textiles, medicines, processed food, and electronic components. This prosperity contrasts starkly with the situation a century ago. At that time the mandarins benefited from nature's bounty, but the peasants who harvested it were kept in abject poverty. The same applied to much of China, but in Zhongshan the downtrodden had a way out—crossing the border to Macau and taking a coolie ship to the railroads of California and the gold mines of Australia.

Tens of thousands of peasants left. Zhongshan's city fathers boast of the half million "native sons" now residing in lands around the globe. Quite a number came back, though, from a sense of patriotism or the desire to show off their newly acquired wealth. Among them was Sun Yat-sen, born in Cuiheng, who led the movement to overthrow the Manchus and become "father of the Chinese Republic."

Cuiheng, where Sun Yat-sen was born in 1866, is on every Zhongshan tour. Its major attractions are contained within a memorial park. One point of interest is the house that Sun built for his parents during a visit in 1892. It is a fine example of China coast architecture, with European-style verandas facing west. This is bad geomancy for traditional Chinese, and it underscored Sun's reputation for rebellion. The interior, however, is traditional, with high-ceilinged rooms, ancestral

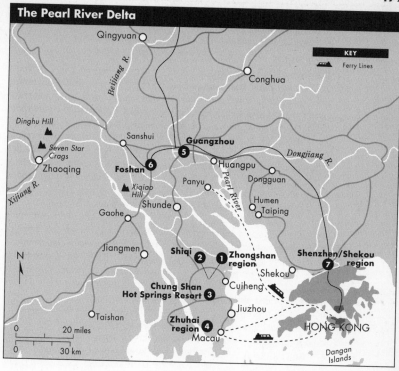

plaques, gilded carvings, and heavy blackwood furniture that includes a roofed Chinese marriage bed. Next door to Cuiheng is the excellent **Sun Yat-sen Museum,** with rooms ranged around a patio, each showing the life and times of Sun as man and revolutionary. The exhibits are well chosen and displayed, with labels in English, Chinese, and Japanese. In addition, there are videos about Sun and Zhongshan.

Also in the park is the **Sun Yat-sen Memorial High School,** with splendid blue tile roofs and a traditional Chinese gateway. It was built in 1934 and has about 700 students. Across from the park is the 242-room **Cuiheng Hotel,** a gracefully designed resort with a pool terrace and good Western and Chinese restaurants (☞ Dining and Lodging, *below*).

② **Shiqi** (formerly spelled Shekkei) is the capital of Zhongshan County, and for 800 years it has been an important market center and inland port. It's about 38 miles (61 kilometers) from Macau and 49 miles (78 kilometers) from Guangzhou and thus a convenient stopover on excursions to the delta area.

Until four or five years ago it was a picturesque port, where a cantilever bridge over the Qi River was raised twice a day to allow small freighters to pass, but the old town has been all but obliterated by modern highrises, and farms that used to surround it are now covered with factories. Nevertheless it can still be interesting to join the throngs who stroll along the riverbanks in the evening, and the **Sun Yat-sen Memorial Hall** and **Xishan Temple,** restored in 1994, are worth a visit. The dining here in Shiqi is exceptionally good.

❸ Chung Shan Hot Springs Resort is more than a place to stay. Built by a Hong Kong millionaire, the complex is a tourist attraction in itself (☞ Dining and Lodging, *below*). It is included as a stopover for lunch on many day tours, so visitors have a chance to explore the complex.

Dining and Lodging

$$ ✕☷ Chung Shan Hot Springs Resort. This vast recreational complex consists of a charming compound of villas with pagoda roofs and Chinese antiques in some rooms, built around a traditional Chinese garden landscaped with classical pavilions beside willow-screened, carp-and-lotus-filled ponds. The English-speaking staff is helpful, and there is a large Chinese restaurant (popular with tour groups) and a smaller Western restaurant. Outside, extensive grounds contain a swimming pool, shooting range, horseback-riding ring, and shopping center. There are also four baths fed by hot-spring water piped from a neighboring valley. The hotel is 15 miles (24 kilometers) from Macau. ⊠ *Zhongshan*, ☎ 760/668–3888, ℻ 760/668–3333. *350 rooms. 2 restaurants, pool, 4 tennis courts, 36 holes of golf, shops. AE, MC, V.*

$$ ✕☷ Fuhua Hotel. Situated beside the river, this high-rise offers superb views. There are two Western restaurants and two Chinese; one of the latter is in its own pavilion with stylishly furnished rooms and excellent food, particularly fish such as baked *garoupa* (grouper) and local pigeon, minced and eaten with plum sauce in lettuce leaves. ⊠ *Sunwen Xi Rd., Shiqi*, ☎ 7654/886–1338, ℻ 7654/886–1862. *420 rooms. 4 restaurants, pool, sauna, shops, bowling, dance club. AE, V.*

$$ ✕☷ Zhongshan International Hotel. This 20-story tower, topped with a revolving restaurant, has become a landmark of downtown Shiqi. Its rooms, restaurants, and service are fairly standard. ⊠ *2 Zhongshan Rd., Shiqi*, ☎ 7654/887–3388, ℻ 7654/887–3368. *369 rooms. 4 restaurants, pool, sauna, bowling, billiards. AE, MC, V.*

$ ☷ Cuiheng Hotel. Situated opposite the Sun Yat-sen Memorial Park, this hotel consists of low-rise wings and bungalows of contemporary, elegant design. It has gardens around the pool and a riding school next door. ⊠ *Cuiheng Village, Zhongshan*, ☎ 7654/552–2668, ℻ 7654/552–3333. *242 rooms. 2 restaurants, pool, dance club. AE, V.*

Outdoor Activities and Sports

GOLF

The **Chung Shan Golf Club** was the first and is still considered one of the best in China. Located half an hour north of Macau, in Zhongshan County, it was designed by Arnold Palmer's company and opened in 1984, with Palmer among the first to try it out. It's a par 72, 5,991-meter course of rolling hills, streams, and tricky sand traps. Professionals who have competed in China's first international golf tournaments here declare it first-class, and local youngsters who have been trained here now make up what amounts to China's national team. A second 18-hole course, designed by Jack Nicklaus, was added a few years ago, making this an ideal championship venue. The clubhouse, with gleaming mahogany paneling and elegant rattan furniture, has a bar, restaurant, sauna, and granite-walled pool, plus a pro shop with everything you'd expect to find in an American or Japanese club. Greens fees for visitors are HK$500 for 18 holes during the week, HK$1,200 on weekends. Caddies cost HK$140 a round, and club rentals cost HK$100. Bookings, transport (via Macau or Jiuzhou), and visas can be arranged through the club's office. ⊠ *38th Floor, Bank of China Building, 1 Garden Rd.* ☎ 2521–0377, ℻ 2868–4642.

Zhuhai

❹ **Zhuhai** was one of the first Special Economic Zones set up in 1980 with special liberal laws to encourage foreign investment. The zone has been extended from an original 5 square miles (13 square kilometers) to 46 square miles (121 square kilometers), complete with a long coastline and many small off-shore islands.

Zhuhai has the highest standard of living anywhere in China. It is also one of the most congenial and clean areas, thanks to its high-tech industrial base, which includes factories producing electronics—Canon has its manufacturing headquarters here—textiles, glassware, TV parts, and computer discs. It is the place where pilots from all over Asia take Boeing simulator courses. Tourism is also important. Every day hundreds of Western visitors cross from Macau and observe hundreds of Chinese tourists, often from remote provinces, who are observing them in return. Domestic tourists come to Zhongshan to pay their respects to Sun Yat-sen, and then they explore the shops and restaurants of Zhuhai, from which you can gaze across at Macau.

Dining and Lodging

$$$ ✕🏨 **Grand Bay View Hotel.** This handsome new hotel stands on the bay between the Macau border and the Zhuhai ferry terminal. It is sumptuously furnished and contains some of the zone's best nightlife and dining, as well as imaginative function areas that include a balcony overlooking the water and Macau. ⊠ *Shui Wan Rd., Gongbei,* ☎ *756/887–7998,*🅵🅰🆇 *756/887–8998. 238 rooms, 4 restaurants, pool, 2 tennis courts, exercise room, billiards, nightclub. AE, DC, MC, V.*

$$ ✕🏨 **Shichingshan Resort.** This very attractive, sprawling hotel has spacious hillside gardens and is opposite the Zhuhai Convention Center. It has good restaurants serving both Chinese and Western food. ⊠ *Zhuhai,* ☎ *756/333–7388,* 🅵🅰🆇 *756/333–3508; in Macau,* ☎ *553–888,* 🅵🅰🆇 *552–735. 115 rooms with bath. 2 restaurants, 2 pools, 2 tennis courts, shops. AE, DC, MC, V.*

$$ ✕🏨 **Zhuhai Resort.** This is a delightful reproduction of a Qing Dynasty courtyard mansion. The **Jade City** restaurant serves excellent Cantonese food, which is also served in private dining rooms. ⊠ *Zhuhai,* ☎ *756/333–3718,* 🅵🅰🆇 *756/332–2339. 340 rooms. Restaurants, bar, 2 pools, 2 tennis courts, health club, conference rooms. AE, DC, V.*

Outdoor Activities and Sports

GOLF

Located in Zhuhai, next to a proposed Formula 1 racing circuit, the **Lakewood Golf Club** is about half an hour by car from Macau, 20 minutes from the Zhuhai Ferry Terminal. It opened its Mountain Course at the end of 1995 and the clubhouse was completed a few months later. Managed by the Club Corporation of America, the club is a joint venture of Zhuhai and Malaysian companies. A Lakes Course and full resort facilities are planned. Greens fees for visitors are HK$600 weekdays and HK$1,200 weekends, while caddies are HK$120 and golf carts HK$240. For details contact the Hong Kong office. ⊠ *Suite 1006, Central Plaza, 18 Harbour Rd., Hong Kong,* ☎ *2877–1128,* 🅵🅰🆇 *2877–8770.*

Guangzhou

❺ **Guangzhou** is still better known as Canton, an English corruption of the Portuguese version of the Chinese name. With a strategic location on the South China coast, it has been a major trading port for almost 2,000 years. It received cargo from the Spice Islands, India, and the Middle East long before Europe knew China existed. It was also the port of export for silk, and centuries ago it began holding semiannual fairs at which the silk was bartered for spices, silver, and sandalwood. From the time the Portuguese settled Macau, Guangzhou became the prime meeting place of East and West. During the 19th century it was a business home for British, American, and European traders.

Throughout its history Guangzhou has shown a rebellious character, and the Cantonese have frequently been at odds with the rulers in the north. Exposure to Western ideas made them more independent, and it is no surprise that the 1911 revolution and the organization of the Chinese Communist Party both started here.

The majority of current foreign visitors to Guangzhou attend trade fairs or are otherwise involved in business. Tourists rarely spend more than a day in the city. Although there are some interesting attractions, Guangzhou is best combined with tours of other parts of the delta.

Shamian Island appeals to those who know something of its history. This is where Western traders set up shop when the island was a sand spit in the Pearl River, linked to the city by bridges that were closed at night. The traders built fine mansions, churches, and even a cricket pitch. Most of the buildings have been renovated to house government and business offices, hotels, and shops.

Yuexiu Park is of general interest, with its array of Krupp cannons, and the 14th-century Zhenhai Tower, which contains the **Municipal Museum** (⊙ Daily 8:30–5:30). Nearby is a modern statue of five goats with sheaves of corn in their mouths. Legend has it that the goats were sent from heaven with gifts of cereals; they have been adopted as the symbol of the city. Sun Yat-sen is, of course, honored in the city where he studied medicine and later celebrated the birth of the Chinese Republic. The **Sun Yat-sen Memorial Hall,** built in 1925, contains a 5,000-seat auditorium.

The **Peasant Movement Institute** is a monument to an early Communist organization. In 1924 Mao Zedong and his comrades set up schools to teach their doctrine. **The Guangzhou Institute,** housed in a Ming Dynasty Confucian temple, has been restored to recapture the atmosphere of a revolutionary's cell.

The **Chen Family Institute** has some magnificent porcelain friezes and stone carvings. The 11th-century Zen Buddhist **Temple of the Six Banyans** (⊙ 8–5:30) has a 196-foot-high pagoda. The 7th-century **Huaisheng Mosque** (closed to tourists during services) was once a beacon for ships. The **Roman Catholic Cathedral** was built in the 1860s and is active again after years as a warehouse. Guangzhou's other attraction is its food (☞ Dining *in* Pleasures and Pastimes, *above*).

Dining and Lodging

$$$ ✕⊞ **China Hotel.** This vast complex of a hotel, with office and apartment blocks, standing opposite the Trade Fair Exhibition Hall and the railroad station, is greatly favored by business visitors because of its convenient location. It is expertly managed by Hong Kong–based New World Hotels. ⊠ *Liuhua Rd.* ☎ *8666–6888,* ⨳ *8667–7014; in Hong Kong,* ☎ *2724–4622,* ⨳ *2721–0741. 1,017 rooms. 6 restaurants, pool, health club, shops, bowling, theater, business services. AE, DC, MC, V.*

$$$ ✕⊞ **Dong Fang Hotel.** This luxury complex is across from Liuhua Park, which has the largest artificial lake in the city. There is an interesting selection of Chinese antiques and carpets in the shopping concourse, and the complex includes an amusement park. Restaurants serve a variety of Chinese regional cuisines as well as Western and Southeast Asian dishes. ✉ *120 Liuhua Rd.,* ☎ *8666–9900,* ℻ *8666–2775; in Hong Kong,* ☎ *2575–5866,* ℻ *2591–0335. 1,300 rooms. 5 restaurants, beauty salon, shops, recreation room, business services, meeting rooms. AE, DC, MC, V.*

$$$ ✕🏨 **Garden Hotel.** In the eastern part of the city, this establishment has some spectacular gardens, including an artificial hill with a waterfall and pavilions. The hotel contains some fine antiques and modern artwork. ✉ *368 Huanshi Dong,* ☎ *8333–8989,* ℻ *8335–0467. 1,112 rooms. 8 restaurants, pool, health club, squash, shops, dance club, business services. AE, DC, MC, V.*

$$$ ✕🏨 **Guangdong International.** The tallest hotel in China, this new landmark is part of a spectacular complex, built as a flagship property by GITIC, China's second-largest financial institution. The hotel occupies the top floors of the 63-story tower, next to a complex with 14 restaurants and lounges, shops, and banquet halls. There are also extensive recreation facilities. ✉ *339 Huanshi Dong Rd.,* ☎ *8331–1888,* ℻ *8331–1666. 402 rooms, 300 suites. 14 restaurants, pool, health club, 2 tennis courts, shops, bowling, business services. AE, DC, MC, V.*

$$$ ✕🏨 **Ramada Pearl.** In the eastern part of the city, this is a full-service, deluxe hotel on the Pearl River with great views of the river traffic. ✉ *9 Ming Yue Yi Rd.,* ☎ *8777–2988,* ℻ *8776–7481. 394 rooms. 5 restaurants, pub, dance club, meeting rooms. AE, DC, MC, V.*

$$$ ✕🏨 **White Swan.** The first international hotel in town, the White Swan occupies a marvelous site, on historic Shamian Island beside the Pearl River. It is a huge luxury complex surrounded by banyan trees and with a landscaped pool and a jogging track nearby. Many rooms have replicas of Chinese antique furniture and porcelain. Even if you don't stay here, visit the lobby and take a look at the spectacular indoor waterfall there. ✉ *Shamian Island,* ☎ *8188–6968,* ℻ *8186–1188; in Hong Kong,* ☎ *2524–0192,* ℻ *2877–0811. 843 rooms. 12 restaurants, pool, health club, shops, dance club, business services, meeting rooms, travel services. AE, DC, MC, V.*

$$ ✕🏨 **Furama Hotel.** This modest hotel is well located beside the river downtown. Rooms are small but adequate, and the **Gourmet Court** restaurant serves excellent Singaporean and Malaysian meals. ✉ *316 Changdi Rd.,* ☎ *8186–3288,* ℻ *8186–3388. 360 rooms. 3 restaurants, bar, business services. AE, DC, MC, V.*

$$ ✕🏨 **Holiday Inn City Centre.** Conveniently located in the financial district, this is a good, reliable place to stay in typical Holiday Inn style. There's an adjoining exhibition center and 800-seat cinema. ✉ *Huanshi Dong, Overseas Chinese Village 28, Guangming Rd.,* ☎ *8776–6999,* ℻ *8775–3126. 431 rooms. 3 restaurants, pool, health club, shops. AE, DC, MC, V.*

Outdoor Activities and Sports

GOLF

Opened in 1995, the **Guangzhou Luhu Golf & Country Club** (☎ 8350-4957 or 8359-5576 ext. 3282) has one of the most convenient locations for golfing visitors, as it occupies 180 acres of Luhu Park, 20 minutes from Guangzhou train station and 30 minutes from Baiyun Airport. The 6,820-yard, 72-par course was designed by Dave Thomas. The club also offers a 75-bay driving range and fully equipped club house. Members' guests and those from affiliated clubs pay HK$500 greens fees for 18 holes on weekdays, HK$800 on weekends. The club is managed by Hong Kong–based CCA and is a member of the International Associate Club network.

Foshan

6 **Foshan,** which translates as "Buddha Mountain," is 12½ miles (20 kilometers) southwest of Guangzhou on the main circuit of the delta region. The drive takes less than 30 minutes on the new expressway. The city's history goes back 1,200 years. At one time it was an important religious center with a population of a million. Today, after centuries of obscurity, it is again a prosperous town with numerous joint enterprises involving overseas cousins.

The legacy of the past is preserved in the city's **Ancestral Hall** (✉ Zumiao Lu St.), with its brilliantly decorated prayer halls and astonishing porcelain murals, all beautifully maintained. To fully appreciate the porcelain figurines, visit Siwan, the district in Foshan's suburbs that has been making porcelain for centuries, and watch craftsmen at work. Some figurines are for sale.

Equally skilled workers are found in the **Folk Art Center**, where intricate paper cutouts are made by hand. Chinese lanterns, fish-bone carvings, and other handicrafts are also produced here. They are for sale at extremely reasonable prices. ✉ *Renmin Lu St., C Daily 8–6.*

Shenzhen/Shekou

7 **Shenzhen** (Shumchun in Cantonese) was just a farming village across the border from Hong Kong until, in the late 1970s, it was designated a Special Economic Zone and became the first "instant China" excursion for foreign tourists. Since then it has been transformed into a bustling industrial center, complete with one of the highest GDPs in China and the attendant pollution. Today most visitors to Shenzhen are Chinese from Hong Kong engaged in business or on family holidays, golfing and relaxing in lavish but moderately priced resorts. Foreign tourists are drawn to Shenzhen's series of theme parks, which provide a condensed tour of the great sights of China and an introduction to the country's culture and peoples. "Splendid China" replicates historical and scenic spots in other parts of the country, and the adjoining **China Folk Culture Village** shows the colorful customs and costumes of the country's ethnic minorities. Designed to appeal to Chinese tourists, the newest park, **Window of the World,** offers reduced-size representations of the world's most famous buildings and natural marvels. The other area of the Special Economic Zone that has developed into a city is Shekou, a major shipping port and headquarters for oil exploration companies.

Outdoor Activities and Sports

GOLF

Opened in late 1994, the **Honichi Golf Leisure Club** in Shenzhen's Baoan District was built primarily for Japanese who were either working in the area or visiting Hong Kong. It has proved popular, however, with many other golfers. One reason is that it is accessible by the high-speed catamaran service between Hong Kong and Shenzhen Airport. Another is the course design, which tests a player with the chance to use all 14 of his clubs during the round. There is a good clubhouse, with a sauna and restaurants. For visitors, greens fees are HK$400 on weekdays and HK$800 on weekends. Caddies are HK$100 and clubs HK$200. For bookings contact the Hong Kong office. ✉ *Room 1205, Mirror Tower, 61 Mody Rd., Kowloon,* ☎ *2312–1308,* FAX *2312–1726.*

Mission Hills Golf Club, in Shenzhen, scored a signal success, against many expectations, when it hosted the World Cup of Golf in 1995. The first 18-hole championship course—designed by Jack Nicklaus—

was only just completed in time, as were the opulent club facilities, which include facilities for basketball tournaments as well as tennis and squash courts, a variety of restaurants, and an indoor/outdoor pool around a stage for concerts or fashion shows. The course proved a winner and 18 more holes have been added, along with every conceivable service of an exclusive country club. For visitors, greens fees are HK$700 weekdays and HK$1,200 weekends; caddies are HK$100 and caddy carts HK$200. There is special bus service from Hong Kong. For details contact the Hong Kong office. ⊠ *29/F, 9 Queen's Rd. Central,* ☎ *2973–0303,* FAX *2869–9632.*

Just across the border between Hong Kong and Shenzhen, the **Sand River Golf Club** can be the quickest to reach, if there's no delay at immigration. Next door to Window of the World park, it offers courses—one is nine holes and floodlit—designed by Gary Player. There is also a large driving range, a fishing lake, and various resort facilities. Greens fees for visitors are HK$600 weekdays and HK$1,000 weekends. Caddies are HK$150. For details contact the Hong Kong office. ⊠ *19/F, SPA Centre, 55 Lockhart Rd., Wanchai,* ☎ *2520–2830,* FAX *2527–6885.*

The **Shenzhen Xili Golf Course** is part of a resort complex close to Shenzhen Bay and just 75 minutes by car from Hong Kong. Managed by Shangri-La International Hotels, it has an 18-hole course, a driving range, tennis courts, a pool, a fitness center, restaurants, and function rooms. The course is open to visitors only on weekdays, when the greens fees are HK$1,000 for 18 holes. Caddies (with carts) cost HK$300, and clubs can be rented for HK$250. For details contact the club's Hong Kong office. ⊠ *14/F, CityPlaza 3, 14 Tai Koo Wan Rd., Tai Koo Shing,* ☎ *2967-2592,* FAX *2967–1972.*

SOUTH CHINA A TO Z

Arriving and Departing

Although there is no shortage of transportation options in and out of Guangdong, you may have trouble finding travel operators who speak English. Ask your hotel concierge for the latest schedules and prices, or call the **China Travel Service** (CTS; ☎ 2853–3533).

Hong Kong–Zhuhai
Fast, modern catamaran ferries make eight round-trips daily to the **pier at Jiuzhou,** with five departures from the China Hong Kong City (CHKC) Terminal (⊠ Canton Rd., Kowloon) at 7:45 AM, 9:30 AM, 11 AM, 2:30 PM, and 5 PM) and three from the Macau Ferry Terminal (⊠ Shun Tak Centre, Connaught Rd., Central) at 8:40 AM, 12 PM and 4 PM). The trip takes 90 minutes. 🎫 *HK$171 from Kowloon, HK$181 from Hong Kong side, including departure tax.*

Hong Kong–Zhongshan
Catamarans make four round-trips daily to Zhongshan Harbor, close to Shiqi, with departures from the **CHKC Terminal.** The trip takes approximately 80 minutes. 🎫 *HK$193 first class, HK$183 economy class, one way, including tax.*

Hong Kong–Guangzhou
There are five express trains daily, departing from **Kowloon Station** (⊠ Hong Chong Rd., Tsim Sha Tsui East) at 8:45 AM, 9:25 AM, 12:45 PM, 3:05 PM, and 5:45 PM. The trip takes just under 2½ hours. The last train back to Hong Kong leaves at 6:15 PM. 🎫 *HK$230–250 one-way.*

A ferry makes the journey every day, departing **CHKC Terminal** at 9 PM; it arrives at dawn, and passengers disembark at 7 AM. There are cabins of different classes and restaurants. ✉ *From HK$202 for a four-berth cabin.*

CAAC, the Chinese airline has frequent flights between Hong Kong's Kai Tak Airport and Guangzhou airport. The trip takes about 20 minutes. ✉ *HK$920 round-trip (plus a departure tax of HK$100 from Hong Kong, RMB90 from Guangzhou).*

Citybus (☎ 2873–0818) has four round-trips a day between Hong Kong and Guangzhou using new vehicles that have toilets, drinks, snacks, reclining seats, and individual air-conditioning and lighting controls. The trip takes 3½ hours, and buses leave from CHKC and Shatin City One in Hong Kong and the Garden Hotel in Guangzhou. ✉ *HK$180 one-way.*

Hong Kong–Shenzhen

There's electric commuter train service throughout the day (first train at 6:08 AM; last train back to Hong Kong at 12:08 AM) from Kowloon Station to Lo Wu at the border. The trip takes about 40 minutes, but expect to spend up to an hour at border checkpoints. ✉ *HK$31 one-way.*

Citybus buses (☎ 2873–0818) make eight round-trips daily to Shenzhen, with six continuing on to Shenzhen Bay theme parks. Buses depart Admiralty Station and CHKC Terminal. Fares depend on the destination and day. ✉ *HK$65 one-way to Shenzhen City weekdays, HK$85 weekends. HK$75 one-way to Shenzhen Bay weekdays, HK$95 weekends.*

Fast ferries make a pleasant one-hour trip to Shekou, with eight departures between 7:50 AM and 4:30 PM daily, from the **Macau Ferry Terminal.** ✉ *HK$119 one-way, including departure tax.*

Booking Your Trip

China Travel Service (CTS; ☎ 2853–3533) is the most convenient place to book tickets to China, although they add a service charge. In recent years, customs and monetary declarations have rarely been checked, and those on group visas have had to ask to get a stamp in their passports. At the Chinese arrival points there are money-exchange counters and duty-free liquor and cigarettes at bargain prices.

Currency

You can easily change foreign currency at hotels and banks in Guangdong; the Hong Kong dollar is a very acceptable second currency here, however, so you probably won't need Chinese RMB.

Guided Tours

The vast majority of tourists on side trips to China take a guided tour, ranging from one to four days. Although travelers in recent years have reported some problems with China Travel Service (CTS), mostly about overcharging for bad accommodations and tours being cut short to make up for transportation delays, it is still much easier for foreigners to get around China with a guide. Tours offered by CTS and Hong Kong travel agents are designed to fit into any normal schedule.

By far the most popular is to **Zhongshan** via Macau, which provides a full and interestingly diverse, if rather tiring, daylong tour. All one-day Zhongshan tours begin with an early departure from Hong Kong to Macau and a bus transfer to the border at Gongbei, in the Zhuhai Special Economic Zone. From here tour itineraries vary, but all spend time in Cuiheng Village, to visit the house built by Sun Yat-sen, hero of the 1911 revolution, and an excellent museum devoted to his life and times. An eight-course lunch, with free beer and soft drinks, is taken in Shiqi, an 800-year-old inland port that has become an industrial city, at the Chung Shan resort, or in one of the "neo–Ching Dynasty" hotels of Zhuhai. Completing the itinerary is a visit to a "typical" farming village, which is kept traditional for tourists. Tours return to Hong Kong in the late afternoon via Zhongshan Harbor. (This tour is often combined with a day and night in Macau, which makes for an excellent balance.) ✆ *Zhongshan tour: HK$880.*

The other established one-day China trip takes in the **Shenzhen Special Economic Zone,** immediately across the border from Hong Kong. This begins with a coach trip to Shenzhen and its prime tourist attraction, known as **Mini Kingdom** or **Splendid China,** a park containing 70 miniaturized historical or scenic wonders of China, complete with a population of thousands of porcelain figurines. ✆ *HK$630.*

Alternatively, a visit is made to the adjoining theme park, **China Folk Culture Villages,** a superb collection of full-size buildings representing the different peoples of China, plus folk art and dance performances. The tour also includes visits to a Hakka village, kindergarten, and market. ✆ *HK$650.*

Thanks to the geographic and historic unity of the delta region, and the recent construction of bridges over the many Pearl tributaries and upgrade of major roads, multiday circular tours have become possible. The basic itinerary is a four-day tour (departs Tues., Thurs., and Sat.), beginning with a fast ferry to Macau. This is followed by a visit to Cuiheng, an overnight stay in Shiqi, a day in Foshan, a night in Zhaoqing, and a night and day in Guangzhou before a return by train to Hong Kong. ✆ *HK$2,520.*

The above examples represent the range of side trips available; other combinations exist. Ask for the "Guangdong Highlights" leaflet from CTS travel. Prices quoted apply per person, double occupancy. Most tours have daily or very frequent departures.

Reliable agents include **Able & Promotion Tours** (✉ 128 Connaught Rd., Central, ☎ 2544–5656, ℻ 2541–4413), **China Adventures** (✉ Room 1030 Star House, 3 Salisbury Rd., Tsim Sha Tsui, ☎ 2736–5662, ℻ 2735–5873), **China Travel Service** (✉ 78 Connaught Rd., Central, ☎ 2853–3533, ℻ 2541–9777; 27 Nathan Rd., Kowloon, ☎ 2853–3534, ℻ 2721–7757), and **International Tourism** (✉ 60–66 Wing Lok St., Sheung Wan, ☎ 2541–2011, ℻ 2541–3254). For a list of additional agents, call the Hong Kong Association of Travel Agents (☎ 2869–8624).

Visas

Travelers in groups of three or more can visit Shenzhen for up to 72 hours visa-free. However, to do so they must buy a package from one of the agents approved by the China Travel Service. Otherwise, visas are required to enter China. Cost depends on how quickly you have it issued. A single-entry visa with a two-day wait costs HK$160; a same-day visa costs between HK$310 and HK$560, depending on time of application. Visas are available from CTS offices and from most travel agents (all add a service charge). One passport-size photo is needed. For groups of 10 or more, travel agents get the visas; you need only supply your passport number to the agent the day before the tour.

10 Portraits of Hong Kong

Impacts and Images

*Food and Drink in Hong Kong
and Macau*

*Doing Business in Hong Kong,
1997 Style*

A Shopper's Paradise

Further Reading

IMPACTS AND IMAGES

HONG KONG IS in China, if not entirely of it, and after nearly 150 years of British rule the background to all its wonders remains its Chineseness—98% if you reckon it by population, hardly less if you are thinking metaphysically.

It may not look like it from the deck of an arriving ship, or swooping into town on a jet, but geographically most of the territory is rural China still. The empty hills that form the mass of the New Territories, the precipitous islets and rocks, even some of the bare slopes of Hong Kong Island itself, rising directly above the tumultuous harbor, are much as they were in the days of the Manchus, the Mings, or the neolithic Yaos. The last of the leopards has indeed been shot (1931), the last of the tigers spotted (1967, it is claimed), but that recondite newt flourishes still as *Paramesotriton hongkongensis,* there are still civets, pythons, barking deer and porcupines about and the marshlands abound with seabirds. The predominant country colors are Chinese colors, browns, grays, tawny colors. The generally opaque light is just the light one expects of China, and gives the whole territory the required suggestion of blur, surprise, and uncertainty. The very smells are Chinese smells—oily, laced with duck-mess and gasoline.

Thousands of Hong Kong people still live on board junks, cooking their meals in the hiss and flicker of pressure lamps among the riggings and the nets. Thousands more inhabit shantytowns, made of sticks, canvas and corrugated iron but bustling with the native vivacity. People are still growing fruit, breeding fish, running duck farms, tending oyster beds; a few still grow rice and a very few still plow their fields with water buffalo. Village life remains resiliently ancestral. The Tangs and the Pangs are influential. The geomancers are busy still. Half-moon graves speckle the high ground wherever *feng shui* decrees, sometimes attended still by the tall brown urns that contain family ashes. Temples to Tin Hau, the Queen of Heaven, or Hung Shing, God of the Southern Seas, still stand incense-swirled upon foreshores.

But the vast majority of Hong Kong's Chinese citizens live in towns, jam-packed on the flatter ground. They are mostly squeezed in gigantic tower-blocks, and they have surrounded themselves with all the standard manifestations of modern non-Communist chinoiserie: the garish merry signs, the clamorous shop-fronts, the thickets of TV aerials, the banners, the rows of shiny hanging ducks, the washing on its poles, the wavering bicycles, the potted plants massed on balconies, the canvas-canopied stalls selling herbs, or kitchenware, or antiques, or fruit, the bubbling caldrons of crab-claw soup boiling at eating stalls, the fantastic crimson-and-gold façades of restaurants, the flickering television screens in shop windows, the trays of sticky cakes in confectionery stores, the profusion of masts, poles and placards protruding from the fronts of buildings, the dragons carved or gilded, the huge elaborate posters, the tea shops with their gleaming pots, the smells of cooking, spice, incense, oil, the racket of radio music and amplified voices, the half-shouted conversation that is peculiar to Chinese meeting one another in the street, the ceaseless clatter of spoons, coins, mah-jongg counters, abaci, hammers, and electric drills.

It can appear exotic to visitors, but it is fundamentally a plain and practical style. Just as the Chinese consider a satisfactory year to be a year in which nothing much happens, so their genius seems to me fundamentally of a workaday kind, providing a stout and reliable foundation, mat and bamboo, so to speak, on which to build the structures of astonishment.

What the West has provided, originally through the medium of the British Empire, later by the agency of international finance, is a city-state in its own image, overlaying that resilient and homely Chinese style with an aesthetic far more aggressive. The capitalists of Hong Kong have been terrific builders, and have made of the great port, its hills and its harbors, one of the most thrilling of all metropolitan prospects—for my own tastes, the finest sight in Asia. More than 6 million people, nearly twice the population of New Zealand, live here in less than four hundred square miles of land, at least half of which is rough mountain country. They are necessarily packed tight, in urban forms as startling in the luminous light of Hong Kong as the upper-works of the clippers must have been when they first appeared along its waterways.

THE TANGS AND the Lius may still be in their villages, but they are invested on all sides by massive New Towns, started from scratch in starkly modernist manner. All over the mainland New Territories, wherever the hills allow, busy roads sweep here and there, clumps of tower-blocks punctuate the skyline, suburban estates develop and blue-tiled brick wilts before the advance of concrete. Even on the outlying islands, as Hong Kong calls the rest of the archipelago, apartment buildings and power stations rise above the moors. Flatland in most parts of Hong Kong being so hard to find, this dynamic urbanism has been created largely in linear patterns, weaving along shorelines, clambering up gullies or through narrow passes, and frequently compressed into almost inconceivable congestion. Some 80% of the people live on 8% of the land, and parts of Kowloon, with more than a quarter of a million people per square mile, are probably the most crowded places in all human history. An amazing tangle of streets complicates the topography; the architect I. M. Pei, commissioned to design a new Hong Kong office block in the 1980s, said it took nine months just to figure out access to the site.

There is not much shape to all this, except the shape of the place itself. Twin cities of the harbor are the vortex of all Hong Kong, and all that many strangers ever see of it. On the north, the mainland shore, the dense complex of districts called Kowloon presses away into the hills, projecting its force clean through them indeed by tunnel into the New Territories beyond. The southern shore, on the island of Hong Kong proper, is the site of the original British settlement, officially called Victoria but now usually known simply as Central; it is in effect the capital of Hong

Kong, and contains most of its chief institutions, but it straggles inchoately all along the island's northern edge, following the track worn by the junk crews when, before the British came at all, adverse winds obliged them to drag their vessels through this strait. Around the two conglomerates the territory's being revolves: one talks of Kowloon–side or Hong Kong–side, and on an average day more than 115,000 vehicles pass through the underwater tunnel from one to the other.

Once the colony had a formal urban center. Sit with me now in the Botanical Gardens, those inescapable amenities of the British Empire that have defied progress even here, and still provide shady boulevards, flower beds, and a no more than usually nasty little zoo almost in the heart of Central. From this belvedere, fifty years ago, we could have looked down upon a ceremonial plaza of some dignity, Statue Square. It opened directly upon the harbor, rather like the Piazza d'Italia in Trieste, and to the west ran a waterfront esplanade, called the Praya after its Macao original. The steep green island hills rose directly behind the square, and it was surrounded by structures of consequence— Government House, where the Governor lived; Head Quarter House, where the General lived; a nobly classical City Hall; the Anglican cathedral; the Supreme Court; the Hongkong and Shanghai Bank. The effect was sealed by the spectacle of the ships passing to and fro at the north end of the square, and by the presence of four emblematically imperial prerequisites: a dockyard of the Royal Navy, a cricket field, the Hong Kong Club and a statue of Queen Victoria.

It has all been thrown away. Today Statue Square is blocked altogether out of our sight by office buildings, and anyway only the specter of a plaza remains down there, loomed over, fragmented by commercialism. Even the waterfront has been pushed back by land reclamation. The surviving promenade is all bits and pieces of piers, and a three-story car park obstructs the harbor view. The cricket ground has been prettified into a municipal garden, with turtles in a pond. Government House and the cathedral are hardly visible through the skyscrapers, the Hong Kong Club occupies four floors of a twenty-four-story office block. Queen Victoria has gone.

This is the way of urban Hong Kong. It is cramped by the force of nature, but it is irresistibly restless by instinct. Except for the harbor, it possesses no real center now. The territory as a whole has lately become a stupendous exercise in social design, but no master plan for the harbor cities has ever succeeded—Sir Patrick Abercrombie offered one in the heyday of British town planning after the Second World War, but like so many of his schemes it never came to anything. Proposals to extend that promenade were repeatedly frustrated down the years, notably by the military, who would not get their barracks and dockyards out of the way; all that is left of the idea is the howling expressway that runs on stilts along the foreshore.

Today beyond Statue Square, all along the shoreline, across the harbor, far up the mountain slopes, tall concrete buildings extend without evident pattern or logic. There seems to be no perspective to them either, so that when we shift our viewpoint one building does not move with any grace against another—just a clump here, a splodge there, sometimes a solitary pillar of glass or concrete. Across the water they loom monotonously behind the Kowloon waterfront, square and Stalinesque; they are limited to a height of twelve stories there, because the airport is nearby. On the sides of distant mountains you may see them protruding from declining ridges like sudden outcrops of white chalk. Many are still meshed in bamboo scaffolding, many more are doomed to imminent demolition. If we look down the hill again, behind the poor governor's palace immolated in its gardens, we may see the encampment of blue-and-white awnings, interspersed with bulldozers and scattered with the laboring straw-hatted figures of construction workers, which shows where the foundations of yet another skyscraper, still bigger, more splendid and more extravagant no doubt than the one before, are even now being laid.

The fundamentals, then, are plain and practical, the design is inchoate, the architecture of a somewhat mixed character; yet Hong Kong is astonishingly beautiful. It is made so partly by its setting, land and sea so exquisitely interacting, but chiefly by its impression of irresistible activity. It is like a cauldron, seething, hissing, hooting, arguing, enmeshed in a labyrinth of tunnels and overpasses, with those skyscrapers erupting everywhere into view, with ferries churning and hovercraft splashing and great jets flying in, with fleets of ships lying always offshore, with double-decker buses and clanging tramcars, with a car it seems for every square foot of roadway, with a pedestrian for every square inch of sidewalk, and funicular trains crawling up and down the mountainside, and small scrubbed-faced policemen scudding about on motorbikes—all in all, with a pace of life so unremitting, a sense of movement and enterprise so challenging, that one's senses are overwhelmed by the sheer glory of human animation.

—By Jan Morris

Jan Morris is the author of more than 20 books, including such best sellers as Journeys, Destinations, and Manhattan '45. In this excerpt from her book Hong Kong, Morris describes the ever-changing face of the city and its intrinsically Chinese character.

FOOD AND DRINK IN HONG KONG AND MACAU

IF YOU ARE COMING to Hong Kong for the first time, there are certain misconceptions that you must leave at home. First, Hong Kong doesn't just have some of the better Chinese food in the world; it has the best.

Such a statement may not find immediate acceptance in Taiwan or the People's Republic of China, but the proof of the pudding is in the eating, as they say in the West, and those Taiwanese and mainland Chinese who can afford it come to Hong Kong to eat. It is historical fact that chefs were brought from Canton to Peking to serve in the Chinese emperors' kitchens, and that for many centuries the Cantonese were acknowledged as the Middle Kingdom's finest cooks.

There is an old Chinese maxim that tells listeners where to find the prettiest girls, where to get married, where to die, where to eat, and so forth; the answer to "where to eat" is Canton (now called Guangzhou in the approved official romanization of Chinese names that also changes Peking to Beijing).

Hong Kong's 6-million-plus population is 98% Chinese, and the vast majority of that number are Cantonese (that includes a significant group of Chiu Chow people, whose families originated around the port city of Swatow). Food is a subject of overriding importance to the Cantonese, and it can be claimed of them as it is of the French, that they live to eat rather than eat to live. Find out how true that statement is on a culinary tour of Hong Kong.

There's no such thing as a fortune cookie in a Hong Kong restaurant; it was the overseas Chinese who came up with that novelty. Chop suey was invented overseas, too. The exact origin is disputed: Some people say it began on the California goldfields; others give credit (or blame) to Australian gold miners.

The Cantonese made an art out of a necessity, and, during times of hardship, used every part of an animal, fish, or vegetable. Some dishes on a typical Hong Kong menu will sound strange, even un-

appetizing—goose webs, for example, or cockerels' testicles, cows' innards, snakes (in season), pigs' shanks, and other things that may not be served at McDonald's. But why not succumb to new taste experiences? Who scorns the French for eating snails and frogs, or the Japanese for eating raw fish, or the Scots for stuffing a sheep's stomach lining?

Visit a daytime dim-sum palace. Served from before dawn to around 5 or 6 PM, the Cantonese daytime snacks of dim-sum are miniature works of art. There are about 2,000 types in the Cantonese repertoire. Most dim-sum restaurants prepare 100 varieties daily. Generally served steaming in bamboo baskets, the buns, crepes, and cakes are among the world's finest hors d'oeuvres. Many are works of culinary engineering—such as a soup with prawns served in a translucent rice pastry shell, or a thousand-layer cake, or the ubiquitous spring roll.

There are hundreds of dim-sum restaurants. The Hong Kong Tourist Association (HKTA) publishes a listing of some of the better ones that welcome tourists. The publication also provides color illustrations of the main dim-sum favorites. Many of the top-rated Chinese restaurants in hotels, and some of the better restaurants, provide (somewhat incongruously) elegant settings for lunchtime dim sum—with bilingual check sheets, waiter service, and private tables. Such class costs about HK$15 or more per basket. History-minded snackers will prefer, preferably in the company of Cantonese colleagues, to visit the culinary shrine of the Luk Yu Teahouse in Central (24 Stanley St.).

Luk Yu is more than a restaurant. It is one of Hong Kong's few historical monuments. It's fitting that a restaurant should be an unofficially preserved monument in this culinary capital of the world. It opened in the early 20th century as a wood-beamed, black-fanned, brass-edged place for Chinese gentlemen to partake of tea, dim sum, and gossip. When it was forced to relocate over a decade ago, everything was kept intact—marble-back chairs, floor spittoons, kettle warmers, brass coat hooks, lock-up liquor cabinets for regular patrons, and a Sikh doorman. Despite the modern air-conditioning, fans still decorate a plain ceiling that looks down on elaborately framed scrolls, carved-wood booth partitions, and colored-glass panels. The ancient wood staircase still creaks as Hong Kong's gentlemen ascend to the upper floors to discuss the territory's government and business.

Modernity has brought the English language, bilingual menus (but not for the individually served dim-sum items), and some good manners to Luk Yu. And so the adventurous tourist will seek out daytime dim-sum palaces where such modern affectations do not exist—as in the authentic teahouses of Mongkok, where local customers still "walk the bird" at dawn (the Chinese tradition—considered very "masculine"—of taking one's caged bird out for a morning stroll).

Birds are also to be eaten, of course. As far as the Cantonese are concerned, anything that "keeps its back to heaven" is fit for cooking. Bird-tasting experiences in Hong Kong should include a feast of quails; smooth, salted chicken; sweet roasted chicken in lemon sauce; and minced pigeon served in lettuce leaf "bowls" (that are rolled up with a plum sauce "adhesive"). Pigeons in dozens of different forms can best be enjoyed in the New Territories, around the new city of Shatin.

Fish can be enjoyed anywhere. Hong Kong is a major port with numerous fishing communities—something easily forgotten by the city-centered visitor. Go to the islands, to **Lamma** especially, for fine seafood feasts. Or take the bus and ferry trip to **Leiyuemun,** where you can choose your dinner from the massive fish tanks, haggle over its price, and take it into any restaurant for cooking and an alfresco feast.

At Causeway Bay, a small fleet of sampans turns dining out into a memorable experience. Your private floating restaurant table bobs past other craft selling shellfish, fresh fruit and vegetables, beer and spirits. There is even a floating Cantonese Opera minitroupe that can be hired to serenade you.

The prime floating experience is, of course, the **Jumbo restaurant** at Aberdeen. It is moored to another floating home of seafood and gaudy multicolored carvings and murals that are a sight worth seeing. The Jumbo, a 2,000-seat three-decker, is a marvel of outrageous ostentatiousness.

THERE'S IS NO SUCH thing as "Chinese" cooking in China. Every good "Chinese" cook has his (or sometimes her) own repertoire that will reflect his clan's origin. Most Hong Kong restaurants are Cantonese. Others concentrate on Pekingese or northern styles, Shanghai specialties, or the other regional styles of Szechuan or Chiu Chow cooking. There are a few spots that offer Hakka-style food, some Mongolian specialty restaurants (featuring hot pots), a Hunanese restaurant, and even a Taiwanese café on Food Street.

Food Street, in Causeway Bay, is a good place for a first-timer to start discovering the variety of food available in Hong Kong. There are now two covered and fountained arcades of relatively well-managed restaurants to suit most tastes and budgets. All around them, in an area that's generally named after the Daimaru department store, are literally hundreds of other cafés and restaurants.

Other favored eating places are in **Wanchai,** once the fictional home of Suzie Wong and now a struggling nightlife area that has run out of sailors. Restaurants have appeared instead, alongside the topless bars, hostess-filled nightclubs, and dance halls that are expensive ways to get a drink in Hong Kong.

In "old" **Tsim Sha Tsui,** on both sides of Nathan Road, from the Peninsula Hotel up to the Jordan Road junction, there is another batch of good, long-established restaurants. And Tsim Sha Tsui East has skyscrapers bursting with a wide variety of eating spots—from grand Cantonese restaurants to cheerful little cafés. There, as everywhere, you'll find not only Cantonese fare but Korean barbecues, Singaporean satays, Peking duck, Shanghainese breads and eel dishes, fine Western cuisine—and junk food, of course.

The **Harbour City** complex, along Canton Road, has many fine spots tucked into shopping arcades or courtyards. **Central,** once morguelike at night, is now a bustling dining district with a warren of trendy bistros and good Indian restaurants up the hillside lanes, on and off Wyndham Street and Lan Kwai Fong. All are much favored by resident expatriates.

THEN THERE are the hotels, culinary competitors full of stylish salons—so stylish it's now hard to find a simple, old-fashioned coffee shop. Travel away from downtown districts and you find more temptations. Every housing estate and community center now boasts at least one brass-and-chrome home of good Cantonese cuisine, often as chic as it is wholesome.

Deciding what and where to eat can be a headache in Hong Kong. There is an embarrassment of riches. This guidebook's restaurant listings will help. Once in Hong Kong, get the HKTA's guide to dining and nightlife. It is free and gives a useful introduction to Chinese regional cuisines, chopstick wielding, dim-sum selecting, and other topics that can confuse a novice.

In simple terms, the Northern or Peking cuisine is designed to fill and warm—noodles, dumplings, and breads of various types are more evident than rice. Mongolian or Manchurian hot pots (a sort of fondue-cum-barbecue) are specialties, and firm flavors (garlic, ginger, leek, etc.) are popular. Desserts, of little interest to Cantonese, are heavy and sweet. Feasts have long been favored in the north, and not just by emperors composing weeklong banquets with elaborate centerpieces such as Peking duck (a three-course marvel of skin slices, sautéed meat, a rich soup of duck bones, and Tien Tsin cabbage). Beggar's chicken, about which you'll hear varying legendary origins, is another culinary ceremony, in which a stuffed, seasoned, lotus-leaf-wrapped, and clay-baked bird releases heavenly aromas when its clay is cracked open.

Farther south, the Shanghai region (including Hangzhou) developed tastes similar to Peking's but with an oilier, sweeter style that favored preserved meats, fish, and vegetables. In Hong Kong, the Shanghainese cafés are generally just that—unostentatious cafés with massive "buffet" displays of preserved or fresh snacks that are popular with late-nighters.

The phenomenal development of a middle class in Hong Kong in recent years has prompted the appearance of grander, glitzier restaurants, for Shanghainese and all other major regional cuisines. Those run by the Maxim's group are always reliable, moderately priced, and welcoming.

The territory's Chiu Chow restaurants also come alive late at night—especially in the Chiu Chow–populated areas of the Western District (on Hong Kong Island) or in parts of western Kowloon. As with Shanghainese and Cantonese cuisine, the Chiu Chow repertoire emphasizes its homeland's marine traditions, especially for shellfish. The exotic-sounding "bird's nest" is the great Chiu Chow delicacy. It's the refined, congealed saliva of nest-building swallows (mainly gathered from Gulf of Siam cliff-face nests). Although it may sound terrible, it is often exquisitely flavored. The dish is also deemed to be an aphrodisiac, as are many of China's most expensive luxury food items. That's why a visit to a Chinese department store should include a shocked glance at the "medicine" counter's natural foods. The prices of top-grade bird's nest, shark's fins, deer horns, ginseng roots, and other time-tested fortifications are staggering. The laws of supply and demand are very apparent on the price tags.

The roughest, simplest fare can appear to be that of the Szechuan region. At first tasting, the fiery peppercorned dishes, akin to both Thai and Indian cuisines, can be tongue-searing. After a while, when the taste buds have blossomed again, the subtleties of Szechuan spices will be apparent—particularly in the classic smoked duck specialty, where camphor wood chips and red tea leaves add magical tinges to a finely seasoned, daylong marinated duck.

Other regional variations (such as those of Hunan or the Hakka people) are not as distinctive as the major regional cuisines and are rarely found in Hong Kong. But any visitor who wants a taste of adventure can find a host of alternatives.

Chinese-influenced Asian cuisines are well represented. Even before the exodus of ethnic Chinese from Vietnam, that nation's exciting blend of native, French, and Chinese cooking styles was popular in Hong Kong. Now there are many cafés and a few smart restaurants specializing in prawns on sugar cane, mint-leaved meals, Vietnamese-style (labeled "VN") salamis, omelets, and fondues. Look, too, for Burmese restaurants.

The most ubiquitous Asian cuisine is the multiethnic "Malaysian," a budget diner's culinary United Nations that includes native Malay, Indian, and Straits Chinese dishes, as well as "European" meals and the Sino-Malay culinary cross-culture of the *nonya* cooking (developed by Malay wives to satisfy Chinese spouses).

Indian restaurants are also popular, and not just with Hong Kong's population of immigrants from the subcontinent. Usually the Indian kitchens concentrate on the northern Moghul styles of cooking, with reliable tandoori dishes. Vegetarians also find pleasures at Indian cafés. Thailand has not been forgotten, and the territory sports more than 24 spicy Thai restaurants.

Northeast Asia is also well represented. Some observers claim that Hong Kong has some of the world's finest Japanese restaurants, which thrive on local seafood catches and still tempt big spenders with their imports of the highly prized Kobe or Matsukaya beef (marbled slices of fine flavor produced by beer-massaged and pampered steers). Smaller spenders welcome the many local Korean cafés, whose inexpensive *bulgogi* (barbecues) provide that country's distinctive, garlicky, marinated meats and the minibuffet of preserved kimchee selections.

Then there's Indonesia, which has given Hong Kong another host of inexpensive, nourishing cafés. From Europe, there is a culinary wonderland of fine French restaurants (mostly in the top hotels), British pubs, German wining-and-dining havens, deli delights, and a sprinkling of delightfully offbeat eating experiences—from Mexican to Austrian, Spanish-Filipino, and Californian.

Although the Cantonese are the world's finest cooks, they are among the least polite waiters and waitresses in the world. The Cantonese are proud, some say arrogant, and their dialect has a belligerent tone and abruptness that translates poorly into English. Don't expect smiles or obsequiousness: Hong Kong isn't Bangkok or Manila. It's friendly in its own abrupt way, and it's certainly efficient, and if you meet smiles as well, count yourself lucky. And give the extra percentage on the tip that the pleasant waiter deserves.

Don't tip at local corner cafés or the few remaining roadside food stalls, since it's not expected. And wherever you eat, at the top or lower ends of the culinary scale, always check prices beforehand, especially for fresh fish, which is now a luxury in Hong Kong. "Seasonal" prices apply to many dishes and can be steep. And note that there are various categories of prized Chinese delicacies on menus—shark's fin, abalone, bird's nest, and bamboo fungus, for example—which can cost an emperor's ransom. Although few Hong Kong restaurants set out to rip off tourists (certainly not those that are sign-bearing members of the HKTA), waiters will of course try to "sell up."

Also, don't settle for the safe standbys for tourists. Sweet and sour pork, chop suey, and fried rice can be marvelous in Hong Kong. But the best dishes are off the menu, on table cards, written in Chinese, advertising seasonal specialties. Ask for translations, ask for interesting recommendations, try new items—show that you are adventurous and the captains will respond, giving you the respect and fine dishes you deserve.

—Barry Girling

A food, travel, and entertainment columnist, Barry Girling has lived in Hong Kong since 1977.

DOING BUSINESS IN HONG KONG, 1997 STYLE

IN MORE WAYS than one, Hong Kong is returning to its roots. The most obvious transition comes at midnight on June 30, 1997, when the Union Jack is lowered from the Government House flagpole in the Central District of Hong Kong Island for the last time. At that moment, China regains sovereignty over the island for the first time since 1842, when Britain officially assumed control.

Indirectly related to Hong Kong's becoming again a part of China is a more subtle change: An ongoing economic transformation that is seeing the one-time colony become closely integrated with the mainland and especially with Guangdong Province, the part of China Hong Kong abuts.

China's opening to world commerce under Deng Xiaoping in the late 1970s came at the perfect time for Hong Kong. Though its population was growing, the territory had nevertheless reached its peak as a manufacturing center. But soon, Hong Kong factories were being shuttered up and moved to Guangdong Province, where labor costs were much cheaper. Hong Kong became the principal gateway to China, benefiting by the more than 20% annual growth of the southern mainland. And its economy shifted to embrace a clean and lucrative set of industries that revolved around trade and financial services.

Hong Kong and China have continued to merge economically even as the political day of destiny draws closer. And, almost inevitably, as China's influence has grown, Britain's has weakened. The decision in 1996 by Swire Pacific, an old-line British trading hong, to sell major parts of its Cathay Pacific Airways and sister company Dragonair to mainland interests typifies the transition. Similar signs of the fading British presence are all around Hong Kong. The Royal Hong Kong Jockey Club, long the essence of colonial British rule, dropped "Royal" from its name. British-influenced place names and street names in Hong Kong—Victoria Park and Queen's Road are two of the more obvious examples—may also come under pressure.

Cosmetic name changes are one thing, but will the essence of Hong Kong—its business culture—also be transformed? Hard to say. But if it does change, it's not hard to guess which habits will be the first to go. Business dress in Hong Kong, formal as ever, seems much closer to a British tradition than to the more laid-back styles in other Southeast Asian business centers such as Singapore and Kuala Lumpur. True, those cities are intensely hot and humid year-round, but a sultry summer day in Hong Kong is more than muggy enough to make you wonder whether a suit is really warranted. Business fashion in China is generally less formal, but it remains to be seen whether China will begin dressing up or Hong Kong dressing down.

Until Hong Kong fashion changes substantially, be sure to wear the lightest possible suit materials you can afford, and always carry an extra supply of handkerchiefs—you'll need them to towel off the sweat. Also, in the summer have an umbrella handy. And keep one eye out for typhoon warning flags in the lobbies of hotels and office buildings. When the No. 8 flag is hoisted, time is running out. Cabs are likely to be few and far between, and the ones you can find will be charging a steep premium. You aren't likely to miss much anyway, since many businesses shut down when the No. 8 shows.

Harder to gauge than the impact of the changeover on fashion will be the effect on language requirements in business. For decades in mainland China, Beijing has sought to make Mandarin the official language in deed as well as in word. But southern Chinese, especially in Guangdong Province, have insisted on retaining their Cantonese dialect, which is as different from the official language as French is from Spanish. Despite the resistance, Mandarin, or *putonghua*—the people's language—has made inroads. Television newscasts in Guangdong today come in both flavors. Hong Kong is likely to be even more resistant to Mandarin. It's true that Mandarin classes are ubiquitous among the downtown Hong Kong high-rises, but some Hong Kongers still are loath to admit they understand the mainland language even when they do. Travelers to France will be familiar with the expressions of feigned lingual bewilderment.

Surprisingly, the changeover is not apt to have an impact on the use of English in Hong Kong. Even Malaysia, the former British colony that bitterly rejected the English language after the nation was formed from a polyglot of British colonies and outposts in 1957, has returned to it on purely utilitarian grounds. With ethnic Chinese holding strong economic influence throughout the region, various Chinese dialects are unquestionably useful, but English remains, arguably, the language of business in Asia.

One Hong Kong trait that is unlikely to change anytime soon is its citizens' single-minded devotion to making money. An American businessman remarked: "I'm from Minnesota. When I wake up in the morning, I'm thinking about fishing. When a Chinese person wakes up, he's thinking about ways to make money." That's an important characteristic to keep in mind, whether you're considering how much *laisee* money to give staff at the Chinese New Year or contemplating gifts for a new business partner. Resist the temptation to skimp.

But don't assume that understanding Hong Kong's lust for money is enough to overcome all cultural differences. For example, Hong Kongers have a keen sense of hierarchy in the office. Egalitarianism may be admired in the U.S., but it is often insulting in Hong Kong. Let the tea lady get the tea and coffee—that's what she's there for. Your assistant or Chinese colleague has better things to do than make copies or deliver messages. You'll only engender animosity if you assign such tasks without appreciating whether they fit with job descriptions. And if you do the jobs yourself, you may be sending the message that the person assigned is incompetent—it's easy to offend unwittingly.

Hong Kong's attraction to business cards is easily explained. Status and hierarchy go hand in hand, and business cards are the tangible evidence of both. For your part, have plenty of cards available. Preferably, they should be printed in English on one side and Chinese on the other. Exchange cards by proffering yours with both hands and a slight bow. Receive a card in the same way. It is polite to examine the card you get immediately upon receiving it, still holding it with two hands, and comment on some aspect of it: your colleague's title is impressive, or the card itself is of high quality. Such a response gives the person you're greeting face: His or her prestige and personal dignity have been publicly acknowledged.

DON'T BE SURPRISED, no matter how late in the day it may be, if you are invited to a meal after you're done making a suitably impressive showing on your first meeting with a business associate. Hong Kongers work late, and they often don't get around to eating dinner until well into the evening. A full day of meetings followed by dinner at 10 PM is not unusual, and it's a good idea to make dinner reservations even when it seems you're unlikely to find a restaurant of any sort still open. The fact is, they are open, and they're probably busy.

It won't hurt to brush up on your use of chopsticks. Silverware is common in Hong Kong, but it might be seen as another face-giving gesture if you try your hand at chopsticks. After all, the conversation is probably in English, and learning to use chopsticks is a fairly easy way to reciprocate a cultural interest.

Of course, all of these things—dress, language, business cards, chopsticks—pale next to some of the meaty questions surrounding the changeover. As uncertain as the impact the transition will have on Hong Kong's business culture may be, the effect on weightier issues is even less clear. For instance, the Hong Kong currency has been pegged to the U.S. dollar since 1982 at a rate that fluctuates in a narrow range near 7.8 Hong Kong dollars to $1 U.S. Publicly, Chinese officials say the peg won't change after 1997. But it is undeniable that the peg has been responsible for a good portion of Hong Kong's inflation, which has fluctuated between 7% and 10% for most of the '90s. In large part that's because the U.S. dollar has lost so much ground to the Japanese yen in the last decade, though the dollar regained strength in 1996. For the time being, the Chinese government already has more on its plate than it can easily swallow, which makes it unlikely that the peg will change soon. But the long run is a different story.

As for taxes, China has pledged not to change Hong Kong's reputation as a tax haven for business. The territory has been able to keep its flat tax rate to just below 15%, partly because it hasn't had to pay for its defense (the British garrison provided protection) and because it hasn't chosen to spend much on social welfare. But the resistance to social spending may be breaking down. Recent budgets have included big increases for social services, and Beijing has begun to voice concern that China will inherit an expanding welfare state, which is not what it bargained for.

Of all the questions hanging over the transition, none is likely to have a bigger impact on business than what becomes of the rule of law. Unquestionably, mainland China is moving in Hong Kong's direction on this issue—attempting to establish a legal framework in which laws are written and contracts enforced in a way that is quite new to the world's oldest culture. Today, Hong Kong is southern Asia's regional headquarters of choice for a variety of multinational American, European, and Asian firms. By itself, that's a powerful incentive for China to want to leave Hong Kong alone—don't tinker with success. But there are those who wonder whether Beijing will be able to keep its hands totally off its expensive new toy, and whether, just by handling, the toy might be damaged.

In other ways, will Hong Kong become more like the mainland, or vice-versa? It will be interesting to see how, to take just one for-instance, Hong Kong's zoning laws will fare under Chinese rule. China essentially has no tradition of zoning. How will a mainland developer feel when told he can't build in Hong Kong because a law prohibits it? Such a case may go a long way toward describing whether Hong Kong is ultimately ruled by laws or by people.

In spite of the questions, it would be short-sighted not to see the Chinese takeover of Hong Kong as, at least in an economic sense, precisely what the city needs. There is no question that China's growth has fueled Hong Kong's economy since the early 1980s. At the time China opened up to the outside world, nearly half of Hong Kong's workers were employed in manufacturing. Today, the fraction is barely one-sixth. In the same period, employment in trade, tourism, and services has gone from 30% to 55%.

Clearly, if Hong Kong is to continue its strong economic performance, it will be on the back of China—providing financial and insurance services, advice, and investment. Hong Kong will most assuredly change after June 30, 1997. And much of the change will be tied to even closer relations with the mainland. The big remaining question is whether Hong Kong will continue to be an international city that caters to foreign interests looking for a comfortable conduit to China, or whether it will be swallowed by the mainland.

—Tim Healy

Tim Healy has reported, written, and edited business news for more than 10 years. He currently writes for Asiaweek, a weekly newsmagazine published in Hong Kong.

A SHOPPER'S PARADISE

WHATEVER YOUR reason for coming to Hong Kong, and whether or not you are a shopper by nature, it is very unlikely that you will leave the place without having bought *something*. Indeed, there's a roaring trade in bargain-priced luggage because so many visitors run out of space in the suitcases they arrived with.

There are several good reasons why Hong Kong is such an extraordinary shopping mecca. The first is its status as a free port, whereby everything, other than alcohol, tobacco, perfumes, cosmetics, cars, and some petroleum products, comes in without import duty. The second is the fact that Hong Kong has a skilled and still relatively inexpensive labor force. Goods made here are considerably cheaper than they will be by the time they reach shop shelves anywhere else in the world. The third factor is the highly competitive nature of the retail business—the result of a local policy of free trade, which encourages everyone to try to undercut his neighbor. To this end, many shops, with the exception of those in the Western and Central districts, stay open until 10 PM. Shops are also humming on Sundays and on all holidays apart from Chinese New Year, when everything closes for at least three days.

What else is special about Hong Kong? For a start, consider the geography of the place. It is very small, and very heavily populated. It has had to grow upward and downward rather than outward, which means that there are shops and small businesses in all sorts of unexpected places. You'll find a trendy fashion designer tucked away on the third floor of a scruffy alleyway building, a picture framer operating out of the basement of a lighting shop, a tailor snipping and stitching in the back room of a shoe shop. Many of the buildings will appear dingy and dirty, and you will be convinced that no self-respecting business can be carried on there. But it can be and it is. And these are the places where Hong Kong residents do much of their shopping. Also disconcerting for people who come expecting to find the streets lined with bargains is the discovery that prices for the same goods vary from sky-high to rock-bottom within a 100-yard stretch of shops. But this is the land of free trade. And it is why shopping around and sticking to reputable establishments are prerequisites to any successful purchase, particularly an expensive one.

By reputable establishments we mean ones that have been recommended by a friend who lives or shops regularly in Hong Kong, by this guidebook, or by the Hong Kong Tourist Association (HKTA) via its invaluable shopping brochure.

All shops bearing the HKTA's red junk logo in their window are supposed to provide good value for money, accurate representation of products sold, and prompt rectification of justified complaints, but if you have problems, call the HKTA (☎ 2801–7177). For complaints about non-HKTA shops, call the Consumer Council (☎ 2736–3322).

The law of the jungle is alive and well in Hong Kong, so be prepared for lots of shoving and pushing on the sidewalks, little respect for taxi lines, a limited amount in the way of gallantry, and an overwhelming urge on the part of sales staff to sell you something, no matter what!

Contrary to popular belief, not everyone speaks English. In the main tourist shopping areas you can probably count on most shop staff speaking some English—but do not assume that they understand all you say, even if they nod their heads confidently. Many of the taxi drivers' English is limited, too, and it can make life easier if you get your destination written down in Chinese by the hotel concierge before you set off. Most taxis now carry a radio microphone that lets you speak to their headquarters, where someone will translate.

Once on the right road, shopping around and bargaining are your golden rules. The pressure from sales staff can be exasperating. If you are just browsing, make this very clear. Don't be pushed into a purchase. Note the details of items and prices on the shop's business card. Always ask about discounts—sizable ones for multiple purchases. You should be able to get a discount just about everywhere except in Japanese department stores and some of the larger boutiques, which sell on a fixed-price basis. When other shops try to convince you that everything is fixed price, don't believe them. You should get a discount of at least 10%, and more likely 40%, from jewelers and furriers.

EQUALLY, DO NOT necessarily believe a salesman when he assures you that his price is his "very best" unless you have done enough shopping around to know that he is offering you a good deal. Never be bashful about asking for a discount. It is the accepted and expected way of conducting business all over Asia.

After checking out the prices in several different shops, you'll have a good idea of how much you should pay. Don't imagine that you will get the very best price (you won't know what it is, anyway); these are generally given only to local Chinese customers. Your best bet is to compare the price with what you might have to pay for such an item back home.

If you are planning to shop in markets, alleys, or market stalls, it's best not to go very dressed up; this will not help your bargaining position. Make sure to inspect the goods you buy very carefully; many of them are seconds. Look closely at lengths of fabric; they may have faults. When you buy clothing, inspect the actual item handed to you. You may have chosen it on the strength of a sample hanging up, but what you are given could be different. It may not be the same size, and it could have more serious flaws.

At the other end of the scale, if you are intending to shop for something important like jewelry or a fur coat, it can work in your favor to dress smartly. It is amazing how much more seriously you are taken if you look the part.

If you do not know much about the commodity you are buying, do not hesitate to ask the salesperson to explain or to show you the difference between, say, a HK$30,000 diamond and a HK$10,000 one of the same size, or the difference between the two mink coats that look similar to you but carry vastly different price tags. Any reputable dealer in these specialist items should be happy to show you what you are getting for the extra money, and how it compares to the less expensive item. The understanding of such factors can help you to make up your mind about which is really the better buy.

Having satisfied yourself that you really want the item and have struck the right price for it, you are ready for the exchange of money. (Although credit cards and traveler's checks are widely accepted, the best prices are offered for cash purchases.) An appropriate guarantee and a fully itemized receipt should be provided by the shop for any major purchase. Such details as the model number and serial number of manufactured goods such as cameras, VCRs, or electronic equipment, or the description of gems and precious metal content in jewelry and watches, should be noted.

Make sure you get a worldwide/international guarantee that carries the name or logo of the relevant sole agent in Hong Kong and that there is a service center in your home town or country. And if you are having something shipped home for you (many shops are geared up for this), make sure that the insurance covers not only loss, but also damage, in transit.

So much for the nuts and bolts. But forewarned is forearmed, which, we hope, will make the experience of shopping in Hong Kong all the more fun. Because fun it certainly is. Whether you are drifting about in the comfort of the air-conditioned shopping malls, exploring the factory outlets of Hung Hom, or poking about in the alleys and backstreets, you are getting a look at the life and guts of Hong Kong. It's as much a cultural experience as a shopping expedition. In a way, that can be the most unexpected bargain of all.

— Patricia Davis

A freelance writer based in Hong Kong, Trish Davis specializes in the arts and consumer affairs. Her shopping columns appear regularly, and her background includes extensive experience with women's magazines and newspapers.

FURTHER READING

JAMES CLAVELL'S *Taipan* and *Noble House* are blockbuster novels covering the early history of the British colony and the multifaceted life found there around the 1950s. Both books provide insights, sometimes sensationalized, sometimes accurate. Robert S. Elegant's *Dynasty* is another epic novel tracing the development of a powerful Eurasian family. It has some simplified history, but it does reveal a lot about the way locals think. Another best-seller set in Hong Kong is John LeCarre's *The Honorable Schoolboy,* a superb spy thriller. On a smaller scale is Han Suyin's *A Many Splendoured Thing.* Another classic novel is Richard Mason's *The World of Suzie Wong,* which covers an American's adventures with a young woman in the Wanchai bar area. Austin Coates's *Myself a Mandarin* is a lively and humorous account of a European magistrate handling Chinese society, and his *City of Broken Promises* is a rags-to-riches biography of an 18th-century woman from Macau.

Maurice Collis's beautifully written classic, *Foreign Mud,* covers the early opium trade and China wars. Colin N. Criswell's *The Taipans: Hong Kong's Merchant Princes* describes the historical inspiration for novels exploring that era. G. B. Endicott's *History of Hong Kong* traces Hong Kong from its beginnings to the riot-wracked 1960s. Trea Wiltshire's *Hong Kong: Improbable Journey* focuses exclusively on recent times. Richard Hughes's *Borrowed Time, Borrowed Place* looks at Hong Kong immediately before the signing of the 1984 Sino-British Agreement that returns Hong Kong to the People's Republic of China in 1997. David Bonavia's *Hong Kong 1997: The Final Settlement* provides history and analysis of the agreement.

Jan Morris's *Hong Kong: Social Life and Customs* is a current primer on the region's daily interpersonal interactions. For younger readers, try Nancy P. McKenna's *A Family in Hong Kong,* part of a series describing families all over the world. G. S. Heywood's *Rambles in Hong Kong* is a personal reflection on the colony. T. Wing Lo's *Corruption and Politics in Hong Kong and China,* published by Taylor & Francis, is an intriguing current criminology study. *Born to Shop Hong Kong: The Insider's Guide to Name-Brand, Designer, & Bargain Shopping in Hong Kong,* by Suzy Gershman, is great for die-hard bargain hunters. And Kevin Rafferty's *City on the Rocks: Hong Kong's Uncertain Future* looks ahead to the not-so-distant break from colonialism.

There are many publications available for businesspeople. Most banks and major realty companies publish economic newsletters for their customers. The American Chamber of Commerce publishes books on Hong Kong and China, including *Living in Hong Kong, Doing Business in Hong Kong,* and *Establishing an Office in Hong Kong,* available to members and nonmembers. The *Far Eastern Economic Review Yearbook* and the Hong Kong Government *Yearbook* are essential reference books; the *Monthly Digest* from the government's Census and Statistics Department may also be useful. *Hong Kong Tax Planning* is, as the name implies, a useful book to cut through the legalese of Hong Kong's tax codes. The China Phone Book Co. publishes a slew of useful publications on China in addition to its telephone and telex directories.

Newspapers

Newspapers and magazines from all over the world are readily available in Hong Kong. The *Asian Wall Street Journal,* the *Eastern Express, International Herald Tribune,* and *USA Today International* print international editions in Hong Kong to supplement the two English-language daily newspapers, the *South China Morning Post* and the *Hongkong Standard.* The *Far Eastern Economic Review* leads the pack in business publications. *Time* and *Newsweek* both print in Hong Kong, and the news weekly *Asiaweek* is published here.

INDEX

A

A Casa Macaense ✕, 158
A Galera ✕, 156
A Lorcha ✕ , 156–157
Aberdeen, 18, 33
Aberdeen Cemetery, 33
Aberdeen floating
   restaurants, 33
Academic Community Hall,
   100
Academy for Performing
   Arts, 28
Admiralty (shopping
   center), 61–62, 117, 120
Alfonso III ✕, 157
Afonso's ✕, 157
Airbuses, xii–xiii
Air travel, xii–xiii, xxvi
complaints, xii
from Britain, xii, xxvi
with children, xv, xxviii
insurance for, xxxi
to Macau, 171
Allan Janny Ltd., 123
Alleys (shopping), 122–123
Amah Rock, 41
A-Ma Temple, 152
American Chamber of
   Commerce, xiv
American Library, 26
American Peking Restaurant
   ✕, 65
Ancestral Hall, 184
Antiques, shopping for, 129–
   130, 168–169
Apleichau Island, 33–34
Aquarium, 34
Art, shopping for, 130–132
Art galleries, 131–132
Art museums, 28–29, 34,
   37, 41, 149–150
Arts, the, 99–102
Arts Centre, 28
Ashoka ✕, 54
ATMs, xix, xxxii
Au Trou Normand ✕, 72
Avenida Almeida Ribeiro,
   147
Avenida do Conselheiro
   Ferreira de Almeida, 150
Aviaries, 27, 154
Aw Boon Haw Gardens, 29

B

Baby-sitting, xxvii
Bali Restaurant ✕, 70
Balichão ✕, 157
Ballet, 102
Bangkok Royal ⌂, 89
Bank of China building, 19
Bazaars, 122–123
Beaches, 111–113, 154
Bela Vista Hotel ✕⌂, 156,
   159–160
Benkay Restaurant ✕, 55

Bentley's Seafood Restaurant
   and Oyster Bar ✕, 59–60
Better Business Bureau, xiii
Beverly Plaza ⌂, 161
Bicycles
in Macau, 172
tours of Asia, xxiii
Big Wave Bay, 106, 112
Binoculars, shopping for, 132
Bird market, 37
Bishop Lei International
   House ⌂, 78
Bishop's Palace, 152
Black Sheep ✕, 69
Bodhi Vegetarian ✕, 70
Bonham Strand East and
   West, 19–20, 116
Booth Lodge (Salvation
   Army guest house) ⌂, 89
Border Gate
   (Macau–China), 150
Botanical Gardens, 18, 27
Bowen Road Courts, 108–
   109
BP International House ⌂,
   88
Buddhism, 29, 42, 151
Bun Festival, 48
Buses, xiii, xxvi–xxvii, 172
Business centers, xiii
Business hours, xxvii
Business organizations, xiii–
   xv
Business services, xiii, 174

C

Cabarets, 93
Cafe Deco ✕, 63
Café Luso ✕, 158–159
Camargue Club ✕, 59
Camcorders, travel with,
   xxvii
Cameras
shopping for, 132
travel with, xxvii
Camões Grotto and Garden,
   149
Camões Museum, 150
Canidrome, 166
Cantonese opera, 101–102
Canton Road, 120
Car racing, 167
Car rental, xv, xxvii, 172
Cargo Handling Basin, 28
Caritas Bianchi Lodge ⌂, 90
Carpets, shopping for, 132
Casa Lisboa ✕, 62–63
Cash machines, xix, xxxii
Casinos, 143, 164–165
Cat Street, 23
Cat Street Galleries, 23
Causeway Bay, 18, 29, 32–
   33
hotels in, 82
restaurants in, 66–67
shopping in, 116–117

Causeway Bay Typhoon
   Shelter, 32
Causeway Centre, 28
Cellular phones and beepers,
   xiii
Cemeteries, 33, 150, 154
Central ⌂, 163
Central District, 18, 19–23
restaurants in, 53–61
hotels in, 76–78
shopping in, 116
Central Market, 20, 116
Central Plaza, 28
Century ⌂, 79
Ceramics, shopping for, 133
Chai Wan, 18
Chambers of commerce, xiv
Chapel of St. Francis Xavier,
   155
Chater Garden, 20
Chek Lap Kok Island, 47
Chen Family Institute, 182
Cheung Chau Island, 48–49
Cheung Chau Warwick Hotel
   ⌂, 49, 91
Cheung Sha, 113
Children
shopping for clothes for, 128
traveling with, xv, xxvii–xxviii
what to see and do with, 26,
   27, 34
China
excursions to, 176–187
exploring, 178–180, 181–
   182, 184
gate from Macau to, 150
golf resorts in, 177–178, 180,
   181, 183, 184–185
guided tours, 186–187
hotels and restaurants in, 177,
   178, 180, 181, 182–183
sports, 180, 181, 183, 184–
   185
transportation into, 185–186
visas, 187
China Ferry Terminal (mall),
   120
China Folk Culture Village,
   187
China Hong Kong City
   (arcade), 120
China Hotel ✕⌂, 182
China Products Company,
   121, 137
Chinese Arts & Crafts
   (stores), 121, 137, 169
Chinese language, xxxi–
   xxxii
Chinese Merchandise
   Emporium, 115, 121
Chinese opera, 101–102
Chinese Opera Fortnight
   (festival), 101
Chinese orchestra, 101
Chinese Restaurant ✕, 69
Chinese University, 41, 43

Ching Chung Koon Taoist Temple, 41–42
Chiu Chau ✕, 159
Chiu Chow Garden ✕, 66
Chocolates, shopping for, 133
Chuk Lam Sim Yuen, 42
Chung Kiu Chinese Products Emporium, 121
Chung Shan Golf Club, 180
Chung Shan Hot Springs Resort ✕⌂, 180
Chung Ying Theatre Company, 102
City Contemporary Dance Company, 102
City Garden ⌂, 83
City Hall, 20, 99
City Hall Libraries, 20
Cityplaza I & II, 108, 117, 120
Clearwater Bay Golf & Country Club, 104
Clearwater Bay Road, 42
Climate, xxv, xxxix
Clothes
to bring, xxiv, xxxiii
factory outlets for, 126–128
shopping for, 123–129, 169
tailor-made, 123–125
Club Lanka ✕, 55
Club 97 (nightclub), 93
Cocktail bars, 93–94
Coloane Island, 155
Coloane Park, 154
Commissions, xv
Computers
shopping for, 133–134
travel with, xxvii
Concerto Inn, 48
Concourse ⌂, 88
Conrad International ⌂, 76–77
Consulates, xv
Continental, The ✕, 68
Convention center, xiv
Copy services, xiv
Cosmetics, shopping for, 138
Couriers. ☞ Messengers
Crafts, 121, 137, 169
Cricket fighting, 110
Cuiheng, 178–179
Cuiheng Hotel ✕⌂, 179, 180
Curios, shopping for, 134–135
Currency, xix, xxxii
Chinese, 186
Customs and duties, xv–xvi, xxvii, xxviii–xxix

D
D'Aguilar Street, 116
Daimaru (department store), 116, 121
Dan Ryan's ✕, 61
Dance, 102
Deep Water Bay, 18, 34, 111
Delaney's ✕, 65
Deli Lamma ✕, 73

Department stores, 121–122, 169–170. ☞ Also specific department stores
Chinese, 121
Japanese, 121–122
Western, 122
Des Voeux Road, 20
Diamonds, shopping for, 135–136
Dining. ☞ Restaurants
Disabilities & accessibility, xvi–xvii, xxix
Discos, 96–97, 164
Discounts, xvii, xxix–xxx, xxxiv, xxxv
Discovery Bay Golf Club, 104
Doctors, xviii, xxxii
Dog racing, 166
Dolphin Discovery Cruise, 23
Dolphin tours, xxi
Dom Pedro V theater, 152
Dong Fang Hotel ✕⌂, 182–183
Dragon boat racing, 166
Dragon Seed (department store), 122
Drama, 102
Drum Rocks, 49–50
Duck's Tongue Island, 33–34
Dyanasty ✕, 64

E
East Asia ⌂, 163
Eastern District, shopping in, 117
Elaine Gallery, 49
Electricity, xxxiii
Electronics, shopping for, 134
Embroidery, shopping for, 137
Emergencies, xvii–xviii
English language, xxxi
Excelsior ⌂, 32, 82
Exchange Square, 20–21

F
Facsimile, xiv
Factory outlets, 126–128
Fan Lau, 106
Fanling, 42
Farmacia Tai Ning Tong, 148
Fat Siu Lau ✕, 157
Felix ✕, 71–72
Fernando's ✕, 154, 157
Ferries, xxxvii–xxxviii, 185
Festival of Asian Arts, 101
Festival Walk, 108
Festivals, 100–101
Film, travel with, xxvii
Film festival, 13
Fishing supplies, shopping for, 138
Flagstaff House, 26
Flamingo ✕, 157
Flower Market, 122
Folk clubs, 96
Fortaleza ✕, 156

Foshan, 184
Four Five Six ✕, 159
Fringe Club, 102
Fuhua Hotel ✕⌂, 180
Fung Ping Shan Museum, 34
Furama ✕⌂, 183
Furama Kempinski ⌂, 78, 116
Furniture, shopping for, 134
Furs, shopping for, 128

G
Gaddi's ✕, 72
Gambling, 110–111
Garden Hotel ✕⌂, 183
Gardens. ☞ Parks and Gardens
Garden View International House ⌂, 78
Gay and lesbian travelers, hints for, xviii, xxx
Gifts, shopping for, 137
Gold Coast ⌂, 90
Gold, shopping for, 170
Golden Crown (nightclub), 93
Golf, 104–105, 166
Government House (Hong Kong), 26
Government tours, xxi
Grand Bay View Hotel ✕⌂, 181
Grande ⌂, 163
Grandeur ✕, 160
Grand Hyatt ⌂, 78
Grand Plaza ⌂, 83
Grand Prix Museum, 145
Grand Stanford Harbour View ⌂, 85–86
Grand Tower ⌂, 86
Granville Road, 117
Grappa's ✕, 62
Great Shanghai Restaurant ✕, 71
Greyhound racing, 166
Grissini ✕, 65–66
Guangdong ⌂, 86
Guangdong International ✕⌂, 183
Guangzhou, 181–182
Guangzhou Institute, 182
Guia ⌂, 162
Guia Hill, 147
Guided tours, xx–xxi, 173

H
Hac Sa beach, 155
Handicrafts, shopping for, 134–135, 169
Han Dynasty burial vault, 38
Happy Valley, 29, 32–33
hotels in, 82
shopping in, 116
Happy Valley Race Course, 18, 29, 110
Harbour City, 117, 120, 193
Harbour Plaza ⌂, 84
Harbour Road Indoor Games Hall, 108

Harbour View International House ▨, 79
Health, xviii–xix, xxx
Health clubs, 108
Helicopters, xxi, 171
Hennessy Road, 28, 117
Henri's Galley ✕, 157–158
Heritage tours, xxi
High Island Reservoir, 106
Hiking, 105–107
Historical museums, 28, 32, 34, 37, 149
History
of Hong Kong, 2–8, 15, 17
of Macau, 142–143
Holiday ▨, 163
Holiday Inn (Macau) ▨, 160
Holiday Inn City Centre ✕▨, 183
Holiday Inn Golden Mile ▨, 86
Hollywood Road, 21, 116, 129
Holy Carpenter Church Guest House ▨, 90
Holy House of Mercy, 148
Hong Kong Academy for Performing Arts, 100
Hong Kong and Yau Ma Tei Ferry Company, xxxviii
Hong Kong Arts Centre, 99
Hong Kong Arts Festival, 100–101
Hong Kong Ballet, 102
Hong Kong Chinese Orchestra, 101
Hong Kong Club, 21
Hong Kong Coliseum, 100
Hong Kong Convention and Exhibition Centre, xiv, 28
Hong Kong Cultural Centre, 37, 100
Hong Kong Dance Company, 102
Hong Kong Dolphin Watch, 23
Hong Kong Fringe Club, 99
Hong Kong Fringe Festival, 100
Hong Kong General Chamber of Commerce xiv
Hong Kong International Airport, xii
Hong Kong International Film Festival, 101
Hong Kong Island
arts, 99–102
beaches of, 111–112
children, activities for, 26, 27, 34
exploring, 17–23, 26–29, 32–35, 36
guided tour of, xx
hotels on, 76–83
libraries of, 26
museums on, 26, 28–29, 32, 34
nightlife, 93–99

parks and gardens of, 20, 26, 27, 29, 33, 34
performance halls of, 99–100
restaurants of, 53–69
shopping on, 115–140
sports and outdoor activities, 104–111
Hong Kong Museum of Art, 37, 130–131
Hong Kong Museum of History, 37
Hong Kong Museum of Medical Sciences, 26
Hong Kong Park, 26
Hong Kong Philharmonic Orchestra, 101
Hong Kong Renaissance ▨, 84
Hong Kong Running Club, 107
Hong Kong Science Museum, 37
Hong Kong Space Museum, 37
Hong Kong Squash Centre, 108
Hong Kong Stadium, 100
Hong Kong Tennis Centre, 109
Hong Kong Tourist Association (HKTA), xxiv
Hong Kong Trail, 105–106
Hong Kong University, 18, 34
Hong Kong Zoological and Botanical Gardens, 27
Hongkong ▨, 86
Hongkong and Shanghai Bank, 21
Hong Lok Street, 37
Hopewell Cer re, 28
Horse racing, xxi, 29, 43, 110–111, 166–167
Hospitals, xviii
Hostels, xxii
Hostess clubs, 98, 164
Hotel Bela Vista ✕, 152
Hotel Nikko ▨, 84
Hotel Ritz ▨, 160
Hotels, 75–91, 159–163. ☞ Also specific hotels
Hou Kong ▨, 163
Hours of business, xxvii
Housing tours, xxi
Huaisheng Mosque, 182
Hugo's ✕, 71
Hunghom, 117
Hung Shing Ye beach, 48, 113
Hurricanes. ☞ Typhoons
Hyatt Regency ▨, 84
Hyatt Regency and Taipa Island Resort ▨, 160

I

Ice skating, 108, 167
Imasa ✕, 70
Imperial ▨, 88
Indochine 1929 ✕, 58

Insurance, xix, xxx–xxxi
International ▨, 90
Isetan (department store), 121
Island Shangri-La ▨, 77
Isshin ✕, 66
Ivory, shopping for, xx

J

J. W. Marriott ▨, 77
Jade, shopping for, 122, 136
Jai Alai Casino, 145, 164
Jardine House, 21
Jardines Bazaar, 117
Jazz clubs, 96
Jewelry, shopping for, 135–136, 170
Jimmy's Kitchen ✕, 59
Jockey Club, 164
Jogging, 107
Johnston Road, 116
Jubilee Sports Centre, 43
Jubilee Street, 21
Judaism in Far East, theme tour of, xxiii
Jumbo ✕, 193
Jumbo Sogo (department store), 116, 121
Junking, 109
JW's California Grill ✕, 61–62

K

Kam Pek, 164
Kam Tin Walled Villages, 42
Kansu Street Jade Market, 38
Kat Hing Wai, 42
Kingsway ▨, 162
Korean Restaurant ✕, 159
Ko Wah ▨, 163
Kowloon, 36–40
children, activities for, 37, 38
exploring, 37–38, 40
guided tour of, xx
hotels in, 83–90
museums in, 37
performance halls of, 100
restaurants of, 69–73
shopping in, 117, 120–121, 122–123
Kowloon ▨, 86–87
Kowloon City Market, 122–123
Kowloon Panda ▨, 91
Kowloon Park, 38, 109
Kowloon Shangri-La ▨, 84–85
Kung-fu, 107
Kung-fu supplies, shopping for, 136
Kun Iam Temple, 151
Kwun Yum Temple, 32

L

La Brasserie ✕, 72
Ladder Street, 116
Lai Ching Heen ✕, 69–70
Laichikok Park, 108

Lakewood Golf Club, *181*
Lamma Island, *48*, *193*
beaches on, 48, 112–113
lodging on, 48
restaurants on, 73
Lancombe ✕, *73*
Landmark (shopping
   complex), *21–22*, *116*,
   120
Lane Crawford (department
   store), *120*, *122*
Language, *xxxi–xxxii*
Lantau Island, *46–48*
lodging on, 47–48
Lantau Tea Gardens, *47*
Lantau Trail, *106*
Laptops, travel with, *xxvii*
Lau Fau Shan, *42*
Law Uk Folk Museum, *32*
Leal Senado (Loyal Senate),
   147
Leather goods, shopping for,
   136–137
Legislative Council Building,
   22
Leighton Road, *116*
Le Tire Bouchon ✕, *60*
Li Yuen Streets East and
   West, *116*, *123*
Libraries, *26*, *147–148*
Lido Bazaar, *117*, *123*
Lighthouse (Macau), *147*
Linens, shopping for, *137*
Lingerie, shopping for, *126*
Lin Fung Miu, *151*
Lisboa 🏨, *162*
Litoral ✕, *158*
Lo So Shing, *113*
Lockhart road, *27–28*, *116*,
   117
Lodging, *xxii, xxviii.* ☞
   Also Hotels
Lok Ma Chau, *42*
London 🏨, *163*
Long Kei ✕, *159*
Lou Lim Ieoc Garden, *150*
Loyal Senate, *147*
Luard Road, *28*
Lucy's ✕, *67*
Luen Wo Market, *42*
Luggage
in air travel, xxviii, xxxiii–
   xxxiv
insurance for, xxx–xxxi
Luk Kwok 🏨, *79*
Luk Yu Tea House ✕, *54*

M

M at the Fringe ✕, *59*
Ma On Shan Country Park,
   106
Macau, *142–174*
accommodations, 144, 159–
   163
climate of, xxxix
currency in, xxxi
exploring, 145, 147–154
guided tours, xxi, 173
history of, 142–143

languages in, xxxii
nightlife, 163–165
1999 changeover of, 143
population and size of, 143
restaurants, 144, 155–159
shopping, 168–170
sports, 165–168
tourist information on, xxiv,
   173–174
transportation in, 172–173
travel from Hong Kong to,
   170–172
Macau Canidrome, *166*
Macau Forum, *145*, *167*
Macau Golf and Country
   Club, *166*
Macau Grand Prix, *167*
Macau International Airport,
   154, *171–172*
Macau International
   Marathon, *167*
Macau Jockey Club, *153*
Macau Raceway, *166*
Macau Tourist Information
   Bureau (MTIB), *xxiv*
MacLehose Trail, *106*
Mail, *xiv–xv, xix*
Main Street, *117*
Majestic 🏨, *88*
Mandarin Oriental (Hong
   Kong) 🏨, *77*, *116*
Mandarin Oriental (Macau)
   🏨, *160–161*
Man Mo Temple, *22*
Man Wa Lane, *115*
Man Yue Street, *117*
Marathons, *167*
Marco Polo 🏨, *87*
Marine mammal theater
   (Ocean Theatre), *34*
Maritime Museum, *153*
Markets, *122–123*
Marks & Spencer, *120*
Martial Arts School, *107*
Matsuzakaya (department
   store), *116*, *121*
Medical assistance, *xviii–*
   xix, xxxii
Memorial Home of Dr. Sun
   Yat-sen, *150*
Messengers, *xiv*
Metropole 🏨, *162*
Middle Kingdom (amusement
   park), *18*, *34*
Mid-Levels area, *22*
Military Club ✕, *156*
Ming Lei Fong (shop), *49*
Miramar 🏨, *87*
Mitsukoshi (department
   store), *116*, *121*
Miu Fat Buddhist Monastery,
   42
Mody Road, *117*
Mona Lisa Theater, *163–164*
Monasteries, *42*, *47*
Money, *xix–xx, xxxii–*
   xxxiii
Montanha Russa ✕, *158*
Monte Fort, *149*

Monte Hill, *149*
Mosque, *182*
Motor racing, *167*
Mozart Stub'n ✕, *58*
MTR (Mass Transit
   Railway), *xxii*
Mughal Room ✕, *54*
Mui Wo Inn 🏨, *48*
Municipal Museum, *182*
Museum of Chinese Historical
   Relics, *28–29*
Museum of Tea Ware, *26*
Museums, *26*, *28–29*, *32*,
   34. ☞ *Also specific*
   museums
Music, *99–100*, *101–102*

N

Nam Yue 🏨, *162*
Nathan Road, *38*, *117*
Nature trail (Macau), *154*
Nepal ✕, *62*
New Astor 🏨, *89*
New Cathay 🏨, *82*
New Century 🏨, *161*
New Territories, *40–46*
beaches of, 112
exploring, 40–43, 46
guided tour of, xx
hotels in, 90–92
parks in, 42
performance halls of, 100
restaurants of, 41
New Town Plaza, *43*
New World 🏨, *87*
New World Center, *117*, *120*
New World Emperor 🏨, *162*
New World Harbour View 🏨,
   79
Newton 🏨, *83*
Nightclubs, *93*, *164*
Nightlife, *xxi*, *93–99*, *163–*
   165
Nim Shue Wan, *47*
Ning Po Street, *40*
Noonday Gun, *32*
North Point, *29*
hotels in, 83

O

O Porto Interior ✕, *156*
Ocean Centre, *120*
Ocean City Restaurant &
   Night Club, *93*
Ocean Galleries, *120*
Ocean Palace Restaurant &
   Night Club, *93*
Ocean Park (amusement
   park), *18*, *34*
Ocean Terminal, *120*
Ocean Theatre (marine
   mammal theater), *34*
Old Citadel (Macau), *149–*
   150
Old Protestant Cemetery
   (Macau), *150*
On Lan Street, *116*, *137*
One Harbour Road ✕, *64*

One Pacific Place
(department store), 122
Opera, Chinese, 101–102
Optical goods, shopping for,
138
Outer Harbor (Macau), 145,
147
Outer Islands, 46–50. ☞
Also specific islands
beaches of, 112–113
hotels in, 47,48, 49, 90–91

P

Pacific Place (shopping
center), 116, 120
Package tours, xxiii, xxxvi–
xxxvii
Pak Sha Chau, 112
Pak Tai Temple, 48
Palacio, 152
Palacio de Macau (casino),
164
Pao Gallery, 130
Papillon ✕, 60
Parachuting, 107–108
Park Lane ⌸, 82
Parks and gardens, 20, 26,
27, 29, 33
in Macau, 150
Passports, xx, xxxiv
Peak Cafe ✕, 63
Peak Tram, xxxviii, 26, 27
Pearl Seaview ⌸, 89
Pearls, shopping for, 136
Peasant Movement Institute,
182
Pedicabs, 172
Peking opera, 102
Peng Chau Island, 49
Penha Hill, 152
Peninsula (⌸; Kowloon),
38, 85
Performance halls, 99–100
Performing-arts ensembles,
101
Perfume, shopping for, 138
Philharmonic orchestra, 101
Photocopying, xiv
Photography, xx
Physicians, xviii
Piano bars, 93–94
Pierrot ✕, 60
Ping Chau, 49–50
Pinocchio's ✕, 158
Planetarium, 37
Po Toi islands, 50
Pok Fu Lam, 34, 106
Police, xvii–xviii
Po-Lin Monastery, 47, 106
Portas do Cerco, 150–151
Post '97 ✕, 59
Post Office (Hong Kong),
xix
Post Office (Macau), 148
Pousada de Coloane ✕⌸,
154, 158, 162
Pousada de São Tiago ⌸,
152, 161
Pou Tai Un Temple, 154

Praia Grande, 151
Praia Grande ✕, 158
Praya Promenade, 49
Precious Lotus Monastery,
47, 106
Presidente ⌸, 163
Prince ⌸, 87
Prudential ⌸, 89
Publications
for disabilities & accessibility,
xvi–xvii
for gay and lesbian travelers,
xviii
for senior citizens, xx
for travelers, xii
on travel with children, xv
Pubs, 94–95, 164

Q

Qi River, 179
Quarry Bay, 18, 29, 68
hotels in, 83
Queen Elizabeth Stadium,
99–100
Queen's Road Central, 22
Queen's Road East, 29, 116,
134
Queen's Road West, 22

R

Rail travel, xxxvii
Ramada Hotel Kowloon ⌸,
89
Rasa Sayang ✕, 159
Regal Airport ⌸, 87–88
Regal Hongkong Hotel ⌸, 82
Regal Kowloon ⌸, 88
Regal Riverside ⌸, 91
Regent, The ⌸, 37, 85
Regent Hotel Shopping
Arcade, 120
Repulse Bay, 18, 34, 36,
111–112, 117
restaurants in, 67
Restaurants, 52–73, 155–
159. ☞ Also specific
restaurants
Restoration Row (Macau),
150
Richmond ⌸, 82
Rickshaws, xxxviii
Ricos ✕, 63
Ritz-Carlton ⌸, 77–78
Rock carvings, 50
Romada Pearl ✕⌸, 183
Roman Catholic Cathedral,
182
Royal ⌸, 161
Royal Canton ✕, 159
Royal Garden ⌸, 88
Royal Hong Kong Golf Club,
104
Royal Hong Kong Yacht Club,
32, 109
Royal Pacific ⌸, 89
Royal Park ⌸, 91
Rua de Cinco Outubro, 148
Rua de Felicidade, 148
Rugby, 111

Rugs. ☞ Carpets
Running, 167

S

Sagano Restaurant ✕, 71
Sai Kung Country Park, 42,
106
Sai Kung Peninsula, 42
Saigon Beach ✕, 65
Sailing, xxi, 109
St. Augustine church, 152
St. John's Cathedral, 27
St. Joseph's, Seminary of,
152
St. Lawrence church, 152
St. Paul's church (Macau),
149
Salisbury YMCA ⌸, 90
Sampans, 32
Sam's Art & Jewellery, 123
San Francisco Steak House
✕, 73
Sanmalo, 147, 148
Santa Casa da Misericordia,
148
São Domingos church, 148
Science Museum, 37
Scuba diving, 109
Seibu (department store),
121
Senior citizens, hints for, xx,
xxx, xxxiv
Sha Ha, 110, 112
Sha Tau, 49
Shamian Island, 182
Shamrock ⌸, 90
Shanghai Street, 40
Shanghai Tang Department
Store, 124
Shatin, 42–43
Shatin Racecourse, 43, 110
Shatin Town Hall, 100
Shaukiwan, 18, 29
Shekkei (Shiqi), 179
Shek O, 18, 36, 105, 110,
112
restaurants in, 69–69
Shek O Country Park, 36
Shek O Thai-Chinese Palace
✕, 69
Shekou, 184
Shenzhen, 184–185, 187
Sheraton Hong Kong Hotel &
Towers, 85
Shichingshan Resort ✕⌸,
181
Shing Mun Reservoir, 53
Shiqi, 179
Shoes and boots, shopping
for, 128–129
Shopping, xx, xxxiv–xxxv,
115–140, 199–200
guided tour for, xxi, 140
in Macau, 117, 168–170
Shopping centers, 117, 120–
121
Shui Hing (department
store), 122
Shun Tak Centre, 120

Sightseeing, *xx–xxi*
Silk Road Bazaar, *48*
Silks, shopping for, *137*
Silvermine Bay, *47, 106*
Silvermine Beach Hotel ⚑,
    47–48
Silverstrand, *112*
Sincere (department store),
    122
Singles, meeting places for,
    98–99
Sintra ⚑, *163*
Skating, *108*
Social clubs, *108*
Sok Kwu Wan, *48*
Solmar ✕, *158*
South China ⚑, *83*
South Lantau Park, *106*
South Side, *33–34, 36*
Space Museum, *37*
Space Theatre, *37*
Specialty stores, *129–140*
Spice Island Gourmet Club
    ✕, *55*
Sporting goods, shopping
    for, *138*
Sports, *104–111, 165–168*
Sports centers, *29, 43*
Spring Garden Lane, *116*
Squash, *108, 168*
Stanley, *18, 67*
Stanley Bay, *36*
Stanley Main (beach), *110,
    112*
Stanley Market, *117, 123,
    137*
Stanley's French Restaurant
    ✕, *68*
Stanley Silk and Linen, *123*
Stanley's Oriental ✕, *67*
Star Ferry, *xxxvii–xxxviii,
    22–23*
Star Ferry Pier, *38, 47*
Statue Square, *23*
Stereos, shopping for, *139*
Student travel, *xxii, xxx,
    xxxv*
Subway, *xxii, xxxv*
Sung Dynasty Village, *38, 40*
Sun Yat-sen, *178–179*
    Memorial Hall, 179
    Memorial High School, 179
    Memorial Home, 150
    Museum, 179
Supatra's Thai Gourmet ✕,
    58
Surfing, *110*
Swimming, *109–110.* ☞
    Also Beaches
Szechuan Lau ✕, *67*

T

Tables 88 ✕, *67–68*
Taikoo Shing, *29*
Tailors, *123–125*
Tai Mo Shan, *43, 106*
Tai O, *47, 106*
Taipa House Museum, *153*
Taipa Island, *153*

Tai Po, *43*
Tai Po Kau Nature Reserve,
    43
Tai Tam Country Park, *106*
Tai Tau Chau, *36*
Tai Wong Temple, *29*
Tamar, H.M.S., 21
Tandoor Restaurant ✕, *54–
    55*
Taoist temple, *41–42*
Tap Mun Island, *43*
Taxes, *xxxiii*
Taxis, *xii, xxxv, 172–173*
Tea and tea equipment,
    shopping for, *139*
Telephones, *xxii, xxxv–
    xxxvi*
Telex, *xv*
Temple of Ten Thousand
    Buddhas, *41, 43*
Temple of the Lotus, *151*
Temple of the Six Banyans,
    182
Temple Street, *40, 123*
Temples, *22, 23, 29, 33, 40,
    41–42, 43, 48*
in China, 179, 182
in Macau, 151, 152–153, 154
Tennis, *108–109, 168*
Thai Delicacy ✕, *65*
Theater, *102, 152, 164*
Three-Five Korean Restaurant
    ✕, *71*
Tiger Balm Gardens, *29*
Tiger's ✕, *61*
Times Square shopping
    center, *116, 120*
Timing the trip, *xxxix*
Tin Hau
    temples of, 33, 40, 43
Tin Hau Temple, *33*
Tipping, *xxxvi*
Tokio Joe ✕, *55*
Tokyu (department store),
    121
Tolo Harbour, *43, 110*
Tom Turk Fitness Clubs, *108*
Tong's Sheets and Linen Co.,
    123
Topless bars, *97–98*
Tour operators, *xxii–xxiv,
    xxxvi–xxxvii*
Tourist information, *xxiv–
    xxv, 173–174*
Toys 'R Us, *120*
Trade information, *xv*
Trains, *xxxvii*
Trams, *xxi, xxxviii*
Translations of documents,
    xxiii–xxiv
Transportation, *xxiv,
    xxxvii–xxxviii, 170–173*
Trappist Monastery, *47*
Travel agencies, *xvii, xviii,
    xxiv*
Traveler's checks, *xxxiii*
Tsak Yue Wu, *106*
Tsim Sha Tsui, *193*
    shopping in, 117

Tsim Sha Tsui East, *40, 120–
    121*
Tsuen Wan Town Hall, *100*
Tsui Museum of Art, *19*
Tuen Mun, *43, 46, 106*
Tuen Mun Golf Centre, *104–
    105*
Tun Wan Beach, *110*
Tung Chung, *47*
Tung Wan, *49, 113*
Turtle Cove, *112*
Tutto Bene ✕, *72*

U

U.S. Government travel
    information, *xxiv, xxxviii*
United Chinese Cemetery,
    154
University of Macau, *154*
UNY (department store),
    121
Upper Lascar Row, *23*
URBTIX (ticket outlets), *99*

V

Va Bene ✕, *60*
Valentino Ristorante Italiano
    ✕, *73*
Verandah, The ✕, *67*
Viceroy, The ✕, *64–65*
Victoria Clock Tower, *38*
Victoria Park, *33, 107, 108*
Victoria Peak, *18, 26, 27,
    105*
Visas *xx, xxxiv, 173, 178*
Visitor information, *xxiv–
    xxv*
Vogue Alley, *117, 125*

W

Wah Fu Estate, *34*
Walking, *xxxviii–xxxix*
Wanchai, *18, 27–29*
    hotels in, 78–79
    restaurants in, 63–66, 193
    shopping in, 116
Wanchai Road, *29, 116*
Wanchai Sports Grounds,
    29
Watches, shopping for, *139–
    140*
Watchman's Tower Rocks,
    49–50
Water, *xxx*
Waterski Club, *110*
Waterskiing, *110*
Water sports, *109–110*
Water World (amusement
    park), *18, 34*
Weather, *xxv, xxxix*
Wesley, The ⚑, *79*
Western District, *18, 19–24*
    shopping in, 115–116
Western Market, *23, 115–
    116, 124*
Western Union, *xix–xx,
    xxxiii*
Westin Resort ⚑, *155, 161*

Wharney ⬚, 79
White Swan ✕⬚, 183
Wilson Trail, 106–107
Window of the World, 184
Windsor ⬚, 89
Windsurfing, 110
Wine Museum, 145, 147
Wine, Portuguese, 145, 147
Wine bars, 95–96
Wing Lok Street, 23, 116
Wing On (department store), 122
Wiring money, xix–xx, xxxiii
Wong Nai Chung Road, 116, 128–129
Wong Tai Sin Temple, 40
Wyndham Street, 116, 137

Wyndham Street Thai ✕, 55, 58

X
Xishan Temple, 179

Y
Yacht clubs, 109
Yan Yuen Shek (Lover's Rock), 27
Yaohan (department store), 121–122, 169–170
Yim Tin Tsai Island, 42
YMCAs, xxii–90
Youth travel, xxii
Yucca de Lac Restaurant ✕, 41

Yue Hwa Chinese Products Emporium, 121
Yuexiu Park, 182
Yung Kee ✕, 54
Yung Shue Wan, 48

Z
Zen ✕, 62
Zhongshan, 170, 186–187
Zhongshan International Hotel ✕⬚, 180
Zhuhai, 181
Zhuhai Resort ✕⬚, 181
Zona Rosa ✕, 61
Zoological and Botanical Gardens, 27
Zuni Icosahedron, 102

NOTES

Lantau: Po Lin Monastery
Lamma
Chinese Opera
Shopping
Man Mo Temple
Temple of 10,000 Buddhas (Shatin) (New Ter's)
Train ride
   Star Ferry
Markets - Bird Cage & Kowloon

Goddess B-Day Celeb.

Victoria Peak, p. 27

Queen's Road - shopping p. 29

Aberdeen, p. 33

Shek O, p. 36

NOTES

I. Hong Kong Island

    A. Central + Western Districts:
        - Bonham Strand (traditional shopping)
        - Queen's Road Central (inexpensive clothes)
        - Star Ferry
        - Wing Lok Street (chops engraved)

    B. From Central to Peak
        - Victoria Peak

II. Kowloon Penin.
    - Bird Market ✓
    - Jade Market ✓
    - Peninsula Hotel
    - Chinese Arts + Crafts
    - Sung Dynasty Village
    - Tin Hau Temple ✓

II. New Territories

    - 6 hr tour
    - Temple of 10,000 Buddhas - Shatin

III. Llama Island

    C. The South Side of HK Island

    - Aberdeen - Tin Hau Temple + floating lunch restaurant

    - Stanley Market

    ○ Opera - City Hall 2734-9009

NOTES   4 taxi's, are numbskull

Maw – 3 men
      – bird cage

Presents   – lapis beads
            – 6 Buddhas
            – Sarah's grad present

- Anya
- Chi
- Bry
- Jason
- Lisa

Stanley Market

Bus 6 or 260 from Central

        30-45 mins

NOTES

CNN✈
Airport Network

Your
Window
To The
World
While You're
On The
Road

Keep in touch when you're traveling. Before you take off, tune in to CNN Airport Network. Now available in major airports across America, CNN Airport Network provides nonstop news, sports, business, weather and lifestyle programming. Both domestic and international. All piloted by the top-flight global resources of CNN. All up-to-the minute reporting. And just for travelers, CNN Airport Network features two daily Fodor's specials. "Travel Fact" provides enlightening, useful travel trivia, while "What's Happening" covers upcoming events in major cities worldwide. So why be bored waiting to board? TIME FLIES WHEN YOU'RE WATCHING THE WORLD THROUGH THE WINDOW OF CNN AIRPORT NETWORK!

Fodor's Travel Publications

Available at bookstores everywhere, or call 1–800–533–6478, 24 hours a day.

Gold Guides

U.S.

Alaska	Florida	New Orleans	Santa Fe, Taos, Albuquerque
Arizona	Hawai'i	New York City	Seattle & Vancouver
Boston	Las Vegas, Reno, Tahoe	Pacific North Coast	The South
California	Los Angeles	Philadelphia & the Pennsylvania Dutch Country	U.S. & British Virgin Islands
Cape Cod, Martha's Vineyard, Nantucket	Maine, Vermont, New Hampshire	The Rockies	USA
The Carolinas & the Georgia Coast	Maui & Lana'i	San Diego	Virginia & Maryland
Chicago	Miami & the Keys	San Francisco	Washington, D.C.
Colorado	New England		

Foreign

Australia	Europe	Montréal & Québec City	Scotland
Austria	Florence, Tuscany & Umbria	Moscow, St. Petersburg, Kiev	Singapore
The Bahamas	France	The Netherlands, Belgium & Luxembourg	South Africa
Belize & Guatemala	Germany		South America
Bermuda	Great Britain		Southeast Asia
Canada	Greece	New Zealand	Spain
Cancún, Cozumel, Yucatán Peninsula	Hong Kong	Norway	Sweden
Caribbean	India	Nova Scotia, New Brunswick, Prince Edward Island	Switzerland
China	Ireland		Thailand
Costa Rica	Israel	Paris	Tokyo
Cuba	Italy	Portugal	Toronto
The Czech Republic & Slovakia	Japan	Provence & the Riviera	Turkey
Eastern & Central Europe	London	Scandinavia	Vienna & the Danube
	Madrid & Barcelona		
	Mexico		

Fodor's Special-Interest Guides

Alaska Ports of Call	Halliday's New England Food Explorer	Nights to Imagine	Wendy Perrin's Secrets Every Smart Traveler Should Know
Caribbean Ports of Call	Halliday's New Orleans Food Explorer	Rock & Roll Traveler USA	
The Complete Guide to America's National Parks		Sunday in New York	Where Should We Take the Kids? California
	Healthy Escapes	Sunday in San Francisco	
Disney Like a Pro	Kodak Guide to Shooting Great Travel Pictures	Walt Disney World for Adults	Where Should We Take the Kids? Northeast
Family Adventures			
Fodor's Gay Guide to the USA	Net Travel	Walt Disney World, Universal Studios and Orlando	Worldwide Cruises and Ports of Call

Special Series

Affordables
Caribbean
Europe
Florida
France
Germany
Great Britain
Italy
London
Paris

Bed & Breakfasts and Country Inns
America
California
The Mid-Atlantic
New England
The Pacific Northwest
The South
The Southwest
The Upper Great Lakes

Berkeley Guides
California
Central America
Eastern Europe
Europe
France
Germany & Austria
Great Britain & Ireland
Italy
London
Mexico
New York City
Pacific Northwest & Alaska
Paris
San Francisco

Compass American Guides
Alaska
Arizona
Canada
Chicago
Colorado
Hawaii
Hollywood
Idaho
Las Vegas

Maine
Manhattan
Montana
New Mexico
New Orleans
Oregon
San Francisco
Santa Fe
South Carolina
South Dakota
Southwest
Texas
Utah
Virginia
Washington
Wine Country
Wisconsin
Wyoming

Citypacks
Atlanta
Hong Kong
London
New York City
Paris
Rome
San Francisco
Washington, D.C.

Fodor's Español
California
Caribe Occidental
Caribe Oriental
Gran Bretaña
Londres
Mexico
Nueva York
Paris

Exploring Guides
Australia
Boston & New England
Britain
California
Caribbean
China
Egypt
Florence & Tuscany
Florida
France

Germany
Ireland
Israel
Italy
Japan
London
Mexico
Moscow & St. Petersburg
New York City
Paris
Prague
Provence
Rome
San Francisco
Scotland
Singapore & Malaysia
Spain
Thailand
Turkey
Venice

Fodor's Flashmaps
Boston
New York
San Francisco
Washington, D.C.

Pocket Guides
Acapulco
Atlanta
Barbados
Budapest
Jamaica
London
Munich
New York City
Paris
Prague
Puerto Rico
Rome
San Francisco
Washington, D.C.

Mobil Travel Guides
America's Best Hotels & Restaurants
California & the West
Frequent Traveler's Guide to Major Cities
Great Lakes

Mid-Atlantic
Northeast
Northwest & Great Plains
Southeast
Southwest & South Central

Rivages Guides
Bed and Breakfasts of Character and Charm in France
Hotels and Country Inns of Character and Charm in France
Hotels and Country Inns of Character and Charm in Italy
Hotels and Country Inns of Character and Charm in Paris
Hotels and Country Inns of Character and Charm in Portugal
Hotels and Country Inns of Character and Charm in Spain

Short Escapes
Britain
France
Near New York City
New England

Fodor's Sports
Golf Digest's Best Places to Play
Skiing USA
USA Today The Complete Four Sport Stadium Guide

Fodor's Vacation Planners
Great American Learning Vacations
Great American Sports & Adventure Vacations
Great American Vacations
Great American Vacations for Travelers with Disabilities
National Parks and Seashores of the East
National Parks of the West

WHEREVER YOU TRAVEL, *H*ELP IS NEVER FAR AWAY.

From planning your trip to providing travel assistance along the way, American Express® Travel Service Offices are always there to help.

Hong Kong

American Express Travel Service
25 Kimberley Road
1st Floor
Tsimshatsui, Kowloon
2/732-7327

2849 78

American Express Travel Service
New World Tower
Ground Floor
16-18 Queen's Road Central
2/801-7300

Travel

http://www.americanexpress.com/travel